Words and Meanings

Words and Meanings

Lexical Semantics across Domains,
Languages, and Cultures

CLIFF GODDARD AND ANNA WIERZBICKA

OXFORD
UNIVERSITY PRESS

OXFORD
UNIVERSITY PRESS

Great Clarendon Street, Oxford, OX2 6DP,
United Kingdom

Oxford University Press is a department of the University of Oxford.
It furthers the University's objective of excellence in research, scholarship,
and education by publishing worldwide. Oxford is a registered trade mark of
Oxford University Press in the UK and in certain other countries

First published 2014
First published in paperback 2016

Published in the United States of America by Oxford University Press
198 Madison Avenue, New York, NY 10016, United States of America

British Library Cataloguing in Publication Data
Data available

Library of Congress Cataloging in Publication Data
Data available

ISBN 978–0–19–966843–4 (Hbk.)
ISBN 978–0–19–878355–8 (Pbk.)

Contents

Authorship note

This book presents results of our collaborative work in lexical semantics over the past five or six years. For consistency, we have employed a joint authorial voice throughout. It may be useful to state, however, that Chapters 4, 5, and 6 were principally authored by Anna Wierzbicka, and Chapters 7 and 8 by Cliff Goddard, in each case with substantial input from the other. Chapters 1, 2, 3, 9, and 10 were jointly authored.

Acknowledgements

This book owes a great deal to our ongoing interactions with colleagues in the NSM research community, both in Australia and overseas. In particular, we have been sustained (as well as challenged) by NSM workshops held twice yearly at the Australian National University. We are also greatly indebted to several cohorts of students who have participated in semantic seminars at the ANU and at the University of New England. They have kept us on our toes, contributed insights, and enhanced the joys of our search for semantic understanding. Warm thanks to them all.

We would like to thank Carol Priestley for her careful and insightful help in preparing the final manuscript. We are grateful to Helen Bromhead, Anna Gladkova, Carsten Levisen, and Zhengdao Ye for helpful comments on various chapters. Other acknowledgements are given below. Part of the research reported in this book was supported by the Australian Research Council.

Chapter 3 is a revised version of an article by Cliff Goddard and Anna Wierzbicka (2007), titled 'NSM analyses of the semantics of physical qualities: *sweet, hot, hard, heavy, rough, sharp* in cross-linguistic perspective', *Studies in Language* 31(4), 765–800.

Chapter 4 is an expanded and revised version of an article by Anna Wierzbicka (2008), titled 'Why there are no "colour universals" in language and thought', *Journal of the Royal Anthropological Institute* 14(2), 407–425.

Chapter 5 builds on Anna Wierzbicka's earlier publications on 'happiness' including: '"Happiness" in a cross-linguistic and cross-cultural perspective', *Daedalus* (2004) 133(2), 34–43; 'What's wrong with "happiness studies": the cultural semantics of *happiness, bonheur, Glück* and *sčast'e*', in Leonid Iomdin et al. (eds), *Word and Language* [in Russian *Slovo i Jazyk*], Moscow: Jazyki Russkoy Kultury, 2011, 155–171; and 'The "history of emotions" and the future of emotion research', *Emotion Review* (2010) 2(3), 269–273.

Chapter 6 is an expanded and revised version of an article by Anna Wierzbicka (2012), titled 'Is pain a human universal? A cross-linguistic and cross-cultural perspective on pain', *Emotion Review* 4(3), 307–317.

Tables and figures

Tables

Figures

1

Words, meaning, and methodology

1.1 Why words matter

Mainstream linguistics in the 20th century devoted startlingly little attention to words. Yet words matter a great deal. They matter in human relations (which are often shaped by names, titles, terms of address and kin terms), in the edifice of human knowledge (to mention only number words, the names of biological species, and the role of terminology in science), and in systems of religion, belief, and values.

"The human spirit thinks with words," wrote the 18th-century German thinker Johann Gottfried Herder, and although Herder's words have often been disputed, they reflect a deep-seated human intuition that words matter. In Isaiah Berlin's elegant paraphrase of Herder's German:

Words, by connecting passions with things, the present with the past, and by making possible memory and imagination, create family, society, literature, history. [. . .] to speak and think in words is to 'swim in an inherited stream of images and words; we must accept these media on trust: we cannot create them'. (Berlin 1976: 168)

Before Herder there was Vico, another great visionary and believer in the fundamental importance of words, of whom Berlin, in his book *Vico and Herder*, wrote: "he was, so far as I know, the first to grasp the seminal and revolutionary truth that linguistic forms are one of the keys to the minds of those who use words, and indeed to the entire mental, social and cultural life of societies" (Berlin 1976: 51). For Vico, these "linguistic forms" which can provide the keys to the mental, social and cultural life of societies, present and past, are, above all, words.

His sensitiveness to words and the philosophical significance of their use can be very modern. So, for example, he notes what has only in our day been analysed and classified as the 'performative functions of words', namely the fact that words themselves need not merely describe or attract attention to something outside themselves, but may themselves be acts or intrinsic elements in action, as, for example, in the part that they play in legal transfers, or religious ceremonial. That words are not invariably used to describe, or command, or threaten or ejaculate or convey images or emotions, but can themselves be a form of action, is certainly a new and important idea. (Berlin 1976: 50)

People speak with words, they think with words, they "do things" with words; to a significant extent, words shape people's lives. Arguably, they also contribute significantly to shaping world affairs. In his book *Available Light*, Clifford Geertz (2000), who was more acutely aware of the importance of words than most linguists, psychologists, historians, or political theorists tend to be, reflected, in particular, on the importance of the words *country, nation, state, society,* and *people* in the world's politics, calling them "the elementary building blocks of global world order" (p. 231). Having discussed at length the meanings of these words as documented (in a historical perspective) in the *Oxford English Dictionary* (*OED*), he wrote:

I bring all this up, not because I think words in themselves make the world go round (though, in fact, they have a lot to do with its works and workings), or because I think you can read political history off from dictionary definitions in dictionaries (though in fact they are among the most sensitive, and underused detectors we have for registering its subsurface tremors).

(Geertz 2000: 234)

The authors of this book do not claim either that words by themselves make the world go round, but we too believe that they have a lot to do with its works and workings. We also share Geertz's belief that while you can't read political history off from dictionary definitions, word meanings are in fact among the most sensitive and underused detectors for registering what is going on in the world—political, social, and mental.

This means, however, that it is extremely important for anyone interested in using these detectors to know how to read what they have registered, accurately and reliably. And here, we would like to point out that dictionary definitions, helpful and illuminating as they can be, are not equal to the task. Word meanings register with great sensitivity what is going on in the world (as interpreted by different human groups at different times), but they register these things, so to speak, in a code, and this code needs to be cracked before the records of these highly sensitive instruments can be read.

To successfully decode complex and culture-specific meanings, for example 'country', 'nation', and 'society', one needs to decompose them into simple concepts which can be found in all languages. Dictionary definitions such as those cited by Geertz from the *OED* cannot reveal the semantic history of the words in question, or show how the meanings encoded in them in present-day English compare with those encoded in other languages, because any such comparison would require a common measure (a *tertium comparationis*), and dictionary definitions are not framed in terms of an independently determined common measure. We will expand on this point below. Here, let us note simply that dictionary definitions are, as a rule, circular.

For example, the *OED* defines *country* as "the territory or land of a nation; usually an independent state", *nation* as "the whole people of a country", and *state* as "the supreme civil power and government vested in a country or a nation" (definitions cited by Geertz on p. 233). Thus, *country* is defined via *nation* and *state*, *nation* via *country*, and *state* via both *country* and *nation*. Such definitions merely take us back and forth between concepts. They can explain neither the current meanings of the words in question nor the changes that the meanings of these words have undergone in the past.

Geertz points out that the words *country*, *state*, and *nation*, whose meanings are geographically and historically "highly localized", have now been taken "as a general paradigm for political development overall and everywhere" (p. 235). Such an imposition of "highly localized" conceptual categories on the world at large is typical of today's increasingly "globalized" thought, transmitted around the world through the first ever global lingua franca—"global" English. The conceptual confusion involved in this process is seldom realized or acknowledged.

First, if the only definitions of *country*, *nation*, and *state* to which speakers of English can have access are circular, not even they can see clearly what the relations between the concepts are. Second, if any cultural outsiders try to find out what these key words of global English mean, they can only find definitions which are as untranslatable into other languages as the words *country*, *nation*, and *state* (after all, these enigmatic words are themselves included in the definitions which are supposed to clarify their meanings.) Both these problems—the circularity and the untranslatability of definitions—can be overcome if the complex and language-specific meanings in question are broken down into simple and cross-translatable components such as 'place', 'people', 'do', 'many', 'all', 'live', 'want', and sixty or so others. This is the methodology of the Natural Semantic Metalanguage (NSM) approach, which underlies all the studies presented in this volume. It will be discussed and explained in more detail shortly (section 1.3).

Words are the essential props in social life. It is thanks to words that people can know what other people think—or at least, what they want to say to others. It is also thanks to words that people can know clearly what they themselves think.

This is not to say that people cannot think without words. To some extent, they can—or so the evidence of natural discourse suggests. Cross-linguistic research indicates that in any language one can say, for example, 'I'm thinking about my mother' without implying that one was thinking in words, or that one would be able to say in words what one was thinking. At the same time, to know exactly what one thought at a particular moment, one has to be able to articulate this thought in words (not only for other people's benefit but for one's own). Again, evidence suggests that in any language one can say, for example, 'I thought like this at that time' and follow this with some words specifying the thought in question.

This is, then, how "ordinary people" think about speaking and thinking: they think that people always speak with words, and that while they don't always think with words, they often do. They also think that if one wants someone else to know something, this, too, is usually best achieved by means of words.

This is the folk model of the human condition, which may or may not be shared by scientists or philosophers. Ordinary people, however, are very much aware of the importance of words in human life. The fact that, while many languages do not have words for 'sound', 'sentence', 'language', 'grammar', or 'sign', apparently all have a word for 'word' (or 'words') (Goddard 2011a) is a striking confirmation of the importance of words in human life and in folk models of human life.

No one is more aware of the importance of words than those who cross language boundaries—immigrants, bilinguals, and "sojourners" or travellers forced to live for extended periods through the medium of a new language. For example, the author of the recent memoir *Dreaming in Hindi*, Katherine Russell Rich (2009), who plunged herself into a new language and new life in India, writes:

In any new language, you discover missing words, as revealing as the ones that exist. In Hindi, I soon learned, you couldn't say 'appointment', or 'minute' or 'second', except with the English loan version. In Udaipur, where only 50 percent of the homes had phones then, you didn't need to. (Rich 2009: 68)

But just as missing English words (in Rich's experience, most of all *privacy*) have an impact on the language-traveller's life and world-view (Besemeres 2005), so do the new words missing from English, in Rich's case, words of Hindi.

Much farther out along the spidery web of time, [. . .] I begin a list of words missing from English: *Leelaa*: the acts of a deity performed for pleasure. *Vidya*: translated as 'knowledge,' but which a friend explained as "having characteristics of knowledge but not itself knowledge. It's symbolic of God's world. A person who knows *vidya* knows everything." And *advait*: roughly, non-duality; and *aanand*: broadly, joy or bliss; and then I toss the paper away. Departure's looming. I can't bear to see, spelled out in black and white, what will become unspeakable once I cross back. Transcendence: that's what I'm going to have to lose. (Rich 2009: 68)

And one last quote, from a memoir titled "Words", by the American historian Tony Judt, born in England, and raised on a multilingual diet of words.

I was raised on words. They tumbled off the kitchen table onto the floor where I sat: grandfather, uncles, and refugees flung Russian, Polish, Yiddish, French, and what passed for English, at one another in a competitive cascade of assertion and interrogation. [. . .] I spent long, happy hours listening to Central European autodidacts arguing deep into the night: *Marxismus, Zionismus, Socialismus*. Talking, it seemed to me, was the point of adult existence. I have never lost that sense. (Judt 2010)

As discussed, convincingly, by Walter Ong (1982), this prominent place of "words" in the folk model of human communication, cognition, and interaction belongs primarily to the spoken word, which is not a "sign" but something that one person can say to another. Spoken words, according to Ong, link people and persons, create communities, and enable ceremonial and religious life.

The interiorizing force of the oral word relates in a special way to the sacral, to the ultimate concerns of existence. In most religions the spoken word functions integrally in ceremonial and devotional life. (p. 74) [...] Because in its physical constitution as sound, the spoken word proceeds from the human interior and manifests human beings to one another as conscious interiors, as persons, the spoken word forms human beings into close-knit groups. [...] What the reader is seeing on the page are not words but coded symbols whereby a properly informed human being can evoke in his or her consciousness real words, in actual or imagined sound. [...] Chirographic and typographic folk find it convincing to think of the word, essentially a sound, as a 'sign' because 'sign' refers primarily to something visually apprehended. [...] Our competency in thinking of words as signs is due to the tendency, perhaps incipient in oral cultures but clearly marked in chirographic cultures and far more marked in typographic and electronic cultures, to reduce all sensation and indeed all human experience to visual analogues. (p. 76)

These are profound observations, which bear on some of the central problems of language, culture, communication and cognition.

1.2 Words in 20th-century linguistics

Given the importance of words in social life, in interpersonal communication, and in people's interpretation of the world, it is astonishing how little attention was paid to them in mainstream linguistics in the 20th century. The founder of general linguistics, Ferdinand de Saussure, built his theory of language on the notion of 'signs', not 'words', and contributed to the marginalization of words in structuralist linguistic research (despite the earlier tradition of French lexicologists like Darmesteter and Bréal). In America, the two 20th-century figures who were most influential in shaping a "linguistics without meaning and without words" were Leonard Bloomfield and Noam Chomsky. Bloomfield's behaviourism made him find all references to mind, concepts, and meaning (including word-meanings) "unscientific". The key word for him was not 'words' but 'forms', and this neglect of words (in contrast to 'forms') was further deepened in Chomskyan linguistics, despite its self-proclaimed anti-behaviourism.

Fifty years ago, linguistics and adjacent disciplines experienced a so-called Cognitive Revolution, whose battle cry was "bringing the mind back in". The key figures in this "revolution" were, in psychology, Jerome Bruner and, in linguistics, Noam Chomsky. But while the word 'mind' did indeed make a comeback, the cognitive science which was the child of that revolution did not bring meaning back. Bruner became disillusioned with the effects of that revolution, which, as he wrote in his (1990) *Acts of Meaning*, "gained its technical successes at the price of dehumanizing the very concept of mind it had sought to re-establish in psychology", with the result that much of psychology became "estranged [...] from the other human sciences and the humanities".

But if much of psychology became dehumanized by its lack of attention to what Bruner called "acts of meaning", the same applied to the dominant linguistic paradigm of the second half of the 20th century, that is, Chomskyan generativism. For decades generative linguists pursued the chimera of "autonomous syntax", i.e. syntax without reference to meaning, function or communication. Ironically, even though the late 20th and early 21st century saw generative linguists rediscovering the theoretical importance of lexical meaning and, to some extent at least, rejecting "syntacticocentrism", their interest in lexical meaning remained extremely syntax-bound. Even Ray Jackendoff (1983; 1990; 2010), who coined the term "syntactico-centrism", is himself primarily interested in "syntactically relevant meaning". He regards meaning content which is not relevant to syntax as falling outside Conceptual Structure. In his model, the words *run* and *jog*, for example, are considered to be conceptually identical, as are *toss*, *throw*, and *lob*. "The first set of verbs will all simply be treated in conceptual structure as verbs of locomotion, the second set as verbs of propulsion." Any differences can be treated as belonging to a non-conceptual visual-spatial mode of representation. By this approach, he declares: "we are relieved of the need for otiose feature analyses of such fine-scale distinctions" (Jackendoff 1990: 34).[1]

Within the generativist fold, two other prominent researchers with a special interest in lexical semantics are Beth Levin and Malka Rappaport Hovav. They too are focused on grammatically relevant meaning. In particular, they are interested in characterizing that part of the meaning of a word that would account for the range of construction types and alternations in which the word participates. In their approach, the key content of most verbs is a single primitive predicate such as ACT/DO, CAUSE, BECOME, and GO, while the rest of the meaning, the "idiosyncratic" elements, are separated out and left unanalysed in a so-called "root" component (Levin and Rappaport Hovav 2005: 71–75). Roots can be very complex, they admit, but their full content does not matter very much. For them the main thing is the general type of root (e.g. state, stuff, thing, place, instrument, manner), because this determines how the root relates to the primitive predicate. All "manner verbs", for example, are given an identical representation: [x ACT _{<MANNER>}] (Rappaport Hovav and Levin 2010: 24).

---

[1] Jackendoff's model of Conceptual Structure is highly schematic and highly abstract. Many of its fundamental terms and concepts, furthermore, are based on English-specific vocabulary, making it markedly Anglocentric. To his credit, however, Jackendoff (2002: 338–339) is also on record as saying: "the requirement of learnability forces us to take the problem of primitives seriously. If children can acquire the fine-scale differences among words, they must have some resources from which the differences can be constructed. Therefore it ought to be a long-range goal for conceptualist semantics to characterize these resources." For reviews of how Jackendoff's program compares with NSM, see Jackendoff (2007) and Wierzbicka (2007a).

A third trend in generative linguistics is so-called "formal semantics". Intellectually this trend descends from philosophical logic but, as Hanks (2007) observes in his review of the underdeveloped state of lexicology in mainstream linguistics: "logic and language are two very different things". Formal semantics concerns itself chiefly with truth-conditional analysis of whole sentences, with a particular focus on "logical words", such as quantifiers and connectives. The meanings of ordinary non-logical words, i.e. the vast bulk of the vocabulary, are hardly dealt with in formal semantics, let alone the meaning differences between the words of different languages.

It is true that with the decline of Chomskyan hegemony towards the end of the 20th century, mainstream linguistics has "greened" in some respects, most notably in sociolinguistics, bilingualism studies, cross-cultural pragmatics, and discourse studies (cf. e.g. Pavlenko 2006; Kecskes and Albertazzi 2007; Pütz and Neff-van Aertselaer 2008; Carbaugh 2005), yet this has still not led to a widespread focus on words and their meanings.

On the contemporary linguistic scene, two communities of scholars have been systematically exploring, in depth and detail, hundreds of words and word meanings. One such community consists of Russian linguists and lexicographers based in Moscow and Montreal and associated with the Moscow School of Semantics and the Meaning-Text Model (see e.g. Mel'čuk et al. 1984–99, I–IV; Mel'čuk 2006; Apresjan 1992; 2000; 2004; 2006; Zalizniak et al. 2005; Paduceva 2004; Iordanskaya and Mel'čuk 2007; Majsak and Rakhilina 2007).[2] The other linguistic research community that has been systematically exploring words and their meanings across many languages is the NSM movement, as represented in the present book (see sections 1.3 and 1.4 for extensive references).

The authors of this book believe that it is time to bring words back in and to recognize them as part of the core business of linguistics. Exploring the meanings of words in a systematic way must not be relegated to the margins, but acknowledged as a vital part of what linguistics is all about,[3] and at the same time as a necessary path to

---

[2] One of the leaders of this program, Igor Mel'čuk, said, over 30 years ago (1981: 57): "Not only every language, but every lexeme of a language, is an entire world in itself." In giving as much serious attention to words and their meanings as they did, these scholars were following an older Russian linguistic tradition, reflected in a translation of a sentence from Ščerba's (1940) 'Opyt obshchei teorii lekikografii' [An Outline of a General Lexicographic Theory], used by Mel'čuk and Žolkovskij (1984) as an epigraph for their book on the Explanatory Combinatorial Dictionary of the Contemporary Russian Language: "And indeed, every sufficiently complex word must actually become the subject of a scientific monograph." In contrast to that older tradition, more recent work by Russian scholars places a much greater emphasis on explaining the systematic aspects of the vocabulary, on an integrated approach to the study of the lexicon and grammar, and on lexical and semantic typology.

[3] We of course do not mean to deny that word meanings are crucial to syntax; on the contrary, we have emphasized this in numerous publications (e.g. Wierzbicka 1988; Goddard and Wierzbicka 2002c). Nor would we deny that understanding syntax is a crucial component of linguistics. Our point is rather that words and word meanings are fundamental to language. To study them only from the point of view of syntax is to let the tail wag the dog.

fully "humanizing" linguistics and reclaiming its place in the humanities, as envisaged centuries ago by Vico.

The Finnish linguist Kanavillil Rajagopalan has written of pragmatics that in the last two or three decades it has undergone an "amazing metamorphosis": "from a component of linguistics to a perspective on language and, in the ultimate analysis [...], a perspective on linguistics" (2009: 335). Semantics, too, is often seen as a component of linguistics rather than a perspective on language and linguistics. Yet meaning is what language is all about. If pragmatics is an important perspective on language and linguistics, semantics is even more so, and for most users of language—speakers and hearers, writers and readers—words are alive and "green", whereas forms, symbols, and abstract formulae may seem cold and distant.

There is a very close link between the life of a society and the lexicon of the language spoken by it. This applies in equal measure to the outer and inner aspects of life. An obvious example from the material domain is that of food. It is clearly no accident, for example, that Polish has words for cabbage stew (*bigos*), beetroot soup (*barszcz*), and plum jam (*powidła*), which English does not; or that English (the language of the old British Empire) has a word for orange, or orange-like, jam (*marmalade*), and Japanese a word (*sake*) for a strong alcoholic drink made from rice. Obviously, such words can tell us something about the eating or drinking habits of the peoples in question.

What applies to material culture applies also to people's values, ideals, and attitudes and to their ways of thinking about the world and our life in it. A good example is provided by the untranslatable Russian word *pošlost'* (cf. Wierzbicka 1997), to which the émigré writer Vladimir Nabokov (1961) devoted many pages of detailed discussion. According to Nabokov, the Russian language is able to express by means of this "one pitiless word the idea of a certain widespread defect for which the other three European languages I happen to know possess no special term" (p. 64). He accepts that some English words—for example *cheap, sham, common, smutty, pink-and-blue, high falutin', in bad taste*—express similar meanings, but for him these English words are inadequate, for first, they do not aim at unmasking, exposing, or denouncing "cheapness" of all kinds the way *pošlost'* and its cognates do; and, second, they do not have the same "absolute" implications that *pošlost'* does:

All these however suggest merely certain false values for the detection of which no particular shrewdness is required. In fact, they tend, these words, to supply an obvious classification of values at a given period of human history; but what Russians call *poshlust* [sic] is beautifully timeless and so cleverly painted all over with protective tints that its presence (in a book, in a soul, in an institution, in a thousand other places) often escapes detection.   (Nabokov 1961: 64)

One could say, then, that the word *pošlost'* (and its cognates) both reflects and documents an acute awareness of the existence of false values and of the need to deride and deflate them. There is no such word, and no such concept, in English (or for that matter, in other languages).

"People can be forgiven for overrating language," says Steven Pinker (1994: 67). They can also be forgiven for underrating it. But the conviction that one can understand human cognition, and human psychology in general, on the basis of English words alone is short-sighted and ethnocentric.

Modern psychology, too, has often shown itself to be remarkably blind to the significance of language in general and of words in particular in both people's mental life and their understanding of themselves and others. A good example of this is the theory of so-called "basic emotions", formulated in terms of English words like *happiness, anger,* and *sadness.* When anthropologists like Catherine Lutz (1988) and Michelle Rosaldo (1980), or linguists like the present authors and their colleagues (Wierzbicka 1997; 1999*a*; 2009*a*; Goddard 1991; 1996*a*; 1997*a*; 2010*a*; Gladkova 2010*a*; 2010*b*; Ye 2001; 2006; Levisen 2012; Priestley 2002), have pointed out that different languages categorize emotions differently and that words for emotions don't match semantically across languages, they have often been accused of being obsessed with words and, by implication, uninterested in psychological reality. A common response to the challenge posed by the work of Rosaldo, Lutz, and others has been: "I am not talking about words, I am talking about emotions"—as if one *could* talk about emotions without using words, as if people could describe and report their emotional experiences without using words. In these theories of human emotions, Anglophone researchers unwittingly absolutize English words, treating them as if they were neutral analytical tools.

To quote a comment from one distinguished psychologist, Richard Lazarus (1995: 255, 259), directed, inter alia, at one of the authors of the present book:

Wierzbicka suggests that I underestimate the depth of cultural variation in emotion concepts as well as the problem of language. [. . .] Words have power to influence, yet—as in the Whorfian hypotheses writ large—they cannot override the life conditions that make people sad or angry, which they can sense to some extent without words [. . .] I am suggesting, in effect, that all people experience anger, sadness, and so forth, regardless of what they call it . . . Words are important, but we must not deify them.

Unfortunately, by refusing to pay attention to words, and to semantic differences between words from different languages, scholars who take this position end up doing precisely what they wished to avoid, that is, "deifying" some words from their own native language and reifying the concepts encapsulated in them. Thus, unwittingly, they illustrate once again how powerful the grip of our native language on our thinking habits can be. As the anthropologist Richard Shweder and his colleagues argue in their chapter in *Handbook of Emotions*, in writing about human emotions there is a constant danger of "assimilating them in misleading ways to an a priori set of lexical items available in the language of the researcher" (Shweder et al.

2008: 424). To assume that people in all cultures have the concept of 'sadness', even if they have no word for it, is little better than assuming that people in all cultures have a concept of 'marmalade'. Moreover, to assume that the emotional experience of people in all cultures can be faithfully described using English words ("all people experience anger, sadness, and so forth, regardless of what they call it"), while denying the same privilege to the words of other languages, is simply Anglocentric (and hence unscientific).

But, it may well be asked, if the words of different languages can vary so greatly, how can one describe anything using English words without succumbing to Anglocentrism? This is why the research finding that, despite all the cross-linguistic variability, some lexical meanings—the very simplest ones—are shared between all languages is of crucial importance. Using these words, we can fashion a non-ethnocentric lingua franca for conceptual analysis.

1.3 Universal words and the NSM methodology of semantic analysis

As Patrick Hanks (2007: 6) has observed, "There is no metalanguage other than words themselves (in one language or another)—or at a pinch derivatives of words such as logical symbols—for expressing thoughts about words." Any approach to describing the meanings of words must therefore recognize the fundamental importance of the metalanguage of description; in particular, it must ensure that the metalanguage is not vitiated by circularity, ethnocentrism, or excessive abstractness. Unfortunately, however, Hanks's ready acknowledgement of the importance of metalanguage issues is the exception rather than the rule in linguistics. Many linguists, including many who count themselves as semanticists, do not so much as mention the word 'metalanguage' and approach semantics without any rigorous theoretical basis. It is also surprising, and, to be frank, embarrassing, how many linguists (as well as psychologists, and cognitive scientists generally) seem to believe that once they have "translated" an ordinary language word into a technical equivalent, the task of semantic analysis has been completed. Nothing could be further from the truth.

At this point, a little history can be useful. As 17th-century philosophers like Arnauld, Descartes, Locke, Pascal, and Leibniz saw clearly, the only way to immunize the metalanguage of semantic description against circularity and/or infinite regress is to base it on a finite inventory of primitive terms. As Arnauld and Nicole put it, in their famous *Logic or the Art of Thinking* (1662):

I say it would be impossible to define every word. For in order to define a word it is necessary to use other words designating the idea we want to connect to the word being defined. And if we then wished to define the words used to explain that word, we would need still others, and so on to infinity. Consequently, we necessarily have to stop at primitive terms which are undefined.   (Arnauld and Nicole 1996[1662]: 64)

Taken alone, this quotation might suggest the idea that the choice of primitive terms can be arbitrary, or a matter of convenience. In fact, however, the same 17th-century thinkers were convinced that primitive terms, i.e. indefinable words, are self-explanatory to the human mind and thus, presumably, universal and innate. The link between the indefinability of certain words, their inherent intelligibility, their universality, and their presumed innateness is particularly clear in the following quote from Pascal:

> It is clear that there are words which cannot be defined; and if nature hadn't provided for this by giving all people the same idea all our expressions would be obscure; but in fact we can use those words with the same confidence and certainty as if they had been explained in the clearest possible way; because nature itself has given us, without additional words, an understanding of them better than what our art could give through our explanations.   (Pascal 1954[1667]: 580)

Where the 17th-century thinkers made little headway was on the practical task of identifying those simple, indefinable words. Of all of them, it was Leibniz (1903; 1890[1675]) who perceived most clearly the required methodology. The "alphabet of human thoughts", as he called it, could only be found by experimental semantic analysis. One has to attempt a very large number of definitions to be able to find out which words can, and which cannot, be defined, and consequently, which words (or word-meanings) can be regarded as elementary building blocks out of which all complex concepts (and word-meanings) can be built. Throughout his life Leibniz worked intermittently on this project, drafting a large number of lexical definitions, but he never brought it to fruition and his semantic definitions remained an isolated phenomenon for almost three centuries (cf. Wierzbicka 2001a). It was only in the mid-1960s that his project was taken up in the work of the Polish semanticist Andrzej Bogusławski (1966; 1970), and subsequently turned into a large-scale research program of empirical/analytical semantic analysis, starting with Wierzbicka (1972). Major benchmarks since have included the numerous studies in Goddard and Wierzbicka (1994), Wierzbicka (1996), Goddard and Wierzbicka (2002c), Peeters (2006b), and Goddard (2008b), along with many other publications.[4]

After nearly forty years of sustained research, both within selected individual languages and across many languages, linguists in the NSM program are prepared to claim that they have discovered the complete inventory of simple universal concepts that are embedded in the lexicons of all (or most) human languages. To say this is not to deny that much further work is necessary, nor does it rule out the possibility of future revisions to the current inventory. The claim is, however, that a plausible, stable, and well-evidenced set of "universal words" has been identified and

---

[4] A bibliography and downloads can be found at the NSM Homepage: https://www.griffith.edu.au/ humanities-languages/school-humanities-languages-social-science/research/natural-semantic-metalanguage-homepage [short URL bit.ly/1XUoRRV].

TABLE 1.1 **Semantic primes (English exponents), grouped into related categories**

I~ME, YOU, SOMEONE, SOMETHING~THING, PEOPLE, BODY	substantives
KIND, PARTS	relational substantives
THIS, THE SAME, OTHER~ELSE	determiners
ONE, TWO, SOME, ALL, MUCH~MANY, LITTLE~FEW	quantifiers
GOOD, BAD	evaluators
BIG, SMALL	descriptors
KNOW, THINK, WANT, DON'T WANT, FEEL, SEE, HEAR	mental predicates
SAY, WORDS, TRUE	speech
DO, HAPPEN, MOVE, TOUCH	actions, events, movement, contact
BE (SOMEWHERE), THERE IS, (IS) MINE, BE (SOMEONE/SOMETHING)	location, existence, possession, specification
LIVE, DIE	life and death
WHEN~TIME, NOW, BEFORE, AFTER, A LONG TIME, A SHORT TIME, FOR SOME TIME, MOMENT	time
WHERE~PLACE, HERE, ABOVE, BELOW, FAR, NEAR, SIDE, INSIDE	space
NOT, MAYBE, CAN, BECAUSE, IF	logical concepts
VERY, MORE	intensifier, augmentor
LIKE~WAY~AS	similarity

Notes: 1. Primes exist as the meanings of lexical units (not at the level of lexemes). 2. Exponents of primes may be words, bound morphemes, or phrasemes. 3. They can be formally complex. 4. They can have combinatorial variants or "allolexes" (indicated with ~). 5. Each prime has well-specified syntactic (combinatorial) properties.

that this can provide the necessary solid foundation for the project of decoding meanings across languages. Strictly speaking, the units we are talking about are not words as such, but word-meanings. These putatively indefinable word-meanings are known as semantic primes and they are 65 in number.

The table of semantic primes above (Table 1.1) is presented in its English version, but comparable tables have been drawn up for many languages, including Russian (Gladkova 2010c; 2012), Polish (Wierzbicka 2002d), French (Peeters 2006b), Spanish (Travis 2002; Barrios Rodríguez and Goddard 2013), Danish (Levisen 2011; 2012), Chinese (Chappell 2002), Japanese (Hasada 2008), Korean (Yoon 2006; 2008), Lao (Enfield 2002), Malay (Goddard 2002a), Mbula/Mangaaba-Mbula (Bugenhagen 2002), Koromu, PNG (Priestley 2012a; 2013), Tok Pisin (Priestley 2008; 2012b), Amharic (Amberber 2008), Arabic (Habib 2011), East Cree (Junker 2008), Finnish (Vanhatalo, Tissari and Idström 2014), and many others.[5] Semantic primes and their

---

[5] Examples of full explications in non-English NSMs can be found e.g. in Goddard and Wierzbicka (2007b), Ye (2004a), Yoon (2004; 2006), Priestley (2012a), Travis (2006), Barrios Rodríguez and Goddard (2013), Peeters (2012; 2013), and Gladkova (2010c).

grammar together constitute a kind of mini-language which can be thought of as the "intersection of all languages". As such, it is an ideal tool for semantic description—hence the term Natural Semantic Metalanguage (NSM).

At the bottom of Table 1.1, a number of important caveats are given in dot-point form. For reasons of space, we will discuss these points only in an abbreviated fashion here. The chief caveat is that the relationship between the semantically primitive meaning and the form that represents it in a given language (known as an "exponent" of the prime) is not one-to-one. An exponent (say, MOVE or TOUCH in English) can have other, non-primitive meanings in addition to its semantically prime meaning. This situation—a word has two or more distinct but related meanings, is known as lexical polysemy. For example, the English word *move* has one meaning (its semantically prime meaning) in a sentence like *I can't move* and a distinct, semantically complex meaning in a sentence like *I'm moving house tomorrow*. Conversely, a given semantically primitive meaning can have more than one exponent in a particular language, with the distribution of the alternative forms often conditioned by the linguistic context. This situation is known as allolexy. For example, in English the words *other* and *else* express the same meaning, *other* being used as a modifier of nouns and *else* as a modifier of indefinite pronouns.

Patterns of polysemy and allolexy are language-specific. Thus, when we say that (for example) English *do* and Spanish *hacer* are exponents of the same prime, this is not the same as saying that *do* and *hacer* are "the same" in all their uses. Both words have additional language-specific meanings, over and above their shared semantically primitive meaning; for example, one additional meaning of *hacer* approximates to English 'make'. Equally, when we say that English *other* and Spanish *otro* are exponents of the same prime, this claim is not disturbed by the fact that English *other* has an allolex *else* that has no counterpart in Spanish.

Many of the counter-claims levelled at the universality of NSM primes have been based on a failure to recognize polysemy or (less commonly) allolexy. Needless to say, it is not enough to assume that just because a particular meaning is a discrete semantic unit in English that it has the same status in every language. A polysemy analysis must always be supported by detailed language-internal argumentation. Lexical polysemy is, however, a fact of life.

The Natural Semantic Metalanguage consists not just of a lexicon, but also of a syntax. Semantic primes are hypothesized to have certain universal combinatorial properties (a "conceptual syntax"), and available evidence indicates that these properties also manifest themselves in all or most languages (Goddard and Wierzbicka 2002c; Goddard 2008b). To give a very brief indication of the kinds of properties involved, it can be mentioned that they include: (a) basic combinatorial possibilities: e.g. that substantives can combine with specifiers, as in expressions like 'this something~thing', 'someone else', 'one place', 'two parts', 'many kinds'; (b) basic and extended valencies of predicates and quantifiers, e.g. that DO has patient and

TABLE 1.2 **Valency frame arrays for three semantic primes** HAPPEN, DO, **and** THINK

something HAPPENS	[minimal frame]
something HAPPENS to someone/something	[undergoer frame]
something HAPPENS somewhere	[locus frame]
someone DOES something	[minimal frame]
someone DOES something to someone else	[patient$_1$ frame]
someone DOES something to something	[patient$_2$ frame]
someone DOES something to someone/something with something	[instrument frame]
someone DOES something with someone	[comitative frame]
someone THINKS about someone/something	[topic of cognition frame]
someone THINKS something (good/bad) about someone/something	[topic + complement frame]
someone THINKS like this: " – – "	[quasi-quotational frame]

instrument valencies such as 'do something to something' and 'do something to something with something', and that ONE allows a partitive option, in expressions such as 'one of these things'; and (c) the complement options of the mental primes, KNOW, THINK, and WANT.

For illustrative purposes, the proposed universal valency and complement frames for three semantic primes (HAPPEN, DO, THINK) are displayed in Table 1.2, using English exponents. Naturally, the entries in Table 1.2 include various English-specific morphosyntactic devices, most obviously, the prepositions *to*, *with*, and *about*. Importantly however, the claim that semantic equivalents of these frames are available in all languages does not entail that other languages realize the frames in an analogous fashion. For example, the patient and instrument roles of DO can be indicated in other languages by case-marking, postpositions, verb serialization, or purely by word-order. Even if prepositions are used in a given language, there is no requirement or expectation that they will pattern in a fashion analogous to English; for example, there is no requirement that the instrument and comitative roles will be marked by the same formal means, as they are in English, i.e. by means of preposition *with*.

As mentioned, the lexical status of some primes has been challenged for some languages, and some of these claims are as yet unresolved. Before commenting on one or two of these, we want to make the point that in far too many cases, as it seems to us, apparently definitive claims that "Language Y has no word for semantic prime X" are advanced on the basis of unreliable or inaccurate data and/or on weak and inadequate argumentation. Here we will give just two examples. In a much-discussed article titled "The myth of language universals", Evans and Levinson (2009) assert that there are "vanishingly few" semantic universals, and they illustrate by saying that the Australian Aboriginal language Guugu Yimidhirr, for example, has no word for 'if'. To back this claim, they cite Haviland's (1979) short grammar of the language (now out of print). In fact, however, Haviland (pp. 151–152) stated: "The related particle *budhi* 'if' signals uncertainty, or questions the possibility of some outcome, sometimes very much like a subordinate conjunction, sometimes in a more modal sense." Haviland cited the apparently conditional sentence *Nyundu budhu dhadaa nyundu minha maanaa bira* [2sgNOM if go.NONPAST 2sgNOM meat get.NONPAST indeed] with two glosses: 'If you go, you'll get meat for sure' and 'Should you go, you'll get meat for sure'.[6]

As an example of weak argumentation, we can refer to Everett's (2005) much-publicized description of Pirahã, a language spoken in the Brazilian rainforests. On Everett's account, Pirahã language and culture appears "extreme" in many ways, most notably by lacking various grammatical and semantic features that are widely viewed as universal. In relation to the semantic claims, we will concentrate here on the supposed lack of any expressions for the semantic prime ALL. The "closest expressions Pirahã can muster", according to Everett, are examples such as the following, where the word *'ogi* 'big' (or a nominalized version *'ogiáagaó* 'bigness') appears to convey the meaning ALL.

a. *Hiaitíihí*   *hi*   *'ogi-'áaga-ó*   *pi-ó*   *kaobíi.*
    Pirahã.people   he   big-be(permanence)-direction   water-direction   entered
    'All the people went to swim/went swimming/are swimming/bathing, etc.'

b. *'igihí*   *hi*   *'ogiáagaó*   *'oga*   *hápií…*
    man   he   bigness   field   went
    'The men all went to the field.'

Despite the free translations, Everett insists that even in these contexts, the Pirahã word *'ogi* means 'big' and not ALL, even though this requires him to assert that the true meaning of the expression *hiaitíihí hi 'ogi* in (a) above is "people's bigness", not 'all the people'. The sentence as a whole, he is saying, means something like 'People's bigness went to swim'. Unfazed by the bizarre, not to say incoherent, quality of this interpretation, Everett does not accept the possibility that *'ogi* is polysemous and can

---

[6] According to Stephen Levinson (p.c. email to Goddard, 4 Apr. 2011), this conclusion was not actually based mainly on Haviland's (1979) grammar, but on Levinson's own unpublished fieldwork. He states that "*budhu* is a dubitative particle, which can implicate but does not code IF". Needless to say, the existence of unpublished field notes does not improve the quality of publicly available data or argumentation. The wording "implicate[s] but does not code" seems to imply the assumption that *budhu* has a single abstract meaning, i.e. "dubitative", in both monoclausal and biclausal constructions. Similar particles in the Australian languages Arrernte and Yankunytjatjara (*peke* and *tjinguru*, respectively) have been analysed as exhibiting polysemy between MAYBE (in single clauses) and IF (in biclausal constructions) (Harkins and Wilkins 1994; Goddard 1994*a*). In view of the sentence cited by Haviland (1979), we would be inclined to think that the same applies to Guugu Yimidhirr.

express two meanings, i.e. either BIG or ALL. According to him, because *'ogi* means 'big' in some contexts, it means 'big' in all contexts.

Further supporting a polysemy analysis of *'ogi*, there is the fact that Pirahã plural pronouns are formed by addition of *'ogi* to the singular (or unspecified) form. It is well known that forms such as 'I-all' for 'we', 'you-all' for 'you (pl)', and 'he-all' for 'they' are common in creoles, and there is evidence that Pirahã pronominal roots have been borrowed from a nearby Tupi-Guarani language, suggesting that Pirahã has passed through a phase of creolization. Everett maintains, however, that the Pirahã word that corresponds to English 'we' truly means something like "my bigness". When challenged, in the same volume, by Wierzbicka (2005a: 641) on the issue of polysemy, Everett simply declined to say anything on the subject[7], asserting instead that "much of Pirahã is largely incommensurate with English" (Everett 2005: 624, n. 5).

To be sure, the lexical status of some proposed primes has been challenged on the basis of better data and argumentation. Bohnemeyer (1998a; 1998b) has argued, for example, that Yucatek Maya lacks words corresponding to AFTER and BEFORE, but he does not deny that relations of temporal sequence can be clearly conveyed in the language. His argument is that this effect is achieved via pragmatic inference based on the combination of aspectual operators (such as the "terminative" or "post-state" *ts'o'k*, roughly similar to English *finish* or *end*), the linear order of clauses, and resumptive topicalization (cf. Bohnemeyer 1998a: 213–215). From an NSM point of view, however, the crucial thing is that if a subordinate clause marked with *ts'o'k* and depicting event A is followed by a main clause depicting event B, then the meaning conveyed corresponds to English 'After A, B'. The fact that the interpretation is different if *ts'o'k* appears instead in the main clause (where it will correspond roughly to 'finish') suggests that *ts'o'k* is polysemous (cf. Goddard 2001a). Bohnemeyer (2003) remains unconvinced, insisting that *ts'o'k* has a uniform Yukatek-specific meaning, unstatable in ordinary English,[8] and that Yucatek Maya and English are radically incommensurate in their temporal semantics. To take another example, in a careful study Junker (2008) reports an apparent lexical gap for the prime PART in East Cree.

---

[7]   All Everett (2005: 643) had to say about semantic methodology was: "All semanticists know that the quantificational properties of a word are revealed by its truth conditions. I have pointed out that Pirahã has no word with the truth conditions of universal quantification." His point is that Pirahã words for 'all' do not imply absolute exhaustiveness, as one would expect of an equivalent of universal quantification, but this overlooks the obvious point that 'all' in natural languages is not the same as universal quantification in logic. Ordinary English 'all' does not entail absolute exhaustiveness either.

[8]   Unlike English *finish* and *end*, Yukatek *ts'o'k* is compatible with punctual verbs such as 'die' and 'wake up'. Hence: "*Ts'o'k* must be assumed to represent a type of phasal operator unattested and probably unparalleled in Indo-European languages... This underlines the status of *ts'o'k* as an operator of temporal coherence rather than merely a lexical verb..." (Bohnemeyer 1998b: 270). It is notable that quasi-aspectual verbs have also been reported to be the usual exponents of BEFORE and AFTER in some Austronesian languages, such as Samoan (Mosel 1994: 349–354) and Acehnese (Durie, Daud, and Hasan 1994: 191–192); cf. Wierzbicka (1994a: 485–487).

In our view, however, her treatment leaves some open questions, because although body-part terminology is arguably the canonical lexical domain for "part-hood" relations, Junker does not indicate how East Cree speakers could go about constructing Cree-internal explications for words like 'head' and 'hands', i.e. how they could express components such as 'one part of someone's body' (for 'head') or 'two parts of someone's body' (for 'hands'). In both cases the debate has not been settled conclusively.

For other exchanges about the supposed non-lexicalization of primes in particular languages, see Khanina (2008; 2010) and Goddard and Wierzbicka (2010) on WANT; Shi-xu (2000) and Chappell (2002: 270–271) on FEEL in Chinese; Myhill (1996) and Durst (1999) on BAD in Biblical Hebrew; Dixon and Aikhenvald (2002) and Goddard (2011a) on WORD; Evans (2007) and Goddard and Wierzbicka (2014) on THINK and KNOW in Dalabon. In all these cases, in our view, the lexicalized status of the primes in question has been sustained.

In short, despite the existence of a handful of unresolved cases, the balance of evidence clearly indicates that semantic primes are expressible by words or phrases in the great majority of the world's languages.[9]

To recapitulate, then, the metalanguage of semantic description employed in this volume, i.e. the Natural Semantic Metalanguage, consists of a small, well-specified vocabulary from which phrases, sentences, and texts can be constructed according to well-specified grammatical rules. Evidence indicates that this highly constrained vocabulary and grammar has equivalents in all or most languages of the world. Consequently, semantic explications framed in this metalanguage can be transposed without loss or distortion of meaning from one language to another. Though in this volume we are using English-based NSM, the explications are not tied to the English language or dependent on the English language in any way. They are explications couched in terms of universal human concepts expressed **through** English, but equally well expressible through Russian, Spanish, Ewe, Chinese, Arabic, Japanese, Korean, Finnish, Mangaaba-Mbula, Koromu, etc.

Up to this point we have been talking about the deepest level of the NSM metalanguage, i.e. the level of semantic primes and their grammar. It must also be noted that many explications include not only semantic primes but also various complex word meanings, themselves decomposable into semantic primes. These

---

[9] If it were to turn out that a minority of languages lack exponents of certain primes, this would call into question the "meta-semantic adequacy" of the languages concerned, i.e. whether they provide the resources for explicating their own meanings in language-internal terms. The expressive power of such a language would be redeemed, of course, if it could be shown to possess one or more language-specific semantic primes which covered the same territory as the missing primes, but this would imply semantic incommensurability in the areas concerned. We deem both of these scenarios unlikely, but if future research established them as fact this would not invalidate the current inventory of semantic primes for the majority of the world's languages, nor would it invalidate NSM analyses based on the current metalanguage.

complex semantic units are known as "semantic molecules". Examples of semantic molecules include 'hand [m]', 'child [m]', 'ground [m]', 'water [m]', 'round [m]', and 'grow (in the ground) [m]'. (Molecules are marked as such in explications with the notation [m].) Using semantic molecules means that explications can be phrased more simply and comprehensibly, but this is not the main rationale for using them. Rather, using semantic molecules in explications embodies a claim about semantic dependency between concepts. For example, by including the molecule 'child [m]' in the explication for *woman*, we are claiming that the concept behind *woman* depends conceptually (in part) on the concept of 'child'. Likewise, by including the molecule 'hand [m]' in the explication for *hold*, it is claimed that from a conceptual point of view, the idea of *holding* something includes the idea of doing something with one's hands. The theory of semantic molecules is introduced, and their use exemplified, in Chapters 2, 3, and 4.

Although the radical restriction in vocabulary and syntax in NSM does not bring with it any loss of expressive power, it does mean a certain loss of idiomaticity. Though many NSM expressions, e.g. 'I want to do something', 'this is not good', 'people think like this', sound like ordinary simple English, some common metalanguage expressions, such as 'this someone', are rather unidiomatic in English. The argument for using them is that despite their non-idiomaticity they are maximally clear, and that alternative expressions such as 'this person' and 'he/she' are not universally translatable and/or introduce additional semantic content. Furthermore, the very fact that explications are composed in restricted vocabulary of simple words gives them an unusual stylistic quality. To put it bluntly, the natural semantic metalanguage is not always very "natural" in its phraseology or discourse conventions, simply because it is a standardized subset of natural language being used in a highly disciplined fashion.

In a classic essay, the logician Tarski (1956[1935]: 267) expressed the view that to pursue the semantics of colloquial language using "exact methods" would necessitate the "thankless task of a reform of this language . . . to define its structure, to overcome the ambiguity of the terms which occur in it"; and in the end it may be doubted "whether the language of everyday life, after being 'rationalized' in this way, would still preserve its naturalness and whether it would not rather take on the characteristic features of the formalized languages". Now that the Natural Semantic Metalanguage exists as a practical reality, we can reassess Tarski's view. We can see that the tiny vocabulary and narrow range of grammatical patterns in NSM does indeed compromise its "naturalness" in certain ways, but—crucially—not to the point that it cannot be understood via ordinary natural language.

As we will show throughout this book, it is possible using NSM to bring precision, rigour, and an often astonishing level of detail into lexical semantics.

1.4 Worlds of words

This brings us back to where we started—to the phenomenal richness and culture-specificity of most words, and to the pervasive role that words play in the lives of individuals and speech communities. Despite the existence of a small set of "universal words", an equally impressive, if not more impressive, fact is the tremendous semantic variability that exists in the vocabulary of the world's languages. In particular, evidence suggests that in every speech community there are certain words which, far from being universal, are in fact unique to one particular language. Such words, which contain a wealth of culture in their meaning, can be called cultural key words (Wierzbicka 1997). Common knowledge of and use of these words binds speakers into a community sharing a mental world and, in Herder's words, "swimming in an inherited stream of images and words" (see Berlin 1976: 168).

The language-specificity of concepts poses challenges and at the same time creates opportunities for language learners, translators, and bilinguals. As the German philosopher Arthur Schopenhauer (in Lefevere 1977: 99) put it, in learning a language "one does not learn words only; one acquires concepts", and doing this both requires and promotes "skill in thinking". Referring to the difficulty of expressing one's thought in classical languages, Schopenhauer expands as follows:

[O]ne most often has to melt down the thought one has to render in Latin, and in this process it is taken apart down to its basic components and then put together again. It is precisely on this that the great challenge posed to the mind by the learning of foreign languages rests.... It follows from this that one thinks differently in every language and also that our thinking is given a new colour and modification each time we learn a new language.

(Schopenhauer, in Lefevere 1977: 99–100)

As emphasized in section 1.1, the Anglophone linguistic tradition has generally paid little attention to word meanings. In contrast, however, outside linguistics many Anglophone writers, literary critics, philosophers, historians, and others have shown an acute awareness of the importance of words and their meanings in human life and in the life of societies. To start with a recent example, Adam Potkay in his book *The Story of Joy: From the Bible to Late Romanticism* (2007) pays a great deal of attention to the role that the English word *joy* played in the conceptualization, and indeed the experience, of this emotion in English-speaking countries. Referring to one of the authors of the present book, Potkay recognizes that "[e]motion terms are themselves culturally freighted":

As the linguist Anna Wierzbicka writes, they "reflect, and pass on, certain cultural models; and these models, in turn, reflect and pass on values, preoccupations, and frames of reference of the society (or speech community) within which they have evolved". (Potkay 2007: vii)

Potkay proposes what he calls a "cultural philology of joy", in which the semantic and cultural history of the word *joy*, and the differences in meaning between English *joy*, German *Freude*, French *joie*, and Italian *gioia* play a significant role.

Older voices which spoke in English about words as important guides to ways of thinking and ways of living include those recalled recently by the British philosopher Thomas Dixon (2008) in his remarkable book *The Invention of Altruism*. Dixon (2008: 30) notes, for example, that Samuel Taylor Coleridge (1825) argued that sometimes "more knowledge of more value may be conveyed by the history of a word than by the history of a campaign". The clergyman and scholar Richard Chenevix Trench, whose insistence on the value of words and their meanings as historical sources was one of the driving forces behind the creation of the *Oxford English Dictionary*, "used the history of words to explore the history of humanity". The Oxford writer Owen Barfield in his *History in English Words* (1953) saw in English words "an imperishable map" of the "inner, living history" of the speakers' souls. C. S. Lewis in his *Studies in Words* (1960) applied the same idea to the moral lexicon of English and many other languages, classical, medieval, and modern. The historian of modern Britain Eric Hobsbawm (1973[1962]) opened his *The Age of Revolution* with the observation: "Words are witnesses which often speak louder than documents" (quoted in Dixon 2008: 30). Hobsbawm illustrated the dramatic development of the English vocabulary during the industrial revolution with words like *factory*, *railway*, *scientist*, and *proletariat*.

As one would expect, Dixon acknowledges Raymond Williams's (1976) book *Keywords: A Vocabulary of Culture and Society* as a milestone in the tradition of word-oriented studies in the English language. He also notes book-length studies of 'enthusiasm', 'purgatory', 'inhibition', 'emotions', 'serendipity', 'democracy', and in particular 'curiosity' (Kenny 2004), "all of which have been at least partly conceived as histories of words" (Dixon 2008: 397). This is the tradition within which he places his own *Invention of Altruism*—a book which should be required reading for anyone interested in historical semantics and/or the history of ideas.[10]

It is somewhat disappointing to reflect on the extent to which mainstream contemporary linguistics is out of touch with scholarship in the humanities, as represented, for example, by C. S. Lewis, Raymond Williams, Adam Potkay, and Thomas Dixon, not to mention the whole discipline of "Begriffsgeschichte" (as represented, for example, by

---

[10] Dixon (2008) documents how the term *altruism*, which was constructed by the French philosopher August Comte and which drew a strong distinction between a person's own good and the interest of others, acquired great popularity in Victorian England and became a key word of the moral rhetoric of the time. It is ironic that this arbitrarily invented word has now acquired the status of a scientific concept and has become one of the key words of post-Darwinian evolutionary biology, conflating (as Dixon argues) animal instincts and human conduct and often confusing parental care, social cooperation, and mutual aid. One does not need to agree with all of Dixon's conclusions and charges to see the potential of his word-based intellectual history for clarifying many confusions prevailing in current ethical and biological debates.

the German scholar Reinhart Koselleck and his best-known English interpreter, Melvin Richter). It is high time for linguistics to reclaim its stake in the study of words—not only syntactically relevant ones, but also those relevant to culture and cognition, to self and society, to humanities, and to science. As we endeavour to illustrate here, linguistics (and in particular the NSM approach) can bring systematic, precise, and empirically based methods to bear on the study of words and meanings. This book is a sustained exploration of semantically complex and culturally important words across a range of domains: physical, sensory, emotional, social, and abstract.

Although they are positioned in cross-linguistic and cross-cultural perspective throughout, our starting points in this book are English words. For NSM investigations into culture-rich words in other languages, the reader can consult, for Russian, Gladkova (2010*a*; 2010*b*; 2012) and Wierzbicka (1992*a*: ch. 11; 1997: ch. 3; 1999*a*: ch. 5; 2002*a*); for French, Peeters (2000; 2006*a*); for Colombian Spanish, Travis (2004; 2006); for Danish, Levisen (2011; 2012); for Malay, Goddard (1996*a*; 1997*a*; 2000*a*); for Ewe, Ameka (2002; 2006; 2009); for East Cree, Junker (2003; 2007); for Chinese, Ye (2004*a*; 2006; 2007*a*; 2007*b*; 2010); for Korean, Yoon (2004; 2007*a*; 2007*b*); and for Koromu, Priestley (2002; 2012*a*; 2012*b*; 2013; forthcoming). NSM studies into other dialects of English include, for Singapore English, Wong (2004*a*; 2004*b*; 2005; 2008) and, for Australian English, Wierzbicka (2002*b*), Goddard (2006*a*; 2009*a*), Peeters (2004*a*; 2004*b*; 2006*a*), and Bromhead (2011*a*). There have also been several extended culture-historical explorations of English conducted in the NSM framework, including Helen Bromhead's (2009) *The Reign of Truth and Faith*, and Wierzbicka's (2006*a*; 2010*a*) twin volumes, *English: Meaning and Culture* and *Experience, Evidence, Sense: The Hidden Cultural Legacy of English*.

This literature may seem rich and diverse, and in a sense it is. Yet, as we show in the present volume, there are whole worlds of meaning that are still unmapped and little understood. It may be no exaggeration to say that the universe of meaning is as vast as the physical universe, and no less awe-inspiring.

2

Men, women, and children

The semantics of basic social categories

2.1 The canonical example of lexical semantics?

The great Danish linguist Louis Hjelmslev produced the classic structuralist semantic analysis of *men*, *women*, *boys*, and *girls* as part of his *Prolegomena to a Theory of Language* (1961[1943]: 69–75). Hjelmslev's program was to progressively reduce complex semantic entities to combinations of a smaller number of simpler semantic elements.

> If, for example, a mechanical inventorying at a given stage of the procedure leads to a registration of the entities of content 'ram', 'ewe', 'man', 'woman', 'boy', 'girl', 'stallion', 'mare', 'sheep', 'human being', 'child', 'horse', 'he' and 'she'—then 'ram', 'ewe', 'man', 'woman', 'boy', 'girl', 'stallion', and 'mare' must be eliminated from the inventory of elements if they can be explained univocally as relational units that include only 'he' and 'she', on the one hand, and 'sheep', 'human being', 'child', 'horse', on the other.   (Hjelmslev 1961: 70)

In other words, *man* implies 'he-human being', *ram* implies 'he-sheep', and *stallion* implies 'he-horse'. Similarly, *woman* implies 'she-human being', *ewe* implies 'she-sheep', *mare* implies 'she-horse'. The shared content of *boy* and *girl* can be captured by means of the element 'child': *boy* is 'he-human being, child' and *girl* is 'she-human being, child'. Hjelmslev urged that the process of reductive analysis be carried through as far as possible: "until all inventories have been restricted, and restricted as much as possible" (p. 71).

Subsequent to Hjelmslev (1961), a similar style of structuralist analysis came to be known as componential analysis (CA). The set of words *man*, *woman*, *boy*, *girl*, and (sometimes) *child*, and apparently comparable sets from various farmyard animal species, was employed in influential linguistics texts, such as John Lyons' (1968) *An Introduction to Theoretical Linguistics*, Adrienne Lehrer's (1974) *Semantic Fields and Lexical Structure*, Geoffrey Leech's (1974) *Semantics*, and Eugene Nida's (1975) *Componential Analysis of Meaning*. The influence of structuralist anthropology was important too. Componential analysis of kinship systems had arisen independently in American anthropology in the works of Lounsbury (1956) and Goodenough (1956), and their analyses of complex kinship phenomena in native American languages commanded tremendous prestige. As D'Andrade (1995: 30) explains, in those days structuralist techniques of kinship analysis did not seem specialized and formalistic, as they do today. "Then such an analysis was experienced as a nearly magical process of discovery in which elegant patterns emerged from an initial jumble of kin terms and kin types." Of course, the set of words *man, woman,* etc. is a very small and humble part of the anthropological picture, but just because it appears to yield so simply and transparently to structural analysis it came to function as canonical introductory material. When Lyons (1968: 470) said that "what is meant by componential analysis is best explained by means of a simple example", and adduced for this purpose sets of words such as *man—woman—child, bull—cow—calf, rooster—hen—chicken*, and so on, he rightly noted that this example "has often been used for this purpose by linguists".

So it was then, and so it is today. Introductory linguistics textbooks, such as Fromkin et al. (2012) and O'Grady and Archibald (2009), routinely adduce feature displays such as those in Figure 2.1 to illustrate what is variously described as componential analysis, lexical decomposition, or semantic feature analysis. To judge from Google searches, countless linguistics lecturers in the USA, Europe, and Australia include similar material in their introductory semantics handouts.

Less frequently, apparently parallel word sets for animal species are used without explicit comparison with the domain of 'humans'. For example, Radford et al. (1999) illustrate meaning decomposition into semantic features by considering "triples" of words such as *ram, ewe, lamb; bull, cow, calf;* and *stallion, mare, foal.* The analysis is essentially the same, but with features such as OVINE, BOVINE, or EQUINE substituted in place of HUMAN.

The choice of the "third feature" (i.e. the one in addition to ±MALE and ±HUMAN) varies somewhat. Sometimes it is ±MATURE, sometimes ±ADULT, sometimes ±YOUNG. In some cases, the textbooks or handouts note analytical problems with the choice of features, such as the existence of functionally equivalent variants

man:	[+HUMAN]	woman:	[+HUMAN]
	[+MALE]		[−MALE]
	[+ADULT]		[+ADULT]
boy:	[+HUMAN]	girl:	[+HUMAN]
	[+MALE]		[−MALE]
	[−ADULT]		[−ADULT]

FIGURE 2.1 Standard feature analysis of *man, woman, boy, girl*

(MATURE, ADULT, YOUNG, etc.). Less commonly, they express a tinge of doubt about characterizing the "female" members of the sets as −MALE, or declare (like O'Grady and Archibald 2009: 197): "Nothing depends on the choice of feature names here; the analysis would work just as well with the feature ±FEMALE as ±MALE." The word *child* usually enters the picture in connection with the point that a particular semantic feature can remain unspecified or neutral. Thus, *child* is unspecified (or neutral) as to the feature ±MALE, paralleling *lamb, calf,* and *foal* in this regard.

If these componential-style analyses of *men, women,* and *children* are profoundly flawed (as we believe they are), their canonical status in the linguistics curriculum can hardly be a matter of indifference to linguists. Imagine the ruckus if it were discovered that introductory chemistry texts included incorrect formulas or described unworkable lab procedures. The twin tasks to be undertaken in the present study are to expose the inadequacies of the canonical analysis and to propose and justify a much more satisfactory analysis. Some of the results have broad-ranging ramifications for cognitive and social psychology and for cultural anthropology. Within linguistics, this case study in semantic analysis will raise issues of semantic methodology. In view of the general revival of interest in meaning and conceptualization that has galvanized linguistics in recent years, it is timely to return to some foundational questions of semantic methodology. We argue that fundamental questions for semantic analysis turn on the issue of semantic metalanguage, and that failure to heed and act on these issues has undermined, and continues to undermine, a great deal of semantic work.

The remainder of the chapter is structured as follows. Section 2.2 reviews traditional componential analysis, drawing out its similarities to and differences from NSM. Section 2.3 first deals with the English words *men, women,* and *children,* proposing original semantic explications in each case and arguing for their superiority over standard analyses. It continues in the same vein with a treatment of *babies, boys,* and *girls.* Section 2.4 reviews the results with respect to the treatment of category structures in mainstream cognitive linguistics, i.e. in terms of prototypes and extensions. In this connection, we examine "hedged" expressions such as *a real man* and *a typical woman,* and we touch on derivationally related words such as *manly, boyish, childish,* and *childlike,* which seem to invoke or activate social stereotypes. In section 2.5 we provide a lexical typological perspective on the meanings we have covered, dealing first with cross-linguistic semantic differences. Drawing on comparisons with Russian, Japanese, and other languages, we show that meanings identical to those expressed by the English words *babies, boys, girls, male,* and *female* are not universal. On the other hand, we argue that despite appearances to the contrary, meanings comparable, or even identical, to the meanings of English *men, women,* and *children* may well be universal in human languages. Section 2.6 contains concluding remarks. Aside from its inherent interest, the study serves to illustrate the application of the concept of "semantic molecules".

2.2 Methodology and metalanguage: componential analysis vs. NSM

How are meanings to be represented? Necessarily, in some kind of notation which can be termed a language of semantic description. What then is the relationship between the language of semantic description and the ordinary language being described? For Hjelmslev (1961), it was clear that the process of reduction was to take place inside the language being described. He saw the descriptions he presented as no different in kind from those of a unilingual dictionary; what was different was rather the systematicity and formalized nature of the analysis process. Consequently: "that which is established as equivalent to a given entity, when that entity is so reduced, is actually the *definition* of that entity, formulated in the same language and in the same plane as that to which the entity itself belongs" (pp. 71–72).

This means, of course, that apparently synonymous expressions in different languages could receive different analyses. For example, Hjelmslev's definitions of Danish 'man' and 'woman' contain the elements 'he' and 'she', which have no analogues in nearby Finnish, and consequently the structural analyses of the Finnish counterparts of 'man' and 'woman' would be quite different. But such an outcome may not have bothered Hjelmslev as a committed structuralist, and may even have been a welcome one for him.

As noted by Lyons (1977; cf. Goddard 1994b), later cohorts of structuralists, including those in the American generativist tradition, preferred to think that once a deep enough level of analysis had been reached, the units of analysis would turn out to be the same across languages: that is, they expected to discover a universal system of meaning representation. Presumably, considerations of this nature were behind the substitution of the terms 'male' and 'female' (or ±MALE) for Hjelmslev's 'he' and 'she'. In fact, some languages lack words for 'male' and 'female' (just as some lack words for 'he' and 'she'), but this fact did not trouble the practitioners of componential analysis, either in linguistics or anthropology, on account of two other divergences from classic linguistic structuralism. The first was to see the semantic analysis as a cognitive or conceptual representation, and not just in terms of formal relationships between linguistic items. The second was the belief that the terms of semantic analysis are not themselves words in a natural language, but rather belong to a technical or formal language of cognitive representation. These two considerations are both part of the conventional wisdom, according to which it does not matter whether or not a particular language has words for 'male' or 'female', because the concepts behind the words *man, woman, boy,* and *girl* depend on the **concepts** of male and female, and these concepts (it is assumed) are universal, whether or not they are lexicalized in a particular language.

In our view, it is futile and self-defeating to retreat from natural language as the language of semantic representation, for the following reasons. First, even if the language of description is a technical one composed of features, logical symbols, and what-not, it still has to be interpretable by the users of the representation. Even if these users are trained experts, such as professional semanticists, they necessarily rely on their native natural languages as they are learning to use their specialized technical system, and they necessarily fall back on their native natural languages when they communicate between themselves about the intended meaning or interpretation of the technical analyses (as when logicians and formal semanticists introduce and discuss the "intuitions" behind their formalisms in ordinary language paraphrases).

Allan (1986: 268) has argued on this basis that any artificial semantic formalism is best viewed as "a degenerate form of a natural language". In order to read and interpret an artificial metalanguage, he argues, what one effectively does is to mentally translate it back into one's native language. In a more recent work, he writes:

> There is no point claiming that the semantic component MALE is a metalanguage symbol and at the same time not the English word *male*. Unless we are carrying out a pointless mental exercise, no matter what symbol we use for this component, the meaning for that symbol must be equivalent to the relevant sense of the English *male*.   (Allan 2001: 272)

It follows that the optimal metalanguage of semantic description is a standardized and regularized version of a natural language, rather than an artificial creation which is covertly dependent on ordinary language in any case.[1]

A second reason for avoiding technical terms in the metalanguage (as mentioned in Chapter 1) relates to the goal of achieving a description that is conceptually realistic, in the sense of capturing the indigenous or "native" conceptualization. A description framed in indigenous categories can have a *prima facie* case for conceptual reality, because it is framed in terms which are used by speakers them-selves on a daily basis, which are recognizable to them, and which are directly accessible to their intuitions. In contrast, a description framed in technical terms, unrecognizable to the people concerned, at the very least requires some kind of special pleading before it can be accepted as modelling the conceptualization of these people. Yet such special pleading is seldom provided by advocates of technical analyses. That there is a serious epistemological issue here usually goes unrecognized in linguistic discussions. Note that we are not saying that abstract technical analyses are necessarily wrong or that they have no place in semantics—only that they require special justification. Other things being equal, a simpler representation framed in natural language is always preferable to a technical one.

---

[1] Commentators sometimes treat NSM as a variety of "componential analysis" (Geeraerts 2006), but this only makes sense if one understands this term as synonymous with decompositional semantics in all its varieties. In our view, it makes much better sense to reserve the term componential analysis (CA) for structuralist, feature-based systems (cf. Goddard 2005*a*).

The principle that semantic hypotheses about indigenous ways of thinking ought to be framed in indigenous terms (Wierzbicka's (1992a: 331) "principle of indigenization") cuts much deeper than this, however. It disqualifies the analyst from using ordinary language words which have no equivalents in the language being described. For example, it would disqualify one from using the term 'adult' in semantic descriptions of the Yankunytjatjara words *wati* 'man' and *kungka* 'woman', because the Yankunytjatjara language has no word corresponding in meaning to 'adult' (Goddard 1996b).[2] Similarly, it would violate the principle of indigenization to describe Yankunytjatjara causative meanings using a putative semantic component CAUSE, because, like most languages of the world, Yankunytjatjara has no verb corresponding to *cause* (though it does have an equivalent to the semantic prime BECAUSE). Violating the principle of indigenization can legitimately be described as "terminological ethnocentrism". Like ethnocentrism in general, it involves imposing alien cultural categories upon people of other languages and cultures, with an inevitably distorting effect.

A third advantage of basing the metalanguage of semantic description as transparently as possible on natural language is methodological. As pointed out by Ruth Kempson (1977), among others, to test and revise hypotheses about meanings depends on our being able to generate predictions about ordinary language use on the basis of the semantic description. The more transparent the relationship between the two, the clearer and more testable the descriptions become. Conversely, as the relationship between the semantic description and the "real" language being described becomes more and more tenuous, the prospect of any real empirical testing evaporates. For example, take the perennial analysis of *x kills y* as [CAUSE *x* (DIE *y*)]. One obvious empirical objection to this analysis is that the range of use of *X caused Y to die* does not match that of *X killed Y*: the version with *kill* demands a "direct" connection between the agent's action and the fatal outcome. The appropriate reaction to such evidence is to revise and improve the analysis, but McCawley (1972) dismissed the relevance of the evidence by claiming that the technical semantic component CAUSE is not identical in meaning to the English verb *cause*. The point is that allowing a disconnect between the language of description and the language being described makes the analysis immune from empirical disconfirmation (see also Allan 2001: 272 above).

One further observation is necessary. Like any analysis, semantic analysis requires a process of reduction: the breaking down of complex meanings into configurations of progressively simpler meanings. From an intuitive point of view, what this means in practice is that a viable semantic analysis must always be phrased in terms which are simpler and more intelligible than the expression being explicated. An analysis of

---

[2] The closest expression is *anangu pulka* [person big], which is closer in meaning to the English word *grown-up* than to *adult*.

father and *mother*, for example, as 'male parent' and 'female parent' can be questioned on this basis, for there is no reason to believe that the meaning of the word *parent* is any simpler than that of *father* or *mother*. The analysis of *child* as 'non-adult human' can be questioned along the same lines, for there is no reason to believe that the meaning of the word *adult* is any simpler than that of *child*. Intuitively, the opposite would seem more likely on both counts, i.e. that *parent* is the more complex term and ought to be explicated as, essentially, 'father or mother'; and that *adult* is the more complex term and ought to be explicated as, essentially, 'someone who is not a child any more'. In addition, it can be noted that *parent* and *adult* are less frequent and acquired later in child language acquisition than *father*, *mother*, or *child*.

Still, in giving these examples we are relying primarily on intuitive judgements of relative semantic complexity, and such judgements can be misleading. The more reliable test is the test of semantic analysis itself. In the carrying through of systematic and progressive semantic analysis, it usually becomes very clear that analysis is viable in one direction, but non-viable in the other. Trying to carry through an analysis in the wrong direction, i.e. trying to explicate the simple (or relatively simple) in terms of the complex (or relatively complex), inevitably leads to circularity—providing, of course, that the analytical process is pushed far enough. On this point, we are at one with Hjelmslev (1961). Semantic analysis must be pursued as far as it can go, until the process terminates in a highly restricted set of meanings that resist further decomposition. Only in this way can we make the semantic content of any complex expression explicit in full detail.

Our primary analytical tool, the NSM metalanguage, has been introduced in Chapter 1. In this chapter, our intention is not to justify or explain the metalanguage any further, but rather to show how it can be used to carry through a detailed set of semantic analyses—of the English words *men*, *women*, *children*, *boys*, and *girls*, and related words in other languages. On the other hand, it is true to say that the exercise can be seen as a test of the expressive capacity of the NSM metalanguage itself. In a very real sense, each and every attempted explication is an experiment, an experiment which tests the adequacy of the analytical tools used to conduct it. Many of the various refinements and improvements to the NSM model over the years have emerged from the crucible of semantic experimentation.

We will shortly commence the analysis proper. In all cases we will be concerned only with the basic descriptive meanings of the words concerned, not with any additional polysemic meanings connected with social attitudes or the like. This raises the question of how lexical polysemy is treated in the NSM approach. This question has been extensively discussed in the NSM literature (cf. Wierzbicka 1996; Goddard 2000b). Briefly, NSM follows the traditional "definitional" approach (Geeraerts 1994). In general, one assumes to begin with that there is but a single meaning, and attempts to state it in a clear and predictive fashion, in the form of a translatable reductive paraphrase (explication). Only if persistent efforts fail is polysemy posited. The next hypothesis is that there are two distinct meanings, and attempts are made to state both in a clear and predictive fashion, and so the process goes, until the full range of application of the word can be captured within the specified range of senses. The paraphrase analysis procedure allows us not only to detect polysemy but also to understand it, because it enables us to "see" and to compare the relevant meanings in detail. Needless to say, this procedure can only be implemented if the principles of good definition are followed. The NSM requirements that meanings be stated as reductive paraphrases, and that their validity be testable by substitution, provide clear guidelines to limit the ad hoc postulation of polysemy. Usually these procedures converge on the same results that would be expected on the basis of standard lexicological tests for detecting polysemy (cf. Cruse 1986): the possibility of directly contrasting the two meanings without contradiction, the existence of different antonyms for the putatively different senses, different syntactic properties attaching to the different senses, the existence of derived forms accepting only one of the senses, different entailments and implications, and so on.

A familiar example is the French word *fille*, which can be used to refer both to daughters and to girls. It would not be possible to formulate a single predictive paraphrase, because any paraphrase broad enough to include both kinds of use would have to say that *fille* meant something like 'female human being', which would be too broad. We therefore posit two distinct meanings for *fille*. In further support of this, it can be pointed out that the conjoined phrase *le garçon et la fille* can only mean 'the boy and the girl' (not 'the boy and the daughter') and that the phrase *le fils et la fille* can only mean 'the son and the daughter' (not 'the son and the girl'). It could also be pointed out that only one of the posited meanings participates in diminutive derivation, i.e. *fillette* can only mean 'little girl', not 'little daughter'. There are also some syntactic frames which allow one meaning but not the other, e.g. *la fille de Marie* can only mean 'Mary's daughter' (not 'Mary's girl').

Closer to home, we can take the English word *child* as an example. Like most dictionaries, we recognize two main senses. *Child*$_1$ is (roughly speaking) a stage-of-life term, and its meaning is one of the main concerns of this study. *Child*$_2$ is not a stage-of-life term, but rather a relational term, implying 'someone's child'. *Child*$_1$ contrasts with the word *adult*, while *child*$_2$ does not. One could say about a woman in her 50s or 60s, for example, that at a family gathering *All her children were there*, referring to her *adult children* (i.e. the expression *adult children*$_2$ is acceptable, while *adult children*$_1$ is self-contradictory). *Child*$_1$ is related to other stage-of-life words, such as *men* and *women*, while *child*$_2$ is related to other relational kin words, such as *mother* and *father*. In a syntactic frame such as *Mary's child*, the word can only have the meaning *child*$_2$. On the other hand, the meaning *child*$_1$ participates in derivatives such as *childish* and *childlike* (see section 2.4), while *child*$_2$ does not. Finally, it is not possible to formulate a single paraphrase that would apply to both uses of *child* and still have predictive power, because any such paraphrase would necessarily be too broad in its application.

With this by way of background, we now turn to a detailed semantic analysis of English *men, women,* and *children,* followed by *boys, girls,* and *babies.*

2.3 Semantic explications for basic social categories

Of the NSM semantic primes, the most important ones that are relevant to the present study are KIND, PEOPLE, BODY, and TWO: because the words *men, women,* and *children* effect a categorization, i.e. a partition into KINDS, of PEOPLE based on a contrast between TWO kinds of BODIES. Beyond this, however, it turns out that a surprisingly rich assortment of semantic primes is needed to flesh out other details connected with the "gender" difference and with the "maturity" dimensions. These include: PART, the time-period expression FOR SOME TIME, the dimension term SMALL, the specifier elements THIS and OTHER, the verbal elements LIVE, DO, and HAPPEN, and the "logical" concepts BECAUSE and CAN,[3] among others. None of these expressions, of course, has been devised specifically for the purpose at hand. They are all necessary for semantic analysis in diverse areas across the lexicon.

Men, women, *and* children

In approaching the set of words *men, women,* and *children,* there are good reasons to start with *children,* counter-intuitive as it may seem at first. Starting with *children* allows us to proceed without immediately confronting the issue of "sex-differentiation", and this is not just a matter of convenience, because, we will see shortly, the distinction between *women* and *men* depends on the capacity of *women* to bring *children* into the world.

As we have seen, the conventional semantic analysis of *children* boils down to 'non-adult human' or 'immature human'. The deficiencies of this analysis should be rather clear by this point, particularly the semantic complexity of the concepts of 'adult' or 'mature'. To "unpack" the semantic complexity of *children* in full detail requires a semantic explication of moderate length and complexity, given in [A] below.[4] Notice that the explication is framed entirely in semantic primes. There are no semantic molecules needed.

---

[3] NSM researchers argue that semantic prime CAN is a unitary and semantically irreducible expression in natural language (Wierzbicka 1996: 103–107; Goddard and Wierzbicka 2002a: 73–75). This means rejecting the artificial distinction between the "*can* of ability" and the "*can* of possibility" which has found its way into linguistics from the logical tradition. Cross-linguistic studies show that languages generally have a morpholexical expression that can be used in contexts such as both 'I can/can't do it' ("ability") and 'bad things can happen' ("possibility").

[4] An earlier version of this analysis (Goddard 2012a) included a component 'people of this kind have lived for a short time, not for a long time'; however, this depended on the use of the semantically complex English perfect construction ('has lived'), which does not have semantic equivalents in many languages. The explication presented here also incorporates several other small improvements over previous analyses, including that presented in the earlier hardback edition of the present book.

[A]   *children*

a.   people of one kind
b.   all people are people of this kind for some time
c.   when someone is someone of this kind, it is like this:
d.   this someone's body is small
e.   this someone can do some things, this someone can't do many other things
f.   because of this, if other people don't do good things for this someone at many times,
        bad things can happen to this someone

The top-most component categorizes *children* as 'people of one kind', while component (b) captures the existential fact that being someone of this kind is a necessary stage in the life of all people. In their reliance on the concept of 'kind', it is fair to say that these two components reflect or express an implicit "essentialism" (Gelman 2005). On the other hand, it is important to remember that an explication is not a claim about reality as such, but about a representation embedded in a language. Line (c) introduces a set of components that characterize a person's situation as a child. Component (d) says that 'this someone's body is small'. (It does seem strange that "smallness" is altogether missing from the traditional analysis.)[5] The final two components, (e) and (f), articulate social properties and relations: that a child is only partially capable ('this someone can do some things, this someone can't do many other things') and consequently that he or she is dependent on other people ('if other people don't do good things for this someone at many times, bad things can happen to this someone').[6]

It is implicit in explication [A] that in the normal course of life people do not remain *children* indefinitely. This brings us to the question of *women* and *men*, which are explicated in [B] and [C] below. Both explications begin with the same set of components. The first component ('people of one kind') establishes the existence of the category and the second ('people of this kind are not children [m]') differentiates it from the category 'children'. In effect, this second component does the same work as the traditional [+ADULT]. Component (c) then establishes that the kind of people in question have a specific body type ('people of this

---

[5] It is a striking fact that morphological diminutives are often derived historically from a word meaning 'child' (Jurafsky 1996).

[6] The explication for the singular 'child' is the same in all respects, except that the initial component is 'someone of one kind', rather than 'people of one kind'. The same applies for 'woman' and 'man', in relation to 'women' and 'men', to be explicated in [B] and [C] below. In addition to its simplicity and inherent plausibility, a subtle semantic observation supporting this analysis is that words like 'child' and 'woman' are more "individualizing" and less species-bound than their plural counterparts; for example, it seems to us that one can think of Aphrodite as a 'woman'—more readily than one can think of all the Greek goddesses together as 'women'. 'Child', 'woman', and 'man' function as semantic molecules in later explications in this study, and are necessary in other areas of the lexicon as well, especially kinship vocabulary (Wierzbicka forthcoming).

kind have bodies of one kind'), which is then subsequently elaborated.[7] These three shared components provide the conceptual backdrop, so to speak, for the twin concepts of *men* and *women*. In reality, of course, things are not so clear cut, but the explications are not intended to be a picture of reality. They are intended to be a picture of the conceptualization implicit in the words *women* and *men*.

How then to characterize the difference between the body types of *men* and *women*? The traditional, and largely unexamined, assumption is that "maleness" is semantically simpler, presumably because some morphological processes treat maleness as the unmarked category. We agree that there is a sense in which maleness is conceptually taken-for-granted relative to femaleness; but this does not necessarily mean that maleness is semantically simpler. From a conceptual point of view, the biological categorization is anchored in the facts of birth and motherhood. Given that we are starting with a categorization based on body types, it is easier and more natural to give a positive specification of the criterial property of women's bodies, namely, their capacity to "have children": hence the final components (d)–(e) in explication [B] for *women*, in which 'child [m]' appears as a semantic molecule.

[B]   *women*

a.   people of one kind
b.   people of this kind are not children [m]
c.   people of this kind have bodies of one kind
d.   the bodies of people of this kind are like this:
e.   inside the body of someone of this kind there can be for some time the body of a
        child [m]

Essentially, components (d) and (e) characterize women's bodies in terms of the capacity to be pregnant ('inside the body of someone of this kind there can be for some time the body of a child [m]'), but without mentioning any details about conception, sexual reproduction, or birth. Presumably, even youngsters learn fairly early in life that this is the explanation for the big tummy of a pregnant woman. Note that the explication in no way implies that an individual woman who cannot have children is not a *woman*. The claim is rather that to say that someone is a *woman* is to say something "generic" about this person: that she is someone belonging to the kind of people whose bodies are of the kind that can have children.[8]

---

[7] It might be asked why gender-specific body-parts are not mentioned. There are two reasons: first, to include terms like 'breasts', 'penis', 'beard' in the explications would incur circularity, because plausible explications for such terms themselves rely on the concepts 'woman' and 'man' (Wierzbicka 2007c); second, this degree of anatomical detail is not very plausible from a cognitive or intuitive point of view.

[8] The claim cannot be accurately glossed simply as "women are the kind of people that can bear children", because this omits reference to the kind of human body involved. It may also be worth noting that, as long observed in the philosophical literature on kinds (cf. Gelman 2005), an individual may belong

The explication for *men* is given in [C] below. Components (a)–(c) are the same as for *women*. After that, rather than characterizing men's bodies in positive terms, a different strategy is employed, namely, contrasting them with women's bodies. Component (d) presents a holistic contrast ('the bodies of people of this kind are not like women's [m] bodies') and component (e) presents a more specific contrast about body-parts: 'some parts of bodies of this kind are not like parts of women's [m] bodies'. In a very real sense, then, the concept of 'men' takes the concept of 'women' for granted.

[C]   *men*

a.   people of one kind
b.   people of this kind are not children [m]
c.   people of this kind have bodies of one kind
d.   the bodies of people of this kind are not like women's [m] bodies
e.   some parts of bodies of this kind are not like parts of women's [m] bodies

Though the explication for *men* in [C] may seem superficially no more complex than either the explications for *women* [B] or *children* [A], in reality it is the most complex of all, because it utilizes both 'women' and 'children' as semantic molecules. Its greater semantic complexity is disguised by the fact that most of the complexity is pre-packaged into these two taken-for-granted concepts.

Babies, boys, *and* girls

In this section, we undertake to explicate the meanings of three more words from the same semantic field in English, and we will begin with *babies*. Despite its high frequency and impressionistically basic status, structuralist treatments rarely mention this word. Perhaps the oversight is due to the absence of comparable terms in the word sets for animal species; or perhaps it is because the basis for the differentiation does not lend itself to a binary feature treatment. On intuitive grounds, it would seem that being a *baby* is the first stage of being a child and that babies are a kind of "extreme" subcategory of *children*: they have very small bodies, are more or less incapable of doing anything for themselves, and are therefore much more dependent than *children* in general.

To formalize these ideas in a semantic explication, we propose [D] below. It follows the same general structure as *children*.

to a given kind without possessing all the attributes of the kind in question; for example, an individual *dog* can have only three legs without ceasing to be a dog, an individual *sparrow* can break a wing and be unable to fly without ceasing to be a sparrow.

[D]   *babies*

a.   children [m] of one kind
b.   all children [m] are children [m] of this kind for some time
c.   when a child [m] is a child [m] of this kind, it is like this:
d.   this child's [m] body is very small
e.   this child [m] can do very few things
f.   because of this, if someone doesn't do many good things for this child [m] at many
          times, very bad things can't not happen to this child [m]

The first notable feature is component (a): *babies* are categorized as 'children [m] of one kind', rather than as 'people of one kind'. (Their ultimate status as 'people' is secure, of course, since *children* are themselves categorized as people.) Certainly *babies* are included in the referential scope of the word *children*; for example, if someone asks how many children are in a room, the count will certainly include any babies present; likewise, one would certainly expect to find some babies among the patients at a children's hospital.[9] The next component, (b), depicts being a *baby* as a necessary stage of childhood. The set of components (d)–(f) that characterize the situation of being a baby are more "extreme" versions of their counterparts in the explication of *children*. Component (d) says that a baby's body is 'very small' (not just 'small'). Component (e) says they 'can do very few things'. This "helplessness" component is rather self-evident from an intuitive point of view, but it is also logically important as a link to the following component (f), which captures a baby's extreme dependency and need for protection. (This final component can be seen as a more extreme version of the corresponding component for *children* in general.)

An additional difference is that with *babies*, the final component refers not to 'other people' in the supportive role, but to 'someone': 'if someone doesn't do many good things for this child [m] at many times, very bad things can't not happen to this child [m]'. Though the existence of a mother is not mentioned as such (nor is it necessary for these roles to be fulfilled by the mother, or even by any single person), the phrasing is more individualist, more "one on one", and this way, it is more suggestive of a mother–child relationship.

It might be queried whether some of the components in the *babies* explication are at odds with those implicit in its molecule 'children [m]'. For example, isn't component (e), 'this child [m] can do very few things', at odds with a more "generous" sub-component in the explication of 'children [m]', namely: 'this someone can do some things'? There is no contradiction, however, because it makes perfect sense to

---

[9] In Yankunytjatjara (Central Australia), the word *iṯi* 'baby' can occur in the generic-specific construction with *tjitji* 'child', i.e. as *tjitji iṯi* (Goddard 1996*b*). Comparable constructions are found in many Australian languages.

say that someone 'can do some things, very few things'. That is, the messages conveyed by 'some' and 'very few' are compatible: the relationship is one of amplification. A similar relationship obtains between the other pairs of components, i.e. between 'small' and 'very small'; and between 'bad things' and 'very bad things'.

Before leaving *babies*, it is worth noting that the concept embodied in this English word is a language-specific one. Many languages have no comparable lexical item. Polish, for example, has no word directly comparable to *babies*, using instead the expression *małe dzieci* 'small children' (there is a less common word, *niemowlęta*, reserved for very young babies). We will return to the issue of language-specificity vs. universality in section 2.5.

Now let us turn to *boys* and *girls*, which, as we have seen above, figure centrally in the canonical structuralist account. Obviously, in their basic descriptive meanings *boys* and *girls* are parallel terms semantically. They are explicated in [E] and [F] below, which are identical except for the provisions linking *boys* with *men*, and *girls* with *women*.

[E] *boys*

a. people of one kind
b. people can be people of this kind for a long time, not for a very long time
c. when someone is someone of this kind, this someone is not a man [m]
d. at the same time, some parts of this someone's body are like some parts of a man's [m] body
e. because of this, after some time this someone can be a man [m]

[F] *girls*

a. people of one kind
b. people can be people of this kind for a long time, not for a very long time
c. when someone is someone of this kind, this someone is not a woman [m]
d. at the same time, some parts of this someone's body are like some parts of a woman's [m] body
e. because of this, after some time this someone can be a woman [m]

Component (a) characterizes *boys* (and *girls*) as 'people of one kind' (the same, in this respect, as with *men* and *women*). It would not be justifiable to regard either *boys* or *girls* as 'children [m] of one kind', as with *babies*, because both terms can be used rather freely about young adults (as occasionally noted in the componential analysis literature, this creates difficulties for an analysis of *boys* and *girls* as [−ADULT]). Of course, adequate explications must be compatible with the explication for *children*, and even with *babies*, because we can readily speak of a *baby boy* or *baby girl* (cf. the classic question about a new born baby: *Is it a boy or a girl?*). At the same time it is necessary to convey the idea that being a boy or a girl is not a long-lived stage of life. The explications meet this desideratum by way of component (b), which says of *boys* and *girls* that 'people can be people of this kind for a long time, not for a very long time'. This is a fairly open-ended specification. It is easy to see that young people in their teens could be viewed as still being *boys* or *girls* because it is possible to think that they have not yet lived for a very long time (given that most adults live much longer).[10]

Components (c) and (d) spell out the relationship with *men* in explication [E] and with *women* in [F]. When someone is a *boy*, this someone is not a man, and yet 'at the same time, some parts of this someone's body are like some parts of a man's [m] body'. Consequently, as stated in (e), there is the potential for this person later to be a man: 'because of this, after some time this someone can be a man [m]'. The same components apply, mutatis mutandis, in the explication for *girls*. In this way, the explications capture the notion that being a *boy* or a *girl* is a stage of life prior to being a *man* or a *woman*. In effect, *boys* are potentially future *men*, and *girls* are potentially future *women*.[11]

Brief review

Reflecting on a set of explications like those presented in [A]–[F], newcomers to NSM often observe that although the wording is relatively simple, an explication taken as a whole is a rather complex structure. Partly this is due to the fact that semantic primes have a fairly complex combinational syntax (which allows for considerable flexibility of expression), and partly it is due to the way which explications are configured in terms of anaphoric and causal relations so that their various components cohere and make sense as a whole. We view this outcome as an empirical finding: it appears to be an empirical fact that many human concepts have this kind of intricate structure.

On account of their overall conceptual complexity, to absorb and fully comprehend an explication often takes a certain amount of time and effort. Furthermore, we readily concede that NSM explications composed in a highly limited vocabulary do not sound like everyday speech, and that for many readers they will be strikingly

---

[10] It may be asked whether this explication is compatible with an assertion like *She's just a girl, yet she's already got two children*. Such a sentence of course carries with it the assumption that the situation being described runs contrary to normal expectations (as predicted by the explication), but there is nothing in explication [F] which would make it contradictory in a strict sense. The fact that a given individual is not yet a 'woman' does not strictly entail that her body is unable to bear children (if anything, there is a hint of this possibility in component (d)).

[11] Explications [E] and [F] do not cover the full range of use of English *boys* and *girls*, on account of polysemy. In certain contexts both words can be used about people who clearly qualify as *men* and *women*; for example, when a middle-aged woman speaks about the *girls* in her tennis group or a middle-aged man addresses his fellow football team members as *boys*; cf. *our boys in uniform*. Typical contexts involve "solidarity". These are not literal descriptive uses, but are polysemic extensions that convey additional semantic content related to the speaker's attitude or point of view. This can readily be seen when we ask whether an objective non-participant could refer to those middle-aged men and women as *boys* or as *girls*. Presumably not.

unfamiliar in style. Indeed, there is an obvious intertextual dissonance between the simple wording of NSM explications and the complex high-register vocabulary of most academic writing. For many readers, explications represent a new genre and the NSM metalanguage a new register, and, as when one encounters any new genre and register, a period of familiarization and stylistic habituation is usually necessary before one feels fully comfortable. Nonetheless, we would insist that these difficulties are quite different in nature and scale from the comprehensibility issues posed by opaque and untranslatable technical terminology.

It is also worth highlighting that though we have framed our discussion in terms of our opposition to structuralist-inspired componential analysis, the account we have developed preserves—and we would say, improves on—the structuralist recognition that there is a significant parallelism and symmetry between the twin pairs of words: *man* and *woman*, *boy* and *girl*. For example, if one glances above to explications [E] and [F] for *girls* and *boys*, it will be immediately apparent that they have exactly the same structure, and that they embody the claim that the semantic relationship between *girls* and *women* is exactly parallel to that between *boys* and *men*.

As for the relationship between *women* and *men*, the NSM account recognizes a substantial parallelism in semantic structure. Explications for both concepts largely follow the same semantic template. Comparing [B] and [C], repeated below for convenience, it will be immediately apparent that they share precisely the same set of components (a)–(c). The two meanings are literally built on the same base or frame, i.e. the assumption that "non-children" can be seen as having bodies of two specific kinds.

[B]   *women*

a.   people of one kind
b.   people of this kind are not children [m]
c.   people of this kind have bodies of one kind
d.   the bodies of people of this kind are like this:
e.   inside the body of someone of this kind there can be for some time the body of a child [m]

[C]   *men*

a.   people of one kind
b.   people of this kind are not children [m]
c.   people of this kind have bodies of one kind
d.   the bodies of people of this kind are not like women's [m] bodies
e.   some parts of bodies of this kind are not like parts of women's [m] bodies

In the case of *women* and *men*, however, the symmetry in meaning is not as complete as that between *girls* and *boys*, because some important components of their respective explications do not have the same structure. As argued earlier, the body type of *women* is characterized by a reference to the capacity to have children, whereas the body type of *men* is characterized by contrast with the body type of *women*. It has been one of the main burdens of our case that the structuralist analysis ([+HUMAN, +MALE, +ADULT] and [+HUMAN, −MALE, +ADULT]) overstates the symmetry of meaning between the concepts of *men* and *women*, while at the same time obscuring genuine relationships. Most importantly, it fails to recognize the chain of semantic dependency that connects the concepts of *children*, *women*, and *men*—a chain of semantic dependency which is made explicit in the way in which the first concept serves as a semantic molecule in the meaning structure of the second one, and the second concept in turn serves as a semantic molecule in the meaning structure of the third.[12]

2.4 Categories, prototypes, and stereotypes

We will shortly turn to issues of cross-linguistic comparison: to what extent are meanings like those of English *men*, *women*, and *children* present in other languages of the world? What can be said about the balance between universality and language-specificity in this semantic domain? Before moving to these cross-linguistic issues, however, we want to reflect on how the NSM approach to the semantics of *men*, *women*, and *children* compares with some other influential trends in linguistic semantics, specifically with the widespread view in cognitive and functional linguistics that lexical categories have a prototype structure and that some members of a category are "more central" than others (Lakoff 1987; Taylor 1995). This will lead us to inquire into so-called hedged expressions, such as *a real man* and *a typical man*, and into derived words, such as *manly*, *boyish*, and *childish*. These have been argued in the literature to provide evidence for a gradient view of category structure, mainly because such expressions appear to highlight or bring into focus certain social expectations associated with the core categories.

---

[12] Would it be possible to construct an equally plausible analysis based on the opposite chain of semantic dependencies, e.g. starting from 'man' as a potential "begetter"? The prospect of multiple equally plausible analyses haunted classical feature analysis (Bolinger 1965; Burling 1969), but the NSM approach avoids this prospect by requiring that explications be both non-circular and conceptually plausible. To start with 'man' as a "potential begetter" would require spelling out the basics of sexual reproduction; roughly, that someone of one kind can do something with part of his body to the body of someone else of the other kind, with the result that inside the body of this other someone, there can be something which is like a part of that someone's body, and which afterwards can be the body of another someone. Although it may be possible to avoid circularity in such a line of analysis, and it would indeed be appropriate for a semantic analysis of a word like *begetter* (or *progenitor*), it would hardly be plausible from a conceptual point of view to include this degree of sexual detail in the semantics of *man*.

The NSM view of "category structure": classical or cognitive, or both?

The NSM position does not fit readily into the stock classifications one often finds in overview discussions of "category structure". Clearly it is not a structuralist approach, and yet (as discussed above in section 2.3), it is mindful of the need to capture and correctly characterize meaning relations, such as various kinds of antonymy and hyponymy, and to identify semantically coherent subdomains within the lexicon (cf. Wierzbicka 1992*b*).

As far as the standard opposition between "classical" and "prototypical" views of category structure is concerned, the NSM position seems to align with aspects of both approaches, while differing from both in other ways. The so-called classical or Aristotelian view is often characterized as the view that nominal categories (roughly, noun meanings) can be captured via a fixed set of necessary and sufficient conditions, thereby implying that category boundaries are fixed and that category membership is an "all-or-nothing" affair (Taylor 1995). Do NSM explications, such as those above, represent a set of "necessary and sufficient conditions"? In a sense, yes they do. Not that it is claimed that every single use of a word necessarily fully conforms to the set of semantic components in its explication, because words may be used in the service of irony, poetry, word-play, and/or other creative or rhetorical purposes. But setting these usage variations and modulations aside, the NSM claim is that when a speaker uses a word in a given sense, he or she expresses the full set of semantic components which constitute its meaning, and conversely, that when the situation and discourse context are compatible with the use of a given word in a given sense, then the word can be so used, if the speaker chooses. This is, essentially, what it means to say that NSM explications aim to be predictive of the actual range of use of a word.

On the other hand, NSM semantic components are unlike classical category conditions in many ways. For one thing, they abound with "subjective" components of all sorts, e.g. components to the effect that something is LIKE something else, evaluational components (involving GOOD and BAD), and dimensional judgements, such as A LONG TIME vs. A SHORT TIME. Such components reflect the inherent subjectivity and anthropocentrism of ordinary language. The NSM approach is strongly opposed to what is variously termed objectivism, referentialism, or correspondence theories of meaning, i.e. to the view that meaning consists in a correspondence between a linguistic expression and the real world. For NSM linguists, meaning is first and foremost a conceptual phenomenon, albeit with social and cultural underpinnings. Many NSM explications, furthermore, incorporate prototypical cognitive or motivational scenarios. All these things set the NSM approach apart from the classical view of category structure.

Is the NSM position, then, more aligned with cognitive linguistics, as in the works of George Lakoff and Ronald Langacker, or with the conceptual semantics of Ray Jackendoff? In different respects, the answer is yes. NSM linguists would certainly echo Taylor's (1995: 83) statement: "For cognitivists...[m]eanings are cognitive structures, embedded in patterns of knowledge and belief" (cf. Fillmore 1985). Likewise, they endorse the strong emphasis in cognitive linguistics on construal and subjectivity in meaning (Langacker 1987; Taylor and MacLaury 1995). An important point of alignment with Jackendoff's work is shared commitment to the existence of a finite set of "conceptual primitives" governed by well-specified principles of combination (Jackendoff 1990). In our view, cognitive linguistics is best seen as a movement or a coalition, rather than as a single approach, and the NSM approach can rightly be seen as one research program in this broad movement or coalition. On the other hand, there are significant differences between the NSM approach and these other cognitivist programs. At the theoretical level, the greatest difference turns on the issue of representation and metalanguage. Most cognitive linguists remain wedded to vocabularies of semantic representation that are complex and English-specific, and they often seem oblivious to the semiotic complexity of their diagrammatic representations (cf. Goddard 2006b; Wierzbicka 2007a; 2007b).

More pertinently to the present study, many cognitive-functional linguists would not accept the NSM position that meanings can be pinned down and clearly stated in discrete propositional terms, because they hold the belief that "linguistic categories have no clear boundaries". Since the influential work of Eleanor Rosch and colleagues in the 1970s (cf. Rosch and Mervis 1975; Rosch 1978), it has become a commonly held position that category membership is a "gradient phenomenon" or "a matter of degree". In his book *Linguistic Categorization: Prototypes in Linguistic Theory*, Taylor (1995: 75–76) argues that so-called "hedges", such as *typical*, *real*, and *strictly speaking*, are "linguistic resources for expressing degree of category membership", for example by distinguishing between central and peripheral members of a category or by re-weighting attributes of a category relative to a larger frame.[13] The word *real*, for example, "highlights attributes conventionally associated with a frame, while at the same time releasing a category from otherwise necessary conditions for membership. A *real man* exhibits to a strong degree stereotyped attributes of masculinity; his gender is not at issue" (p. 97). Taylor's discussion builds on Lakoff's (1987: 74–84) well-known treatment of the meaning of *mother*, in which expressions such as *real mother* play an important part. Lakoff argues that "there is more than one criterion for 'real' motherhood" (p. 75), and that this constitutes evidence for a cluster model of radial polysemy.

On the basis of these discussions, we assume that many cognitive linguists could be uncomfortable with what they could see as the excessively "categorical" nature of the meaning structures we have proposed for *men*, *women*, and *children*, and related words, and we suppose that they would turn to expressions such as *a typical man, a*

---

[13] Ironically, Lakoff (1987: 45) goes to some lengths to argue that prototype effects do not necessarily implicate degrees of category membership, hence disavowing his earlier stance on hedges in Lakoff (1972).

typical woman, a real man, and so on, in an attempt to demonstrate both that the concepts of *man* and *woman* are both less well delimited than in our account and also that they are semantically richer, i.e. that they include components (albeit peripheral) related to social attitudes, gender roles, and the like. Morphologically related expressions such as *manly, womanly*, and *childlike* might also be adduced as evidence that the concepts of *man, woman*, and *child* are associated with particular gender role stereotypes. We therefore think it worthwhile to examine such expressions in some detail.

A typical woman, a real man, *etc.*

Phraseological data from English corpora show that *(a) real man* is a common collocation in English, and that *(a) real woman* is also well attested, though it is less common than *real man*. At the same time, *a typical woman* is quite common, and probably not less so than *a typical man*. For example, when we consulted in Wordbanks Online (on 4/2/2008) we found that the frequency of *a real man* was much higher than that of *a real woman* (30 vs. 19), whereas in the case of *a typical man* and *a typical woman* it was the other way around (1 vs. 4). Since the absolute figures involved were small, we went on to compare the figures for these four phrases on the internet, using the Google search engine. The results were rather similar. As shown in Table 2.1, the figures for *real man* were two to three times higher than those for *real woman*, whereas the figures for *typical man* and *typical woman* (though smaller in absolute terms) were much closer to one another.

With all the qualifications which need to be added in relation to Google searches as a linguistic tool (cf. Fletcher 2007; Schmied 2006; Wierzbicka 2009c), these results confirm the intuitions of native speakers of English whom we have consulted: there is a strong stereotype of *a real man* among English speakers, which is not matched by an equally strong stereotype of *a real woman*. There is no corresponding asymmetry in the case of *a typical man* and *a typical woman*.

What do such contrasts in collocatability tell us about the meanings of the words *man* and *woman*? As we will seek to show in this section, they tell us a lot—but not about the meanings of *man* and *woman*. Above all, they tell us a great deal about stereotypes widespread among speakers of English and reflected in English phraseology. They also tell us something interesting about lexical semantics—but again, not about the words *man* and *woman*. Rather, they throw an interesting light on the meaning of the words *typical* and *real*.

TABLE 2.1 **Google "hits" for four English collocations (rounded)**

	real man	*real woman*	*typical man*	*typical woman*
2.2.08	3 million	1 million	100,000	100,000
8.5.08	3.8 million	1.5 million	130,000	99,000

We will begin with *typical*, since it is simpler to deal with. We would propose the semantic explication in [G] below. As one can see, it claims that to describe someone as a *typical* person of a particular kind (*man, woman, Englishman, scholar*, etc.) is to invoke a certain identifiable stereotype about how people of this kind behave. The reference to a stereotype is spelt out in component (b) ('many people think about people of this kind like this: – –'); cf. Stollznow (2006).

[G]   *X is a typical man (woman, scholar, Jewish mother, etc.).*

a.   X is someone of one kind
b.   many people think about people of this kind like this:
c.   "these people often do some things, other people don't often do these things"
d.   X is like this, X often does these things

The phrase *a typical Jewish mother* sounds very natural in English because there is a well-known stereotype of a Jewish mother in English-speaking countries. This stereotype is not lexically encoded either in the word *Jewish* or in the word *mother*, but in a sense the existence of a recognizable stereotype is implied in the word *typical* (cf. Lakoff 1987: 85–87). What applies to *a typical Jewish mother* applies also to *a typical woman, typical man*, etc.

The word *real* presents a more complex picture than does *typical*. As argued extensively by one of the present authors (Wierzbicka 2002c), *real* is an English cultural key word, with a high frequency, rich phraseology, and extended polysemy. Its various meanings are interrelated and are linked with different syntactic frames. The topic is large and cannot be treated at length here, but the observations below should be sufficient for the present purposes. The first essential point is that noun phrases with the word *real* involve different categories of nouns, both human and non-human. We will be concerned only with human nouns, as shown in (i) below. Other categories include: (ii) "non-human concrete", (iii) "non-human abstract", (iv) "non-human linguistic". Each of these deserves lengthy discussion, but that would take us too far afield here.

   (i)   a real person; a real hero/scoundrel; a real man
   (ii) real flowers; real money
   (iii) a real disaster; a real coincidence; a real war; a real drought
   (iv) real sense of the word; real sense of the term; a real sense

Our second point is that even the "human noun" category designated here as (i) is heterogeneous, and that at least three distinct subcategories need to be distinguished here, depending on the type of head noun. The first are nouns with the meaning 'people' or 'person', as in expressions like *real people, a real person, a real human being*. These expressions are used in opposition to mannequins, ghosts, apparitions, and so on. A second and more populous subcategory consists of inherently evaluative nouns that include the semantic component 'very good' (as in *a real hero, a real saint, a real superwoman*) or 'very bad' (as in *a real scoundrel, a real bastard*). The third subcategory—which is the one of interest to us—consists of human nouns which are not inherently evaluative; for example, *a real man, a real woman, a real scholar, a real polyglot, a real expert, a real artist*. As these examples suggest, and as the contrasts below confirm, this sense of *real* highlights somebody's (perceived) ability to do something: *a real polyglot* can do something that other people can't (speak many languages), *a real expert* can provide expertise (*real expertise*), *a real artist* can produce art (*real art*), and so on. All these expressions, we would argue, crucially involve someone's capabilities—what this someone CAN DO, in implicit contradistinction with the lesser capabilities of some other people.

The semantic component CAN DO does not need to be part of the meaning of the head noun in order to "activate" the CAN DO interpretation of the adjective *real*, but it has to be compatible with it, in a way that makes sense to speakers of English. For example, the high frequency of *a real man* in English speech is no doubt related to the widespread (in English-speaking countries) stereotype of men as capable of doing some things (as reflected, for example, in the meanings of words like *manly* (see below) and *manliness*). To describe someone as *a real man* is to say that this man satisfies these stereotypical expectations, unlike some other men (see components (d) and (e)), and, furthermore, that 'it is good if someone can be like this'.

Our explication of the relevant sense of the word *real* is as follows:

[H]   *X is a real man (scholar, polyglot, . . .).*

a.   X is someone of one kind
b.   many people think about people of this kind like this:
c.   "people of this kind can do some things, other people can't do these things
            at the same time, people of this kind don't do some other things"
d.   X is like this
e.   not all people of this kind are like this
f.   it is good if someone is like this

The collocation *a real woman* is less salient in English than *a real man*, because it is more difficult to interpret, as there are no salient, widely agreed on stereotypes of what some women can do (that other women cannot). At the same time, the collocation *a real woman* features prominently in discussions about gender, sexuality, the portrayal of women in the media, social expectations about women, and women's changing expectations and ideals. For this reason, no doubt, this collocation occurs a lot in the materials displayed on the Web, in entries like the following ones: *We need a "REAL WOMAN" Manifesto; Three Teens Define "A Real Woman"; Check out How to Be a Real Woman*. The collocation *a real man* is not a similarly contested one, or not to the same degree, and it appears to be used much more widely with reference to concrete individuals, with the implications spelled out in explication [H].

For example: *Aaron Ralston is a real man and one tough son of a bitch....Captain Petursson is a real man in every sense of the word.*

It can be useful to compare some parallel phrases with *real* and with *typical*. A *real man* is someone who can do some things (broadly speaking, identifiable by speakers of English), which is seen as "a good thing". By contrast, a *typical man* is someone who often does some things (not 'can do', but 'does')—things which are also, broadly speaking, identifiable by speakers of English, but which are not seen as of any particular value. Broadly speaking, *real* (as in *a real man*) is approbatory, whereas *typical* (as in *a typical man* or *a typical woman*) can be seen as rather disparaging. As a final example, let us contrast the implications of the phrases *a typical scholar* and *a real scholar*. A *typical scholar* is probably absent-minded and impractical, because there is a recognizable stereotype to this effect. A *real scholar* need not be either absent-minded or impractical but has to be, roughly speaking, inquisitive and persistent in the pursuit of knowledge. Obviously, this difference in interpretation is not due to different meanings of the word *scholar*. These observations square up well with explications [G] and [H].

One conclusion from this discussion is that semantic analysis of words like *real* and *typical*, combined with corpus techniques, can be an effective tool for social psychology (including the study of stereotypes, prejudices and preconceptions). Our principal concern here, however, is with the lexical semantics of words like *men* and *women*. On this matter, our conclusions are: first, that modifiers such as *real* and *typical* do not function to indicate degrees of category membership; and second, that the stereotype of men as capable of doing some things (more so than women) is not part of the meaning of the words *man* and *woman* as such.

Adjectives based on social category terms

It might be thought that derived words such as *manly, boyish, girlish, childish*, and *childlike* show that social attitudes are included in the meanings of social category words. Don't these derived words incorporate social attitudes? And if so, doesn't this have implications for the meanings of the base words from which the derivates are formed? In this section we will address this question briefly but directly, by explicating several of these words. To begin with *childish*, consider explication [I]. According to the explication, to describe someone as childish is, essentially, to say that although this person is not a child any more, they give the impression of being 'like a child', and that this is being seen in a negative light. The wording of component (b) is vague enough to be compatible with different ways in which such an impression could be formed, such as, for example, from someone's general behaviour, demeanour, or interactional style. The main point, however, is that 'child [m]' in its plain descriptive sense functions as a semantic molecule in the explication.

[I] *Robin is childish.*

a. this someone (Robin) is like this:

b. when people are with this someone for some time, they can think about this someone like this:

c. "this someone is not a child [m] any more

d. at the same time, this someone is like a child [m]

e. it is not good if someone is like this"

A similar style of explication seems appropriate for the adjectives *boyish* and *girlish*, with two qualifications. First, for these words the (b) component should refer more directly to the "visual" impression ('when people see this someone for some time'). Second, there is no implicit negative evaluation; on the contrary, *boyish* at least conveys something like affection (an endearing quality), as shown in expressions such as *boyish good looks* and *boyish charm*. The overall meaning can be captured as shown below. Although the details of the explication may be open to revision, it is clear that 'boy' is required as a semantic molecule. (Strictly speaking, 'boy' is better seen as a derivational base (or [d] element), rather than as a semantic molecule (see Chapter 11), but this point is not relevant here.)

[J] *Peter is boyish.*

a. this someone (Peter) is like this:

b. when people see this someone for some time, they can think about this someone like this:

c. "this someone is not a boy [m] any more

d. at the same time, this someone is like a boy [m]"

e. when people think like this about someone, they can feel something good towards this someone because of this

It is notable that neither [I] nor [J] contains any explicit spelling-out of social attitudes or expectations about children or boys. The explications allude to the existence of such attitudes or expectations, inasmuch as they take it for granted that observers could agree that someone **seems** 'like a child' or 'like a boy', but they do not articulate the content or even indicate much about the basis on which such judgements might be made. Some other derived adjectives are a little more specific in this regard, as we can see from the example of *childlike*. It is typically used in phrases such as *childlike innocence, childlike trust, childlike faith, childlike naivety.* The key idea can be captured as in explication [K], i.e. that although we are talking about someone who is no longer a child, this person still thinks about other people 'like a child [m] thinks about people'. As with *boyish*, this appears to be a potentially endearing quality, as captured in component (d).

[K]   *childlike:*

a.   people can think like this about someone:
b.   "this someone is not a child [m] any more
c.   at the same time this someone thinks about people like a child [m]
               thinks about people
            because this someone doesn't think bad things about people"
d.   when people think like this about someone,
            they can feel something good towards this someone because of this

Words like *manly* and *womanly* (and for that matter, *masculine* and *feminine*) convey a much richer—and more contestable—set of implicitly approved gender role expectations. The word *manly*, for example, seems to be predicated on the presupposition that in general 'men are not like women': that men are motivated to do many things because they think differently from women, and equally that they prefer not to do many things because they think differently from women (cf. phrases such as *manly activities*, and sentences such as *It isn't manly to cry*). The evaluative stance embodied in the English word *manly* not only approves the implicit generalization about the behaviours and capabilities of men, it seems equally to envisage (with implied disapproval) that not all men are like this. The (less common) word *womanly* seems to embody and project a similar portfolio of assumptions and evaluations. It would take us too far off track to delve into the complexities behind these "gender-loaded" English words here. For present purposes, our claim is simply that implicit expectations and evaluations about gender roles presuppose conceptual categories such as 'men', 'women', 'boys', and 'girls'.[14]

After this excursion into the phraseology and morphology of *men, women, children,* and related words in English, we return to our main project, and specifically to the question of cross-linguistic differences.

2.5 Cross-linguistic differences

Up to this point we have been explicating the meanings of English words, but the question can be asked: are any of these meanings lexico-semantic universals (Goddard 2001a)? That is, do all languages have lexical meanings precisely matching the meanings we have captured for *men, women, children, babies, boys,* and *girls*? And if not, can we say anything about the range of variation for comparable concepts in

---

[14] Rhetorical tautologies such as *Men are men* and *Boys will be boys* also invoke and reflect conventional attitudes (Wierzbicka 1987a).

the languages of the world? Initially, these questions might seem strange, for in general there is little reason to believe that semantically complex meanings transcend the barriers of particular languages and cultures. Despite the conviction that monolingual speakers often have that their own language "carves nature at its joints" (as Plato put it), the vast majority of complex meanings are undoubtedly language- and culture-specific. On the other hand, cultures do not vary without limit either (cf. Keesing 1994). Anthropologist Donald Brown's (1991) review of proposed "human universals" includes several which would seem to imply some kind of universal distinction between 'men' and 'women', including: a system of kinship, some form of marriage, sexual regulations, and standards of sexual modesty.

Since the 1990s, NSM researchers have built up a lot of experience in the search for lexical semantic universals. To establish that there is an exact semantic match between putatively identical word-meanings across two or more languages requires detailed analytical work and high quality information on the languages. As a heuristic, then, it is often easier first to try to **dis**confirm a proposed lexical universal by seeking out apparent counter-examples where either: (a) there is reportedly no word at all for the putative universal meaning, or (b) there are reportedly two or more words dividing the territory of the putative universal meaning, i.e. lexical elaboration. Most proposed lexical universals can be fairly readily disconfirmed if we adopt this search strategy (Goddard 2001a). However, before jumping to conclusions on the basis of reports of either situation, it is always necessary to look carefully for language-internal evidence for polysemy and/or for possible lexicalization of formally complex expressions. It is never enough to take dictionary entries, or even reports from field linguists, at face value, without scrutinizing them and, where necessary, extending the data. If we apply these principles to word-meanings of the kind we are interested in, the provisional result is that 'men', 'women', and 'children' appear to be strong candidates for universally lexicalized meanings, while the remaining terms can be decisively disconfirmed as lexical universals. In this section, we will first deal with the "negative" results, i.e. we will demonstrate that 'boys', 'girls', 'male', and 'female' are not lexico-semantic universals. We will then move to the proposed genuine universals.

Language-specific social categories

The meanings of the English words *boys* and *girls* are demonstrably language- and culture-specific, because there are other languages that do not have semantically identical words. In Russian, for example, there are two words—*devočki* and *devuški*—which cover the same territory as English *girls*. Neither is a hyponym of the other and neither corresponds precisely in meaning to the English word *girls*. Russian *devočki* 'girl children' is used for girls who are specifically children. It contrasts with another Russian word, *devuški*, which is used for young females who are no longer children but are not yet necessarily regarded as women either. The two words are explicated in [L] and [M] below.

There are several differences between the explications. For *devočki*, the (b) component reads: 'people of this kind are children [m]', while for *devuški* the corresponding component has it that: 'people of this kind are not children [m] any more'. For *devočki*, component (c) suggests a moderate time period ('for some time, not a very long time'), while for *devuški* the comparable component explicitly rules out a lengthy period ('someone can't be someone of this kind for a very long time'). For *devočki*, component (d) refers to similarities between parts of the girl's body and parts of a woman's body (as in the explication for English *girls*), while for *devuški* the comparison is a holistic one: 'this someone's body is like a woman's [m] body'. Although each component is a little different from its counterpart, the differences all align in a consistent fashion—as though *devuški* were at each point going one step further than *devočki*. The final parts of the two explications diverge, however. For *devočki*, the final component is simply 'because of this, after some time this someone can be a woman [m]'. For *devuški*, however, there is a pair of final components that capture a dual perspective, so to speak. These are "attitudinal" components, expressing the idea that people can think of a *devuška* in two ways: either as a woman (component (e)) or as someone who will soon be a woman (component (f)).

[L]   *devočki* [Russian, 'girl children']

a.   people of one kind

b.   people of this kind are children [m]

c.   someone can be someone of this kind for some time, not for a very long time

d.   when someone is someone of this kind, some parts of this someone's body are
        like some parts of a woman's [m] body

e.   because of this, after some time this someone can be a woman [m]

[M]   *devuški* [Russian, 'young women, girls who are not children any more']

a.   people of one kind

b.   people of this kind are not children [m] any more

c.   someone can't be someone of this kind for a very long time

d.   when someone is someone of this kind, this someone's body is like a woman's [m]
        body

e.   because of this, people can think about someone of this kind like this: "this someone is
        a woman [m]"

f.   at the same time people can think about someone of this kind like this:
        "after a short time, this someone will be a woman [m]"

A parallel contrast exists between Russian *mal'čiki* 'boy children' and *junoši* 'boys who are not children any more'. We will not present explications here, but it will be apparent how they can be constructed on the model of the explications above.[15] The conclusion is that in this domain English and Russian have somewhat different systems of ethno-classification embedded in their lexicons.

The English words *male* and *female* are also demonstrably language-specific, as mentioned earlier. This fact has special significance, because when an English-speaker is called upon to generalize about what words like *men* and *boys*, or *women* and *girls*, have in common, the terms *male* and *female* come to mind almost irresistibly. Since, furthermore, the words *male* and *female* can be applied not only to people but also to a great variety of different kinds of creatures (animals, birds, fish, frogs, spiders, etc.), it is quite understandable that they (or analogues such as [+MALE] and [−MALE]) have been adopted as basic components in almost all systems of componential analysis. Nevertheless, it is not difficult to find languages that lack equivalents to *male* and *female*. In fact, in typological perspective English is rather unusual in having words that can apply broadly across so many different kinds of living things. Comparable concepts in many other languages are restricted to 'kinds of animals [m]'; for example, the Polish nouns *samiec* 'male' and *samica* 'female' are typically restricted to animals, and in colloquial language would not readily be applied, for example, to reptiles and insects.

Explications for English *female* and *male* are given in [N] and [O] below. The two concepts are similarly structured, so we can review them together. To say of any living thing that it is *female* (or *male*) implies a dichotomy of classification (if something could be *female* but is not, then it is necessarily *male*). Hence component (a) reads: 'a living thing of one of two kinds'. Component (b) then sets out the basis for the twofold classification. It rests ultimately on an analogy with people's bodies. Notice that the first line of this component reads: 'there are two kinds of many living things...'.[16] Component (c) states that 'women's [m] bodies' (or 'men's [m] bodies', as the case may be) 'are of one of these two kinds'. Then finally, in component (d) 'the body of this living thing' is identified as being of 'this kind'.

[N]   (*it's a*) *female* (*dog, chicken, fish, frog, spider, etc.*)

a.   a living thing of one of two kinds
b.   there are two kinds of many living things
         because there are two kinds of bodies of many living things,
         like there are two kinds of people's bodies
c.   women's [m] bodies are of one of these two kinds
d.   the body of this living thing is of this kind

---

[15] There are also extended uses, as in the case of English *boys* and *girls*; but these require separate treatment.

[16] The NSM expression 'many living things' does not include plants, however, or at best only marginally so.

[O]   (*it's a*) *male* (*dog, chicken, fish, frog, spider*, etc.)

a.   a living thing of one of two kinds
b.   there are two kinds of many living things
          because there are two kinds of bodies of many living things,
              like there are two kinds of people's bodies
c.   men's [m] bodies are of one of these two kinds
d.   the body of this living thing is of this kind

The English concepts of *male* and *female*, then, refer back to a human model, relying on 'men [m]' and 'women [m]' as semantic molecules. Like so many other concepts (Wierzbicka 1985*a*), they are implicitly anthropocentric or, to coin a phrase, "crypto-anthropocentric".

Are 'men', 'women', and 'children' language-universal social categories?

Having argued the case that the meanings 'boys', 'girls', 'male', and 'female' are language-specific, we would now like to argue for the opposite position in relation to 'children', 'women', and 'men'. Naturally a claim to universal status is much more difficult to establish, and we do not want to say that our case is definitive at this point in time; nevertheless, we believe it is persuasive and worthy of consideration.

The concept 'children' seems to have a fairly strong prospect of universal status. It is true that some languages appear to have no gender-neutral term answering to the singular 'child'—as in Spanish, where *niño* and *niña* normally designate a male child and female child, respectively. But the Spanish masculine plural *niños* can be used about 'children' generally, and even in singular contexts there is a default choice (*niño*) when the gender is unknown, or known but irrelevant, e.g. *Para ella es difícil conseguir trabajo porque tiene un niño* 'It is difficult for her to get work because (she) has a child'. At present we are not aware of any data that would conclusively disconfirm 'children' as a universally lexicalized meaning. In addition, there are theory-internal reasons for believing it to have this status, in particular, its role as a foundational semantic molecule inside the concepts of 'women' and 'men'.[17]

Turning now to 'men' and 'women', it might seem at first that there are clear semantic differences between languages in their nearest equivalent words, but on closer examination these differences seem to recede in importance. One such

---

[17]   From a lexical typological point of view, one can expect some "child-specific" vocabulary items to exist in all languages, requiring the semantic molecule 'children [m]' in their explications, e.g. the names of children's games, such as (to give English examples) *chasings, peek-a-boo, mothers and fathers*; names for toys, dolls, etc.; words for any child-specific clothing or childcare items or practices, *crib, cradle, bib, nappy, lullaby, bedtime story*, etc. Many languages have special vocabulary for use with small children—words such as *horsie, wee, choo-choo*, and the like. The concept of 'playing' (or something similar) is likely to be commonly lexicalized, and it too arguably refers to 'children [m]' as part of its prototypical characterization (Alexander 2006).

difference is that the equivalents of words for 'men' and 'women' are sometimes conflated with social information about seniority or age level. In Pitjantjatjara, for example, *wati* 'man' normally refers only to initiated men, and there are two words for 'woman'—*kungka* and *minyma*—depending on the age and associated seniority of the individual. However, there is language-internal evidence that *wati* and *minyma* are polysemous, having both a general meaning (identical with those of English *men* and *women*) and a specific meaning (including the additional social information). For example, the words *wati* and *minyma* are freely used when it is necessary to speak about men and women in general, without regard to their social status, e.g. to discuss sexually transmitted diseases, or to discuss ritual or economic division of labour. The word *wati* is also routinely used about non-Aboriginal men, for whom initiation is not normally an option and is certainly not expected (cf. Goddard 1996b). Conversely, it hardly makes sense to speak of white men as *tjitji* 'children', though "technically" they are from a ritual point of view. An uninitiated Aboriginal man, on the other hand, can certainly be described as a *tjitji* 'child', when his initiation status is the issue; and in this context it is possible to contrast the two meanings of *wati*, which clearly establishes the polysemy: *Wati nyaratja wati wiya, tjitji* 'That man is not a man (initiated man), (he's) a child'.

The most interesting potential counter-examples to the universality of 'men' and 'women' are posed by languages (usually classifier languages) that express these meanings via phrasemes or compounds, rather than by morphologically simple words. Superficially these phrasemes or compounds take the form 'male people' and 'female people', respectively, but as we will argue in a moment, such glosses are not semantically accurate. The following data is representative:

Japanese:	*otoko no hito*	'men'	[*hito* 'people']
	onna no hito	'women'	
Cantonese:	*nàahmyán*	'men'	[*yán* 'people']
	néuihyán	'women'	

It can be no coincidence that the word for 'people' is involved, given that the meanings in question both begin with the component 'people of one kind'. On the other hand, it is not possible to neatly divide the meanings expressed by these phrases into two parts, one of which is semantic prime PEOPLE and the other something like 'male' or 'female', because expressions like Japanese *otoko no hito* and Cantonese *nàahmyán* (putatively, 'male people') cannot be used to refer to male children—even though male children surely qualify as male people. Nor can the modifier elements be used about anything but humans: hypothetical expressions such as **otoko no inu* ["male" dog] and **néuih-kai* ["female" chicken] are quite impossible (the appropriate Japanese expressions are: *osu no inu* 'male dog', *mesu no inu* 'female dog'). It therefore would not make sense to say that the modifiers literally mean 'male' or 'female' in these contexts.[18] As far as we know, the referential range of the Japanese and Cantonese expressions shown above correspond exactly with those of English *men* and *women*. Until and unless some specific semantic differences are identified, we provisionally conclude that the meanings of these phrasemes and compounds match those of English *men* and *women*.

From the point of view of semantic and cultural typology, a strong case can be made that the social categories of 'men', 'women', and 'children' are universals of social cognition.[19] The semantic and cultural aspects of the case are intertwined, and turn on presumed universals of culture and lexicon. All documented cultural groups, for example, have concepts and practices that correspond to some extent to "marriage": i.e. to long-term unions between men and women that result in the birth of children (Brown 1991; Foley 1997). Of course, the conditions and assumptions involved vary considerably from culture to culture, and have varied across the ages, but to capture the common elements behind these concepts and practices, and the lexical items that go with them, the concepts of 'men', 'women', and 'children' are surely essential.

Likewise, all documented cultural groups have some knowledge of sexual reproduction and some system of ideas and values regulating sexual behaviour. The concepts of 'men' and 'women' are surely essential foundations of any such system of ideas and values. Relatedly, as far as we know, every language has words for gender-specific parts of the body, such as breasts, penis, and beard (Andersen 1978; Brown 1976). Of course, in many languages the words for some or all of these parts may incorporate social taboos and may normally be avoided, or be replaced by socially acceptable substitutes, indirect locutions, or the like; but this does not change the fact that, as far as we know, all cultures recognize an important difference between the body types of 'men' and 'women'—that these concepts are part of a common human model of the human body (cf. Wierzbicka 2007c). Again, particular cultures may recognize an additional "third gender" and/or recognize ways of "gender-shifting" (as in many Oceanic societies), but this doesn't mean that they go without the categories of 'men' and 'women'.

As far as we are aware, all reported cultural groups have some cultural ideas about gender-specific roles and responsibilities, and about preferred or proscribed behaviours between the sexes. How could such roles and behaviours be characterized without some reference to the concepts of 'men' and 'women'? At the lexical level, most languages and cultures have a large inventory of gender-specific tools, practices,

---

[18] There is often formal evidence that the phrasemes are lexical compounds. For example, in Cantonese *néuihyán* 'woman' (lit. 'female person'), the second morpheme *yán* has rising tone, but as a separate word *yàhn* 'people, person' has low-falling tone. This kind of tone change indicates that the combination has been lexicalized (Matthews and Yip 1994: 26).

[19] In Swadesh's (1972[1960]) 100-item Basic Vocabulary List, 'woman' and 'man' are items 16 and 17, the very first nouns. Oddly, 'child' does not make it onto the list.

and occupations. Modern Anglo culture is typologically unusual in its drive to minimize the "gender-specific",[20] but even in modern English many items of gender-specific clothing remain, such as *dress, skirt, bra, panties, lingerie, stockings, pantyhose,* and (perhaps) *necklace* and *bracelet,* whose meanings involve 'women' (and 'girls') as semantic molecules.

The universality of "kinship" systems and family groupings also argues for 'women' (or more precisely, 'woman') as a semantic and conceptual universal. This is because the indispensable minimal unit of biological kinship is the mother–child relationship. Foley (1997: 134) calls it "the basic atom of kinship systems": "The link between mother and child is the basis of genealogy, the basic axis of structure in all kinship systems" (cf. Scheffler 1978; Wierzbicka 1992a: ch 9; in press b).

In summary, there is persuasive, if not conclusive, evidence from both lexical-typological semantics and from cultural typology that the concepts of 'men', 'women', and 'children' are foundational conceptual categories for the social domain.

2.6 Concluding remarks

As reviewed in section 2.1, the standard componential analysis of *men, women, boys,* and *girls* has a canonical status in the introductory linguistics curriculum. We have shown that this analysis is deficient and have proposed an analysis which is more precise, descriptively more predictive of semantic relationships and distributional facts, and based on a theoretically sound and empirically well-grounded methodology of semantic analysis. The old analysis should not disappear from textbooks and introductory lectures altogether, but in our view it should be retained mainly for its historical value—as an exemplar of a superseded approach, much as the concepts of phlogiston and the ether are still mentioned in chemistry and physics texts. The basic ideas behind componential features such as [±HUMAN], [±ADULT], and [±MALE] can be much more revealingly, and much more precisely, "unpacked" in terms of semantic components written in empirically established universal primes, such as PEOPLE, KIND, PART, BODY, TWO, LIKE.

We have also ventured into the area of lexical typological semantics, exploring and identifying a number of important semantic differences between several concepts in the English domain of stage-of-life words and gender descriptors and comparable words in several other languages. It has become apparent that the meanings behind English words such as *boys* and *girls* are not language-universal but language-specific; likewise, the meanings of the English words *male* and *female* are not universal but language-specific. In contrast, we have argued that evidence suggests that the

---

[20] The general direction of cultural and lexical change has been extending what were previously "men's" items to women also. Consequently, only a few items of men's clothing remain: *jocks, tie,* and *waistcoat.*

meanings 'men', 'women', and 'children' may be lexical and conceptual universals. Despite their relative complexity, these "basic social categories" appear to be prime candidates for the status of universal semantic molecules. If so, they represent a few shared building blocks across the enormous diversity of ways of thinking about people and their ways of life which are embodied in the social lexicons of the world's languages.

3

Sweet, hot, hard, heavy, rough, sharp

Physical-quality words in cross-linguistic perspective

3.1 'Kinds', 'parts', and qualities

How do people think about the physical world? Here as elsewhere, the best evidence comes from languages. The empirical cross-linguistic work conducted in the NSM framework suggests that there are three important universals in this respect: (i) all languages reflect a wide-ranging categorization in terms of 'kinds'; (ii) all languages reflect a view that things of different kinds have certain specifiable 'parts'; and (iii) all languages reflect a view of the world in which certain properties—either permanent or transient—are attributed to things.

To begin with the first of these universals, evidence suggests that every language has a word for the conceptual prime KIND, and numerous words identifying certain 'kinds of things'. This applies, in particular, to the domain of living things, and to the domain of artefacts. In both these domains, every language reflects its own categorization. Concepts like *bird*, *fish*, or *tree* are of course far from universal, and "lower-level" categories like *ant*, *butterfly*, *snail*, or *lizard* need not match across language boundaries either (Goddard 2001a). All languages, however, have a vocabulary differentiating different 'kinds of living things'; roughly, in the sense of Berlin's (1992) "folk genera" (cf. Wierzbicka 1985a). Similarly, names for categories of human artefacts such as *cup* and *mug*, *hammer* and *scissors*, *spade* and *spoon* do not necessarily match in meaning across languages, even in those parts of the world where comparable objects are used. Every language, however, has a large set of words for different kinds of artefacts. Turning now to the second universal, all languages have words for kinds of things which imply the presence of certain specifiable PARTS in all, or most, things of a given kind. For example, the word *elephant* implies the presence of a *trunk*, the word *butterfly*, the presence of *wings*, and the word *bee*, the presence of a *sting*. Similarly, the word *bicycle* refers to two *wheels*, the word *jug* to a *handle*, and so on. Like KIND, the element PARTS is a conceptual prime, surfacing as a fundamental element in the conceptual ontologies of all languages.

This chapter focuses on the third universal mentioned at the outset: all languages show that their speakers attribute to things—both individual things and kinds of things—certain qualities, either temporary or permanent. Often, but by no means always, the words for such qualities come in pairs of apparent opposites. For example, in English there are words *hot* and *cold*, *hard* and *soft*, *rough* and *smooth*, and *heavy* and *light*. It is important that the "qualification" of things implied by such adjectives (or in some languages, verbs, cf. Dixon 1982) be distinguished from categorization implied by nouns for 'kinds of things' (such as *butterfly* or *spoon*). From a semantic point of view, *butterflies* are a 'kind of living thing', and *spoons* a 'kind of thing made by people', whereas *heavy things* or *hard things* are not conceived of as 'kinds of things' at all. While categorization is based on the concept KIND, "qualification" is based on the conceptual prime LIKE.

The main task to be undertaken in this chapter is to map out exactly how descriptors like *sweet*, *hot*, *hard*, *rough*, *heavy*, and *sharp*, and their "opposites", can be analysed in terms of LIKE and the other semantic elements. For the most part our treatment focuses on English, but we adduce some initial cross-linguistic comparisons from French, Polish, and Korean, both to demonstrate that there can be significant cross-linguistic differences in this domain and also to show that the approach developed here can be extended to other languages. We hope to lay the groundwork for more comprehensive semantic studies of physical-quality terms across a wide range of languages.

3.2 Qualities based on taste: *salty, sweet, sour*

To begin with properties whose conceptualization is relatively transparent, let us consider a sentence like *This soup is salty*. Clearly, it is intended by the speaker as a description of an objective property of a particular bowl of soup. At the same time, it is a description which characterizes the objective property in question via reference to a certain kind of sensation which it can produce in people. This particular sensation ('salty') can be identified with reference to a particular prototype—salt. This was in fact how Leibniz (1903) approached the task of defining taste words in Latin. Thus, under the heading *Sapor* 'taste' he offered the following:

> *insipidum cujus sapor nullus aut tenuis. Caeteri non melius quam exemplis osten-*
> *duntur.* 'tasteless—which have little or no taste. The others can best be shown by
> means of examples.'
> *acris ut piperis* 'sharp/hot—like that of pepper'
> *amarus ut bilis* 'bitter—like that of bile'
> *salsus ut salis vesci* 'salted—like that of salt'
> *dulcis ut saccari* 'sweet—like that of sugar'
> *acidus ut aceti* 'acid—like that of vinegar'
> *austerus ut in pomis immaturis* 'sour—like that of unripe fruit'

Elaborating on this starting point from Leibniz, we would propose the semantic explication in [A] below for English *salty*. Some brief comments are in order about its general format or **template**, which is shared to a large extent by other concepts explicated throughout the present study. The explications begin with the component 'this thing is like this:—', thereby portraying what follows as an attributed quality or property of the thing being described. The next component begins to specify this quality by stating, 'if some parts of someone's mouth [m] touch this thing, this someone can feel something in these parts because of it.'[1] The potential for physical contact (touching) to arouse a localized sensation appears to be a crucial part of the semantic structure of physical-quality concepts generally. In the case of taste concepts, the locus of this physical touching and the resultant sensation is of course the mouth; as indicated by the notation [m], 'mouth' is a semantic molecule, not a semantic prime. The next component specifies that as a result of the sensation produced in this fashion, the experiencer can acquire some knowledge: 'because of this, this someone can know something about this thing.' In a sense, the experience is an "informative" one. The content of this knowledge is then characterized by reference to a potential inference or thought. To a large extent, the differences between different physical-quality concepts reside in the nature of such potential inferences. In the case of *salty*, the nature of the inference is very specific and indeed self-evident: namely, that the thing in question contains salt. Obviously this presupposes that 'salt' can be separately explicated without circularity; see Wierzbicka (1985a: 193–194).[2] (In explication [A] the expression 'a lot of' can be regarded as an idiomatic equivalent of semantic prime MUCH~MANY.)

[A]   This thing (e.g. soup) is *salty*.

a.   this thing is like this:

b.   if some parts of someone's mouth [m] touch this thing,
            this someone can feel something in these parts because of it

c.   because of this, this someone can know something about this thing

d.   because of this, this someone can think like this:
            "there is a lot of salt [m] in this thing"

---

[1] Two further points need to be mentioned. First, further investigation may be required as to whether component (b) should be phrased in terms of 'some parts of the mouth' or 'somewhere inside the mouth', or some combination thereof. Second, sentences about how things "taste", e.g. *This tea tastes sweet*, will require a more complex format of explication: more subjective, focused more explicitly on the quality of the sensory experience, and expressing a degree of "epistemic reserve". Presumably, they ought to follow a similar pattern to sentences involving the other senses, e.g. *Those rocks look wet*, *He sounds upset*. One possibility is that to say *This tea tastes sweet* is to say, in part, that 'when I taste it, I can think that it is sweet, I don't say I know it'; and similarly, that to say *Those rocks look wet* is to say, in part, that 'when I look at those rocks, I can think that they are wet; I don't say I know it', etc. The verbs *taste* and *look* of course also need to be decomposed.

[2] The literal reference to *salt* is as one would expect, given the direct morphological relationship between *salt* and *salty* (cf. *sugar* ~ *sugary*). It should be noted, however, that the literal presence of salt is not essential for something to **taste** *salty*, since people know that a salty taste can be due to the presence of some chemical ingredient other than salt.

We suggest that the same semantic template can be applied in the explication of *sweet*, as shown in [B] below. To describe something as *sweet* is to say that if parts of the mouth are in contact with this thing, there can be a localized sensation (in the mouth) which gives rise to some knowledge, which in turn licenses a certain inference. The inferential scenario is more extensive than for *salty*. It first recognizes the pleasurable quality of sweet things, in component (f): 'when something like this is in someone's mouth [m], this someone can feel something good in their mouth [m] because of it.' Then it links this property with the potential presence of some special substance, in component (g): 'something can be like this if there is a lot of something of one kind in it.' Note the element of "likeness": the potential inference is not that there **is** such a special substance in this thing, but rather that things can be like this if they have some special substance in them. A final component (h) acknowledges the existence of some kinds of things which are always, i.e. inherently, *sweet*, thereby providing a kind of conceptual link with honey, fruits, and the like (see Wierzbicka 2009d).[3]

[B]   This thing (e.g. tea, orange) is *sweet*.

a.   this thing is like this:
b.   if some parts of someone's mouth [m] touch this thing,
c.   this someone can feel something in these parts because of it
d.   because of this, this someone can know something about this thing
e.   because of this, this someone can think like this:
f.   "when something like this is in someone's mouth [m], this someone can feel something good in their mouth [m] because of it
g.   something can be like this if there is a lot of something of one kind in it"
h.   things of some kinds are always like this

Explication [C] below applies the template to *sour*, and in this case the inferential section is more complex still. Note that explication [C] accounts for the quasi-antonymical relationship between *sweet* and *sour* by the presence in the potential inference section of a component which stands in direct opposition to the corresponding component in *sweet*: namely, 'when something like this is in a person's mouth [m], this person can feel something bad in their mouth [m] because of it'. Furthermore, according to [C], the meaning of *sour* has some additional content which has no counterpart in the meaning of *sweet*, namely, recognition by the experiencer that sourness can cause parts of a person's face (see the explication for 'face' in Wierzbicka 2007c) to move involuntarily, i.e. the characteristic "puckering" associated with sour things, and that this can serve as a sign or symptom to other people of what the person is experiencing.

---

[3] In new work since 2014, ways have been found to simplify the explications presented in this chapter, while retaining the key themes of physical contact linked with subjective construal.

[C]   This thing (e.g. soup) is *sour*.

a.   this thing is like this:

b.   if some parts of someone's mouth [m] touch this thing,

c.   this someone can feel something in these parts because of it

d.   because of this, this someone can know something about this thing

e.   because of this, this someone can think like this:

f.   "when something like this is in someone's mouth [m], this someone can feel
                something bad in their mouth [m] because of it

g.   because of this, parts of this someone's face [m] can move, not because this
                someone wants it

h.   if other people see this, they can know what this someone feels because of this"

i.   things of some kinds are always like this

Some comment is in order at this point on the use of semantic molecules such as 'salt', 'mouth', and 'face' in the above explications. Any use of a semantic molecule in an explication presupposes that the molecule can be explicated independently without recourse to the word in whose explication it appears, otherwise circularity would result. Explications of body-part words are provided in Wierzbicka (2007c) and Priestley (in press). As for 'salt [m]', Wierzbicka (1985a: 193–194) presents an explication of *salt* that defines it, essentially, as a white substance which people add in small quantities to various foods to make them taste better.[4]

The scheme of analysis developed for tastes in this section can be extended to take in other taste and flavour words such as *bitter*, *savoury*, and *pungent* in English, and their counterparts in other languages (cf. Kerttula 2005; 2007); but we will not undertake this now, since our focus is on sensory qualities generally and we want to move on to consider a range of different sensory quality words, starting in the next section with *hot* and *cold*. The examples considered so far make it clear, however, why words for "sensory qualities" are based on the concept LIKE, rather than KIND. If I say that the soup on the table in front of me is *salty*, I do not mean that it belongs to a category of salty soups. I am just saying what this particular soup is like. Likewise, if I say that the tea I am drinking is *sweet*, I am not saying that it belongs to a particular category of tea ('sweet tea'). I am only saying what this particular tea is like.[5]

---

[4] *Sugar*, in contrast, can be defined as a sweet white substance which is not normally eaten by itself, but which is an ingredient of various kinds of food which people eat for pleasure (such as cakes, pastries, and lollies), and which people sometimes add to drinks. An attraction of such analyses for *salt* and *sugar* is that they bring to the surface the parallelism between the two: both are "additives", but they are added to foods of different kinds, for a different kind of purpose in each case.

[5] The lexicalized expression *sweet potato*, on the other hand, does represent a conceptual category, i.e. a 'kind'.

3.3 "Temperature words": *hot, cold,* and *warm*

The *Collins Cobuild Dictionary of the English Language* (1991) defines the English words *hot* and *cold* as in (a) below, via *temperature. Temperature,* in turn, is defined via *heat,* as in (b). Given the perennial circularity plaguing most traditional dictionaries, one is not too surprised to see *heat* sending us back to *hot* (though with a detour, via *warmth*), as in (c). Thus, *hot* is defined via *temperature, temperature* via *heat,* and *heat* either directly or indirectly via *hot.*

> (a) hot—something that is hot has a high temperature, e.g. *The metal of the tank is so hot I can't touch it.*
> cold—something that is cold has a very low temperature, e.g. *The concrete floor is freezing cold.*
> (b) temperature—the temperature is the amount of heat that something has or that is in a place.
> (c) heat—warmth or the quality of being hot.
> warmth—warmth is a moderate amount of heat that something has.

The futility of such circular definitions hardly requires further discussion (see Wierzbicka 1996: ch. 9; Goddard 1998). It is obvious that the best way to get out of the vicious circle is to find an external reference point for the quality described by the word *hot.* In this particular case, it is also obvious where such an external reference point can be found, and the fact that in many languages the word corresponding to *hot* is derived from the words for burning or fire makes it doubly so: the idea of 'hot' is based on the idea of 'fire'. People know that they will feel a certain recognizable sensation if they touch things which a short time before were in fire. In describing something as *hot,* one draws a kind of comparison with this experience and with this sensation. This commonsense interpretation of the meaning of *hot* can be set out in a formal fashion in explication [D]. The semantic molecule 'fire' occurs in this explication (cf. Goddard 2010b). Note that recognizing 'touching' as the ultimate basis for knowing that something is *hot,* as in [D], by no means denies the fact that one can sometimes deduce that something is hot in other ways—for example, if one sees steam coming off some water.

[D]   This thing (e.g. tea, kettle) is *hot.*
a.   this thing is like this:
b.   if a part of someone's body touches this thing,
c.   this someone can feel something in this part of the body because of it
d.   because of this, this someone can know something about this thing
e.   because of this, this someone can think like this:
f.   "something can be like this if a short time before it was in a place
                  where there was fire [m]"

As for *cold* (in expressions like *cold water* and *very cold water*), it is explicated in [E] via an inferential scenario with two crucial components: one referring to 'ice [m]' and the other the converse of the corresponding component with *hot* (the molecule 'ice [m]' can be independently explicated in terms of more basic molecules 'hard' and 'water').

[E]   This thing (e.g. water, milk) is *cold*.

a.   this thing is like this:
b.   if a part of someone's body touches this thing,
c.   this someone can feel something in this part of the body because of it
d.   because of this, this someone can know something about this thing
e.   because of this, this someone can think like this:
f.   "ice [m] is always like this
g.   something can't be like this if a short time before it was in a place
            where there was fire [m]"

The link between the concepts 'hot' and 'cold' and the concept TOUCH is intuitively clear. In his *Essay*, John Locke (1959[1690]) wrote about it as follows:

There are some ideas which have admittance only through one sense, which is particularly adapted to receive them. Thus, light and colours as white, red, yellow, blue (. . .) come in only by the eyes. All kinds of noises, sounds, and tones, only by the ears. The several tastes and smells, by the nose and the palate. (. . .) And if these organs, or the nerves which are the conduits to convey them from without to the audience in the brain (. . .), are any of them so disordered as not to perform their functions, they have no postern to be admitted by; no other way to bring themselves into view, and be perceived by the understanding. The most consider-able of those belonging to touch are heat and cold, and solidity.   (Vol. I, pp. 148–9)

Like explications of *sweet* and *salty* proposed earlier, the explications of *hot* and *cold* in [D] and [E] are both objective and subjective. They are based both on embodied human experience with fire and on an inferred comparison with a prototypical situation and a prototypical sensation.

In his *Essay*, Locke distinguished between "primary" and "secondary" qualities of things (or "bodies") and he placed *hot* and *cold* squarely in the latter category: they are "ideas" produced in us by certain properties of the things so described, properties which bear no resemblance to our "ideas" and "sensations":

The ideas of primary qualities of bodies are resemblances of them, and their patterns do really exist in the bodies themselves, but the ideas produced in us by these secondary qualities have no resemblance to them at all. There is nothing like our ideas existing in the bodies themselves. They are, in the bodies we denominate for them, only a power to produce those sensations in us, and what is sweet, blue or warm in idea, is but the certain bulk figure and motion of the insensible parts, in the bodies themselves, which we call so.   (Vol. I, p.173)

Thus, heat is not an inherent property of fire: things are hot (or cold, warm, etc.) only by virtue of "the ideas they produce in us" (p. 174): "The same fire that at one distance produces in us the sensation of warmth, does, at a nearer approach, produce in us the far different sensation of pain." Neither pain nor heat, Locke argues, are in the fire: both are "ideas" in us.

The explications proposed here are consistent with Locke's observations. When people say of an object that it is *hot* or *cold* they are of course saying something about that object, not about themselves. All they manage to say about this object, however, is what effect it would have on people touching it, and this effect is described by reference to a prototypical situation; namely, something having recently been in fire.

The English word *hot* is, of course, not only used to ascribe a "physical property" to objects; it can also be used about places, i.e. to say something about "ambient" temperature. In many languages, different words are used in these two situations. In our view, English *hot* is polysemous: the word *hot* means something somewhat different in relation to places, as opposed to objects. The temperature required for a place to qualify as *hot* is no doubt lower than for a thing to qualify as *hot*, and this reflects a conceptual difference, namely, that the concept of a "hot place" is characterized not only by reference to the presence of fire in a place but also by reference to the possibility of the sun beating down overhead. Needless to say, it is very natural that an environmental concept such as 'sun' should play a part in the concept of "ambient hotness".[6]

[F]   It is *hot* in this place now.

a.   this place is like this:
b.   if someone is in this place now, this someone can feel something in their body
              because of this
c.   because of this, this someone can know something about this place
d.   because of this, this someone can think like this:
e.   "a place can be like this when there is fire [m] in it
f.   a place can be like this when the sun [m] above it is like fire [m]"

By a further but very straightforward polysemic extension, the word *hot* can be used to report a person's subjective experience, e.g. to say *I'm hot*. As explicated in [G], in this usage the word *hot* refers to the bodily sensation associated with being in a "hot place"; hence, the meaning 'hot [m]', in its ambient sense, functions as semantic molecule in the explication.

[G]   *I'm hot.*

a.   I feel something bad in my body now
b.   someone can feel something like this when they are in a place where it is hot [m]

---

[6] The semantic molecules 'sun', 'sky', and 'fire' are explicated in Goddard (2010*b*).

Explications for the corresponding senses of English *cold* follow. Ambient *cold*, explicated in [H], follows the same pattern as ambient *hot*, except that the inferential components are in a converse relationship with those for ambient *hot*. Explication [I], for experiential expressions like *I'm cold*, follows the same pattern as *I'm hot*.

[H]   It is *cold* in this place now.

a.   this place is like this:
b.   if someone is in this place now this someone can feel something in their body
              because of this
c.   because of this, this someone can know something about this place
d.   because of this, this someone can think like this:
e.   "a place can't be like this when there is fire [m] in it
f.   a place can't be like this when the sun [m] above it is like fire [m]"

[I]   I'm *cold*.

a.   I feel something bad in my body now
b.   someone can feel something like this when they are in a place where it is cold [m]

Similar explications can be proposed for various senses of the English word *warm*. According to explication [J], when speaking of a thing being *warm*, the implied comparison is with something having been NEAR fire some time ago. The idea of being 'near fire [m]' provides a "weaker" version of the corresponding component with *hot*, which referred to being 'in a place where there is fire [m]'. At the same time, the vagueness of the expressions 'near fire' and 'some time before' are compatible with the rather wide range of actual temperature values which can be covered by *warm*. An additional component is required to account for the intuitive link between *warmth* and "good feeling". The final component of [J] represents the recognition that something *warm* can be pleasant to touch (and a similar component would be needed for *cool*)[7].

[J]   This thing (e.g. soup, milk, bottle) is *warm*.

a.   this thing is like this:
b.   if a part of someone's body touches this thing,
c.   this someone can feel something in this part of the body because of it
d.   because of this, this someone can know something about this thing
e.   because of this, this someone can think like this:
f.   "something can be like this if some time before it was near fire [m]"
g.   if a part of someone's body touches something when it is like this,
h.   this someone can feel something good in this part of the body because of it

---

[7]   This treatment by no means exhausts the polysemy of English *warm*. It has another meaning, roughly 'no longer cold', applying to things which can be expected to be cold, as in expressions like *warm beer*; and yet another meaning in relation to clothing of the kind intended to keep one warm in cold weather, e.g. *a warm coat*.

Explication [K] applies to the ambient sense of *warm*, as when one speaks of being in a *warm place*. In addition to the "weakened" version of the prototypical component involving fire, there is also a weakened version of the prototypical component involving the sun, namely, 'a place can be like this if the sun [m] is above it.'[8]

[K]   It is *warm* in this place.

a.   this place is like this:
b.   if someone is in this place this someone can feel something in their body
c.   because of this, this someone can know something about this place
d.   because of this, they can think like this:
e.   "a place can be like this if there is fire [m] near it
f.   a place can be like this if the sun [m] is above it"
g.   if someone is in a place when it is like this,
h.   this someone can feel something good in their body because of it

Despite the possibility that meanings such as 'fire' and 'sun' may be universally lexicalized (Goddard 2001a), complex meanings based on them, such as *hot*, *cold*, *warm*, and *cool*, do not match up perfectly across languages, as documented in Koptjevskaja-Tamm and Rakhilina (n.d.; 2006) in relation to Swedish, Russian, and English (cf. Sutrop 1999). Nonetheless, we believe that the approach developed here is flexible enough to capture meanings and to pinpoint meaning differences across languages, as well as within individual languages. Though space prevents an extended treatment of this matter here, we will adduce a single example: French *chaud*, which covers the area divided in English between *hot* and *warm* and is regarded as a translation equivalent of both English words. Its meaning can be represented as in [L]. The key component is 'something can be like this if a short time before it was near fire [m]'. If one compares the wording of this component with those for English *hot* and *warm*, it can be seen that the reference to being 'near fire' explains why *chaud* corresponds partially to *warm*. On the other hand, in the case of *chaud* the temporal modifier is different: not 'some time before' (as in English *warm*), but rather 'a short time before'. This explains why the range of application of French *chaud* partly overlaps with that of English *hot*.

[L]   Ceci est *chaud* ('this is warm/hot'). [French]

a.   this thing is like this:
b.   if a part of someone's body touches this thing,
c.   this someone can feel something in this part of the body because of it
d.   because of this, this someone can know something about this thing

---

[8] Regarding the ambient sense of *warm* and comparable terms in Russian and/or Swedish, while we agree with Koptjevskaja-Tamm and Rakhilina (n.d.; 2006) that they are related to the normal human body temperature, we point out that the semantic explication does not refer explicitly to body temperature. In our view, the relation to the human "comfort zone" is sufficiently reflected by the reference in the explication to a person feeling 'something good in their body' as a result of being in a *warm* place.

e.   because of this, this someone can think like this:
f.   "something can be like this if a short time before it was near fire [m]"
g.   if a part of someone's body touches something when it is like this,
h.   this someone can feel something good in this part of the body because of it

Dictionary definitions like the one quoted from the *Collins Cobuild Dictionary* ('something that is hot has a high temperature') can create an impression that *hot* refers to a mysterious inherent property of the object: "temperature". This is a huge step backwards from the kind of analyses developed 300 years earlier by Locke. "Temperature" is an abstraction, based on the concepts 'hot' and 'cold', and it should itself be explicated via these concepts, not the other way around (see Chapter 9 below).

In addition, using the concept of temperature in the definitions of *hot* and *cold* denies the embodied and subjective character of these concepts, clearly recognized in Locke's analysis (echoed and reinforced in modern times by certain streams of thought in cognitive linguistics and cognitive science generally, e.g. Varela, Thompson, and Rosch 1991; Lakoff and Johnson 1999; cf. Wilson 2002). It also introduces a pseudo-scientific perspective which is absent from the meaning of the words *hot* and *cold* themselves. Koptjevskaja-Tamm and Rakhilina (n.d.) reach a similar conclusion: "[T]emperature concepts are strongly embodied and anthropocentric, and an adequate semantic description of these terms has to be founded on an anthropocentric, rather than on a scientific dominant [i.e. basis]."

3.4 *Rough* and *smooth*

Many different kinds of prototypes are embodied in the meaning of words describing physical properties. Some of these refer, as we have seen, to some prototypical situations, such as having been recently in or near fire. Others may refer to the internal structure of the objects themselves. Consider, for example, the English word *rough*. In Locke's framework, "roughness" is clearly a one-sense quality, based on touch: one cannot hear or smell that something is *rough*, and though one may sometimes think that something is *rough* from the look of it, the only way to know for sure is by touch. Prototypical "roughness" is conceived in terms of a surface with lots of small variable parts (something like a 'bumpy' surface). If one moves one's hand while touching such a surface, one can experience a sensation of a particular type which is indicative of this feature of the object ('many small parts of this thing are not like the other parts'); at the same time one can recognize that touching such a surface in certain ways can be unpleasant. For example, running one's hand across the bark of a tree, one can detect the variegated surface structure and at the same time recognize that if one scraped or brushed against it quickly it could hurt or chafe.

These ideas can be represented in a formal semantic explication as in [M]. (English *rough* can also be used in collocations like *rough terrain*, referring to a property which can be detected by means of one's feet and legs rather than hands, but this exemplifies a distinct, albeit related, meaning.) For explications for *hand*, see Wierzbicka (2007c), Goddard (2012a).

[M]   This thing (e.g. bark, cloth) is *rough.*

a.   this thing is like this:
b.   if someone's hand [m] moves when it is touching this thing,
c.   this someone can feel something in this hand [m] because of it
d.   because of this, this someone can know something about this thing
e.   because of this, this someone can think like this:
f.   "many small parts of this thing are not like the other parts"
g.   if a part of someone's body moves when it is touching this thing,
h.   this someone can feel something bad in this part because of it

Closely related to English *rough* is *smooth*, and it is not surprising that the two words are usually presented in dictionaries as opposites. To some extent, this is justified. Explication [N] for *smooth* presents the critical inference in terms of "homogeneous parts" ('all parts of this thing are like all the other parts'), which could be seen as an implicit contrast with the variegated structure implied by *rough*. Likewise, the final component of [N] is analogous to that of *rough*, except that the potential feeling associated with touching smooth things is characterized as a good feeling (rather than as a bad feeling). On the other hand, the two words are not fully symmetrical. To see this, it is enough to think of food products like *smooth* peanut butter and *smooth* ricotta cheese, or drinks called *smoothies*. *Smooth* peanut butter is opposed to *crunchy* rather than to *rough*, smooth ricotta is presumably contrasted, on some level, with cottage cheese, with its visually and tactilely detectable "curds", and a *smoothie* is a milky drink containing some fruit which is blended so well with the milk that its presence cannot be detected by the tongue. These examples from the area of food show that "smoothness" can be detected not only with one's hand but also with one's tongue, and relatedly, that "smoothness" is not such an explicitly "surface" property as is "roughness". For this reason, explication [N] refers not to a person's hand as the prototypical source of the tactile sensation, but rather to a 'part of someone's body', thereby allowing for the tongue, cheek, etc. to play this role.

[N]   This thing (e.g. silk, a baby's skin, peanut butter) is *smooth.*

a.   this thing is like this:
b.   if a part of someone's body moves when it is touching this thing,
c.   this someone can feel something in this part because of it
d.   because of this, this someone can know something about this thing
e.   because of this, this someone can think like this:

f.   "all parts of this thing are like all the other parts"[9]
g.   if a part of someone's body moves when it is touching this thing
h.   this someone can feel something good in this part because of it

As with *hot* and *cold*, so with *rough* and *smooth*: the meanings of apparent equivalents to these words are not necessarily exactly the same in other languages. In Polish, for example, the word closest in meaning to English *smooth*—Polish *gładki*—would be more accurately described as an opposite of English *rough*, rather than as an exact equivalent to *smooth*. *Gładki* refers exclusively to surfaces and cannot be applied to things like peanut butter, ricotta cheese or fruity milk drinks. It is explicated in [O].[10]

[O]   This thing (e.g. wood) is *gładki* (i.e. has a "smooth" surface). [Polish]
a.   this thing is like this:
b.   if someone's hand [m] moves when it is touching this thing,
c.   this someone can feel something in this hand [m] because of it
d.   because of this, this someone can know something about this thing
e.   because of this, this someone can think like this:
f.   "all parts of this thing are like all the other parts"
g.   if someone's hand [m] moves when it is touching this thing,
h.   this someone can feel something good in this hand [m] because of it

The natural counterpart of *gładki* in Polish, namely *szorstki*, is not an exact opposite either. For the most part, it is comparable to English *rough*. Interestingly, *szorstki* is derived (etymologically) from the noun *sierść* (previously *szerść*) referring to the stiff, "bristly" hair of a dog, presumably seen in contrast to the soft fur of a cat, perceived as pleasant to the stroking hand. From a synchronic point of view, however (and this is the main point of difference with English *rough*), Polish *szorstki* is quite strongly associated with stubble on a man's face. Accordingly, this has been included as part of the conceptual prototype in explication [P].

[P]   This thing is *szorstki* (i.e. has a rough, bristly, coarse feel). [Polish]
a.   this thing is like this:
b.   if someone's hand [m] moves when it is touching this thing,
c.   this someone can feel something in this hand [m] because of it
d.   because of this, this someone can know something about this thing
e.   because of this, this someone can think like this:
f.   "some very small parts of this thing are not like the other parts"

[9] Or alternatively: 'someone can't say about this thing: "some of its parts are not like the other parts"'.
[10] Admittedly, *gładki* is sometimes used in relation to the surface of a lake, e.g. *gładka tafla jeziora* 'a *gładka* sheet of the lake', but this is clearly a metaphorical extension, describing the surface of a lake as if it were a sheet of glass.

g.   if someone's hand [m] moves when it is touching this thing
h.   this someone can feel something bad in this hand [m] because of it
i.   someone can feel something like this if this someone's hand [m] moves
j.   when it is touching some parts of a man's [m] face [m]

Though there is clearly scope for more far-reaching studies of "tactile" physical-quality concepts across languages, these contrastive examples from English and Polish are sufficient to show that such concepts are language-specific. They do not simply name objective language-independent properties of things "as such", but rather embody certain language-specific interpretations of aspects of the physical world.

3.5 *Hard* and *soft*

Along with *rough* and *smooth*, another pair of words that identify what from an English speaker's point of view are important physical qualities are *hard* and *soft*. The fact that all four of these words have a wide range of extended and metaphorical uses underscores their importance in the view of the world associated with the English language. Of the four, however, by far the most important is *hard*, a concept which apparently constitutes a recurrent "semantic molecule" in the meaning of numerous other English words, verbs as well as nouns. Consider, for example, the semantic domain of the human body. Even the most rudimentary definitions of words like *teeth* and *bones* would have to include the component 'hard'. On the other hand, there do not appear to be any body-part terms which would require, or justify, the inclusion of the descriptors 'rough' or 'smooth'. Similarly, among verbs of physical activity, there are many which include in their meaning a reference to things which are 'hard' (e.g. *to chop*) or 'not hard' (e.g. *to tear*), but none to 'rough' or 'smooth'.[11]

The *Collins Cobuild Dictionary* (1991) defines English *hard* as follows: 'something that is hard is very firm and stiff rather than soft to touch and usually not easily bent or broken.' This is not very helpful, since the words *firm*, *stiff*, and *soft*, through which *hard* is being defined here, are no less complex than *hard* itself, and the same applies to *bent* and *broken*. Modern lexicography, grappling with the semantics of physical-property words, is largely unaware of the insights of 17th-century philosophers like Locke, on which it could very profitably draw. In the case of *hard*, Locke's notion was that it refers to the "cohesion of the parts", referring to how "separable and how movable the parts were" (1959[1690]: vol. I, p. 154). These objective aspects, however, are only one half of the story. The other half has to do with the subjective effect that touching things produces in people. Locke wrote about it like this:

---

[11] This does not mean that one cannot *chop* soft things, such as lettuces or tomatoes; but the conceptual category of *chopping* is founded on a prototypical situation of someone dealing with 'something hard' (Goddard and Wierzbicka 2009).

hard and soft are names that we give to things only in relation to the constitutions of our bodies; that being generally called hard by us will put us to pain sooner than change figure by the pressure of any part of our bodies; and that, on the contrary, soft, which changes the situation of its parts upon an easy and unpainful touch.   (p. 154)

The importance of the subjective aspect of the concepts *hard* and *soft* can be appreciated if we compare them with concepts like *breakable* or *fragile*: the words *breakable* and *fragile* do not refer to people's sensations, as *hard* and *soft* do. It is significant that in everyday English speech "subjective-cum-objective" words like *hard* and *soft* appear to be much more common than purely "objective" ones like *fragile, brittle,* or *durable* (not to mention technical and scientific ones like *adhesive, glutinous,* or *viscous*). Evidently, the "subjective-cum-objective" mode plays a greater role in everyday conceptualization of the world than the purely "objective" mode characteristic of technical and scientific discourse.

Explication [Q] for *hard* refers to the "unyielding" or "impervious" quality of hard things, such as rocks, teeth, and bones. This is not very different from Locke's idea that hard objects resist our attempts to separate or move their parts. The basic insight is that often people want to do something to an object so that some parts of it are not the same as they used to be; for example, they may want to break it, to scratch it, or to make something out of it. If such an object is **not** *hard*, they can do it with their hands alone. If it is *hard*, they have to do it with something else—a knife, an axe, or some other tool. Bearing in mind that this objective property is detectable by touch, we can propose the explication below. (*Hard* also has a separate meaning, *hard₂*, in examples such as *a hard bed*, describing things which can be expected to be 'soft', but which are not so; see below.)

[Q]   This thing is *hard*.

a.   this thing is like this:
b.   if someone's hand [m] moves when it is touching this thing,
c.   this someone can feel something in this hand [m] because of it
d.   because of this, this someone can know something about this thing
e.   because of this, this someone can think like this:
f.   "if someone wants to do something to this thing with the hands [m]
g.   because this someone wants some parts of this thing not to be
                   where they were before,
h.   this someone can't do it if this someone doesn't do something
                   with something else at the same time"

Soft, which may appear to be completely symmetrical with respect to *hard*, in fact appears to focus more specifically on the "movability" of the object's parts. Perhaps the main interest of things described as *soft* is that of providing comfort to the human body: people value *soft* pillows, cushions, beds, chairs, carpets, and so on, because when their bodies press upon such objects, these objects "give in" in a way which is agreeable to the body, and this "giving in" means that some parts of the object pressed by the body move. (The main interest of things described as *hard* is different: people can use "hard" things like stones, wood, and metal to transform their environment so that it would offer protection and facilitate transport, by building walls, roads, fences, and so on, to make things which can last and which can make everyday life easier and more manageable, such as furniture, cooking utensils, tools, and so on.) Accordingly, we would propose the following explication of *soft*:

[R]   This thing is *soft*.

a.   this thing is like this:
b.   if a part of someone's body moves when it is touching this thing,
c.   this someone can feel something in this part because of it
d.   because of this, this someone can know something about this thing
e   because of this, this someone can think like this:
f.   "if a part of someone's body moves when it is touching a thing like this,
g.   parts of this thing can move at the same time because of it
h.   this someone can feel something good in this part of the body because of it"

Explications [Q] and [R] are compatible with various asymmetries in the range of use of *hard* and *soft*. For example, the phrase *soft fur* does not have a counterpart in **hard fur*, and though some carpets can be described as *soft* (*a soft carpet*), it would not make sense to describe a carpet as *hard* (**a hard carpet*). Similarly, *hard* does not always have an opposite in *soft*. For example, some apples can be described as *hard*, but normally apples are not described as *soft* (unless they are cooked). It is not the case, then, that the same range of objects can be described as either *hard* or *soft*. This confirms that "hardness" is not conceptualized as an absence of "softness", or vice versa. Rather, the two are based on qualitatively different prototypes.

One last aspect of the concepts *hard* and *soft* which warrants attention here concerns the part of the body envisaged as the source of the sensation. As we saw earlier, Locke linked both concepts with "the pressure of any part of our bodies". In the case of "softness", this formula may be appropriate, given the salience of *soft pillows* (pleasant for the head), *soft beds* (pleasant for the whole body), *soft carpet* (pleasant for the feet), and so on in the discourse about "softness". The sensation of "hardness", however (as conceptualized through the English word *hard*), appears to be linked in a special way with the hands: stones, wood, metal, shells, bones, nuts, and so on, are all *hard* to the hands that handle them.

The concept encoded in the English word *hard* differs in this respect from its counterparts encoded in many other languages. For example, in Polish the word *twardy* covers a range of use divided in English between *hard* and *tough*. In English, apples which are difficult to bite can be described as *hard*, but meat difficult to bite would normally be described as *tough* rather than *hard*, whereas in Polish *twardy* would be used in both cases. There is a similar difference in range of use between English *soft* and its closest Polish counterpart, *miękki*. Meat which is easy to bite is described in English as *tender* rather than *soft*, whereas in Polish such meat is described by the same word, *miękki*, which is used for "soft" foods of any kind, and for any other "soft" things, e.g. pillows. This suggests that it may be justified in the explications of Polish *twardy* and *miękki* to refer not to 'hands' specifically, but rather to 'some parts of the body' (to allow for the teeth, as well as hands).

[S]   This thing is *twardy* ("hard-tough") [Polish]

a.   this thing is like this:
b.   if some parts of someone's body move when they are touching this thing,
c.   this someone can feel something in these parts because of it
d.   because of this, this someone can know something about this thing
e.   because of this, this someone can think like this:
f.   "if someone wants to do something to a thing like this with some parts of the body
g.   because this someone wants some parts of this thing not to be
                    where they were before
h.   this someone can't do it if this someone doesn't do something
                with something else at the same time"

[T]   This thing is *miękki* ("soft-tender") [Polish]

a.   this thing is like this:
b.   if some parts of someone's body move when they are touching this thing,
c.   this someone can feel something in these parts because of it
d.   because of this, this someone can know something about this thing
e.   because of this, this someone can think like this:
f.   "if a part of someone's body moves when it is touching a thing like this,
g.   some parts of this thing can move at the same time because of it
h.   this someone can feel something good in this part of the body because of it"

It is true that in English, too, cooked vegetables (e.g. pumpkin) can be described as *soft* (if they are well cooked or overcooked) or *hard* (if they are undercooked), just as in Polish they can be described as *twarde* (plural) or *miękkie*, despite the fact that cooked vegetables are normally not handled with one's bare hands. As we have seen, however, in Polish these words apply to cooked meat as well as cooked vegetables, whereas English draws a conceptual distinction between the two. This suggests that in English undercooked *hard* vegetables are seen as somewhat similar to *hard* raw vegetables or fruit, whose "hardness" can be felt with one's hands, whereas in Polish, on the other hand, undercooked vegetables are seen as similar to both raw vegetables or fruit and to "tough" meat: in all these cases, *twardość* is expressed in terms of their effect on some parts of the body, be they hands or teeth.

3.6 *Heavy* and *light*

Heavy and *light* are not mentioned by Locke among the physical properties based on touch, and understandably so: one can't find out whether something is *heavy* or *light* by merely touching it. How does one find it out, then? If we were to believe dictionaries, we would think that one does it by putting things on scales: usually, dictionaries define *heavy* in terms of "weighing". For example, *Collins Cobuild* offers the following definition: 'something that is heavy weighs a lot more than is usual and is often difficult to move.' As one might expect, however, *weight* itself is then defined, circularly, via *heavy*: 'if something weighs a particular amount, this amount is how heavy it is.'

The second part of the *Collins Cobuild* definition is more useful: *heavy* things are indeed 'difficult to move', especially if one wants to move them to a place that is far away. But difficult in what sense? Things can be difficult to move for many reasons aside from heaviness (e.g. they can be too big, or be awkwardly shaped, or unwieldy). This brings us back to the subjective aspect of "heaviness": how do people assess things as *heavy* or *not heavy*? In the absence of scales, the obvious way is to try to lift or pick them up. If something is *heavy*, when we do this the feeling in our arms and backs will tell us clearly enough that it would be physically stressful to try to move this thing to a distant place with our bodies alone. These considerations lead us to the following explication:

[U]   This thing is *heavy*.

a.   this thing is like this:
b.   if someone does something to this thing with some parts of their body
c.   like people do something to a thing when they want it to be above the place
                    where it is,
d.   this someone can feel something in their body because of it
e.   because of this, this someone can know something about this thing
f.   because of this, this someone can think like this:
g.   "if someone does something to this thing for some time with parts of their body
h.   because this someone wants it to be in a place far from the place
                    where it was before,
i.   this someone can't not feel something bad in their body because of it"

If this explication is correct, the concept of "heaviness" indeed includes the idea that moving a heavy object (with one's body alone) would be difficult, in a specific sense: that doing so necessarily brings about unpleasant feelings in the body, and that one can anticipate this by reference to the sensation one feels when one attempts to lift such things. The concept of "lightness" can be explicated in a converse fashion, as follows.

[V]   This thing is *light*.

a.   this thing is like this:
b.   if someone does something to this thing with some parts of their body
c.   like people do something to a thing when they want it to be above the place where it is,
d.   this someone can feel something in their body because of it
e.   because of this, this someone can know something about this thing
f.   because of this, this someone can think like this:
g.   "if someone does something to this thing for some time with parts of their body
h.   because this someone wants it to be in a place far from the place where it was before,
i.   this someone does not feel something bad in their body because of it"

Thus, *heavy* and *light*—like *hard* and like *rough*—turn out to be "subjective-cum-objective" kinds of word. Things that are heavy (or light) have to **feel** heavy (or light). If something never feels heavy when lifted then it is not heavy, just as something that never tastes sweet is not sweet, no matter how much sugar it may contain.

3.7 Sharp

The last physical-quality word to be discussed here is *sharp*. Intuitively, *sharp* is another touch-related concept, like *rough* and *smooth* or *hard* and *soft*: some things **feel** "sharp" to the exploring hand. It could be suggested, however, that "sharpness" is a purely objective property, whose definition does not require any reference to the sensation produced by a person's hand upon contact with a "sharp" object and to a resulting judgement.

In our view, there are two kinds of evidence which militate against such an assumption. The first is a test based on combinability with the word *feel*. Consider the contrast between the two groups of sentences in (a) and (b):

(a)   I felt how rough (smooth) it was.
       I felt how heavy (light) it was.
       I felt how hard (soft) it was.
       I felt how hot (cold) it was.

(b)   ?I felt how fragile it was.
       ?I felt how breakable it was.
       ?I felt how water-resistant it was.
       ?I felt how stretchy it was.
       ?I felt how strong it (the material) was.

The adjectives in group (b) do not readily combine with the verb *feel* because they refer to "objective" properties of certain objects, independent of any sensation that human beings may experience in contact with them. Those in group (a), on the other hand, do combine with *feel* because there is in their meaning an appropriate "hook": a reference to a feeling in a part of a person's body.[12] Applying this test to *sharp*, we can see that it belongs to group (a), not to group (b): *I felt how sharp it was.*

Second, if we deny the subjective, experiential aspect of the meaning of *sharp*, it would be hard to account for the fact that the word is commonly used as a warning—much more so than, for example, the word *heavy*. If a heavy object were to land on somebody's head, the effect could be as hurtful and as damaging as a cut caused by a sharp object; nonetheless, *heavy* is not normally used as a warning, the way *sharp* is. This suggests that in the case of *sharp*, a reference to the potential injury and pain is built into the meaning of the word itself. The fact that *sharp* is frequently used to describe a particular kind of pain (cf. Nicholls 2003) points in the same direction.

Explication [W] incorporates the anthropocentric and pain-related aspect of *sharp*, along with other aspects which parallel those discussed in connection with earlier explications.

[W]   This thing is *sharp*.

a.   this thing is like this:
b.   if someone's hand [m] touches some parts of this thing,
c.   this someone can feel something in this hand [m] because of it
d.   because of this, this someone can know something about this thing
e.   because of this, this someone can think like this:
f.   "if this thing moves when some parts of it are touching something else,
g.   something can happen to this other thing because of it
h.   it can happen in one moment
i.   when it happens, some parts of this thing can be inside this other thing
                because of it
j.   if this other thing is a part of someone's body,
k.   this someone can feel something bad in this part because of it"

Given how important the concept of "sharpness" is for speakers of English, one might expect that the word *sharp* would have its exact equivalents in all other languages. This, however, is not the case: here as elsewhere, the vocabulary of different languages reflects different ways of conceptualizing the physical world. For example, Korean (Kyung-Joo Yoon, p.c.) distinguishes lexically between "sharp" (*ppyocokha-*)

---

[12] On the basis of this test, one could motivate a terminological distinction between "qualities" and "properties". Being *breakable* or *water-resistant* could be termed a "property" of the thing so described, but being *sweet*, *hard*, or *smooth* could be called a "quality", or at least a property which is also a quality. The point is that in the latter case there is an implicit reference to a qualitative experience.

needles and "sharp" (*nalkhalop-*) knives, and native speakers of this language express surprise that two "so different" concepts should be covered in English by the same word. (Korean has a third word comparable to *sharp*, which is also applicable to blades, but not to needles.)

In fact, the conceptual differences between English *sharp* and its two Korean counterparts are quite small. They can be captured by means of the following contrasting components:

> *sharp* (e.g. about a needle or knife): 'some parts of this thing can be inside this other thing because of it'
>
> *ppyocokha-* (e.g. about a needle or thorn): 'one small part of this thing can be inside this other thing because of it'
>
> *nalkhalop-* (e.g. about a knife): 'some parts of the edge [m] of this thing can be inside this other thing because of it'

For English *sharp*, the component which refers to the "penetrating effect" describes the penetrating parts of the item as 'some parts of this thing', a formulation which is equally compatible with a point or a blade. For Korean *ppyocokha-*, the penetrating part is described as 'one small part', compatible with a point or tip but not with a blade. For Korean *nalkhalop-*, it is described as 'some parts of the edge [m] of this thing', compatible with a blade but not with a point or tip (cf. Goddard and Wierzbicka 2009).

3.8 Metaphorical extensions: Polish vs. English

Some of the most interesting questions about physical-quality words arise from the observation that apparent close equivalents in different languages exhibit different kinds of metaphorical extension. Some extensions appear to be attested in many languages; for example, the use of words comparable to *hot* and *cold* (and/or *warm* and *cool*) in relation to interpersonal good and bad feelings. Others appear to be culture-specific to a greater or lesser degree, sometimes even unique. The productivity of particular extensions also varies from language to language. To what extent are such differences attributable to differences in the literal meanings of the apparent translation equivalents? What other factors, such as differing cultural norms and differing cultural models, are involved? Limitations of space preclude a thorough treatment here, but we would like to briefly consider some examples from Polish and English to illustrate how the present approach allows a start to be made on such questions, and to indicate the directions it would take. We will compare extensions of the Polish words *ciężki* 'heavy' and *ostry* 'sharp' with their closest counterparts in English.

One of the authors recently received a letter from a Polish friend in which the writer contemplated emigration from Poland and summed up his dilemma in the words: *Wyjechać ciężko i zostać ciężko*, literally 'it is heavy (adv.) to leave and it is heavy to stay'. In English, one would say *It's hard to leave and it's hard to stay*, but one couldn't use the word *heavy*. By contrast, in Polish one can use *ciężko* 'heavy' in such a context but one couldn't possibly use *twardo* 'hard'. Is this difference significant, or is it just a phraseological quirk of the two languages?

When we explore many other metaphorical extensions of *ciężki* 'heavy' in Polish and of *hard* in English, we see that what might seem at first sight a mere phraseological quirk is in fact evidence of a far-reaching semantic and cultural difference. The point is that "heaviness" (of life and its different manifestations) is a general theme of Polish folk philosophy, manifesting itself in numerous collocations, whereas "hardness" is similarly a general theme in the folk philosophy reflected in the English language.

Common collocations with the Polish adjective *ciężki* 'heavy' include: *ciężkie życie* 'heavy life', *ciężki los* 'a heavy fate', *ciężka choroba* 'a heavy illness', *ciężkie zmartwienie* 'a heavy sorrow/trouble', *ciężkie czasy* 'heavy times', *ciężka walka* 'heavy struggle', *ciężkie przejścia* 'heavy events-gone-wrong', *ciężkie przeżycia* 'heavy experience', *ciężka praca* 'heavy work' (e.g. preparing for exams), and so on. These collocations suggest a view of life as a heavy burden that one simply has to carry.

In English, such imagery is virtually absent (except for a few phrases like *a heavy burden* and *a heavy responsibility*). Generally speaking, a difficult life tends to be interpreted in English through the images of "hardness": *a hard life*, not **a heavy life*; *hard times*, not **heavy times*; *a hard struggle*, not **a heavy struggle*; *hard work*, not **heavy work* (in the relevant sense), and so on.

The Polish phraseology linking aspects of life with "heaviness" builds in particular on the component 'this someone can't not feel something bad because of it', in the meaning of *heavy* (or rather, of *ciężkie*) as a physical-quality word; cf. explication [U]. All the collocations with the adjective *ciężki* quoted here imply this component, even if the noun modified by it does not imply any feelings, bad or otherwise. For example, neither *życie* 'life' nor *los* 'fate/destiny' implies any bad feelings, but *ciężkie życie* and *ciężki los* do. Similarly, phrases combining the adverb *ciężko* with a verb imply bad feelings, even if the verb does not imply any feelings at all (as in *ciężko wyjechać, ciężko zostać* ('[it's] heavy to leave, [it's] heavy to stay').

When used as physical-quality words, both *heavy* and *ciężki* imply 'bad feelings in one's body' (one feels something bad in one's body when one carries something heavy and one just has to put up with it). Polish collocations like *ciężkie życie* 'a heavy life' or *ciężkie czasy* 'heavy times' build on this component, implying that life is like a heavy burden that one simply has to carry.

On the other hand, when *hard* and *twardy* are used as physical-quality words, they do not imply that if one tried to move some parts or separate them from the others one would feel something bad in one's body. Rather, they imply that one might need to use an instrument for this (see explications [Q] and [S]). Arguably, therefore, English collocations like *a hard life* or *hard times* suggest a different view of life than

Polish collocations like *ciężkie życie* 'a heavy life' or *ciężkie czasy* 'heavy times': in one case, living is seen as being like carrying a heavy burden, and in the other, like trying to change the shape of a hard object.[13] In particular, the image of hardness in English collocations suggests difficulties which possibly can be overcome (through determination, effort, and resourcefulness), whereas comparable Polish collocations with the adjective *ciężki* suggest burdens which simply have to be borne.

Turning now to the Polish word *ostry* and its English counterpart *sharp* (cf. explication [W]), we can observe that the metaphorical range of the Polish word is notably wider than that of its English counterpart. In the domain of speech acts at least, Polish *ostry* is used very widely indeed, whereas comparable collocations with English *sharp* are restricted, by and large, to the expression *a sharp rebuke*. Even so, this single collocation is sufficient to give English speakers an insight into the figurative potential of "sharpness" in this domain: *a sharp rebuke* is a rebuke which is meant to be hurtful, as well as sudden and momentary. In Polish, there are several common collocations comparable in both these qualities, hurtfulness and momentariness. They include: *ostre słowa* 'sharp words', *ostra nagana* 'a sharp reprimand', *ostra krytyka* 'sharp criticisms', *ostry atak* 'a sharp attack', as well as *ostro krytykować* 'to criticize [someone] sharply', and *ostro atakować* 'to attack [someone] sharply'.

Trying to identify the meaning of the words *sharp* and *ostry* as used in relation to speech, it is good to start with simple sentences such as *She spoke sharply*. The quality of potential hurtfulness is evident here. What is perhaps less evident is that the suddenness implied by *sharply* suggests a concurrent feeling on the part of the speaker, presumably anger. This is supported by the oddness of sentences like ?*She decided to speak to him sharply*. One doesn't decide in advance to speak to someone sharply, because *sharply* implies unpremeditated speech resulting from anger or annoyance felt at the time of speaking.

Given that the Polish words *ostry* and *ostro* have the same implications as their English counterparts, the fact that they are used more widely suggests that cultural, rather than strictly semantic, factors are involved. The limited use of *sharp* in English in relation to speech seems to be related to "Anglo" cultural scripts which discourage criticizing the addressee, especially on impulse, "without a good reason". There is independent evidence for such cultural scripts.[14] As discussed, for example, in Wierzbicka (2006a: ch. 1; 2012a), Eva Hoffman (1989), who immigrated to North America from Poland at the age of 13 and discovered there what she perceived of as new rules for speaking, noted: "You don't criticize the person you are with, at least

---

[13] The English word *heavy* can also be used in a figurative way, e.g. in the phrase *a heavy heart*, and here, too, *heavy* implies that the person in question 'can't not feel something bad'. In English, however, the range of such collocations is rather limited, whereas in Polish the model in question is productive and the collocations based on it are numerous.

[14] For background on the theory of cultural scripts, and for studies in a range of languages, see Goddard and Wierzbicka (2004), Goddard (2006d), and Wierzbicka (2002a; 2002b; 2004b).

not directly." Similar "rules" have been discovered and commented on by other cross-cultural writers, for example, the Australian-born son of Jewish Hungarian parents Andrew Riemer (1992), and the daughter of Ukrainian immigrants to Britain Marina Lewycka (2005).

As discussed in earlier NSM work (e.g. Wierzbicka 2003*a*; 2007*f*), there is also a cultural norm in English against "hurting people's feelings", which has no counterpart in Polish or Russian (or, one might add, Ukrainian or Hungarian). Speaking to people "sharply" is inconsistent with this rule, as it is bound to "hurt their feelings". This does not mean of course that speakers of English never speak to other people sharply: the existence of the phrase *a sharp rebuke* in itself testifies that they do. But the phraseological evidence suggests that the range of situations in which they do so is more specific and more constrained: people are sometimes prepared to *rebuke* someone else *sharply* when they feel that it is "worth" expressing their anger and hurting the addressee's feelings in order to influence their behaviour (and when they are in a position to do so). On the whole, however, *speaking sharply* is to be avoided.

As this discussion indicates, metaphorical extensions of physical-quality words can provide important evidence for cultural models (cf. Holland and Quinn 1987; Gibbs and Steen 1999; Dirven, Frank, and Pütz 2003): in the realm of the metaphorical, "physical semantics" and "cultural semantics" intertwine. While it is of course of interest to search for universal tendencies in this area, we would urge that it is at least as important to explore the concomitant cross-linguistic differences, and to try to reveal the cultural underpinnings of language-specific metaphorical transfers.

3.9 Concluding remarks

It has often been asserted that the most secure basis of human knowledge lies in sensory experience, in so-called "sense data": we touch things, we feel their hardness, their smoothness, their sharpness, and so on, from this we derive knowledge of what they are like (hard, smooth, sharp, and so on), and we can build our knowledge of the world on that. As we have seen, however, even apparently objective properties like "hardness", "smoothness", and "sharpness" are constructed through particular languages and may differ somewhat from language to language. Moreover, within each language—for example, English—the structure of lexical concepts like *hard, smooth,* and *sharp* reflects a recognition that these concepts are derived from bodily experience and from judgments based on that experience. A sentence like *This thing is hard* is not **as** subjective as *This thing feels hard*, and it does purport to convey some reliable information about the thing in question. At the same time, however, it implicitly indicates that the information relates to embodied human experience which often involves manipulation of things. For example, a word like *hard* relates to the experience of doing things to objects with one's hands, and a word like *heavy* relates to the experience of carrying things from place to place.

The importance of concepts like 'hard', 'heavy', and 'sharp' is reflected in the fact that they often function as semantic molecules in the structure of other concepts, in particular, verbs of physical activity. For example, in English, the verb *chop* refers in its meaning to the kinds of things which are prototypically chopped as being 'hard', and the verb *tear* refers to the kinds of things which are prototypically torn as being 'not hard'. *Chop, cut*, and *slice* all refer in their meaning to the "sharpness" of the tool with which the activity in question is carried out (Goddard and Wierzbicka 2009).

We can hypothesize, therefore, that all languages will have words reflecting the same semantic template, involving TOUCH, FEEL, KNOW, and THINK, employed in this study: touching something with a part of the body, feeling something in that part, knowing something about that thing because of it, thinking about that thing in a certain way because of it. We can expect that all languages will have some such words involving specifically the body-parts 'hand' and 'mouth'. We can expect that in all languages the semantics of such words will hinge crucially on the component LIKE THIS. Furthermore, we can expect that some physical-quality concepts (such as 'hard' and 'sharp') are integral to the meanings of various words about KINDS used for categorizing living things (like animals and plants), non-living natural things (like rocks and stones), and things made by people—either directly or via the role they play in the meanings of various words for PARTS. For example, *rocks* and *bones* can be expected to be conceptualized as 'hard', *cats* and *tigers* as animals which have 'sharp claws', and so on.

Do all languages have words (whether adjectives or verbs) comparable in meaning to English *hot, hard, rough, heavy*, and *sharp*? The examples from Polish, French, and Korean which we have discussed in this chapter suggest that we can expect considerable variation in this area. There is certainly no reason to expect that all languages will have words corresponding in meaning exactly to the English words. At the same time, we can expect some commonalities arising from existential commonalities of human experience, such as the need to be careful with fire, to cut meat, to carry things, and also from bodily and cognitive experiences such as touching things and finding out what they are like.

For a long time it was widely assumed that all languages have "colour words", and this is a myth that dies hard (Lucy 1997; Saunders 1992; Saunders and van Brakel 1995; Wierzbicka 1990; 2005*b*; 2006*c*; 2007*d*; 2008*a*; and Chapter 4 below). Even so, it is clear that the domain of "visual semantics" exhibits many commonalities and recurring features, such as the contrast between light and the absence of light, or the prominence of bodily and environmental prototypes such as blood, vegetation, sky, and earth. What then of "physical-quality words" like 'hard' and 'soft', or 'heavy' and 'light', or 'sharp'? What range of commonalities and recurring features do these words exhibit across languages? The domain of "qualitative" physical-property words such as those discussed in this chapter is ripe for cross-linguistic investigations.

4

From "colour words" to visual semantics

English, Russian, Warlpiri

4.1 'Colour semantics' vs. 'visual semantics'

In his *English as a Global Language* David Crystal (2003: 15) observes: "There is no shortage of mother-tongue English speakers who believe in an evolutionary view of language ('let the fittest survive, and if the fittest happens to be English, then so be it') or who refer to the present global status of the language as a 'happy accident'. There are many who think (....) that a world with just one language in it would be a very good thing." Linguists usually do not agree, and neither do anthropologists. Nonetheless, in practice it seems that sometimes linguists and anthropologists behave as if they believed that English is indeed the fittest. This is done by implicitly absolutizing some concepts which are lexically encoded in English, and giving them a fundamental status in human cognition. The concept of 'colour' is a good case in point, as is also the idea of "colour universals" based on English words like *white, black, red, blue,* and so on.

It has often been pointed out that many languages, e.g. in Australia, Papua New Guinea, and Asia, do not have a word for 'colour' (cf. Conklin 1964; Bulmer 1968; Kuschel and Monberg 1974). On the face of it, therefore, 'colour' is not a universal concept, at least not demonstrably so. It is (demonstrably) a very important concept in English, and of course in many other languages, but by no means in all. To assert, as is often done, that speakers of such languages nonetheless **think** in terms of 'colour' (although they never speak about 'colour') is to impose on those languages a conceptual grid alien to them. The claim that speakers of languages without a word for 'colour' nonetheless have a **concept** of 'colour' is to go beyond empirical evidence. In any case, without a word for 'colour', a putative concept of 'colour' could not be a coin in the speakers' shared conceptual and communicative currency.

This being so, the popular idea that there are some "colour universals"—conceived of as empirical universals of language and thought—is self-contradictory. There can be no universals in how people habitually think and talk about colour, given that in many languages people don't talk about colour at all but instead focus their attention on other aspects of what they see (aspects for which there may be no word in English).

This basic point—which Anna Wierzbicka has been making for many years (e.g. Wierzbicka 1990; 1996; 1999*b*; 2007*d*; 2008*a*; in press *a*; cf. also Lucy 1997)—has often been rejected on the basis of the axiom that the absence of a word does not prove the absence of a concept. Thus, if English happens to have a word for 'colour' and the Papuan language Kalam (Bulmer 1968) does not, this supposedly does not indicate that 'colour' is not as real in the thinking of the Kalam people as it is in the thinking of the speakers of English. The absence of a word for 'colour' in Kalam is said to be merely a "lexical gap". The same convenient axiom has been invoked in support of many other putative human universals, for which there just happen to be words in English, though not in some other languages—in particular, many so-called "basic human emotions", such as 'sadness' (for which Tahitian, for example, has no word at all, as documented by Levy 1973). Again, the absence of a word for 'sadness' in Tahitian is said to be "just a lexical gap". Such an insouciant attitude to troublesome lexical data from different languages implies that English really is the fittest language of all: a language which just happens to have words for everything fundamental in human thought.

Even if it is true that the absence of a word does not prove the absence of a concept, how can we prove the **presence** of a concept for which there is no word? And if we want to search for human universals in an unbiased way, shouldn't we try to rely, as far as possible, on concepts which **are** lexically recognized in all languages, rather than those which happen to be lexicalized in English?

Empirical work undertaken within the NSM theory of language and thought has shown that while many languages do not have a word for 'colour', all languages have a word for 'see'. For example, in all languages one can say things like: 'I don't see anything' or 'I see many people' (cf. Goddard and Wierzbicka 2002*c*). It makes more sense to ask about the universals of seeing than any putative "universals of colour" (cf. Goddard 1998; 1999; Wierzbicka 1996). It makes sense to ask, in the first instance, how people in different cultures talk, and think, about what they see—rather than ask about how they talk, and think, about 'colour'. "Visual semantics" is wider and more fundamental than the "semantics of colour", and to explore fruitfully the semantics of colour (with respect to languages like English), we need to do so in the context of a more fundamental inquiry into the semantics of seeing.

As evidence from the recent literature on bilingual experience shows, the structure of the experiential world differs, to some extent, from language to language (cf. Besemeres 2002; Besemeres and Wierzbicka 2007; Pavlenko 2006). There are in fact many different experiential worlds, and if we try to explore them through shared human concepts, rather than through English alone, we can hope to get closer to the experiential worlds inhabited by the speakers of languages other than English. The fact that we may never be able to capture those worlds fully or perfectly is not a good reason not to try to get as close to them as possible.

4.2 'Blue' and its two Russian counterparts

We will first illustrate differences in the conceptualization of the visual world with the Russian words for referring to the colour of the sky. As is well known, Russian doesn't have a word corresponding to the English word *blue* (and English doesn't have words corresponding to the Russian words *goluboj* and *sinij*). From an English speaker's point of view, *goluboj* and *sinij* are, roughly speaking, 'light blue' and 'dark blue', two varieties of 'blue'. From a Russian speaker's point of view, however, they cannot be that because there is no concept of 'blue' in Russian (just as there is no concept in English which would cover the combined range of *yellow* and *orange*). What do these words mean, then, from a Russian speaker's point of view?

Using NSM, we can explicate these meanings (both in English and in Russian) on the basis of prototypes phrased in terms of the environmental molecules 'sky', 'sun', 'day', and 'sea' (see Goddard 2010*b*) as follows:

[A]   X is *goluboj*. [Russian]

a.   when people think about the colour [m] of X, they can think like this:
b.   "it is like the colour [m] of the sky [m] at times when people can see the sun [m]
c.   at those times the colour [m] of the sky [m] on all sides of the sun [m] can be like this"

[B]   X is *sinij*. [Russian]

a.   when people think about the colour [m] of X, they can think like this:
b.   "the colour [m] of the sky [m] can be like this during the part of the day [m]
            when people can't see the sun [m] any more
c.   the colour [m] of the sea [m] can be like this"

The English word *blue* can be explicated along similar lines (but differently from both *goluboj* and *sinij*):

[C]   X is *blue*. [English]

a.   when people think about the colour [m] of X, they can think like this:
b.   "the colour [m] of the sky [m] can be like this at many times during the day [m]
c.   it can be like this when people can see the sun [m]
d.   it can be like this when people can't see the sun [m]
e.   the colour [m] of the sea [m] can be like this"

This explication of *blue* does not give this word a privileged status in relation to *goluboj* and *sinij*; at the same time, it accounts for the fact that the denotational range of *blue* covers, more or less, the combined ranges of *goluboj* and *sinij*.

For a more comprehensive picture, we will also include here the explication of the Polish word *niebieski* (from *niebo* 'sky'), which is different from all three: *blue*, *goluboj*, and *sinij*.

[D]   X is *niebieski*. [Polish]

a.   when people think about the colour [m] of X, they can think like this:
b.   the colour [m] of the sky [m] can be like this at many times during the day [m]
c.   it can be like this when people can see the sun [m]
d.   it can be like this when people can't see the sun [m]

The evidence supporting the claim that the four words (*goluboj*, *sinij*, *niebieski*, and *blue*) are indeed associated with the prototypes indicated above has been discussed elsewhere (see e.g. Wierzbicka 1996; 2005b; 2006c; 2008a). But the main argument in favour of the proposed prototypes is their explanatory power: they account both for the similarities and for the differences in the use of these words, both for the overlaps in their use and for their different boundaries.

The fact that the prototype of the Russian word *goluboj* is restricted to only one type of sky, bright-light sky on a sunny day, accounts for the relatively narrow denotational range of this word (comparable not to that of the English word *blue* but to that of the English compound *sky-blue*). The fact that the prototype of *blue* includes the bright-light sky on a sunny day, whereas the prototype of *sinij* does not, explains why the range of *sinij* is skewed towards darker colours than that of *blue*. The fact that the prototype of the Polish word *niebieski* takes in a wider range of different skies than either *goluboj* or *sinij* explains why *niebieski* can be darker than *goluboj* and lighter than *sinij*. At the same time, *niebieski* cannot be as dark as the English *blue*, whose prototype includes many different kinds of sky and doesn't even fully exclude the night sky.

This comparison of the meanings of the English word *blue* and its closest counterparts in Russian and Polish illustrates the fundamental differences between the NSM approach to visual semantics and the traditional Berlin and Kay (1969) style approach. For example, in one of his more recent papers, Kay (2004) insists that the English word *blue* stands for a "phenomenally basic color" and should be taken as a semantic primitive in terms of which Russian *goluboj* and the Polish *niebieski* should be defined (and also, that the basic Hungarian word *piros*, which is equivalent to neither the English *red* nor the English *pink*, should be defined via *red*). To quote:

All the [Natural Semantic Metalanguage] analyst needs to do is take the phenomenally basic colors: black, white, red, yellow, green and blue [i.e. the English colour words—AW] as primitives and define other color words such as words for pink or light blue (Russian *goluboj*, Polish *niebieski*) or light red (but darker than pink = Hungarian *piros*) in terms of these.

(Kay 2004: 242)

Using the English words as primes seems to Kay to be the obvious thing to do:

Assuming that the meanings of color words *must* be based on some non-color prototypes (Wierzbicka) makes a plausible case for her particular choices, but the argument rests entirely on the supposition that *red, green, yellow,* and *blue* cannot simply mean 'red', 'green', 'yellow' and 'blue' at the perceptual and conceptual level.   (Kay 2004: 243)

The suggestion that both Russian *goluboj* and Polish *niebieski* should be described in terms of the English words *light* and *blue* misses the point (discussed in detail in Wierzbicka 1996) that the range of use of the Polish word *niebieski* is different from that of the Russian word *goluboj* or that of the English expression *light blue*. Unlike *goluboj* (or *pink*), *niebieski* is not necessarily a light colour, and it is commonly used in combination with modifiers like 'light', 'dark', or 'bright': *jasno-niebieski* 'light-niebieski*', *ciemno-niebieski* 'dark-niebieski*', *jaskrawo niebieski* 'bright *niebieski*'.

Furthermore, to suggest that *blue* is "phenomenally basic", whereas *niebieski, goluboj,* or *sinij* are not, is deeply ethnocentric. The use of "non-colour prototypes" such as the sun, the sky, and the sea frees us from such ethnocentrism. It is also an approach which can be tested in consultation with native speakers and, in the case of languages like English, Russian, and Polish, through patterns of use evident from corpora.

The English word *blue* does not represent pure, unadulterated reality any more than *goluboj* or *sinij* do. All these words embed language-specific construals. These construals can be unpacked and compared through universal human concepts (such as SEE, LIKE, and WHEN) and through widespread conceptual molecules (such as 'sky', 'sun', and 'day').

The comparison of the English word *blue* and its closest counterparts in Russian has important theoretical implications. In particular, it undermines even the scaled-down claims of the proponents of the B&K paradigm, such as those made in Regier, Kay, and Cook (2005), an article provocatively entitled "Focal colors are universal after all". In this article, the authors affirm that there is "a universal tendency for the named color categories of languages to be based on favored precepts selected from restricted regions of color space" (2005: 8390) and they link those "favored precepts" with prototypes, claiming that in the large sample of languages examined by them, "best example choices for color terms in these languages cluster near the prototypes for English *white, black, red, green, yellow* and *blue*" (2005: 8386, Abstract).

The "best example" of the Russian categories *goluboj* and *sinij* cannot cluster near the prototype for the English word *blue*, because the prototype of *goluboj* is different from the prototype of *sinij*, and the "best examples" are in each case different, too.

As Wierzbicka has argued for many years, there are indeed "favourite areas" in visual semantics, and these can be explained in terms of visually salient environmental prototypes such as the sky, the sun, the sea, fire, grass and trees, and day and night (as well as the salient bodily prototype of blood). But these environmental (and bodily) reference points do not translate into cross-linguistically stable foci, because they can be conceptualized differently in different languages (cf. Biggam 2004). For example, the sky can be conceptualized as "the sky that people can see on a sunny day" (as in the case of *goluboj*) or as "the sky that people can see at many times during the day (whether or not they can see the sun at the same time)", as in the case of *niebieski*. They can also conceptualize the sky as visually comparable to the sea (as in the case of *blue*, and—in a different way—in the case of *sinij*).

It is not true, therefore, that, as Regier et al. (2005) put it, "focal colors are universal after all". What **is** true is that there are commonalities in visual semantics and that many of these commonalities can be linked with commonalities in human visual experience and in people's shared conditions of life on planet Earth (under the sky, and the sun, amidst vegetation, in the rhythm of days and nights). They are also related to some commonalities in people's bodies, such as (above all) the visually salient and vitally important blood.

4.3 Languages without a "colour concept": an illustration

As we have seen, English and Russian do not share the concept of 'blue', but they do share the concept of 'colour'. As already mentioned, however, many languages do not have a (lexically embodied) concept of 'colour' at all, and do not have "colour words" as such. The concept of 'colour' emerges in a language when people become interested (often, because of new technologies) in distinguishing purely "chromatic" aspects of appearance from other aspects, such as, for example, darkness, shininess, vividness or brightness, which may have more to do with visibility or visual conspicuousness than with specific prototypes. It is not an accident that languages which have no word for 'colour' have no specific "colour words" either. They may of course have words which, from the point of view of English, are "words for colours", but these words do not include the concept of 'colour' in their meaning. When "colour words" emerge in a language a word for 'colour' emerges too (often by borrowing). For example, the language of Aboriginal teenagers in Central Australia includes now both the word *kala* and more specific loanwords like *yala-wana* and *blu-wana* (from 'yellow one', 'blue one') (Langlois 2004: 157).

But if we want to compare the visual semantics of English with that of languages which don't have a word for 'colour', and if we want to do so from a maximally neutral epistemological perspective, not from an Anglocentric one, we can only use SEE, not 'colour', as our conceptual anchor point, because it is SEE, not 'colour', that all languages share.

Consider, for example, the following visual descriptors used by the speakers of the Australian language Warlpiri (Hargrave 1982; Laughren et al. 2006): *yalyu-yalyu*, literally 'blood-blood', *karntawarra-karntawarra*, literally 'ochre-ochre', *yukuri-yukuri*, literally 'grass-grass',[1] *walya-walya*, literally 'earth-earth', and *kunjuru-kunjuru*, literally 'smoke-smoke'. The form of these words provides a clue to their meaning as it is understood "from the native's point of view": they all appear to imply that what the speaker sees is likened to some prototype—blood, ochre, grass, earth, or smoke. This is often confirmed by folk definitions such as the following one for the word *kunjuru-kunjuru* cited in the *Warlpiri–English Encyclopedic Dictionary* (Laughren, Hale, and Warlpiri Lexicography Group 2006): *kunjuru-piya*, i.e. 'like smoke' (offered while describing a particular flower).

When the Warlpiri Dictionary glosses *kunjuru-kunjuru* as 'dark blue, smoky grey, purple', it seems clear that the purpose of this gloss is to help an Anglo reader to get some idea of the word's referential range rather than to capture its meaning from an insider's point of view. By contrast, an NSM explication of *kunjuru-kunjuru* would try to capture the latter, and while it would be more explicit than the folk definition, it would be in line with it:

[E]   This is *kunjuru-kunjuru*. ('smoke-smoke') [Warlpiri]

a.   when people see this they can think about it like this:

b.   "this is like *kunjuru* [m, smoke]

c.   when people see *kunjuru* [m] somewhere, they can see something like this"

Crucially, the Warlpiri visual descriptors can be explicated along the lines proposed here in Warlpiri itself—a point which we will illustrate with a tentative explication of *yukuri-yukuri* (roughly, 'grass-grass') whose Warlpiri version was kindly provided by Mary Laughren.

[E']   This (X) is *yukuri-yukuri* (*Nyampu=ju yukuri-yukuri*).

a.   kuja=ka=lu yapa-ngku nyampu nya-nyi, kaji=ka=lu=nyanu kuja wangka-mi:
       when people see this they can think like this:

b.   "nyampu=ju yukuri=piya"
           "this is like *yukuri*"

c.   kuja=ka=lu yapa-ngku yukuri nya-nyi nyarrpara, nyampu-piya (marda) ka=lu nya-nyi
       when people see *yukuri* somewhere, they can see something like this

The *Warlpiri Dictionary* glosses *yukuri* as 'green vegetation, new growth, fresh vegetation, alive (of plants)', and quotes a folk definition: "*yukuri* is the green vegetation—grass and trees—after rain and when everything is green [*yukuri-yukuri*] like when it is not dead and waterless—when the foliage and grasses are alive and

---

[1]   The *Dictionary* also describes *yukuri* as green, fresh vegetation, or new growth.

green." The explication in [E/E'], which does not rely on English words *colour* or *green*, attempts to capture an insider's point of view and uses only words which do have Warlpiri equivalents.

Anthropologist Diana Young (2005: 64–65) writes about 'green-ness' in Central Australia like this: "The earth in the Western Desert is red but after heavy or prolonged rain, and the immediate germination of opportunistic seeds, the ground begins to turn a brilliant green." As Young points out with respect to two related Central Australian languages, Pitjantjatjara and Yankunytjatjara, "the bright green of new plant growth occurs only where there is moisture. *Ukuri wiru* or in English 'really green' is a phrase [Yankunytjatjara and Pitjantjatjara] people often use about country, or plants." The same applies to Warlpiri, where the corresponding phrase is *yukuri-yukuri-nyayirni*. Thus, *yukuri-yukuri* does not mean 'green'; it refers not to (any) green but to "brilliant green", and it means that something so described 'looks like the earth where it is covered, after rain, with fresh new growth (*yukuri*)'.

Given that Warlpiri visual descriptors can be readily explained in Warlpiri itself, and in a way consistent with native speakers' intuitions (as reflected e.g. in folk definitions), it is hard to see any justification for saying that 'really', unbeknown to themselves, Warlpiri people think in terms of categories lexicalized in English—such as 'colour' and 'green'—and not in terms of categories lexicalized in Warlpiri itself. The Warlpiri Dictionary is a priceless resource, and we do not mean to criticize it here. Our disagreement is with the B&K paradigm (cf. Wierzbicka in press *a*), within which a word like *yukuri-yukuri* is glossed as 'green' (or 'grue') and regarded as a "colour word" (Kay et al.1997: 48).

4.4 The Warlpiri visual world

The main features: an overview

What can the world look like to people who are not interested in 'colours'? In this section, we will probe this question in relation to Warlpiri, using as our main database the *Warlpiri Dictionary*. Generally speaking, the Warlpiri people appear to be particularly interested in four aspects of what they see—all four different from 'colour', with which speakers of languages like English are clearly preoccupied. Things which attract their special attention are:

1. those which (regardless of their colour) are visually conspicuous in a given place, highly noticeable against the background;
2. those which (regardless of their colour) *shine* somewhere in one's surroundings—often in the distance;
3. those which (regardless of their colour) are visually striking because they are not 'the same all over' but present striking visual contrasts and patterns (e.g. they are spotted, striped, or flecked);

4. those which strike the onlookers as looking like some familiar and visually conspicuous features of the environment (commonly occurring local minerals, fresh vegetation after rain, the characteristic local soil, the smoke of evening camp fires, and so on).

In the *Warlpiri Dictionary*, the English glosses, definitions, and translations reflect a preoccupation with colour, but the Warlpiri folk definitions and folk comments themselves do not, and in fact no word for 'colour' appears in the Warlpiri parts of the *Dictionary* at all.

As Hale (1959) noted nearly half a century ago, one can't ask in (traditional) Warlpiri the question 'what colour is it?', and one would normally render this question as *Nyiyapiya nyampuju?*, literally, 'what is it like?' [*nyiya* 'what', -*piya* 'like', *nyampuju* 'this']. If one wanted to be more precise, one could of course say in Warlpiri the equivalent of 'what does it look like?' or 'what is it like when people see it?', but not 'what colour is it?'. Thus, for Warlpiri speakers, the question 'what colour is it?' simply does not (did not) arise. It is likely that the absence of "colour talk" in traditional Warlpiri was linked with the absence of any "colour practices" such as dyeing which involve giving 'colour' to a whole piece of cloth. On the other hand, the Warlpiri have an extremely rich visual discourse of other kinds, and a rich visual art, including body painting and ground painting that are based on pigments, designs, and eye-catching visual contrasts (cf. Isaacs 1999).

Visual conspicuousness

The *Warlpiri Dictionary* (Laughren et al. 2006) includes many words which suggest "visual conspicuousness" without specifying any particular source of it and it often lists a number of possible sources. For example, the reduplicated form *pirarr-pirarrpa* (from *pirarr(pa)*, glossed 'bright, light coloured, shiny, whitish') is defined in the *Dictionary* as "bright colour or light colour (white, yellow, orange, red, silver) as opposed to dark colours (black, blue, green, purple)", and in addition it is glossed as 'bright colour, yellow, orange, light colour, shiny'. In fact, it seems clear that the meaning of *pirarr-pirarrpa* does not refer to 'colour' at all: what unites the range including elements like 'yellow', 'orange', 'silver', 'light', and 'shiny' is not colour but high visibility (against a different background).

Another word, *junyuku*, is glossed as 'bright colours on body, dressed-up, brightly decorated, flash', and it is given the following folk definition: "*Junyuku* is what we call it like when they paint *yawulyu* designs on someone and put a white band on her head and a bunch of Major Mitchell cockatoo feathers. Or when somebody puts a very nice dress, "Hey! Look at that woman! That dress really makes her look flash.'"

Yet another word, *warntiril-pari*, is similarly glossed, with reference to 'bright colours', as 'coloured, brightly coloured, reddish in colour, ripe colour (of fruit), bright colour, colourful'. In fact, the folk definition offered in the entry of this word suggests that what this word means is not 'colour' but again, roughly speaking, 'high visibility (against a background)'. The English translation of this folk definition, which relies on 'colour', is, we think, misleading: "*warntirilypari* is something that is light coloured or multicoloured, like when people paint themselves across the nose or the forehead, either in white or red. That *is warntirilypari*. Or a multicoloured shirt is colourful or colours on a dress—white or red or green."

The fact is that the Warlpiri folk definition itself includes no words like 'coloured', 'multicoloured', or 'colourful'; it only includes words like *yalyuyalyu* (lit. 'blood-blood', i.e., roughly speaking, 'looking like *yalyu*—blood') and *yukuri-yukuri* (lit. 'grass-grass', i.e., roughly speaking, 'looking like *yukuri*—grass after rain'). The Warlpiri speaker is giving **examples** of what would be regarded as *warntirilypari*, and what unites these examples is, we would argue, not 'colour' but high visibility.

Things shining somewhere at some time

If the visual semantics of languages like English reflects a preoccupation with colour, that of Warlpiri suggests a preoccupation with things "shining" somewhere in the speaker's environment. (For the importance of "shining" in other Australian languages, see Jones and Meehan 1978). The *Warlpiri Dictionary* presents a large number of words referring to "shining", and the discourse of "shining" reflected in the accompanying folk comments is rich, distinctive, and culturally revealing. Some examples:

- The verb *jalarlany-ma-ni* is glossed as 'shine, be shiny', and it is illustrated with the following examples: 'There they are shining [*jalarlany*] over there'; 'After rain the rocks are shiny [*jalarlany*].'
- The noun *liirl(ki)* is glossed as 'light, white, clear, pale, bright, shining, shiny' and is defined specifically with reference to sunlight: 'of surface which reflects sunlight without absorbing any visible rays'. The verb *liirl-nyina-mi* is glossed as 'be white, shine, glow, glisten, sparkle' and is provided with the definition 'x reflect light'. The *Dictionary* notes that this verb evokes a particular prototype: a place which is normally a source of water but is currently dried up, for example: 'If a white rocky hill shines [*liirl-nyinakarla*] in the distance, then we call it *liirlpari*'; 'Water shines [*liirl-nyinami*]—in soakages, rockholes. Ghost gums (stand out) white [*liirl-nyinami*]'; 'Take a hill which sparkles [*liirl-nyinakarla*] from a long way off, then the hill is shiny [*liirlpari*], white.' As these examples illustrate, the stem *liirl* suggests (prototypically) not so much a permanent quality of an object as something that visually "stands out" in a particular place at a particular time.
- Another word glossed as 'shining from afar' is *pirltarr-ku*. The reduplicated verb *pirltarrku-pirltarrku-wapa-mi* is defined as 'x be bright and easily seen against surroundings' and glossed as 'be highly visible, be bright and stand out'. This is

illustrated with the following sentence: 'They can easily bone you walking around (in bright clothes) so that you can be easily seen in the distance'.

The entry for one further "word of shining", *ratarata*, does not refer to visibility in the distance, but it too refers to standing out against the surroundings: 'typically used of something white which stands out on a dark surface'. The examples support this: 'There's a lot of edible sap glistening right there'; 'we can see them [drops of water] glistening on the grass'; 'the white [...] flakes shine on the Red River Gums', and so on. (For further examples, see Wierzbicka 2008*a*.)

All this suggests that traditional Warlpiri culture encouraged paying attention to 'something shining somewhere', especially in the distance, and deriving therefrom information about what is happening in one's surroundings. In particular, it encouraged paying attention to possible sources of water, and in Central Australia rocks shining in the distance could suggest the presence of rockpools.

For a nomadic people living essentially in a natural world (and in a desert), such a focus of attention is clearly more relevant than that associated with discriminating between abstract "colours"—a mental habit which makes sense in a world full of manufactured objects, where many objects of one kind can differ from other objects of the same kind in colour alone. The elaboration of "shiningness" in the Warlpiri lexicon is a shining example of the principle of cultural elaboration in general—an important principle which some culture-blind linguistic writings have tried, and failed, to undermine (see e.g. Pinker 1994; Pullum 1991).

Visual patterns and contrasts within an object

When one reads English translations of Warlpiri sentences in the domains classified in the *Dictionary* as 'colour' and 'perception' one comes, again and again, up against the curious word 'variegated'. *Variegated* is not a colloquial English word, but in general, English dictionaries tend to link it with patches of different colours, especially in relation to leaves.

In Warlpiri sentences, on the other hand, the words translated into English as 'variegated' are not linked with 'colours', and apply above all to the bodies of animals. Clearly, they stand for concepts which are salient in the Warlpiri view of the world but have no equivalents in English. For example, the word *kuruwarri-kuruwarri* is glossed as 'variegated, striped, patterned'. This is illustrated with the following folk comments: 'The plains goanna is big and broad, and variegated'; 'We call the blue-tongued lizard variegated—the blue-tongued lizard is variegated. Pretty. Short and small'; 'The black-nosed snake is variegated. Pretty. Striped.' As the last two examples suggest, 'variegation', at least of the kind described with the word *kuruwarri-kuruwarri*, tends to be linked with aesthetic appreciation.

There are 24 folk sentences with the reduplicated form *kuruwarri-kuruwarri* scattered throughout the *Dictionary*, and in 18 of them it is translated as 'striped'.

The remaining six instances, however, make it clear that this word doesn't mean 'striped', as it is also applied to 'designs' on the wings of butterflies, or to 'markings' on the chest of a particular kind of bird. In such cases, expressions like 'mixed colours,' 'pretty coloured', or 'colourful designs' are used instead.

Another 'variegated'-type word is *piirrpiirrpa*, glossed as 'half white, brown and white, whitish, speckled with white', and illustrated with the sentences '[*Jalalapiny-pinypa*] is what we call one whose feathers are speckled with white' and 'The belly [of the Bush Turkey] is speckled with white'. The English phrase 'speckled with white' suggests a conceptual distinction between 'speckled' and 'white', but in Warlpiri the concept is clearly unitary. The noun *piirrpiirrpa* is related to the 'pre-verb' *piirr(pa)*, glossed as 'painting, daubing, smearing', and to the verb *piirr-pi-nyi*, glossed as 'paint with kaolin, cover with pipe-clay, whiten, smear with white'; and it seems clear that all these concepts are related.

Some insight into the Warlpiri ways of thinking reflected in such untranslatable Warlpiri words is provided by folk comments like the following one (in the English entry for the word *jalajirrpi*): 'The [*jalajirrpi*] is a white one. It doesn't have any other colours, is not flecked or speckled with colours. Its body is the same (colour) all over.'

The repeated mention of 'colours' in the English translation above has no direct basis in the original Warlpiri sentence. The phrase 'speckled with colours' translates here the Warlpiri word *jiirlpari-jiirlpari,* which is glossed in its own entry as 'dappled, flecked, mottled, spotted, spotty' and is defined as 'having small round marks'. There is no mention of 'colours' in the Warlpiri folk comments, and the interest of the Warlpiri speaker evidently lies in the presence of patterns or visual contrasts between different places on the bird's body, that is, in the question of whether or not all parts of the body look the same. Similarly, insects called *yuljulju* (praying mantis) are described as 'all green; their bodies and wings are green—all of them including their hind legs. They are green all the way down their legs.' Likewise, birds called *kalwaju* are described as follows: 'The heron, its legs are all white really all the way down.'

Folk comments referring to the presence or absence of patterns and contrasts in the visual appearance of some species occur repeatedly in the *Dictionary*, and point to an aspect of the visual world which is evidently of special interest to Warlpiri speakers.

The English translations of Warlpiri folk comments offer expressions like 'splotches of colour', 'blotches of colour', or 'multicoloured' to render concepts which in Warlpiri indicate striking visual contrasts (as in stripes, spots, and other patterns) rather than different colours. For example: 'The body is really like a leaf, but smaller. It's just spotted [*mawurlpari-mawurlpari*]—green and black spots on the yam grub. Like stripes and spots [*mawurlpari-mawurlpari*] as well'; 'The butterflies have small hairy bodies, which are multicoloured [*mawulpari-mawulpari*] and beautiful. Their bodies are yellow, white, black, with little blotches of colour, spots on them.' Elsewhere in the *Dictionary*, the same butterflies are described in one sentence as *mawulpari-mawulpari* and *jiirlpari-jiirlpari*, which is rendered in English as '[having] small coloured patches and little spots'. But a bird called *jarrawarnu* is also described as *mawurlpari-mawurlpari*—a folk comment translated into English as 'black and white like a magpie'.

Other words which focus on striking visual contrasts and patterns within one thing (usually, an animal body) are *warntukul-pari* and *wartirlkirri-wartirlkirri*, the first of which is defined as 'pattern of contrasting patches of black and white', and the second as 'striped, banded, cross-wise markings'.

Obviously, it is not possible to propose explications for all the "variegated"-type Warlpiri words within the confines of this chapter, but a few brief NSM-style observations on the meaning of some of these words are in order. Thus, *mawul-pari-mawulpari* ('spotted, flecked, dappled, variegated, splotchy') implies, it seems, that when people see something so described 'they can see many very small things in one place' and that 'these things don't all look the same'.

The word *jiirl-pari-jiirl-pari* (glossed as 'dappled, flecked, mottled, spotted, spotty' and derived from *jiirl-pari*, which is glossed as 'small and round') appears to mean that 'people can see many very small round things in a place' and that 'they all look the same'. The word *piirr-piirrpa* (glossed as 'half white, brown and white, whitish, speckled with white') and derived from *piirl(pa)* 'painting, daubing' appears to mean that these things look like (Aboriginal) people's bodies painted (smeared) in some places with kaolin (white clay). Another word, *wartirlkirri-wartirlkirri* (glossed as 'striped, banded, crosswise markings'), appears to imply that something so described 'looks as if something had moved many times from one side of this thing to another'.

To close this section, let us return to the word *kuruwarri-kuruwarri*, with which we started. Reading the gloss 'variegated, striped, patterned,' one would think that *kuruwarri-kuruwarri* is a purely visual descriptor focusing on some physical and geometrical feature of an object's appearance. Such an assumption, however, is contradicted by the meaning of the non-reduplicated form, glossed as 'mark, design, drawing, painting, pattern' and defined as follows: "visible pattern, mark or design associated with creative Dreamtime (*jukurrpa*) spiritual forces: the mark may be attributed to these forces, or it may symbolize and represent them and events associated with them."

In the light of this definition and other information given in the *Dictionary*, it seems clear that *kuruwarri* is a key cultural word in Warlpiri linked with ceremonial and religious life, and that the meaning of the reduplicated form *kuruwarri-kuru-warri* is not about 'stripes' and other forms of 'variegation' (patches, blotches, spots etc.), but rather about visual patterns which look like markings made somewhere by someone to convey some meaning (as in some of the senses of *kuruwarri* itself). This close semantic link between the reduplicated and non-reduplicated form is particularly clearly visible in sentences where the two forms occur together, with reference to the same visual pattern. For example: 'The Black Kite doesn't have any stripes [*kuruwarri-kuruwarri*] on its wings. Its body is all reddish-brown, even including its wings.' However, the Grey Falcon has 'striped [*kuruwarri*] feathers, especially its wing feathers'. In fact, the word *kuruwarri* itself is sometimes translated in the *Dictionary* as 'stripes', whereas elsewhere it is rendered as 'designs' or 'markings'.

We are suggesting, then, that to describe a kind of lizard or bird as *kuruwarri-kuruwarri* is a bit like saying that the patterns on the wings of some insects look like hieroglyphs—or indeed, some culturally important information "coded" in Aboriginal paintings. So here is a tentative explication:

[F]   This thing is *kuruwarri-kuruwarri*. [Warlpiri]

a.   when people see this they can think about it like this:
b.   "this is like kuruwarri [m]
c.   when people see kuruwarri [m] somewhere, they can see something like this"

This could be elaborated with the following component:

d.   people can see something like this in a place
        if someone did something to something in this place
            because this someone wanted people to know something about something

As noted by Morphy (2006: 304) (with special reference to the Yolngu people of Northern Australia):

the design on the back of a turtle is seen as its design in much the same way as the design painted on a human body is seen as belonging to and representing a clan. A myth, for example, explains the origin of the pattern on the turtle's shell, how it was put there, and why it takes the form it does. Myths explaining the form of natural designs are analogous to those relating to cultural designs; indeed, natural and cultural designs are frequently seen as two manifestations of the same thing.

Those 'cultural designs', intimately linked with Aboriginal mythology, are equally relevant to Aboriginal art (in particular, painting) as they are to the natural environment. In Yolngu, the key term *miy'tji*, which "can be roughly glossed as 'a painting' [...] can also be used to refer to any regularly occurring pattern or design, whether it is natural or cultural in origin. The pattern made by interlocking sections of a turtle's shell, the thin spirals engraved by insects on the bark of the scribbly gum, and the chequer-board pattern in black and white on the cone shell are all alike *miny'tji*" (2006: 304).

Morphy goes on to discuss the importance of patterns and designs in Aboriginal art and aesthetics, and to emphasize the key role of cross-hatched lines, geometrical patterns, "the shimmering effect of the cross-hatching, the appearance of movement, the sense of brightness" (2006: 316). Judging by the material collected in the *Warlpiri Dictionary*, the same preoccupation with contrasting and eye-catching patterns characterizes everyday discourse in other Australian languages.

Visual descriptors such as those discussed in this section reflect the same emphases—not on colours, but on contrasting patterns, lines, and circles, the appearance of movement, and the seemingly purposeful and meaningful creative action reflected and encoded in the appearance of things (on related features of Australian Aboriginal art in general and "desert art" in particular, see e.g. Isaacs 1999). English does not have a word for the concept behind *kuruwarri-kuruwarri*, yet nobody would claim that there is a "lexical gap" in English here and that the concept is really there even though there is no word for it. What applies to the absence of *kuruwarri-kuruwarri* from English applies also to the absence of 'colour' from Warlpiri. It is not a matter of lexical gaps, it is a matter of different ways of looking at the world.

Visual semantics and visual discourse: getting closer to "the native's point of view"

The differences between Warlpiri and English lexical semantics are linked with differences in the prevailing mode of discourse. Generally speaking, Warlpiri speakers appear to be far less interested in describing and identifying objects on the basis of their inherent visual characteristics than in noting some striking features of their surroundings (and possibly alerting others to them). For example, in the case of the culturally elaborated domain of "shiningness", the attention is usually directed not at whether or not some particular object is 'shiny' but at the fact that "something is shining somewhere in the environment, especially in the distance".

In the case of reduplicated visual descriptors like *yukuri-yukuri* ('grass-grass') or *yalyu-yalyu* ('blood-blood'), the speaker appears to be interested not so much in describing a particular object or distinguishing between some objects on the basis of their inherent visual characteristics as in drawing attention to something visually striking in his or her surroundings. Phrases like 'very white', 'bright white', 'really green', 'very red', 'very black', and 'bright green' are very common in the English translations of the Warlpiri folk comments, and they often render the Warlpiri suffix *nyayirni*, as in *kardirri-nyayirni* 'very white'. Such phrases suggest that the speaker notes something visually striking about the referent (especially against the background) rather than noting an "objective" and potentially distinguishing permanent characteristic.

Entries like that of the words *jaljalja* (noun) and *jaljalja-mani* (verb) are very characteristic in this respect. The noun is glossed as 'white and striking, white feather, white plumage', and the verb as 'stand out (of white feathers, typically as head ornament), be white and stand out'. Both words are also given the following definition: 'x (white plumage) be very visible in head-dress of yDAT (=human) in contrast with its location'. The accompanying folk comments are: '*jaljalja-mani* is when a feather is very white and when a person has very white feathers in his hair', and 'The (white) feathers are standing out very white on the person's head and forehead.'

The theme of "high visibility", of something that visually "stands out" in a place, is a recurring motif in the entries assigned by the *Dictionary* to the semantic domains designated as 'colour' and 'perception'. Both 'colour' and 'perception' are of course English concepts, concepts for which Warlpiri itself has no words. What the Warlpiri people whose voices are recorded in the *Dictionary* seem interested in is neither 'colour' nor 'perception' but 'seeing', in particular, what people can see in a particular place at a particular time. To reiterate our main point, Warlpiri visual descriptors like *yalyu-yalyu* or *walya-walya* are in fact not "colour terms", and the focus of attention in Warlpiri visual discourse is on noting what is happening in one's surroundings at a particular time, not on describing particular objects or particular places and assigning to them some permanent visual characteristics. Insofar as permanent visual characteristics *are* assigned to certain kinds of referents (usually, living things) they are likely to refer to visual patterns and "markings" rather than to something like colours.

This comes across in the volume of Warlpiri stories collected by Peggy Rockman Napaljarri and Lee Cataldi (1994), which includes five animal stories: 'The two kangaroos', 'The two snakes', two stories entitled 'The two dogs', and one entitled 'The spotted cat'. The English reader expecting to hear about the colour of the dogs or the kangaroos would be disappointed, but the "spottiness" of the "spotty cat" is prominently stressed (in the monomorphemic name of the living kind in question). As for the snakes, the readers only hear what **one** of them looked like: "it was a big snake, a rainbow serpent, a very large rainbow serpent." To an Anglo reader, the word 'rainbow' may suggest "multicolouredness", but what appears to matter to the Warlpiri storyteller is that the snake in question was visually very prominent. In any case, from a Warlpiri point of view a rainbow is not seen as 'multicoloured' but as having two contrasting parts: as the folk definition cited in Hale (1959) and translated by David Nash (p.c.) put it, "we call rainbow [*pararri*] that which stands high, *yukuri-yukuri* [lit. 'grass-grass', *AW*]; then across underneath it's *yalyu-yalyu* [lit. 'blood, blood', *AW*]". Thus, even in the case of the rainbow, the Warlpiri speakers are struck by the visual contrast, not by the "multicolouredness" which is so striking to the English speaker.

Two methodological conclusions arising from these considerations concern, on the one hand, the value of folk definitions and, on the other, the challenges facing those who want to translate them into other languages (e.g. English). As pointed out by none other than the pioneer explorer of the Warlpiri thought-world, Ken Hale (Hale and Casagrande 1967), folk definitions can give outsiders (e.g. Anglos) priceless insights into ways of thinking of a culturally distant people (e.g. the Warlpiri). The *Warlpiri Dictionary*, which contains a wealth of folk definitions, is an unsurpassed treasury in this respect. On the other hand, to be intelligible to outsiders, folk definitions need to be supplied with translations, and if these translations are not very carefully crafted, it is easy to introduce into them concepts and ways of thinking which are alien to the original. The frequent use of the word 'colour' (and its derivates like 'blue-coloured', 'multicoloured', or 'colourful') in the English translations of the Warlpiri folk definitions is a good case in point.

Translations of this kind are re-coding what the Warlpiri consultants are saying into the categories of the translators' own native language (in this case, English). If subsequently such translations—taken for genuine "folk definitions"—are regarded as a source of insight into the indigenous categories, the conceptual intrusions stemming from the translators' own habitual ways of thinking risk being accepted as evidence for "conceptual universals".

The difficulties inherent in translating folk definitions are of course real enough, and naturally, in many cases the translations cannot render the indigenous meanings accurately and have to be approximate. Generally speaking, however, the more such translations rely on simple and universal human concepts such as SEE, PLACE, HAPPEN, THE SAME, and LIKE, the less extraneous material they will risk introducing.

Thus, the metalanguage of universal semantic primes provides a bridge between the conceptual world of the indigenous consultants and that of the linguist or anthropologist. It offers a tool for improving the fidelity of (translated) folk definitions as well as for articulating the indigenous meanings in linguistic explications, and thus for getting closer to the "native's point of view".

4.5 Deconstructing the 'colour' concept

Colour, like shape, appears to be an aspect of human cognition so intimately bound up with perception that any attempt to understand it analytically may seem perverse. This applies to words like *blue, green, long*, or *round* as much as to the more general words *colour* and *shape* themselves: to most people, words of this kind are likely to seem basic and non-decomposable.

But hidden as the meanings of the words *colour* and *shape* are, these words too stand for concepts with a complex internal structure that can also be identified. The very fact that not all languages have words like *shape* and *colour* shows that these are culture-specific conceptual artefacts rather than innate elementary concepts. Wierzbicka (2006b; 2007d) has explored the concept of 'shape' in detail elsewhere. In the remainder of this chapter we want to explore the concept of 'colour'. The hypothesis is that the concept of 'colour' refers to a kind of knowledge: knowledge that is grounded in visual experience. Roughly speaking, colour is one of the things that we can know about an object when we see it—if we turn our mind to one aspect of what we see and abstract it from all the others.

If we want to describe what we see, we can do it globally, for example, by saying that it looks like a cat or an orange, or we can analyse what we see into separate "properties", such as size, shape, colour, shininess, patterns, or brightness. 'Colour' is one such property: it is objective in the sense that it is something we can KNOW about an object because of what we see, but it is also a matter of construal, because it depends on how we THINK about what we see.

This is not, however, the full story. In this section we will argue that the seemingly simple concept of 'colour' includes at least three aspects which distinguish it from the meanings of other physical descriptors: first, its inherent link with the concept of 'seeing', second, its link with daylight vision, and third, the expectation that this aspect of visual experience can be captured in a word of a particular kind (i.e. one of the "colour terms").

To begin with the first of these three aspects, we can recall here Leibniz's observation that the notion of 'colour' is definable ("resolubilis") because it implies something that can be perceived through seeing (1999[1685]: 1289). Undoubtedly, the concept of 'colour'—in contrast to concepts linked with other physical properties— relies exclusively on visual information. Tactile physical properties like 'softness' and 'smoothness' can be established by touch rather than by sight, and properties of shape can be established by either touch or sight (e.g. people can come to know that something is round either by seeing or touching it: cf. Wierzbicka 2007d; Goddard and Wierzbicka 2007a); but colour can only be determined by seeing—and this is not something that we know **about** colours, but is inherent in the very concept of 'colour'.

For a full definition of 'colour', however, we need more than just the observation about seeing as a source of knowledge, if only because, as noted by Leibniz, the same observation applies also to 'light'. Leibniz himself tried to deal with this problem by defining the word *coloratus* 'coloured' as "what can be perceived about a surface without touching it" (1999[1685]: 1286). But clearly this is not adequate: first, because surfaces are not the only things that can be coloured (think, for example, of the rainbow), and second, because we can perceive, for example, the shininess of a shiny apple without touching the apple, and yet shininess is not a colour.

This brings us to the second of the three aspects of 'colour' mentioned at the outset. To think about an object in such a way as to isolate its colour from its overall appearance, we need to think about the conditions under which we can obtain that one particular kind of knowledge about this object. Suppose, then, that we see this object in a very dim light, perhaps at night, without the benefit of an artificial light— could we then find out what colour it is? Presumably not—the dim light may be sufficient to allow us to discern the object's shape and size, and to see some lines, some patterns or some fluorescence on the object's surface, but not its colour.

So this is how, it seems, we can isolate colour from other categories in terms of which we can think about what we see: it is the kind of that thing people can find out about an object by looking at it in good light (prototypically, in daylight). The question 'what colour is it?' implies a certain way of thinking about the object in question. This way of thinking assumes that if people see this object in a good light they can acquire a particular kind of knowledge about it.

The third aspect of the 'colour' concept links the knowledge acquired through seeing with a particular word (rather than with a phrase or some longer description). When someone asks about a shirt or a balloon 'what colour is it?' they expect to hear in reply a word like *blue* or *red* chosen from a restricted set of words, so called "colour terms". The boundaries of this set may be a little fuzzy, but the main members are clear, and for English, they would coincide more or less with B&K's eleven. The fact that the word *colour*—in contrast to words like *size, texture,* or *temperature*—is very often used in the plural is no doubt related to that idea of a set of words. (Other words which form such sets are the names of days or weeks, months, and kin terms.)

[G]   What *colour* is this thing (X)?

a.   people can think like this about many things:
b.   "if someone sees this thing at some time when people can see things well,
c.   this someone can know something of one kind about it because of this"
d.   I want to know something of this kind about this thing (X)
e.   when someone knows something of this kind about something,
f.   this someone can say it with a word of one kind
g.   I want to know with what word people can say something of this kind about this thing (X)

In languages like Warlpiri (Hanunoo, Mursi, Bellona, etc.) the question 'what colour is this thing?' does not arise because the way of thinking implied by the word *colour* and specified in components (a), (b), and (c) above is not part of the culture and is not lexically encoded.

As the explication above indicates, there is something quasi-terminological about "true colour words" (those which incorporate in their meaning the semantic molecule 'colour' present in English and many other languages but by no means universal). This observation chimes in with the B&K intuition expressed in their phrases "basic colour terms" and "colour naming". It does seem to speakers of languages like English that words like *blue, red, green,* etc. form a certain set of words, and that they name something.

Some students of Australian languages are convinced that Australian languages have a "covert category" (either identical or comparable to the English 'colour'). We agree that Warlpiri has a covert category of place-related visual appearance, associated with the use of reduplication (one of the uses; for other uses of reduplication in Warlpiri, cf. Nash 1986), but as any unbiased consideration of the examples below must make clear, the meaning of that covert category cannot be equated with 'colour'. From a formal point of view, this category can be distinguished from other types of reduplication in that the root is a mass noun (designating a substance):

yalyu 'blood', *yalyu-yalyu* 'it looks like blood'
walya 'earth', *walya-walya* 'it looks like earth'
kunjuru 'smoke' [as in campfire smoke], *kunjuru-kunjuru* 'it looks like smoke'

karntawarra '[one kind of] ochre', *karntawarra-karntawarra* 'it looks like [this kind of] ochre'
yulyurdu 'smoke' [as in cigarette smoke], *yulyurdu-yulyurdu* 'it looks like smoke'
yukuri 'lush new growth', *yukuri-yukuri* 'it looks like lush new growth'

The glosses given above for the reduplicated forms are only approximations. More precisely, the meaning of the category in question (lexically covert but clearly marked morphologically) can be stated (both in English and in Warlpiri) along the following lines:

> when people see some things somewhere at some times, they can think like this:
>   "this is like something else (blood/earth/smoke/ochre/fresh grass, etc.)
>   people can see something like this when they see a place where there is this other thing"

To say that *yalyu-yalyu* 'blood-blood' and *karntawarra-karntawarra* 'ochre-ochre' are "basic colour terms" (and mean 'red' and 'yellow'), whereas *walya-walya* 'earth-earth' and *kunjuru-kunjuru* 'smoke-smoke' are "non-basic colour terms" (cf. Kay 2004), or to suggest that e.g. *kunjuru-kunjuru* means 'purplish' or 'grey-coloured' rather than, essentially, 'looking like smoke', is to fail to recognize an indigenous semantic category and to replace it with meanings and distinctions derived from English (and from the B&K theory). By contrast, the meaning assigned to this category in the explication above is not only easily expressible in Warlpiri itself but also is in line with Warlpiri folk comments explaining e.g. *kunjuru-kunjuru* 'smoke-smoke' as *kunjuru-piya* 'like smoke'.

The Warlpiri people do of course see 'colours' and can be very sensitive to differences which an English speaker would think of as differences in colour. Judging by linguistic evidence, however, what we may see as a 'colour' (e.g. brown or purplish) they may see as 'something that looks like something else' (e.g. earth or smoke).

In her piece "How do we know what they see?" Jane Simpson (2006) writes, with special reference to Warlpiri:

> Showing a large number of speakers a large number of Munsell colour chips and asking them how to describe them is a way of reducing the level of bias created by attempts to elicit or understand word meanings through gathering texts and translations of those texts. The stimulus is as close to independence from language as one can get.

Unfortunately, it is not as simple as that. In fact the Munsell colour chart is not a culture-independent "physical stimulus" but a semiotic object with the cultural-specific concept of 'colour' embedded in it. By its very structure it introduces the tacit assumption—alien to Warlpiri speakers—that "colour" is a conceptual domain separate from others, and the reliance on this culturally alien preconception blinds researchers to bona fide indigenous meanings, including the indigenous covert category articulated above. Furthermore, the behaviourist (or neo-behaviourist) reliance on 'stimuli' and 'response to stimuli' (describable in English but not in Warlpiri) precludes treating Warlpiri speakers as conversational partners, capable of understanding the meaning of their own words.

In principle, then, there is nothing wrong with the idea of "covert categories"—if there is language-internal evidence for them and if the hypothetical "covert category" can be plausibly explicated in the indigenous language itself. The idea that Warlpiri has a "covert category" which can be articulated in English but not in Warlpiri itself is evidently ethnocentric.

As noted earlier, the "kind of knowledge" linked with the abstract word *colour* is separated in English from other kinds of knowledge, such as those linked with the abstract word *shape*. "Shininess", "brightness", and the presence of visual patterns (spots, stripes, etc.) are not recognized in colloquial English as distinct, identifiable "kinds of knowledge", but 'shape' is, and so is 'colour', which is conceptually separated from all other aspects of visual appearance. A language like Warlpiri, on the other hand, does not classify (or "pigeon-hole") people's knowledge about the visual world in this way, and does not separate "colour appearance" from visual appearance in general.

For example, the English parts of the *Warlpiri Dictionary* are full of references to things described as 'bright white', where the expression 'bright white' often translates Warlpiri monomorphemic words such as *warntikirli*. Elsewhere in the *Dictionary*, the same words are translated as simply 'white', but it seems clear that the Warlpiri meanings do not fully separate "brightness" from "hue". They are global visual descriptors, like *gold* and *silver* in English, not colour words (Wierzbicka 1996).

The claim that in Warlpiri 'colour' is not separated from other aspects of visual appearance can also be supported with the observation that in Warlpiri so-called "colour-terms" like *yukuri-yukuri* 'it looks like new growth', colour cannot be separated from the contrast between "light" and "dark". For example, English expressions like *dark green* and *light green* have no counterparts in Warlpiri. (One cannot put together words like *yukuri-yukuri* and *maru* or *maru-maru* 'dark' and obtain a meaning equivalent to 'dark green'; Mary Laughren, p.c.)

The existence of expressions like *dark green* and *light green* in languages like English shows that in these languages 'colour' as such is conceptually separated from "light". In languages like Warlpiri, on the other hand, it is not. As the rich material included in the *Warlpiri Dictionary* documents, Warlpiri people can be very interested in what things and places look like. They do not, however, talk about 'colours'. Whether or not they have a concept of colour (a question which, ultimately, cannot be resolved, because one cannot prove the absence of something), they simply do not have "colour talk". Instead, they differentiate other aspects of visual appearance in ways that English speakers do not.

4.6 Concluding remarks

The methodology on which the Berlin and Kay approach relies—the use of the Munsell colour chart—is simpler and easier to apply than semantic analysis of the kind advocated here. As Dimmendaal (1995), Lucy (1997), and others have pointed out, the use of the Munsell chart provides a simple mechanical procedure which does not require any in-depth knowledge of the language (a fact which may have contributed to the popularity of the B&K paradigm). Yet the price to pay for this simplicity was high:

a whole level of analysis is missing from the basic color term tradition, namely, no attention whatsoever is paid to what the various terms actually mean in the sense of what they typically refer to, their characteristic referential range. Yet somehow a tradition that ignores these issues is supposed to provide a way of discovering semantic universals.   (Lucy 1997: 335)

The NSM approach to visual semantics takes a similar view: the most important question of all is what the various words used in different languages actually mean; not just in terms of referential range, but above all in terms of the speakers' conceptualizations. But to establish what words actually mean one needs a suitable metalanguage. Ordinary English cannot serve this purpose: to try to articulate indigenous meanings in ordinary "full-blown" English, drawing freely on those layers of English vocabulary which are culture-specific, means to fall into the same trap of Anglocentrism that the Berlin and Kay paradigm does.

This applies both to the articulation of indigenous meanings and to the identification of universals: it would be Anglocentric to try to articulate semantic universals using English words which lack equivalents in many other languages, for example, *colour* (Wierzbicka 2014). Semantic universals can only be established by observing real human speech, in many languages, and trying to identify the commonalities of linguistic usage. The most important ones among them are words with matching meanings—for example, SEE.

If we want to elucidate other people's ways of thinking without an Anglocentric bias we need to confine ourselves, in our representation of meanings, to that subset of English which matches the intersection of all other languages. By relying on this intersection we can reconcile two fundamental aspects of language and thought, often seen as irreconcilable: relativity and universality. The universal human concepts lexicalized in all languages form a basis for vast numbers of conceptual configurations, most of which are language-specific. At the same time, they provide a common measure for describing and comparing those configurations across languages and cultures. This applies to visual semantics as much as to any other conceptual domain.

5

Happiness and human values in cross-cultural and historical perspective

5.1 Capturing a complex idea in simple and universal words

In her book *Death Talk: The Case against Euthanasia and Physician-Assisted Suicide*, the founding director of the McGill Centre for Medicine, Ethics and Law at McGill University, Margaret Sommerville (2001: xiv), writes: "One challenge of 'globalization' is to find a language and vocabulary that will cross the boundaries of religion and of ethnic and national origin (the boundaries of culture) and capture the profound realities of the human spirit that can give meaning to our lives—and deaths."

In our view, this applies to "happiness" as much as to death, to what the ancient Greeks called "eudaimonia" as much as to what they called "euthanasia". As this chapter tries to show, ordinary English cannot provide us with a vocabulary that would enable us to cross the boundaries of religion and culture. This is why the English word *happiness* is not an adequate tool for exploring themes such as the human desire for a good life. To explore such themes from a global and trans-cultural perspective we need to problematize, and to deconstruct, English cultural concepts which are usually taken for granted, such as those encoded in the English words *happy* and *happiness* (see Wierzbicka 2004c; 2009a).

In his novel *The Slap*, the Australian writer of Greek descent, Christos Tsiolkas (2008), allows his hero, Hector, to experience a moment of happiness one morning:

He would rise, grab a pair of track-pants [...] and then perform a series of nine stretches, each of which he would hold to a count of thirty. [...] Then he'd go to the kitchen and switch on the coffee percolator before walking to the milk bar at the end of the street to buy the newspaper and a packet of cigarettes. Back home, he would pour himself a coffee, walk out on the back verandah, light a smoke, turn to the sports pages, and begin to read. In that moment, with the newspaper spread before him, the whiff of bitter coffee in his nostrils, the first hit of strong tobacco smoke, whatever the miseries, petty bullshits, stresses and anxieties of the day before or the day ahead, none of it mattered. In that moment, and if only in that moment, he was happy.

As this example illustrates, the adjective *happy*, used in a sentence like *He was happy*, implies above all that someone feels something good for some time. In addition to the 'good feeling', however, *happy* implies a certain frame of mind. This frame of mind can be described with reference to 'good things happening' to a person and things that this person can do (as they want). One can 'be *happy*' for a short time, as in the passage from Tsiolkas' novel, or for a long time, as in the sentence *Darwin had a long and happy life*, but the mental scenario implied is the same in both cases (in Darwin's case, 'he *often* thought like this for some time' and 'felt like this for some time').

The passage in Tsiolkas' novel offers a very good illustration of what the word *happy* means in contemporary English. At the same time, it offers a good illustration of an **idea**: the idea of 'happiness' that is passed on by speakers of English through the word *happy* and its derivatives. This mental scenario includes the following thoughts:

> many good things are happening to me now as I want
> I can do many things now as I want
> this is good

As the passage makes clear, Hector's life is not free of miseries, "bullshits", stresses, and anxieties, but at the moment he is not thinking about those. His attention is fully focused on the positives, on the good things that are happening to him and the things he can do just as he wants. There can be no doubt that the presence of such positive thoughts causes the hero to 'feel something good'.

Building on this, we can propose here an explication of the sentence *He was happy*.

[A]   *He was happy.*
a.   this someone thought like this for some time at that time:
b.   "many good things are happening to me now as I want
c.   I can do many things now as I want
d.   this is good"
e.   because of this, this someone felt something good at that time
f.   like people feel at many times when they think like this for some time

Later in the chapter we will return to this explication and discuss it in some detail. To begin with, however, some further background will be helpful.

5.2 Can happiness be a global concern?

In his book *Happiness: A History*, historian Darrin McMahon writes (2006: xiv):

Happiness has occupied a particularly prominent place in the Western intellectual tradition, exerting its influence on many aspects of Western culture and thought. As the late Harvard historian Howard Mumford Jones once pointed out [...], a history of happiness would be 'not merely a history of mankind, but also a history of ethical, philosophic, and religious thought'.[1]

McMahon points out (with reference to Wierzbicka's 2004c paper on the subject) that "the manner in which men and women understand happiness—how they propose, and whether they expect, to achieve it—varies dramatically across cultures and over time" (McMahon 2006: xiv). He also comments: "As the recent international success of the Dalai Lama's *The Art of Happiness: A Handbook for Living* makes clear, the search for happiness is now a global concern, one with roots, however shallow or deep, in many different cultural and religious traditions." But can one really say that "happiness" is a global concern, given that most languages of the world don't have a word corresponding in meaning to the English word *happiness*? McMahon (2006), who is quite exceptional in recognizing the depth of cross-cultural and cross-temporal differences in this area, is nonetheless inclined to agree with William James's Anglocentric and ahistorical perspective on the subject: "In the end, William James may well have been right. Perhaps happiness is, was, and ever shall be the ultimate human end in every time and place" (p. xiii).

How can it be valid to say that "happiness" is the ultimate human goal and ultimate human concern in every time and place if most languages of the world do not have a word (or a phrase) for it? To say, or to imply, that modern English just happens to have a word for the ultimate concern of all people around the globe, now and in the past, is profoundly Anglocentric. If we want to understand other people's concerns and values, we surely need to look at **their** words, and **their** concepts, rather than glibly assume that English happens to get it just right.

Here we would like to look more closely at what McMahon says about the Dalai Lama's book *The Art of Happiness*, which he describes as "incongruous" (p. 471)— though no more so "than a 1990 work by the evangelical Christian Billy Graham, *The Secret of Happiness*, or R. L. Kremnizer's *The Ladder Up: Secret Steps to Jewish Happiness*, or the many other titles that one could cite from centuries-old religious traditions now pressed into service at the altar of the truly modern god" (p. 472).[2]

The characterization of "happiness" as "the truly modern god" seems very apt, but is it true that the Dalai Lama is pressing the Buddhist religious tradition into service at the altar of this new god? Or is it rather the case that by translating one of the Dalai Lama's Tibetan key words into English as "happiness", the publishers of his book have been able to market it as one of the new books on how to be happy, for which there is now clearly a great demand in the Western world?

---

[1] Jones (1953: 63).
[2] In this passage, McMahon appears to be referring to Graham's (1990) movie/video, based on his 1985 book of the same title.

The question is, we believe, very important because it bears on the possibilities of a meaningful global discourse on values, ways of living, human rights, and choices facing individuals and nations in the 21st century and beyond.

5.3 Can the Dalai Lama reconcile Buddhism with "a pursuit of happiness"?

McMahon (2006: 471) writes:

Is there not something deeply ironic, we might ask, about the international publishing success of a book entitled *The Art of Happiness: A Handbook for Living*, written by a Buddhist? Its author, the Dalai Lama, is by all accounts a wise and kindly man. But the fundamental revelation of the Buddha, the first of his "Four Noble Truths", is that all life is suffering. Somehow this seems to have been forgotten.

As we see it, there is nothing in the content of the Dalai Lama's book which would not be consistent with the Buddha's "Four Noble Truths", including the Buddha's fundamental tenet that life is inseparable from suffering. What the Dalai Lama is talking about is not "happiness", but something closer to "spiritual welfare". The Tibetan expression is *bdewa*, which we will try to explicate very shortly.[3] If we gloss it, provisionally, as "spiritual welfare", we can say that the Dalai Lama is actually proposing this as an **alternative** to "happiness", and that he uses the English word *happiness* in a strategic way. The tacit message to his readers is this: you want to know how to achieve the ultimate goal of your life, and I can tell you—and in the process I will show you how your ultimate goal in life can be redefined, so that it is both achievable and worthwhile.

To compare the concept of 'happiness' encoded in present-day English (e.g. in phrases like *the secret of happiness*) with the Dalai Lama's idea rendered in English as *happiness*, we need a common measure. Universal human concepts such as 'want', 'feel', 'think', 'good', and 'bad' provide such a measure. Using these concepts as a common measure we can explicate the two concepts as in [B] and [C] below:

[B]   *Happiness* (as in 'money doesn't bring happiness')

a.   it can be like this:
b.   someone thinks like this for some time:
c.   "some good things are happening to me now as I want
d.   I can do many things now as I want
e.   this is good"

---

[3] For information on the Tibetan key word *bdewa*, and for helpful discussion of Tibetan Buddhism in general, we are indebted to William Foley.

f.   because of this, this someone feels something good at that time
g.   like people feel at many times when they think like this for some time
h.   it is good for this someone if it is like this

This is clearly not the Buddhist ideal, but equally clearly it is not what the Dalai Lama means in his book *The Art of Happiness*. The Dalai Lama's ideal does not depend on whether or not good things are happening to us, or whether we can do things as we want. As he says again and again, his ideal can be achieved "through training the mind" (p. 14), regardless of what happens to us, and regardless of what we can or cannot do.

Apart from the claim that his ideal can be achieved entirely through the training of the mind, the Dalai Lama hints at what he really means by using English words and expressions such as "calm", "inner peace", "contentment", "cultivating kindness and compassion", and "patience and tolerance".[4] All these are English-language concepts, not Tibetan ones, but they point to a conceptual configuration which can be articulated in simple concepts shared by English and Tibetan. It can be done as follows:

[C]   The Dalai Lama's ideal translated into English as *happiness*:

a.   it can be like this:
b.   someone doesn't often think like this:
c.   "I want many good things to happen to me
d.   I don't want bad things to happen to me"
e.   at the same time this someone often thinks like this:
f.   "very bad things happen to all people, very bad things happen to all living things
g.   all people often feel something very bad, all living things can feel something very bad
h.   I am like all other people, I am like all living things
i.   I want to think about all people like this: 'this someone is someone like me'
j.   I want to think like this about all living things
k.   I want to feel something good towards all other people
l.   I want to feel something good towards all living things"
m.   because this someone thinks like this, it is like this:
n.   this someone doesn't often feel something bad towards other people
o.   this someone doesn't often feel something bad towards any living things
p.   this someone often feels something good towards all other people
q.   this someone often feels something good towards all living things
r.   because it is like this, this someone can always feel something good
s.   it is good for this someone if it is like this

---

[4] See also Dalai Lama and Mehrotra (2008).

If we articulate the two concepts, the English 'happiness' and the Tibetan 'bdewa', in this way, we can see that they are very different from one another and that in fact they only share some framing components, and none of the actual content of the cognitive scenario. One key difference is that the English concept refers to external circumstances and to the experiencer's wants directed at external events and actions, whereas the Buddhist concept refers exclusively to what happens in the person's mind and heart. This is consistent with the Dalai Lama's insistence that "happiness" is entirely a question of training one's mind: it is not pursued in the outside world but in one's own thoughts.

The training of the mind described by the Dalai Lama consists largely of emptying one's mind of certain thoughts, and of the attachments, fears, anger, and the like arising from such thoughts. Furthermore, the positive thoughts underlying the Buddhist concept focus on what the Dalai Lama's translator renders as "compassion" and "kindness", linked with the idea (constantly emphasized by the Dalai Lama) that 'I am like all other people', indeed, like all living things, because all people, and all living things, suffer.

The feelings implied by the English *happiness* and the Tibetan/Buddhist *bdewa* are also different. The English word implies actual good feelings, whereas the Buddhist concept implies, first, the absence of hostile feelings towards anyone and anything, second, good feelings towards all people and all living things, and third, a constant potential for good feelings, independent of anything that happens to us.

Given that the two ideals—that of 'happiness' and that of 'bdewa'—are so different, it clearly makes little sense to talk about "the Dalai Lama's conception of happiness". Strictly speaking, he has *no* conception of 'happiness', just as Americans have no conception of 'bdewa'.

The Dalai Lama's book *The Art of Happiness* starts with the sentence: "I believe that the very purpose of our life is to seek happiness" (p. 13). The co-author of the book, the American psychiatrist Dr Howard C. Cutler, MD, comments: "With these words, spoken before a large audience in Arizona, the Dalai Lama cut to the heart of his message." It would be closer to the truth to say that with these words, the Dalai Lama enticed the Arizona audience into listening to him and into hearing the unspoken message "don't seek happiness, seek *bdewa*". This is not to suggest that the use of the word *happiness* was either a mistranslation or an act of conscious deception. Rather, it was probably a strategy—the same strategy which (as we will see shortly) Socrates used when he offered his interlocutors wisdom and virtue as a path to *eudaimonia* (a word usually translated into English as *happiness*). In effect, the Dalai Lama's main message was: "You want what is good for you. You call it *happiness* and I don't mind. But I will tell you what is really good for you, and how to find it." In addition, he is conveying a more specific message about 'good feelings', along the following lines: "You want to feel something good, most of the time. If you train your mind in the way I recommend, you can always feel something good."

To people who read the Dalai Lama's book in full, the substitution of *happiness* for *bdewa* may not be too misleading, and may help to make the connection between his ideal and theirs. But to those who merely leaf through the book there is a real danger of confusion and miscommunication.

Arguably, even the Dalai Lama's co-author, the psychiatrist Dr Cutler, is at times confused and misled by the constant use of the English word *happiness*. For example, he writes (p. 16):

The purpose of our existence is to seek happiness. It seems like common sense, and Western thinkers from Aristotle to William James have agreed with this idea.

It is certainly not the case, however, that Western thinkers from Aristotle to William James have agreed that the purpose of our existence is to seek happiness. Various Western thinkers have had very different ideas about the purpose of our existence, and the use of the English word *happiness* to label them all conceals those differences and creates an impression of unanimity where there is none.

Certainly Aristotle wasn't talking about *happiness* because he was talking about *eudaimonia*, and the two words, *happiness* and *eudaimonia*, don't mean the same any more than *happiness* and *bdewa* do. Moreover, even if the same word is used (perhaps for strategic reasons), the ideals referred to in this way can be very different. This will be illustrated with a discussion of Socrates in section 5.9. Before that, however, we want to talk about German thinkers such as Nietzsche and Freud.

5.4 "Civilization and its discontents": English *happiness* vs. German *Glück*

There is a striking difference in the attitudes to "happiness" between the philosophers of the English and the German language, which is clearly correlated with the semantic differences between the words *happiness* and *Glück* (the German dictionary equivalent of *happiness*), *happy* and *glücklich*. The main difference is that philosophers writing in German were much less likely to present *Glück* (or *Glückseligkeit*) as the aim of human life than the Anglophone ones, relying on the English word *happiness*. For example, according to Kant, "Das menschliche Leben, auch das geschichtliche, ist nicht auf *Glückseligkeit* als höchstes Ziel eingestellt, wenn auch von Natur aus jeder nach Glückseligkeit strebt" ("Human life, including life in history, is not oriented to happiness as the highest goal, even if by nature, everyone strives after happiness" (Eisler 1961: 211)).

Nietzsche famously declared, "Man does not strive after happiness, only the Englishman does that" ("Maxims and Arrows", quoted in Nussbaum 2004: 60). As Martha Nussbaum notes, he "expressed his scorn for Englishmen who pursued that goal rather than richer goals involving suffering for a noble end, continued striving, activities that put contentment at risk, and so forth" (p. 61).

Schopenhauer argued that "happiness" (*Glück*) was impossible: "Everything in life proclaims that earthly happiness is destined to be frustrated, or recognized as an illusion" ("Alles im Leben giebt kund, dass das irdische Glück bestimmt ist, vereitelt oder als eine Illusion erkannt zu werden" (Schopenhauer 1913[1844]: ii.736)).

Max Weber, in *The Protestant Ethic and the Spirit of Capitalism* and in other writings, also spoke with some scorn of what McMahon (2006: 353) paraphrases as "The Capitalist Ethic and the Spirit of Happiness": "Scoffing at 'optimistic dreams of happiness' and at politics based on its pursuit as 'flabby eudaimonism', he granted no place in his political economy for these mundane quests." McMahon (2006: 359) also quotes Weber's speech delivered in 1894 and included in his collected *Schriften und Reden* (Writings and Speeches, ed. Mommsen and Aldenhoff 1993[1894]: 339–340): "I believe that we must renounce human happiness [*Glücksgefühl*] as the goal of social legislation."

Finally, Freud founded psychoanalysis on the assumption that "the intention that man should be 'happy' [*glücklich*] is not included in the plan of 'Creation'", and that the most one can hope for is "the transformation of hysteric misery into common unhappiness (*gemeines Unglück*)".

What we call 'happiness' [*Glück*] in the strictest sense comes from the (preferably sudden) satisfactions of needs which have been dammed up to a high degree, and it is from its nature only possible as an episodic phenomenon. [...] We are so made that we can derive intense enjoyment only from a contrast and very little from a state of things. Thus our possibilities of happiness are already restricted by our constitution.   (Freud 1949: 27–28)

By contrast, modern philosophers and writers of the English language, from the early 18th century on, have often expressed the view that the aim of human life is to seek happiness. One celebrated statement of this idea comes from "the pillar of the English Enlightenment" (McMahon 2006: 363), the poet Alexander Pope:

> Oh, happiness! Our being's end and aim!
> Good, pleasure, ease, content! Whate'er thy name:
> That something still which prompts th' eternal sigh,
> For which we bear to live, or dare to die...

Even in Anglophone literature, however, the idea that happiness is "our being's end and aim" emerged relatively late and was the product of its particular time and place. McMahon (2006: 363) quotes, in this connection, Thomas Carlyle's claim that "'Happiness our being's end and aim' is at bottom, if we will count well, not yet two centuries old in the world", commenting that "Carlyle's chronology was nearly flawless" (he wrote in the 1840s) and that "with regard to the dramatic transformation that this new idea was working in the world, the irascible Scot was equally astute".

As Carlyle observed in the ironically titled chapter "Happy" of his book *Past and Present*, "Every pitifulest whipster that walks within a skin has had his head filled with the notion that he is, shall be, or by all human and divine laws ought to be, 'happy'" (McMahon 2006: 363). This was a new idea of 'happiness', which emerged, as McMahon notes, in 18th-century England and quickly spread in English discourse.

Simplifying the main story we can say that until the 18th century, *happiness* and *Glück* both referred to 'very good feelings' which cannot endure, and which most people experience rarely or not at all. From the early 18th century on, however, *happiness* started to refer to 'good' rather than 'very good' feelings, with the concomitant expectation that these 'good feelings' could be achieved by many people and could be experienced often and for long periods.

The whole idea of "the greatest happiness of the greatest number", launched in 1728 by Francis Hutcheson and popularized later by Jeremy Bentham to the point of becoming recognized as "a prominent idea in English politics", was based on the assumption that what people want and need is not some peak experiences, which can be achieved rarely and only by a few, but 'good' experiences, which can be achieved (at least to a degree) by a great number of people, and which can become the goal of social and political endeavours. As a result of the success of this idea, the very meaning of the word *happiness* changed. Roughly speaking, it changed from 'rare very good feelings' to 'widely accessible good feelings'. The fact that the word *happiness*, which was previously ungradeable (like *bliss*), came to be thought of as gradeable and as standing for something measurable (calculable) reflected a significant change in the word's meaning.

The meaning of the German word *Glück* (and of its counterparts in most other European languages) did not undergo a similar change in meaning. Consequently, when Kant, Schopenhauer, Nietzsche, Weber, or Freud wrote about *Glück*, they were not writing about the same thing as Bentham, John Stuart Mill, Darwin, or William James. Arguably, when Nietzsche attacked the "English" idea of *happiness* as something that only "the Englishman" strives for, he was reacting not only to an idea widespread in the English-speaking world but also to the divergent meanings of the words *happiness* and *Glück*.

This point does not seem to have attracted any attention in philosophical discussions of "happiness", largely no doubt because in English translations *Glück* is usually rendered as *happiness*, and vice versa, and also because ideas expressed by individual writers (and their followers) are seldom distinguished in philosophical literature from ideas which have become so widespread in a given society as to become entrenched in the meaning of key words.

Thus, Martha Nussbaum (2004), in her article on happiness, Bentham, and Mill, chides Nietzsche for generalizing from Bentham's view of "happiness" to the "English happiness" in general; and she points in particular to the poet William Wordsworth as someone who in his poetry showed an understanding of "happiness" quite different from Bentham's. This, however, misses the point that the understanding championed by Bentham became subsequently so widespread in the English-speaking world that it came to be entrenched in the new meaning of the word *happiness* itself. Nothing like that happened in the German-speaking world, where the words *Glück* and *glücklich* continued to be used, essentially, in the same sense, from Martin Luther to Sigmund Freud and beyond.

In 18th-century France, too, the Jacobins promoted a program of universal *bonheur* ("happiness"), akin to Bentham's. But in France the idea failed to spread widely in the society at large, and did not effect a change in the meaning of *bonheur* analogous to that which occurred in the meaning of *happiness*. Consequently, in France, too, objections were raised to the English idea of "happiness", which from the perspective of French speakers may also have seemed too close to pleasure and comfort. *Bonheur* ('happiness') is not the same thing as *plaisir* ('pleasure'), declared Rousseau ('On Public Happiness', section 3 in Rousseau 1994: iv.40) with perhaps a hint of scorn for the new English *happiness*[5]—a scorn echoed and amplified a century later by Nietzsche.

Of course modern English, too, distinguishes the word *happiness* from words like *pleasure*, *contentment*, and *comfort*. Nevertheless, *happiness* is closer semantically to these other words than *Glück* and *bonheur* are to their closest German and French counterparts. *Happiness*—like *pleasure*, *comfort*, and *contentment*—implies feeling something 'good' rather than something 'very good', and does not imply something rare, unusual, and ephemeral.

The adjective *happy* has gone even further in the direction of "devaluation" than the noun *happiness*, by developing new valency options such as *happy with*. A sentence like *I'm happy with the arrangements* does not imply any "happiness" whatsoever (let alone *Glück* or *bonheur*). It emphasizes the absence of 'bad feelings' and dissatisfaction more than the presence of any particular 'good feelings'.

Glück has still preserved its semantic link with 'luck' and 'good fortune', which has totally evaporated from the English *happiness*. *Glück haben* ('to have *Glück*') still means in German something like 'to be lucky', and *zu meinem Glück*, something like 'luckily for me'. But even when *Glück* is used in the sense closer to modern English *happiness*, it still doesn't mean the same as *happiness*, as is quite clear from Freud's discussion of *Glück* in his key work *Civilization and its Discontents*. Setting aside as unanswerable the question "What is the purpose of human life?", Freud turns to "the less ambitious problem, what the behaviour of men themselves reveals as the purpose and object of their lives, what they demand of life and wish to attain in it", and declares, "the answer to this can hardly be in doubt: they seek happiness [*Glück*], they want to become happy [*glücklich*] and to remain so" (Freud 1949: 76).

The translator has rendered the German words *Glück* and *glücklich* here as "happiness" and "happy", but Freud's own comments make clear that he meant

---

[5] On Rousseau and happiness, see Salkever (1978) and Grimsley (1972).

something else: "There are two sides to this striving, a positive and a negative; it aims on the one hand at eliminating pain and discomfort, on the other at the experience of intense pleasures. In its narrower sense the word 'happiness' [*Glück*] relates only to the last" (p. 27). If *Glück*, as discussed by Freud, implies the elimination of pain and discomfort and the experience of intense pleasure, then it is hardly surprising that Freud does not see "the pursuit of *Glück*" as a realistic project for humanity, or any part of it: "The goal towards which the pleasure-principle impels us—of becoming happy [*glücklich*]—is not attainable; yet we may not—nay, cannot—give up the effort to come nearer to realization of it by some means or other" (p. 39).

As noted by the American co-author of the Dalai Lama's *The Art of Happiness*, the psychiatrist Cutler, Freud's views on "happiness" left little room for what is now called "positive psychology", and Freud's huge influence on modern psychiatry and psychology in general led to a focus on disorders, depression, anxiety, and neuroses.

From that standpoint, the [Dalai Lama's] claim that there was a clearly defined path to happiness seemed like quite a radical idea. As I looked back over my years of psychiatric training, I could rarely recall having heard the word "happiness" even mentioned as a therapeutic objective. Of course, there was plenty of talk about relieving the patient's symptoms of depression or anxiety, of resolving internal conflicts or relationship problems, but never with the expressly stated goal of becoming happy.   (Dalai Lama and Cutler 2002: 14)

Similarly, the psychologists David Myers and Ed Diener (1995) start their frequently cited article "Who is happy?" with the observation: "Books, books and more books have analysed human misery. During its first century, psychology focused far more on negative emotions, such as depression and anxiety, than on positive emotions, such as happiness and satisfaction" (p. 10). They note with approval that this is now changing quite dramatically. In another article, Biswas-Diener, Diener, and Tamir (2004: 18) declare that "in the last few decades there has been something of a revolution in the scientific study of happiness".

No doubt the revolt of Anglophone psychiatrists and psychologists against Freud and the radical turn from investigating "abnormal bad feelings" to studying "normal good feelings" had many causes. One component, however, may well have been linguistic: the everyday concept of 'being happy', on which English-speaking psychologists relied in their everyday lives, simply didn't fit Freud's teachings as read in English translations. In the second half of the 20th century the English word *happy* did not refer to "intense pleasures" or to the elimination of all pain and discomfort. Since most psychologists in English-speaking countries were reading Freud in translation, i.e. through the prism of the English language, sooner or later a revolt was perhaps inevitable.

We are not suggesting, needless to say, that the lexical differences between German and English were the cause of different philosophical orientations. It makes more sense to assume that these differences arose for cultural and historical reasons. But once these differences in prevailing philosophical orientations found their reflection in the meaning of cultural key words such as *happy* and *happiness* in English and *Glück* and *glücklich* in German, the clash between the prevailing new orientation of Anglo culture, imprinted on colloquial English, and the older orientation reflected in Freud's writings became particularly jarring. This may well have contributed to the success of "positive psychology" in the English-speaking world, with journals such as *The Journal of Positive Psychology* and *The Journal of Happiness Studies* attracting more and more attention.

5.5 The semantic history of "happiness" Part I ("happiness" in England)

The story of "happiness" in English begins with good fortune. In the case of the adjective *happy*, this meaning is often associated with an impersonal construction, as in the following examples from the *OED* (modernized spelling):

It was happy for them that the weather was so fair.   (1533)
It proved very happy for me.   (1734)

The *OED* defines the meaning as "having good 'hap' or fortune; lucky, fortunate; favoured by lot, position, or other external circumstances". Essentially the same meaning is also clearly present in some *OED* examples with a personal subject, as in the following sentence from Defoe's *Robinson Crusoe*:

I was so happy as not to be thereabouts at that time.   (1719)

The noun *happiness* could also be used in this (or a very similar) sense, defined by the *OED* as "good fortune or luck in life or in a particular affair; success, prosperity". Two examples:

This also [...] was a part of her happiness that she was never overlaid with two great worries at once.   (1614)

It is a very great happiness, and particular Providence of God, that the sea and rivers here seem [...] to contest   (1705)

We can represent this older meaning of *happiness* (*happiness$_1$*) as follows:

[D]   *happiness$_1$*

a.   it can be like this:
b.   some very good things happen to someone
c.   not because this someone does something
d.   things like this don't often happen to people
e.   this someone can feel something very good because of this

Over the same period, roughly the 16th–18th centuries, the words *happy* and *happiness* were also used to refer to a person's state of mind, as in the following examples, the first from the *OED* and the second from Stevenson's (1957) *Book of Quotations*:

Full as an egg was I with glee,
And happy as a king.   (1732)

There is an hour wherein a man might be happy all his life, could he find it.

(George Herbert, 1593–1633)

As both these quotes illustrate, 'being *happy*' in that sense was something rare and unusual: perhaps only one hour in one's whole life, perhaps something that only kings rather than ordinary folk could expect to experience for an extended period. The *OED* defines this meaning as "having a feeling of great pleasure or content of mind, arising from satisfaction with one's circumstances or condition". For the corresponding meaning of the noun *happiness* it offers this: "the state of pleasurable content of mind, which results from success or the attainment of what is considered good". The *OED*'s examples include the following:

Like beast [that] hath no hope of happiness or bliss.   (1591)
Let it suffice thee that thou know'st Us happy, and without Love no happiness.   (Milton, 1667)

We can explicate this second meaning of *happiness* (*happiness$_2$*) as follows:

[E]   *happiness$_2$*
a.   it can be like this:
b.   someone thinks like this for some time:
c.   "something very good is happening to me now
d.   this is very good
e.   things like this don't often happen to people
f.   I can't want anything more now"
g.   because of this, this someone feels something very good for some time
h.   like people feel at many times when they think like this
i.   it is good for this someone if it is like this

The *OED* does not clearly distinguish the meaning of *happy*, which it defines as "having a feeling of great pleasure", from what it calls "a weakened sense: glad, pleased", and it puts the two in the same category. In fact, however, the shift from *happy* as a rare and intense state to *happy* as a common and moderate one was a phenomenon of great cultural and historical significance.

What the *OED* calls the "weakened sense" of *happy* was in fact a linguistic embodiment of the 18th-century idea that what mattered in life most was not some elusive and perhaps unattainable bliss but rather attainable pleasures and comforts. Alexander Pope's paean to "happiness" in his *Essay on Man*, which was quoted earlier, testifies to this lowering of the horizons. On the one hand, Pope's poem seems to suggest that "happiness" is a high ideal which makes life bearable and which is worth dying for. On the other, however, this seemingly high ideal is virtually equated with (one might say) more pedestrian and prosaic ones such as pleasure, ease, and contentment.

The discourse of "happiness", which spread like wildfire in 18th-century England, became clearly linked with the notion of maximizing pleasure in relation to pain. The new quantitative language of "happiness" became epitomized in Bentham's tenet that "it is the greatest happiness of the greatest number that is the measure of right and wrong" (quoted in McMahon 2006: 212).

When "happiness" came to be seen as quantifiable, as a matter of more or less, the concept underwent a profound transformation. We have already commented on one aspect of this transformation: the conceptual shift from 'feeling something very good' to 'feeling something good'. A closer semantic analysis of the changing use of *happy* and *happiness* suggests that the shift from 'very good' to 'good' was accompanied by other conceptual changes as well. As "happiness" (or at least a certain amount of it) came to be seen as widely accessible, (indeed, as "the natural human condition": McMahon 2006: 218), there was no longer room for the component 'things like this don't often happen to people'. At the same time, the notion of "being filled to the brim" (or as full as an egg) also lost its justification: "happiness" was no longer conceived of in the extreme sense of 'I can't want anything more now' (comparable to *bliss*), but rather, in terms closer to *contentment*: 'I don't want anything more now.'

Furthermore, as the new quantitative language of "happiness" brought it closer to *pleasure* (and further away from *bliss*), it introduced an implicit connection between "happiness" and the absence of pain. The common 18th-century talk of a calculus of pleasure and pain (the "felicific calculus": McMahon 2006: 204) brought the absence of pain (and other bad feelings) into the conceptual orbit of "happiness". As a result, "happiness" came to be seen in terms of what is absent (roughly speaking, pain) as well as what is present (roughly speaking, pleasure). Taking all these interrelated developments into account, we can present the new meaning of *happy* and *happiness* which established itself in 18th-century English, as follows:

[F]   *happiness*$_3$

a.   it can be like this:
b.   someone thinks like this for some time:
c.   "something good is happening to me now
d.   this is good
e.   I don't want anything more now"
f.   because of this, this someone feels something good at that time
g.   like people feel at many times when they think like this
h.   it is good for this someone if it is like this

In his life of Johnson, Boswell (1766) wrote: "Happiness consists in the multiplicity of agreeable consciousness" (Stevenson 1958: 854). This is a very 18th-century definition. The word *agreeable* suggests 'good' rather than 'very good' feelings, and the word *multiplicity* implies both a quantitative perspective and a confident expectation that such "agreeable consciousness" can often be attained. In the background, there is an implied contrast between *agreeable* and *disagreeable* and an implied question concerning the balance between the two.

Evidently, it was this "weakened" sense of *happiness* which made the English concept significantly different from those embedded in words like *bonheur* and *Glück* and which attracted the attention of critics like Nietzsche. It was also this "weakened" sense of *happiness* which became transported from England to America—giving rise to further conceptual and semantic developments to which we will turn shortly. First, however, it will be in order to consider briefly the link between the present-day comparative studies of "happiness" across various human groups and societies and the philosophical and semantic developments in 18th-century England.

5.6 The semantic history of "happiness" Part II ("happiness" in America)

It is widely agreed that Thomas Jefferson's phrase "the pursuit of happiness", which next to "liberty" can be seen as the cornerstone of the American Declaration of Independence, had an extraordinary impact on the history and ethos of America. The large volume of literature on what exactly Jefferson meant by this phrase bears testimony to its perceived importance in the history of America and, indirectly, of all English-speaking societies.

> We hold these truths to be self-evident; that all men are created equal; that they are endowed by their creator with inalienable rights; that among these are life, liberty, and the pursuit of happiness.

As McMahon (2006: 314) points out, for Americans, the stakes in the debates about the meaning of Jefferson's phrase are high, "for they place on the table nothing less than the country's self-image, a central tenet of its 'civil religion'. And to others, the matter is hardly less important, for in a direct way, it speaks to what has gradually become a global concern: the place of happiness in the American way of life."

Jefferson himself called the Declaration of Independence an "expression of the American mind" (McMahon 2006: 316), and the celebrated phrase "the pursuit of happiness" came to stand for one of the central defining aspects of that collective mind. Arguably, it was also a phrase which, through frequent repetition in many dominant areas of public life, shaped a new meaning of the word *happiness* itself. The core of this transformation lay in a new emphasis on being able to **do** many things as one wants, in addition to having good things **happen** to us, as we want.

A careful reading of the American foundational documents and other political literature of the time suggests a clear shift from a focus on, roughly speaking, pleasures, to one on "doing things as one wants—and enjoying it". One new phrase which clearly played an important role in the thinking of Jefferson and other founding figures was *public happiness*, which referred, in particular, to free participation in public life.

In a paper for the Virginia Convention of 1774, which, as Hannah Arendt (1973: 127) points out, in many respects anticipated the Declaration of Independence, Jefferson declared that "our ancestors" when they left the "British dominions in Europe" exercised "a right which nature has given all men, [...] of establishing new societies, under such laws and regulations as to them shall seem most likely to promote public happiness" (quoted by Arendt, p. 127). As Arendt also points out, this new ideal of 'public happiness' "consisted in the citizen's right of access to the public realm, in which his share in public power—to be 'a participator in the government of affairs', Jefferson's telling phrase—is distinct from the generally recognized right of subjects to be protected by the government in the pursuit of private happiness".

It is true that the Declaration of Independence speaks of "pursuit of happiness", not of "public happiness", and that "the chances are that Jefferson himself was not very sure in his own mind which kind of happiness he meant when he made its pursuit one of the inalienable rights of man" (Arendt 1973: 127). Nonetheless, as Arendt also observes, one thing is clear: for Jefferson, 'happiness' was very much a matter of doing things, and doing things as one wants, rather than merely having good things happen to us. As she further points out, Jefferson's vision of the afterlife, expressed playfully in a letter to John Adams, is a striking illustration of the fact that he understood "happiness" in terms of activity and, prototypically, activity in a public arena: "May we meet there again, in Congress, with our ancient Colleagues, and receive with them the seal of approbation 'Well done, good and faithful servants'." Arendt comments on this passage as follows (p. 131):

Here, behind the irony, we have the candid admission that life in Congress, the joys of discourse, of legislation, of transacting business, of persuading and being persuaded, were to Jefferson no less conclusively a foretaste of eternal bliss to come than the delights of contemplation had been for medieval piety. [...]

In order to understand how truly extraordinary it was, within the context of our tradition, to see in public, political happiness an image of eternal bliss, it may well be that for Thomas Aquinas, for example, the perfect beatitude consisted entirely in a vision, the vision of God, and that for this vision the presence of no friends was required.

Jefferson's vision of the afterlife is an excellent illustration of how the American dream, from the start, included the idea of purposeful activity: "happiness" was not expected to be handed down to people on a platter but was to be the product of human effort and human actions.

Barack Obama, in his book *The Audacity of Hope* (2008: 85), states that "a careful reading of our founding documents reminds us just how much all of our attitudes have been shaped by them". There can be little doubt that this observation applies also to the phrase "the pursuit of happiness" and to the understanding of *happiness* which was influenced by it. Arendt (p. 128) remarks that "none of the delegation [to the Assembly] would have suspected the astonishing career of this 'pursuit of happiness' which was to contribute more than anything else to a specifically American ideology", quoting in this context the historian Howard Mumford Jones (1953: 16), who called the Jeffersonian right to the pursuit of happiness "the ghastly privilege of pursuing a phantom and embracing a delusion".

But whether the astonishing career of the phrase was beneficial or detrimental in its effects on the "American mind", it seems clear that the thinking crystallized in this phrase did lead to a new concept of 'happiness' and a new meaning of this key word (*happiness₄*)—first, apparently, in American English and then in Anglo-English in general.

[G]   *happiness₄*

a.   it can be like this:
b.   someone thinks like this:
c.   "some good things are happening to me now as I want
d.   I can do many things now as I want
e.   this is good"
f.   because of this, this someone feels something good
g.   like people feel at many times when they think like this
h.   it is good for this someone if it is like this

According to this explication, the Jeffersonian concept of *happiness₄* differs from the Benthamian concept of *happiness₃* in two main respects: first, it carries with it an "active" component 'I can do many things now as I want', and second, it does not include the component of, roughly speaking, "contentment" ('I don't want anything more now'). The more active character of *happiness₄* is suggested, to some extent, by the phrase *the pursuit of happiness* itself. While this phrase originated in early 18th-century England and can be found, for example, in Locke's *Essay*, it is only in America that it became a catchword.

It is interesting to note in this connection Martha Nussbaum's (2004) comparison of two influential conceptions of "happiness" which emerged in the English-speaking world, one from the 18th and the other from the 19th century. In the first, Jeremy

Bentham virtually identified "happiness" with pleasure (and the avoidance of pain)—i.e. essentially, with "good feelings" caused by good things happening to us—and did not pay any particular attention to **actions** as a potential source of "happiness". As Nussbaum (p. 63) puts it, "activity [...] plays no special role in Bentham's system". By contrast, in the second one, John Stuart Mill links "happiness" very much with doing as well as happening. As Nussbaum notes (p. 65), the famous passage of Mill's *Utilitarianism* "shows Mill thinking of pleasures as very like activities, or [...] as experiences so closely linked to activities that they cannot be pursued apart from them".

Nussbaum discusses these two different views of "happiness" as differences between two individual philosophers, Bentham and Mill. It is important to note, however, that these differences are correlated with changes in the meaning of the word *happiness* itself. While the more "active" meaning of *happiness* appears to have first crystallized in America, (perhaps under the influence of Jeffersonian discourse), it clearly spread with time to the entire "Anglosphere", and is reflected also in the writings of Mill.

Moving now to the other two differences between *happiness$_3$* (epitomized by Bentham and Benthamian English discourse) and *happiness$_4$* (epitomized by Jefferson's phrase "the pursuit of happiness" and consistent with Mill's conception), it will be noted that in America, "happiness" was no longer thought of as something that one may seek and hope to find, but rather as something that one can freely, and relentlessly, pursue. The component 'I don't want anything more now' has not been included in the cognitive scenario of *happiness$_4$*, partly because it does not seem fully consistent with the idea of relentless pursuit. Furthermore, the new component 'I can do many things now as I want' invites an expectation of further wants, which can also be freely pursued: I can do many things now and I *will* do many things now because I do want more good things to happen.

Some further justification for the semantic innovations attributed here to *happiness$_4$* comes from the meaning of *happiness$_5$*, to which we will now turn.

5.7 "Happiness" as an emotion

In his *The Descent of Man* (1871) Darwin wrote: "The lower animals, like man, manifestly feel pleasure and pain, happiness and misery. Happiness is never better exhibited than by young animals, such as puppies, kittens, lambs, etc, when playing together, like our children" (1989[1871]: 21.73). When one compares this quote with the 16th-century one adduced earlier, "Like beast [that] hath no hope of happiness or bliss" (1591), one can appreciate the long and winding path from *happiness$_2$*, understood as a rare and quintessentially human experience inaccessible to beasts, to Darwin's *happiness* (*happiness$_5$*), which is best manifested in young animals.

McMahon (2006: 410) quotes Darwin's remark scrawled in his notebook in 1838: "He who understands [a] baboon [will] do more towards metaphysics than Locke", and comments that "the field of happiness would be profoundly altered by the force of his speculation". It is difficult to establish if or to what extent Darwin's writings may have contributed to the emergence of yet another meaning of the word *happiness* (*happiness₅*), but it is clear that "happiness" conceived as an emotion which can be manifested in both animals and humans is not the same "happiness" the pursuit of which was declared a century before to be an inalienable human right. "The pursuit of happiness" was not meant to be the pursuit of an emotion.

In the 20th century, however, the adjective *happy* came to be widely used in English as a perceived opposite of the word *sad* (rather than of *unhappy*), and *happiness* came to be treated in many contexts as an emotion term, on a par with words like *sadness, anger, fear,* and *surprise*. In particular, facial expressions with upturned and downturned corners of the mouth came to be seen as "a happy face" and "a sad face", respectively.

This is consistent with Darwin's idea that "happiness", like fear and rage, can be manifested in the behaviour of animals, and that even lower animals "are excited by the same emotions as ourselves" (*Descent of Man*, 21.73). But clearly, by attributing "happiness" to playful kittens, speakers of English are not ascribing to them any particular thoughts (e.g. 'good things are happening to me now as I want' or 'I can do many things now'). Rather, they are attributing certain feelings to them. These feelings, too, can be described with reference to a certain prototypical cognitive scenario, but only indirectly, by comparison with certain situations involving people rather than animals. This leads us to the following explication:

[H]   *happiness₅*
       (e.g. the 'happiness' shown in someone's face, or in the behaviour of some kittens)

a.   it can be like this:
b.   someone feels something good for some time,
c.   like people feel at many times when they think like this:
d.   "something good is happening to me now, as I want
e.   I can do something now as I want
f.   this is good"

There is no reference in this explication to any actual thoughts, but only to feelings **like** those of someone who has certain thoughts; and there is no evaluative component (i.e. no component 'it is good for this someone if it is like this').

In her essay "Happiness as achievement", Julia Annas writes:

When it is asked what happiness is, a first answer may well be that it is some kind of feeling. Being happy is easily taken to be feeling happy—as when I wake up in the morning—a kind of smiley-face feeling. [. . .] The point that these are the contexts which first occur to many people when they are asked about happiness indicates that our notion of happiness has indeed been affected by the notion of smiley faces, feeling good, and pleasant episodes.   (Annas 2004: 45)

Indeed, we can clarify different ways of looking at human life, its purpose, and its dilemmas by getting away from the complex, polysemous, and untranslatable English word *happiness* and by relying instead on simple and universal human concepts, such as 'good' and 'bad', 'do' and 'happen', 'want', 'think', and 'feel'. We will illustrate this last point, in relation to Socrates, in the concluding section of the chapter.[6]

5.8 "Happiness" and good fortune: English vs. French and Russian

If one compares the present-day English discourse of "happiness" with, for example, the discourse of *bonheur* in French or of *sčast'e* in Russian, one is struck by the absence of certain speech-and-thought practices and resources in English which are very much present in other European languages.

To begin with, in French and in Russian, people can exclaim *Quel bonheur!* or *Kakoe sčast'e!*, meaning a combination of subjective emotion and objective good fortune. In English, however, one cannot exclaim *What happiness!* to convey the same combination of ideas. This absence of a link between subjective "felicity" and objective "good fortune" in the scope of modern English *happiness* is highlighted in the absence from modern English of words like *malheur* in French (an opposite of *bonheur*) and *nesčast'e* in Russian (an opposite of *sčast'e*). In French one can exclaim not only *Quel bonheur!*, but also *Quel malheur!*, and in Russian, not only *Kakoe sčast'e!*, but also *Kakoe nesčast'e!* In English, however, one could only exclaim *What a misfortune!*, thus dissociating the bad thing that happens to us from its subjective result (and at the same time downgrading the event from "calamitous" to merely "bad").

The close link between a subjective emotion (a 'very good' or 'very bad' feeling) and what happens to a person (something 'very good' or something 'very bad') can be illustrated with a sentence from Tolstoy's novel *Resurrection*:

---

[6] It should be noted that there is no *happiness₆* in English (at least not yet) which would correspond to the adjective *happy* used in sentences like *I'm happy with the arrangements* or *I'll be happy to show you how to do it*. The implications of *happy* in such phrases can be compared with those of expressions like *I don't mind, I have no objections, That's fine,* or even *okay*. It is, one might say, *happy* used as a token of interpersonal cooperation. This meaning of *happy* can be explicated along the following lines:

I'm happy with (these arrangements, this solution, this proposal, etc.):
I say: I don't think about it like this: "this is not good, I don't want it to be like this, I want you to do
    something else"
    I can think about it like this: "this is good"
    when I think about it like this, I can feel something good

"Čto že ėto: bol'šoe sčast'e ili bol'šoe nesčast'e slučilos' so mnoj?" sprašival on sebja.

(Tolstoy, *Voskresenie*, p. 67)

"What is the meaning of it all? Is it a great joy, or a great misfortune, that has befallen me?" he asked himself.   (Tolstoy, *Resurrection*, p. 63)

The hero, Nekhludov, has just seduced an innocent girl who was in love with him and with whom he was in love himself—and he is not sure whether what happened was a *bol'shoe sčast'e* (a great *sčast'e*) or a *bol'shoe nesčast'e* (a great *nesčast'e*). The English translation (by Louise Maude) renders *sčast'e* as *joy* here, and *nesčast'e* as *misfortune*, but this loses the Russian idea that *sčast'e* and *nesčast'e* are direct opposites, and that they both depend on what **happens** to a person, and not only on the person's thoughts and feelings.

This is another illustration of the fact that the ethos embodied in modern English leaves relatively little room for notions like "fate", good and bad fortune, luck, and chance (in relation to human life), and places a far greater emphasis on what people **do**, as well as on how they think and feel, than on things which are not subject to their control (cf. Besemeres and Wierzbicka 2009). What has disappeared from this new vision of human life is, as McMahon (2006: 477) puts it, "what the ancient Greeks were prepared to ascribe, in the wisdom of their ignorance, to the gods, fortune, the luck of birth, or the simple nature of things".

5.9 Socrates on "happiness" and a good way to live

McMahon writes: "In the history of happiness, as in the history of philosophy, Socrates is a pivotal figure" (2006: 24). He elaborates: "From the moment Socrates declared that happiness should be the goal of good living, human beings have searched for its secret without end" (p. 461).

This is a striking and somewhat disturbing statement. Did Socrates really declare that "happiness should be the goal of good living"? If Socrates chose to drink hemlock rather than to save his life, did he do it in the name of a search for happiness? And if so, then "happiness" in what sense? As McMahon (p. 25) puts it, "Socrates grounds his search for happiness in natural human longing." He quotes the dialogue *Enthydemus* in which Socrates asks his companions rhetorically: "What human being is there who does not desire happiness?"

Unlike many other commentators, McMahon does pay a good deal of attention to the fact that Socrates spoke in Greek, not in English, and therefore could not have used the English word *happiness*. Moreover, McMahon does look into the question of what Greek word Socrates used in this context, and notes (p. 487) that he did not use the word *eudaimonia* (usually rendered in English as 'happiness') but the expression *eu prattein*, literally 'doing well' or 'living well'. Nonetheless he comments (with a reference to Julia Annas' (1999) study *Platonic Ethics, Old and New*): "It is clear from

the context, however, that the expression is used synonymously with *eudaimonia*."
This merely leaves us with two further questions, however: first, what exactly did
eudaimonia mean in ancient Greek, and second, what exactly did Socrates mean by
either *eudaimonia* or *eu prattein*?

McMahon is very aware of the semantic pitfalls which can be associated with the
use of the same word (e.g. *happiness*) in relation to different systems of ideas. For
example, he says:

> Certainly, the desire for pleasure must be counted a universal trait, in animals and human
> beings alike. But by "happiness", Socrates has something else in mind—something loftier,
> grander—a higher good that lies beyond mere enjoyment or satisfaction of the senses. And
> whether human beings instinctively long for that is far less clear. Only when we realize that
> Socrates declares happiness a natural human longing at the very moment that he invents it as a
> new, and apparently realizable, form of desire do we begin to suspect that the elusive
> something for which we naturally yearn may be less inherent to our nature than originally
> thought.   (McMahon 2006: 25)

But this still does not answer the crucial question: what did Socrates mean by his
phrase *eu prattein*?

For all people who are inclined to revere Socrates as one of humanity's great
teachers and who are willing to learn from him, it is important to know whether or
not he really taught that "happiness" was the goal of human life; and if he didn't teach
that, then what did he teach?

Nietzsche, who, like many philosophers and historians, saw Socrates as a pivotal
figure in the history of human ideas, and indeed as the "vortex and turning point of
Western civilization" (*The Birth of Tragedy*, p. 94), nonetheless saw Socrates as
someone who made a fundamental error with disastrous consequences for Western
civilization. This error consisted, in his view, in equating "reason" with "virtue" and
with "happiness" (*Vernunft* = *Tugend* = *Glück*) and in presenting "happiness"
(*Glück*) as achievable.

> Kurz, die Entnatürlichung der Moralwerte hatte zur Konsequenz, einen enttastenden Typus
> des Menschen zu schaffen,—"den Guten", "den Glücklichen", "den Weisen":—Socrates ist ein
> Moment der tiefsten Perversität in der Geschichte der Werte.   (*Der Wille zur Macht*, p. 298)

> Briefly, the de-naturalization (making unnatural) of moral values had as a consequence the
> creation of a degenerate type of man—"a Good Man", "a Happy Man", "a Wise Man":—
> Socrates is a moment of the deepest perversity in the history of values.   [translation, *AW*]

What Nietzsche appears to hold against Socrates most is that he—like 18th-century
English thinkers such as Bentham—regarded "happiness" as attainable, and attainable through reason. This equation between Socrates and Bentham, between the
"happiness of Socrates" and the "English happiness" epitomized by Bentham, is made
by Nietzsche quite explicitly. McMahon (p. 430) paraphrases Nietzsche's view of this
point as follows:

This fundamental Socratic error—so central to all subsequent classical thought—had been embraced ever since. It was precisely this same false equation that animated the thinking of the Enlightenment, with its insistence on bringing happiness to humanity through the triumph of reason.   (McMahon 2006: 430)

But if "English happiness" (i.e. "happiness" in Bentham's sense) stood, as Nietzsche put it, for "comfort and fashion (and, as the supreme goal, a seat in Parliament)" (*Beyond Good and Evil*, p. 139), then clearly this had very little in common with Socrates' ideal of *eu prattein*. Translating *eu prattein* ("good doing/ good living") as "happiness" leads to confusion and makes Socrates' real ideal unrecognizable. Using NSM, we can elucidate this ideal as follows:

[I]   Socrates' ideal of *eu prattein* ('doing well/living well'):

a.   it can be like this:
b.   someone often thinks like this:
c.   "I live for some time, I want to live well
d.   I know that I can live well if I know some things well
e.   I know well that when I do good things this is always good for me
f.   I know well that if I do bad things this is always bad for me
g.   I know that if I live like this, this will be good for me
h.   I know that if I live like this, when something bad happens to me
                it cannot be bad for me"
i.   because this someone thinks like this, this someone lives well
j.   because of this, this someone can be someone good
k.   at the same time, this someone can always feel something good
l.   it is good for this someone if it is like this

The idea articulated in this explication is of course very different from that expressed in the English word *happiness*, in any of its meanings. It is also different from that linked with *eudaimonia* by other ancient Greek speakers and authors. But Socrates does not reject or attack the word *eudaimonia*, as used by others, just as the Dalai Lama does not reject or attack the word *happiness* as used by others. Rather, he uses the word *eudaimonia* (along with *eu prattein*) to connect with the thinking of other people, and with their conscious desire for 'good things' and 'good feelings'— just as the Dalai Lama is prepared to use the English word *happiness* to encourage people to search for something else (*bdewa*). A reference to 'feeling good' is included in the explication of the Socratic ideal of *eu prattein* presented here. It is, however, combined with, and subordinated to, references to 'being good' and 'living well'.

In her introduction to Plato's *The Symposium*, the classicist C. C. Sheffield (2008: xvi) highlights the differences between the English word *happiness* and the Greek *eudaimonia*, as it was used by Socrates, and the dangers inherent in translating Socrates' concept as *happiness*:

Happiness is quite often conceived as a subjective state to be determined from the inside, so to speak. If happiness is the sort of thing that individuals decide upon for themselves on the basis of how they feel at any given moment, for example, then how can philosophical analysis determine whether or not we are happy? This highlights the difficulties in translating *eudaimonia* as 'happiness'. *Eudaimonia* was considered not just to be a subjective feeling of pleasure, or contentment, or the mere satisfaction of an individual's desires (whatever these may be). What is under consideration here is whatever it is that makes a life worthwhile, that is, the success, or flourishing, of a human being who can be considered to be living well.

As this passage illustrates, commentators on Plato's dialogues are often aware of the deep semantic differences between, on the one hand, *happiness* and, on the other, concepts like *eudaimonia* and *eu prattein* (as used by Socrates). They often think, however, that there is simply no other way of talking about these Greek ideas than by resorting to the English word *happiness*. For example, Julia Annas (1999: 37) writes:

If we are not to give up on finding an overall interpretation which will make sense of Plato's various positions about virtue and happiness, we must find a way of fitting Socrates' moral intransigence into a theory of happiness. The first major obstacle to this lies in our own assumptions about happiness. For us, both at the everyday level and in more theoretical discussions, happiness figures in a rather different way from the ancient conception, so that, although there is no better translation for *eudaimonia* than *happiness*, we find some of the moves that are made in the ancient discussions surprising or hard to accept, and have to be aware of this in order to understand why Plato proceeds as he does.

As we see it, however, the main obstacle lies not so much in "our own assumptions about happiness" as in our assumptions about languages and words. We are inclined to assume that the only way to explain complex Greek (Tibetan, etc.) concepts (e.g. *eudaimonia*, *bdewa*) in English is to use some complex English concepts (such as *happiness*).

There may indeed be no better one-word translation for *eudaimonia* in English than *happiness*. However, if we allow ourselves to use, in addition, an extended paraphrase formulated in simple and universal human concepts we can elucidate both the Greek and the English concept very accurately, and show exactly what the differences and the similarities are.

We are not suggesting, needless to say, that such extended paraphrases could be used directly in the literary translations of Plato's dialogues. Rather, we are suggesting that they can be used in commentaries added to literary translations, and in secondary literatures elucidating the ideas expressed in primary sources. Of course, elucidations formulated in complex English words such as *wisdom* and *virtue* in the case of Socrates, or *calm*, *patience*, and *compassion* in the case of the Dalai Lama, can also be very useful. We submit, however, that it is only the use of simple and universal human concepts, such as 'do' and 'happen', 'good' and 'bad', and 'live' and 'feel', which enables us to identify the different ideals accurately, explicitly, and without any conceptual distortions.

It is refreshing, and illuminating, to hear McMahon (2006) speaking of a historical shift in Western civilization from 'wanting to be good' to 'wanting to feel good', precisely because he is formulating this insight in simple and universal human concepts. Such a simple formulation does help us to see something of the big picture. As we see it, the big picture is not simply a shift from 'wanting to be good' to 'wanting to feel good', but rather a shift from a triple goal of 'wanting to live well', 'wanting to be good', and 'wanting to feel good' to just one of these goals, 'wanting to feel good'. Furthermore, as we have tried to show here, the use of the same simple and universal human concepts allows us also to fill in the details and to portray more exactly the different views of human life offered by different philosophical, religious, and cultural traditions.

As noted earlier, psychologists Biswas-Diener et al. (2004: 18) declared a decade ago: "In the last few decades there has been something of a revolution in the scientific study of happiness":

A combination of radical new thinking and sophisticated methodology has allowed psychologists to add substantially to our understanding of this concept that has historically been the domain of philosophers and theologians. For the first time, we are able to measure happiness.

From a semantic and cross-cultural perspective, such claims seem problematic. From this perspective, it is not clear what exactly psychologists are measuring when they are engaged in "measuring happiness". Nor is it clear that the practice of quantifying self-reports formulated in untranslatable English phrases represents radical new thinking or sophisticated methodology. We hope to have shown in this chapter that a methodology based on simple and universal human concepts is more reliable and holds greater promise.

6

Pain: is it a human universal?

The perspective from cross-linguistic semantics

6.1 The need for a multilingual and multicultural perspective on pain

As noted by the clinical psychologist Ephrem Fernandez and the anaesthesiologist and psychiatrist Ajay Wasan (2010: 450), "pain is a global problem, with one in five persons suffering moderate to severe levels of chronic pain ... (World Health Organization, 2004)". The social, economic, and psychological costs of pain worldwide are immeasurable. As Fernandez and Wasan further note (with reference to Cordell et al. 2002), "pain ... is now deemed to be the most common reason why people seek medical care. The ubiquity and magnitude of pain have prompted professional organizations [...] to recommend that pain be assessed as 'the fifth vital sign' along with pulse, blood pressure, respiration, and body temperature" (p. 450).

There is, however, one crucial difference between the four traditionally recognized vital signs and the newly recognized fifth one: whereas pulse, blood pressure, respiration, and body temperature can be measured by instruments, people's pain can be known to others, including health professionals, mainly through talking. This is why effective communication about pain has to be a vital concern in modern societies—a concern shared by health professionals, counsellors, and "language professionals", above all linguists.

As a recent paper in the journal *Pain* (Strong et al. 2009: 86) states, "Pain is a largely subjective experience and one which is difficult to convey to others, and relies significantly on language to be communicated. The language used to describe pain is therefore an important aspect of understanding and assessing another's pain."

But the language used to describe pain is subject to significant cross-cultural variation. This often causes additional miscommunication and confusion in the case of people crossing linguistic and cultural boundaries. For example, in Australia, this applies in particular to migrants and indigenous Australians. Different ways of thinking about pain, linked with different languages and cultures, colour the way people of different linguistic and cultural backgrounds speak about and express their pain when they speak English. This aspect is often overlooked in the huge literature on pain, which largely focuses on medical and social aspects without regard to the cross-cultural and cross-linguistic perspectives.

Words and phrases used to describe pain do not match in meaning across different languages. For example, in Russian there is no distinction between pain and ache; the noun *bol'* and the verb *bolit* cover both. At the same time, Russian distinguishes between *bol'* and *muka* (roughly, an extremely intensive 'pain', for example, 'pain' under torture). Furthermore, common Russian phrases such as *ščemjaščaja bol'* and *nojuščaja bol'* have no equivalents in English. The verb *ščemit'* when used in a physical sense means 'press, pinch, squeeze', and the verb *nyt'*, 'moan, whine' (the root in *nojuščaja bol'*). The *Oxford Russian–English Dictionary* describes both these kinds of *bol'* ('pain') as 'aching', but from a Russian perspective they are two different kinds of pain (and neither of them corresponds to the English *ache*). Evidence suggests that such different ways of conceptualizing pain continue when Russian speakers immigrate to English-speaking countries.

In different cultural traditions there are different cultural scripts for expressing, and talking about, pain. A degree of cross-cultural training is therefore essential in understanding other people's pain. In the past, this fact was not given much attention in English-speaking countries, but recently it has been increasingly recognized in publications in the areas of nursing and palliative care. For example, Mary Narayan, a trans-cultural nurse consultant in Vienna, writes: "People from different cultures conceptualise and describe pain using different cognitive frameworks. Being asked to characterise pain using an unfamiliar descriptive context may result in inadequate pain control" (2010: 41).[1]

To illustrate the importance of talking about pain, it will be useful to adduce some brief quotes from a newspaper article entitled 'Helpline for nagging pain' by Mark Metherell, a health correspondent for the Sydney Morning Herald (23 November 2009):

Nagging pain, which many non-sufferers might think modern medicine has made a thing of the past, has emerged as a significant problem for nearly 40 per cent of Australians with chronic disease.

A new chronic disease management program, which has signed up 10,000 participants, has found that lower-back pain and other areas of pain are among the five most prevalent conditions suffered by people with chronic conditions. [. . .]

The patients are part of a new and rapidly expanding approach to chronic disease care: telephone-based counselling in which nurses, dieticians and exercise physiologists advise and support patients.

---

[1] See also Weber (1996), Weissman, Gordon, and Bidar-Sielaff (2004). For some notable linguistic publications on pain, see Diller (1980), Halliday (1998), Lascaratou (2008), Sussex (2009), Patharakorn (2010), Reznikova et al. (2012). For particularly insightful older publications, see Fábrega and Tyma (1976*a*; 1976*b*). For more recent NSM work, see Goddard and Ye (in press).

Obviously, telephone-based counselling is language-based: it is not about **assessing** pain but about **understanding** pain, and it requires an ability to understand words and phrases used by "ordinary people", often people of many different linguistic and cultural backgrounds. Such understanding can have far-reaching practical and economic consequences, as the following quotations from Metherell's article indicate.

The proactive approach, in which the trained counsellors call the patients regularly to give personalized guidance, has been shown in trials to have reduced hospital admissions by 17 per cent. [...]

The chief medical officer of HCF, Andrew Cottrill, said [...] the fund had invested $100 million in My Health Guardian, which it was hoped would reduce the need for hospital care and reduce pressure on insurance premiums. The managing director of Healthways, Australia, Tim Morphy, [...] said federal policy experts had pointed out that "chronic disease is the tsunami coming through our health system" and the federal Health Minister, Nicola Roxon, had called for more chronic-disease support services.

Two further quotes reflect the perspective of patients: "for patients to get regular calls from counsellors offering support and guidance in dealing with pain was often of significant benefit" (...). "The 10,000[th] participant to sign on to My Health Guardian, Raymond Moore of Crookwell in southern NSW, said that knowing he could have a conversation on the phone with a professional 'gives me a great deal of comfort'."

The experiences of many immigrants in Australia (and no doubt those of many indigenous Australians) suggest that having a conversation with a professional (even face-to-face) can also be a source of frustration and additional distress (Yoon 2007a: 119). Undoubtedly it can be good to be able to talk to someone about one's pain, but it is even better to talk and to be understood.

As the excerpts quoted above illustrate, talking about pain is a key aspect of dealing with pain. But talking about pain effectively is not easy. The "Helpline for nagging pain" article quotes a health consultant, Katherine McGrath, as saying that "the identification of pain was an important element in chronic disease". It is important to note, however, that often "the identification of pain" requires some cross-cultural understanding and some training in cross-cultural communication.

This applies not only to physical pain but also to mental pain. As Christopher Dowrick, a medical scholar and general practitioner, writes in his book *Beyond Depression* (2004: 68),

the main conclusion I wish to draw is that there are no reliable or agreed diagnostic boundaries between these varied mental and somatic problems which are so commonly present in psychiatry and in primary care. Depression, anxiety, and alcohol misuse overlap with each other. All in turn can be related in various ways to physical problems such as low back pain and chest pain, or can merge into patterns of symptoms which doctors find difficult to explain.

Dowrick sees these difficulties as related to difficulties in communication: "communication between doctors and patients may be an important factor in determining how patients present their problems" (p. 68). Furthermore, in a section entitled "Lost in translation", Dowrick comments: "Words that we take for granted, like depression, do not translate readily into other languages and cultures" (p. 122). Referring to the work of one of the present authors (Wierzbicka's 1999 book *Emotions Across Languages and Cultures*), he elaborates: "It is not just that specific words like depression do not exist in certain languages. It is more that different cultures and languages are constructed in such different ways that there may be no room for a concept like depression, rendering it virtually meaningless" (p. 23).

The emergence of modern (English-based) diagnostic systems has, according to Dowrick, enhanced the professional prestige of psychiatrists. The concept of depression is used in diagnosis "as a bulwark against uncertainty and confusion" (p. 12). In fact, however, "our decision to accord depression the status of a diagnosis may derive not so much from our scientific knowledge as from our system of values" (p. 12). What applies to 'depression' and 'anxiety', distinguished lexically in English but not necessarily in other languages, applies also to lexical distinctions such as those between 'pain' and 'ache', 'sore' and 'hurts', 'pain' and 'agony', or between different types of pain listed, for example, in the McGill Pain Questionnaire (Melzack 1975).[2]

In discussing problems in communication about depression and pain between doctors and patients, Dowrick emphasizes the relevance of cross-cultural and cross-linguistic semantics, and in particular the usefulness of the NSM approach.

6.2 Problems with the official definition of 'pain'

The definition of 'pain' approved for publication by the Council of the International Association for the Study of Pain in Kyoto in November 2007 and available on the IASP's website reads: "An unpleasant sensory and emotional experience associated with actual or potential tissue damage, or described in terms of such damage." This is a technical definition, formulated in a language which could be hard to understand for many ordinary speakers of English and sufferers of pain. This chapter endeavours to show that a psychologically more plausible definition can be constructed in terms of simpler and cross-translatable words.

---

[2] The initial "Overview" of the McGill Pain Questionnaire states that this questionnaire "has been translated into many languages". One wonders at the level of accuracy achieved in such translations, given that most of the words used in it have no exact semantic equivalents in other European languages, not to mention non-European ones. To quote two Finnish medical scholars (Ketovuori and Pöntinen 1981: 252), who tried to render the McGill Pain Questionnaire (MPQ) in Finnish: "In the English-speaking world, the MPQ is invaluable in examining pain in patients, in portraying manifestations of the pain and in following treatment [...]. But when attempting to adjust the MPQ for use in non-English speaking areas, its value is greatly diminished since both attribute meanings and intensity scales defy translation"; see also Patharakorn (2010).

The IASP scientific-sounding definition of 'pain' is of course not entirely out of touch with the ordinary meaning of the English word *pain*. As will be argued below, it is right on the crucial question of whether 'pain' is a unitary concept always referring to a psychological state (Merskey 1994) or whether, on the contrary, it stands for two distinct categories, one physical and the other psychological (as argued e.g. by Marmaridou 2006). The IASP definition mentions both a 'sensory' and an 'affective' dimension, but doesn't treat *pain* as having two distinct meanings.

Nonetheless, it would be hard to argue that the IASP definition captures accurately what ordinary speakers of English mean by the word *pain*. This is not a satisfactory state of affairs because *pain* is not a technical term confined to the use of the medical profession but, on the contrary, a word which doctors need in order to communicate with their patients. When a doctor asks a patient "tell me about your pain" it is important that the two should be using this crucial word in the same sense, and it would be unrealistic to expect this sense to be a technical one, posited by medical practitioners.

What does the word *pain* mean, then, in ordinary English, and how does this meaning differ from that given in IASP's 'official' definition?

One thing that is clearly problematic is the choice of the word 'unpleasant' as a characterization of the subjectivity of pain. For example, to describe the experience of a woman screaming in childbirth as 'unpleasant' would be a curious case of English understatement—curious and clearly inappropriate. There is a long tradition in Anglophone philosophy and psychology of dividing feelings (or 'sensations') into 'pleasant' and 'unpleasant', but to do so is to do violence to ordinary English usage. From the point of view of ordinary English, it would be clearly inappropriate to describe 'ecstasy' or 'joy' as 'pleasant' sensations, and the sensations of a person undergoing torture as 'unpleasant'. The words *pleasant* and *unpleasant* are just not used that way in ordinary English.

It is true that ordinary speakers of English—and for that matter any other language—distinguish 'good feelings' and 'bad feelings' (cf. Wierzbicka 1999*a*). In itself, this distinction does not give us a sufficient basis for defining 'pain', but it does suggest one component towards such a definition: a person who is 'in pain' is feeling 'something bad'. But someone who has an 'itch', or a 'cramp', or a 'stitch' is also feeling 'something bad', and yet they are not feeling 'pain', so obviously, there is more to 'pain' than that. The IASP definition is right in associating the subjective 'bad feeling' with an objective bodily basis, insofar as it mentions 'tissue damage'. Of course 'pain' (even 'physical pain') is not **necessarily** accompanied by something like 'tissue damage', for example, 'phantom pain' is not, but the **concept** of 'pain' is undoubtedly associated with a prototypical situation where, roughly speaking, something 'damaging', or potentially damaging, is happening to a part of a person's body.

This is only a very rough way of putting it, however. The word 'damage' is problematic in a number of ways. Most obviously, it refers to a post-factum result of something untoward that happens to a part of a person's body, not to the untoward event itself. Arguably, however, a prototypical 'pain' situation is one where the 'bad feeling' is perceived as being concurrent with a 'bad event' affecting some part of the body. For example, when one steps on a sharp stone 'something bad' happens to the foot (the stone presses against it) and the person feels something bad in that foot because of this. Whether or not the pressing and the feeling are really concurrent or whether the former slightly precedes the latter is immaterial from a 'naïve' point of view: for an ordinary speaker of English, the contact of the foot with the sharp stone and the feeling in the foot caused by it are occurring at the same time.

The word 'damage' used in the IASP definition of 'pain' suggests a perspective which may belong more to a doctor than a patient: a person experiencing 'pain' is less likely to think about it in terms of future 'damage' than in terms of what is happening right now (when it hurts). 'Damage' implies, essentially, that something bad has happened to an object and that as a result, this object is not like it was before (perhaps not as good as it was before). This explanation sounds more naïve than the word 'damage' itself, because the somewhat technical ring of the word 'damage' helps conceal the 'objective' evaluation. It might be asked: who says that what happened was 'something bad'? Bad from what point of view? According to what criteria? Nonetheless that is precisely what the word *damage* implies: something bad happened to an object, subsequently the object is damaged, and the change is presented by the speaker as bad. There is also a functional perspective here. For example, 'damaged goods' may not be able to fulfil their intended function very well, or at least they are depreciated in their material value.

In any case, the folk concept of 'pain' (and this is the concept which matters most in communication between doctors and patients) is not conceived in terms of subsequent 'damage', but rather in terms of a process, or event, concurrent with the bad feeling. Importantly, this process itself is thought of as 'something *bad*' happening to part of one's body—a construal which (apart from the temporal aspect) corresponds to the intuition behind the word 'damage'. For example, if I feel uncomfortable in the chair in which I am sitting, I 'feel something bad' in my body and don't want it to be like this, but I wouldn't think of this uncomfortable feeling as 'pain' because I don't construe it as 'something bad happening to part of my body'. Thus, for an adequate prototypical cognitive scenario of 'pain' all three components are needed: feeling something bad in part of one's body, thinking that something bad is happening to that part, and wanting it not to be like this. This leads us to the following explication:[3]

---

[3] For an earlier analysis of the language of 'pain' through NSM, see Nicholls (2003).

[A]   *She felt pain.*

a.   she felt something bad at that time
b.   like someone can feel when it is like this:
c.   something bad is happening to a part of this someone's body
d.   this someone feels something bad in this part of the body because of this
e.   this someone can't not think like this at this time: "I don't want this"

The components of this explication are of course not meant to specify the "truth conditions" of the explicated sentence but rather, parts of the "ordinary meaning". Furthermore, as component (b) shows, the indented components—(c), (d), and (e)—describe a certain prototype which provides the speakers with a reference point for the whole range of sentences with the word *pain*. In particular, the sentence *She felt pain* does not imply that something bad was happening to part of the person's body, but rather that the feeling in question can be **likened** to that of a person who is in such a situation (and who, as a result, feels something bad in that part of his or her body).

In some ways this explication is very different, both in style and in content, from the IASP definition. At the same time, the two agree in some crucial respects: above all, they both refuse to draw a sharp line between 'physical pain' and 'psychological pain', while at the same time proposing localized 'physical pain' as a paradigmatic reference point for all kinds of 'pain'. Furthermore, as we will discuss in more detail below, the word *sensory* in the IASP definition points, indirectly, to the importance of the concept BODY as a conceptual component of 'pain'. Both the words *sensory* and *emotional* point to the importance of FEEL as another conceptual component; and the words *emotional* and *experience* point to the relevance of a person's consciousness, and thus of the conceptual component THINK.

But while the concept of 'pain' involves FEEL, BODY, and THINK, it also involves, crucially, the concept WANT. Prototypically at least, 'physical pain' is a feeling against which the body rebels, as it were. Of course, such an instinctive rejection of 'pain' by the sufferer can be overcome and he or she may welcome 'pain' as a salutary, useful, or enriching experience (as in Brand and Yancey's (1997) book *The Gift of Pain: Why We Hurt and What We Can Do About It*); but prototypically at least, there is an 'I don't want this' reaction, which is part of the very concept of 'pain'. All these conceptual ingredients of 'pain'—'body', 'feel', 'think', and 'don't want'—play a pivotal role in the explication (or definition) of 'pain' proposed here.

Explication [A] treats 'pain' as a unitary concept, applicable to both physical and emotional pain. As noted earlier, physical pain is accorded here a privileged status as a reference point for all 'pain'. At the same time, however, the implication is that (so-called) psychological 'pain' is not being treated here as metaphorical. The main arguments for seeing English 'pain' as a unitary conceptual category can be delineated as follows:

First, there is the argument from Occam's razor: polysemy should never be posited without necessity. Of course, polysemy is pervasive in ordinary language, but in each case when it is posited a case needs to be made for it, and the ultimate criterion is always whether or not an adequate uniform definition can be devised. For example, the English word *bank* has to be treated as polysemous because it is impossible to construct a meaningful definition which would apply both to *bank* as a financial institution and *bank* as the raised ground along the edge of a river. This is not, however, the case with *pain*, because a unitary definition is possible, as explication [A] shows.

Second, *pain* is often used in English in a general sense, without any distinction being drawn between different kinds of it. This point can be illustrated with two examples, one from Matthew Henry's commentary on the biblical book of Job, and one from Shakespeare's *Romeo and Juliet* (see Stevenson 1958):

So great was the extremity of his pain and anguish that he did not only sigh but roar.

(Matthew Henry's Commentary on Job)

One fire burns out another's burning; One pain is lessen'd by another's anguish.

(Shakespeare)

As any reader of the book of Job knows, Job's sufferings were both physical and psychological, and no sharp distinction between the two is drawn in his monologues: he pours out his misery in passionate language full of images and similes and he does not analyse it into different kinds. As for the Shakespeare quotation, the reader neither knows nor cares whether *pain* refers here to physical or psychological suffering, and the most likely interpretation is that it is meant to refer to all kinds, without distinction. In fact, Shakespeare provides two different illustrations, one psychological and one physical:

One desperate grief cures with another's languish,
Take thou some new infection to thy eye
And the rank poison of the old will die.

Third, the word *pain* is commonly contrasted in English with the word *pleasure*, which also makes no distinction between physical and psychological pleasures. For example (from Stevenson 1958):

Our pains are real things, and all
Our pleasures but fantastical.   (Samuel Butler, *Upon the Weakness of Man*)

Under pain, pleasure,
Under pleasure, pain lies.   (Emerson, *The Sphinx*)

Pain past is pleasure.   (Thomas Fuller, *Gnomologia*)

For all the happiness mankind can gain
Is not in pleasure but in rest from pain.   (Dryden, *The Indian Emperor*)

If pleasure was not followed by pain
Who would forbear it?   (Samuel Johnson, *The Idler*)

As the explications below make clear, the overall structure of the two concepts, 'pain' and 'pleasure', is quite similar (though not identical). This explains why *pain* tends to be contrasted in English with *pleasure*, rather than with other 'positive emotion' terms, such as *joy* and *happiness* (cf. Wierzbicka 1992c; 1999a). The unitary (non-polysemous) character of *pleasure* supports the unitary (non-polysemous) analysis assigned here to *pain*.

[B]   *He felt pleasure.*

a.   he felt something good at that time
b.   like someone can feel when it is like this:
c.   something is happening to part of this someone's body
d.   this someone feels something good in this part of the body because of this
e.   this someone thinks like this at this time: "I want this"

[C]   *He felt pain.*

a.   he felt something bad at that time
b.   like someone can feel when it is like this:
c.   something bad is happening to part of this someone's body
d.   this someone feels something bad in this part of the body because of this
e.   this someone can't not think like this at this time: "I don't want this"

Like *pain*, *pleasure* too does not need to be physical: there are pleasures of the mind and pleasures of the body. When one compares *pleasure* with *joy*, however, the difference between the two prototypes with respect to embodiment becomes clear: there are *pleasurable sensations* but not *joyful sensations*, and there is *spiritual joy* but not *spiritual pleasure*.

The explications of *pleasure* and *pain* presented here are analogous, but not strictly symmetrical. The main difference between the two lies in the psychological reaction to the sensation: 'this someone thinks like this' (in *pleasure*) and 'this someone can't not think like this' (*pain*). This difference in the phrasing of the last component reflects the perception that, roughly speaking, it is easier for people to ignore "pleasurable sensations" than pain.

6.3 How can one ask questions about 'pain' helpfully and effectively?

From a practical point of view, far more important than how to define 'pain' is the question of how doctors can find out about the pain that their patients feel. Questionnaires such as the McGill Pain Questionnaire (Melzack 1975) are of limited value here, because they use a kind of language that "ordinary people" would normally not use and which in fact might not be intelligible to them. For example, part of the McGill Pain Questionnaire headed by the question "How does your pain change with time?" instructs the respondent to choose one of the following responses:

"continuous/steady/constant", "rhythmic/periodic/intermittent", and "brief/momentary/transient". Many patients in English-speaking countries would find some of these prompts unfamiliar and not fully understandable. They belong to a register of English which is unfamiliar, not only to many immigrants, but also to many monolingual speakers of English.

The part of the Questionnaire entitled "How strong is your pain?" offers general prompts which are also neither colloquial (and thus more accessible to the general public, including second language learners) nor translatable into other languages. They are: *mild, discomforting, distressing, horrible,* and *excruciating.* Of these five, only *mild* and *horrible* are colloquial, but even here, the choice does not correspond well to the way "ordinary people" tend to speak about very bad pain: as Collins Wordbanks Online shows, *terrible pain,* with 186 entries, is a much more common collocation in English than *horrible pain,* with just 12 hits.

We suggest that an approach grounded in simple and universal human concepts would be more helpful in trying to find out about people's pain. A good point of departure in reflecting on this matter is to think about children. Presumably it would not be very helpful to ask a child questions such as "Is your pain intermittent? Is it periodic? Is it transient?" because most children would not understand them. They would, however, understand questions formulated in simple words such as the following ones:

1. Where does it hurt?
2. Does it hurt all the time?
3. Does it hurt all the time in the same way?
4. When it hurts does it hurt for a long time?
5. Does it hurt very much?
6. Does it hurt so much that you think about it all the time?
7. Does it hurt so much that you can't think about anything else?
8. Does it hurt always in the same place?
9. Does it hurt so much that you can't do anything?
10. Does it hurt so much that you think "I can die because of this"?
11. Is it like this: it hurts at some time, after this it doesn't hurt for some time, after this it hurts (again) like before?

Apart from the verb *to hurt,* which we have substituted here for the more abstract noun *pain* and which will be discussed in more detail later, practically all the other words used in the questions above are semantic primes which, evidence suggests, can be found in all languages. Moreover, these words have been put together in ways which are also universally available, that is, they have been combined into questions in accordance with the rules of universal grammar. As a result, these questions are not tied to the English language, but can be readily asked in any language. They can also be addressed, through English, to people whose English is very limited, including immigrants or people from ethnic or indigenous minorities in English-speaking countries. If necessary, questions such as those formulated above can even be asked through interpreters, since they are formulated in terms that can be readily transferred across languages.

Admittedly, the questions about pain which can be asked through simple and universal human concepts relate to the Questionnaire section "How does your pain change with time?", not that titled "What does your pain feel like?". We would not claim that the 'quality' of pain can be easily conveyed in simple sentences based exclusively on universal human concepts. We would suggest, however, that it can be conveyed to a considerable degree through simple sentences that include primes and widespread (though not universal) semantic molecules, such as 'sharp' and 'fire' (Goddard 2010b; 2012a; Goddard and Wierzbicka 2007).

The use of words like *sharp* and *burning* in people's descriptions of their pain suggests that in thinking and talking about their pain people often rely on certain images. These images relate to 'bad things' which can actually happen to some parts of people's bodies, such as cutting oneself on something sharp or burning oneself. Memories of such events, experienced or witnessed, appear to be often drawn upon as a source of ideas of what it would feel like if something like that was happening inside a person's body. Contrary to what one might expect, the number of such images which widely occur in ordinary 'pain talk' in English and in many other languages is actually quite limited, and the two just mentioned appear to be the most common ones.

The long list of adjectives offered as prompts in the "What does your pain feel like?" section of the McGill Pain Questionnaire is likely to be bewildering and even unhelpful to many 'ordinary' speakers of English. Pain descriptors such as *flickering, quivering, pulsing, beating, pounding, pumping, boring, drilling,* or *lacerating* are normally not used in colloquial English when people try to tell others about their pain. If doctors in Anglophone countries want to elicit information about their patients' pain, it may be more productive to ask detailed questions about its location, intensity, and temporal pattern rather than about its 'pure quality'. To the extent to which such information can be elicited at all (beyond a few commonly used descriptors such as *sharp* or *burning*), the most productive approach may be to ask general questions such as "tell me about your pain", "what does your pain feel like?" or "when it hurts what is it like?", rather than to use more obscure and possibly mystifying prompts such as *pulsing, pumping,* or *lacerating*.

6.4 *Pain* and related concepts (*hurt, ache, sore*) in English

In reflecting on the meaning of *pain* and on the place of the concept of 'pain' in the life of speakers of English, it is useful to consider how young children in English-speaking countries talk about their painful experiences. Do they talk about *pain* (using the word *pain*)? Not exactly: what they often do talk about is that something 'hurts'.

At first sight, it may seem that *hurt* is just another word for 'pain' (at least physical pain) and that the two words essentially mean the same. We argue, however, that this is not the case. First of all, the verb *hurt* refers to a localized bodily occurrence, whereas the noun *pain* (even physical pain) can sometimes be conceived as global; one can say, for example, *She is in pain* without referring to any particular part of the body, and in fact without even thinking in such terms. The verb *hurt*, on the other hand, normally requires a subject, and this subject identifies a part or an area of the body which is the one that 'hurts' (e.g. *my eyes are hurting*). Even a sentence like *I was hurting all over* refers to different (unidentified) body-parts, whereas the sentence *I was in pain* does not (and it does not imply that "I was in pain *all over*").

The grammatical difference between *pain* (an abstract noun) and *It hurts* (a sentence with a subject, if only a 'dummy' one) points in the same direction: *It hurts* suggests a more localized and also a more short-term feeling, linked with an identifiable locus and an immediately preceding cause.[4] For example, children know that an injection will 'hurt', and that it will hurt roughly in the place where the needle goes in, at the time when it goes in.

In his memoir *My Year Off: Rediscovering Life After a Stroke,* the British writer Robert McCrum (1998: 91) writes: "Even the good nurses have no idea how much they can hurt, how much hurt they can cause by wrenching my left arm, which is still totally paralysed and helpless, at the wrong moment." This sentence illustrates what appears to be a prototypical scenario for the word *hurt* (when used as a transitive verb): someone does something to a part of someone else's body and because of this, just after this, this other person feels something bad in that part of the body. The actions and the bad feeling are very close in time, and typically they both last for a short time.

Of course, *hurt* can also be used in relation to long-term sensations, and to sensations with internal causes. For example, one can say *My eyes are hurting* (intransitive use of the verb *to hurt*). But even in this case the sensation is localized, and its cause is usually known. *Pain*, on the other hand, while typically localized, can also be diffuse, chronic, and unrelated to any identifiable external causes, and when it is attributed to some identified external cause, it is seen through the prism of a less concrete situational scenario. For example, in McCrum's account of his experiences with different nurses, the sentence with *hurt* ("they can hurt") is followed by one with *pain*: "There's one nurse who causes pain every day." But here, the focus of attention is on the nurse, rather than on the particular experiences of 'hurting', for the passage

---

[4] It is true that the sentence *It hurts* can have two different interpretations, one physical and one emotional, but these really are two different senses of the word *hurt* (only one of which, the emotional one, corresponds to the noun *hurt*), whereas *She was in pain* has only one sense.

continues: "She is loud, brash and infuriating. I think she must be insecure." To take another example, in his autobiography *The Seven Storey Mountain* Thomas Merton (1955[1948]: 95–96) refers to an infected tooth with four different words: *sore, ache, hurt,* and *pain,* each time with a different emphasis:

At first I thought I was only out of sorts because of the **sore** foot and a bad tooth**ache**. The thing [the tooth] was **hurting** me, and I wanted to get rid of it as soon as possible. That night—that sleepless night—was spent in a fog of sick confusedness and general **pain**.

The word *toothache* presents the bad feeling as localized (diffusedly) inside the tooth, prolonged, and due to internal causes. The word *pain* refers to a 'general' (non-localized) feeling. The word *hurt* (used here transitively) presents the tooth as an 'alienable' (removable) cause of the feeling. The word *sore,* in *sore foot,* presents a fourth point of view: here, the feeling is strictly localized, but not in a diffuse way like *ache,* and not necessarily as located **inside** the body-part, prolonged, and due to external causes.

Thus the English lexicon, and its lexicogrammar, offer speakers several prototypical scenarios for situations which in some other languages may be linked with just one word and one prototypical scenario. For example, *earache* suggests that something bad is happening inside the ear (presumably, an infection of the inner ear), whereas both *sore* and *hurt* could be used in relation to the outer ear, but with somewhat different implications. In particular, *sore* implies a certain duration, whereas *hurt* is compatible with a momentary feeling (e.g. caused by an injection or a bee sting). Furthermore, while both *sore* and *hurt* imply a prior event triggering the bad bodily feeling, in the case of *sore,* this prior event can occur some time before the bad bodily feeling, whereas in the case of *hurt,* it (prototypically) comes a short, or even very short, time before the feeling. By contrast to both *sore* and *hurt,* in the case of *pain,* the "bad thing" happening to a body-part is conceptualized as concurrent with the bad feeling.

The duration of the feeling implied by *sore* links it with *ache.* What sets *ache* apart from all the other words in this field is its reference to something happening 'inside' part of the body. Interestingly, the verb *to hurt* is usually not used in relation to internal body-parts. For example, *My stomach hurts* is unlikely (though not impossible), whereas *My foot hurts* is common. In our explications (below), we have not sought to account for this by positing for *hurts* a component like 'this part of my body is not inside the body', which would be implausible from a cognitive point of view. Instead, we have presented the putative cause of the "bad bodily feeling" as preceding the feeling and presumably known and observable. This link between *(My) stomach hurts* and an identifiable, immediately preceding cause can be illustrated with the following examples (from Collins Wordbanks Online):

- "…You've got to hear the Terrible News, especially if you're going to visit Sam tomorrow. You may as well be prepared." "My **stomach hurts**. My stomach hurts already, and I haven't even heard the news yet."
- It's the day I get to have fun with my family and eat until my **stomach hurts**.
- She catches Charlotte's eye and then, suddenly, they're both laughing so much they're choking, until Julie can't breathe and her **stomach hurts**.

By contrast, *stomach ache* can be chronic and have no easily identifiable cause, as the following example illustrates:

- Agitation, especially among nonverbal patients, is sometimes due to hunger, soiled bedclothes, a cold room or a hot room, or even an actual ailment like a **stomachache** or back pain (arthritic and digestive problems tend to become worse at night for many persons). Before patients are put to bed, make sure they have been toileted and fed, appropriately medicated against chronic aches and pains and comfortably bedded down.

These different conceptualizations specific to English can be accurately portrayed and clearly compared through the explications in [D]–[F]. In many other languages, not these but other distinctions would be drawn.

[D]   *It hurts!*

a.   something is happening to a part of my body at this time
b.   because something bad happened to it a very short time before
c.   I feel something bad in this part of my body because of this
d.   I don't want this

[E]   *Her bones (legs) are aching.*

a.   she feels something bad inside part of her body [bones, legs, etc.] at this time
b.   like someone can feel when it is like this:
c.   something is happening inside part of this someone's body for some time
d.   this someone feels something bad in this part of the body for some time
e.   this someone thinks like this at this time: "I don't want to feel something like this"

[F]   *He has a sore foot (finger, throat).*

a.   he feels something bad in one part of his body [foot, etc.] at this time
b.   like someone can feel when it is like this:
c.   this someone feels something bad in a part of their body for some time, not a very long time
d.   because something bad happened to this part of this someone's body some time before
e.   when this someone thinks about this part of the body, this someone thinks like this:
               "I don't want to feel something like this in this part of my body"

[G]   *He feels pain.*
a.   he feels something bad at this time
b.   like someone can feel when it is like this:
c.   something bad is happening to a part of this someone's body
d.   this someone feels something bad in this part of the body because of this
e.   this someone can't not think like this at this time: "I don't want this"

Since children speak (and presumably, think) in terms of *it hurts* rather than *pain* (or *ache*, or *sore*), one may well wonder if the model encoded in *it hurts* is not more widespread across languages than that associated with *pain* (or *ache*, or *sore*). The expression *it hurts* can be used not only to **describe** what someone feels but also to **express** one's feeling, and for this reason too it is more likely to have counterparts in many languages of the world than *pain*. However, 'it hurts' is not a universal concept either, as we can see looking no further afield than at French. The closest French counterpart of *it hurts* is probably *ça fait mal*, but, as we will see in section 6.7, the conceptualization is different in each case. Anticipating the discussion, we can note that the expression *it hurts* appears to have its conceptual prototype in a situation where a "painful" sensation follows an identifiable event (e.g. an injection, or 'hurting' one's foot against a rock). By contrast, the French expression *ça fait mal* evokes a prototype where the event and the sensation are concurrent.

One interesting and important topic which cannot be discussed here at length, but which deserves at least a quick mention, is the semantic history of the 'pain' concept in English. The fact that in older English one could speak of "pain of teeth" (or "pain in teeth"), whereas in contemporary English this is not possible, is a good indication of a change in the meaning of the word *pain*. One example from the *OED* is: *that milk that men use...for pain of teeth* (1450). In contemporary English, one can speak of a *back pain* or *chest pain*, but not "head pain", "throat pain", and "ear pain", or "pain of (the) head", "pain of (the) throat" or "pain of (the) ear". "Pain of teeth" (or "pain of the teeth") is completely out of the question. One hypothesis consistent with such facts is that *pain* used to imply a real cause of a bad sensation, rather than a mere prototype, along the following lines:

[H]   *pain of (the) teeth*
a.   something bad is happening to a part of someone's body
b.   this someone feels something very bad in this part of the body because of this
c.   this someone thinks like this about this at this time: "I don't want this"

What this suggests is that in older English the "very bad feeling" in a part of the body was conceptually linked with some localized physical cause (harm), whereas in contemporary English the attention is focused on the feeling alone, conceptually dissociated from the bodily cause.

In contemporary English the main pattern for *pain* is locational, as is *pain in the neck*. Compounds such as *chest pain* and *back pain* are possible with words which themselves refer to an area of the body, rather than a part of the body; and they don't imply that it is the area which is the cause (rather than merely the location) of the "bad feeling". For example, *chest pain* (or *chest pains*) suggests that something bad is happening to the heart rather than to the chest. The bad feeling is localized in the chest. The older collocation "pain of teeth"—paralleled, for example, by the Polish expression *ból zębów* (to be discussed later)—indicates a shift from a double conceptualization of 'pain' (process and sensation) to a single one ("sensation"). But the matter requires further investigation.

6.5 No 'pain' concept in Australian Aboriginal languages?

Pain is a human universal: presumably, all people feel it sometimes, in some ways. As we have been emphasizing, however, this does not mean that in all cultures and societies people think and talk about it in the same way. The **concept** encoded in the English word *pain* is not a universal human concept, and the English word *pain* does not translate very easily across all languages.

Let us consider an example of a language which does not seem to have an exact counterpart of the English word *pain*, the Australian Aboriginal language Yankunytjatjara (Pitjantjatjara). According to the *Pitjantjatjara/Yankunytjatjara to English Dictionary* (Goddard 1996b), the closest counterpart of *pain* in this language is the noun *pika*. The dictionary assigns to this noun four distinct meanings, which are glossed in English as follows: 1. pain, something that hurts. 2. a sore, wound. 3. illness, disease. 4. a fight, conflict. The derived adjective *pikatjara* is assigned two meanings: 1. sick, ill, wounded, injured; and 2. sick, ill, wounded, injured person or animal. When *pika* refers to a wound or a sore (*pika₂*), it indicates a place in the body where something bad is happening and where the 'bad feeling' is located. When it refers to an illness (*pika₃*), it indicates that something bad is happening in part of a person's body, causing the person to feel something bad somewhere in the body. When *pika* is used in relation to a fight (*pika₄*), it implies a desire to inflict bodily harm on someone and to hurt them.

Pitjantjatjara *pika* is not used to refer to what English might construe as "psychological pain". Although the language has a rich emotional vocabulary, including many words comparable to *sorrow*, *sadness*, *grief*, and the like, *pika* is not a word which could be used in a similar way. Rather, when it is used in a sense broadly comparable to that of 'pain' (and not in the sense of 'wound', 'illness', or 'fight'), it always refers to a bad feeling located in a particular part of the body and associated with a physical cause.

In fact, when *Pika!* is used as an exclamation its meaning appears to come very close to that of the English exclamatory sentence *It hurts!*

[I]   *Pika!*

a.   something bad is happening to a part of my body at this time
b.   I feel something bad in this part of my body because of it
c.   I don't want this

In the explication above we have presented the cause of the "bad bodily feeling" as concurrent with the feeling itself rather than as an immediately preceding event which triggers that feeling, as in the case of *hurt*. If this is correct, *pika!* would be closer, in this one respect, to the English *pain* than to the English *(it) hurts*. (To establish this point conclusively would require further investigation.)

A descriptive use of *pika* is illustrated in the *Pitjantjatjara/Yankunytjatjara to English Dictionary* with the sentence *Kuṯuṯu pika ngaṟala, nyangakutu tjunkupai*, glossed as 'if there is chest pain, you put (ointment) around here'. We could hypothesize for this use of *pika* the following explication:

[J]   There is *pika* in his chest.

a.   something bad is happening to a part of his body [his chest] at this time
b.   he feels something bad in this part of the body because of this
c.   he thinks like this at this time: "I don't want this"

Another type of sentence with *pika* in the relevant sense are those which can be glossed in English as '*pika* is biting him' or '*pika* is eating him'. These sentences, too, refer to a feeling of '*pika*' due to a bodily cause. They may differ in intensity from sentences with the phrase which can be glossed literally as 'there is *pika* (e.g. in his chest)' ('this someone feels something *very* bad'), and they may include in their meaning a simile ('like someone can feel when something is biting this someone'); but here too the overall structure of such sentences appears to be closer to that of English sentences with the verb *to hurt* than sentences with the noun *pain* (although it may match *pain* in one respect, the perceived simultaneity of the cause and the effect).

We cannot here undertake a detailed investigation of the different uses of the word *pika* or of its closest counterparts in other Australian Aboriginal languages. Let us mention, however, one other example: the word *murrumurru*, which appears to be central to the "discourse of pain" in another Central Australian language, Warlpiri. The *Warlpiri Dictionary* defines this word as follows: "state of physical discomfort or pain caused by a malfunction of some part of the body". Clearly, this definition interprets the Warlpiri concept through the prism of the English language, inasmuch as there are no Warlpiri words corresponding to *physical, discomfort*, and *malfunction*. Less obvious, perhaps, is that the definition takes for granted some Anglo cultural scripts that encourage "understatement". The Warlpiri consultant quoted in the entry for *murrumurru* refers to spear wounds, knife wounds, and infected wounds as typical situations when people feel *murrumurru*: clearly, it is not a matter of mere "discomfort", it is a matter of "pain" (usually, it seems, severe "pain").

Warlpiri has many words and phrases referring to negative emotions of various kinds, but *murrumurru* is not one of them. As the wide range of examples in the *Warlpiri Dictionary* illustrates, *murrumurru* is used specifically for physical pain.[5] In some respects, then, the main word for something like 'pain' in Warlpiri, too, is closer to the English verb *hurt* than to the English noun *pain*. And yet *murrumurru* doesn't mean the same as *hurt* either, because *hurt* (as in *It hurts*) normally refers to a "painful" sensation in a particular part of the body, whereas *murrumurru* can be conceptualized as global. Thus, a sentence like

Murrumurru   karnaju   purda-nyanyi.
pain   PRES-1sg   feel

is comparable to the English sentence *I'm in pain*, whereas a sentence which specifies the cause of *murrumurru* as being located in a particular part of the body can be interpreted as 'I am in pain with regard to part X of my body'. For example

Ngaju ka-rna   murrumurru-jarri   miyalu.
I PRES-1sg   paining-INCHOATIVE   stomach
'I'm hurting (in) the belly.'

could loosely be glossed as 'I'm in pain with regard to the stomach' (both examples were provided by Mary Laughren).

More precisely, the conceptualization implied by both Warlpiri sentences above can be portrayed as follows:

something bad is happening somewhere in my body
I feel something bad in my body because of this
I don't want to feel like this

Thus, in Warlpiri the experience of *murrumurru* appears to be conceptualized as global, regardless of whether or not a specific body-part which gives trouble is mentioned. This is different from both *pain* and *hurt*.

To conclude, 'pain' is a concept which generalizes over some bodily bad feelings (triggered by 'bad' bodily events) and some non-bodily bad feelings perceived as comparable to those bodily ones. Languages like Yankunytjatjara and Warlpiri, which otherwise have a rich emotional vocabulary, appear not to have lexicalized such a concept. At the same time, they have a rich vocabulary for experiences of

---

[5] Mary Laughren and David Nash, who are leading experts on Warlpiri, have both confirmed (p.c.) that to the best of their knowledge *murrumurru* refers only to physical pain. For the sake of completeness, we must mention that there is one example in the *Warlpiri Dictionary* which does lend itself to an interpretation in terms of emotional pain: it refers to causing someone to feel *murrumurru* in their stomach "by saying something bad to them". However, both Laughren and Nash agree that this is likely to be a reference to what is perceived as a physical bad feeling in the stomach experienced by the addressee on hearing that bad thing.

"pain" in the body, but these experiences too are conceptualized somewhat differently than they would be in English, and the relevant words do not match in meaning English words such as *hurt*, *ache*, and *sore* any more than they do *pain*.

6.6 English *pain* vs. French *douleur*

At first sight, the French *douleur* may seem identical in meaning to the English *pain*. A closer look, however, reveals that there are significant differences between the two.

First, while both *douleur* and *pain* can range over emotional as well as physical experiences, *douleur* evokes emotions far more than *pain* does. This is recognized, at least implicitly, by the comprehensive *Collins–Robert English–French Dictionary* (1987), which assigns to *douleur* two meanings, one glossed in English as 'pain' and the other as 'distress, grief'. Given that *pain*, too, can refer to emotional suffering ('distress, grief'), it might seem unnecessary to present this word as a suitable gloss for only one kind of *douleur* (*douleur*₁) and to posit another sense, *douleur*₂, which can only be glossed as something other than *pain*. In fact, however, the intuition behind the dictionary treatment of the two words seems sound: *douleur* is used in French far more in relation to emotions than *pain* is in English.

One piece of evidence for this difference comes from the opposites of the two words. While *pain* is routinely contrasted in English with *pleasure*, *douleur* is frequently contrasted with *bonheur* 'happiness'. For example, in Camus's novel *The Plague*, when one of the protagonists, Rambert, becomes reunited with his wife, he cries, and he doesn't know himself if his tears come from his present *bonheur* or from the preceding and long suppressed *douleur* (Todd 1996: 360).

Here are some fuller examples from French websites:

*Tu enfanteras dans la **douleur**, tu allaiteras dans le **bonheur**.*
'You will give birth in *douleur* [pain?], you will nurse your child in happiness.'

*Mon accouchement: de la **douleur** au **bonheur** le plus total.*
'My experience of giving birth: from *douleur* [pain?] to the most complete happiness.'

*Ma vie est tristement belle. Des averses de **bonheur**. Des cyclones de **douleur**.*
'My life is sadly beautiful. Showers of happiness. Cyclones of *douleur* [pain?].'

*Le **bonheur** de Jean-Pierre est un affront à la **douleur** qui les habite et dont ils lui attribuent la responsabilité.*
'Jean-Pierre's happiness is an insult to their continuing *douleur* [pain?], which they blame him for.'

*Sans apprentissage de la **douleur**, le **bonheur** n'est pas solide.*
'Without an apprenticeship in *douleur* [pain?], there can be no solid happiness.'

*Mon enfant, ma **douleur**, mon **bonheur**.*
'My child, my *douleur* [pain?], my happiness.'

The French counterpart of *pleasure*, *plaisir*, is not normally contrasted with *douleur*, just as the English word *pain* is not normally contrasted with *happiness*. These differences between the opposites of *pain* and *douleur* appear to be connected with three other differences between the two words. First, *douleur* suggests a greater intensity of 'bad feeling' than *pain*: one can of course speak in English of *a great pain*, as one can speak in French of *une grande douleur*, and one can speak of a *légère douleur*, as one can speak of *a slight pain*, but English expressions such as *a flickering pain*, *a pulsating pain*, and *a throbbing pain* could hardly be translated into French with the word *douleur*. *Une douleur intermittente*, comparable to *an intermittent pain*, is possible, but it is not colloquial, and in any case doesn't say anything about the intensity of the feeling. More colloquial expressions are *une douleur qui lance* and *une douleur lancinante*, which are comparable to *a shooting pain*, but these expressions suggest a more intense "pain" than that associated with adjectives likes *flickering* and *pulsating*. The intensity of the prototypical French *douleur* is also reflected in common collocations with "extreme" adjectives, such as *une douleur atroce* ('atrocious'), *une douleur déchirante* ('tearing'), and *une douleur cruelle* ('cruel'). In English, comparable experiences would be more likely to be described with the word *agony* than with the word *pain*.

Second, English *pain* is often spoken of as localized, so much so that expressions like *pain in the neck* have acquired a second, figurative meaning; and one can readily speak of *pain* in an infected finger or toe. By contrast, *douleur* is normally not localized. To speak of a localized 'pain' in French one would normally use the word *mal* (which, when used as a noun, can mean 'illness' or 'evil', and when used as an adverb means 'badly'), not the word *douleur*. For example, to ask 'Where does it hurt?' or 'Where is the pain?' one would say *Où avez-vous mal?* (literally, "Where do you have *mal*?").

A third dimension of contrast between *douleur* and *pain* is that, prototypically, *douleur* is extended in time, whereas *pain* can be either prolonged or momentary. This extended nature of *douleur* is particularly salient in the case of the plural form, *les douleurs*, but the singular, too, suggests a certain duration. For example, in the case of an injection, the word *mal* rather than *douleur* would normally be used: *Ça fait mal!* Of course in English, too, one would be more likely to say in this situation *It hurts!* than to use the word *pain*, but one could also speak, for example, of *the pain of an injection*, whereas *la douleur de la piqûre* is judged to be somewhat marginal in French.

We are not suggesting that *douleur*, in contrast to *pain*, has two meanings, one emotional and one physical. On the contrary, we believe that such putative polysemy, posited by many French dictionaries, is untenable. This is implicitly recognized in the French online dictionary *Trésor de la langue française online dictionary*, which, having decided on polysemy of *douleur*, feels then forced to posit not two but three meanings: (A) physical, (B) psychological, and (C) indistinguishable. An example of category C offered by this dictionary comes from Balzac:

Louis Lambert souffrit donc par tous les points où la douleur a prise sur l'âme et sur la chair. 'Louis Lambert suffered through all the points where *douleur* gets a hold on the soul and on the flesh.'

To our way of thinking, such "indistinguishable" uses of *douleur* show that in fact there is no polysemy here but the meaning is unitary, with some components referring to the person and some to this person's body. In this respect, *douleur* is similar to *pain*: both are unitary and both have a prototype based on the body. What is being argued here is that while in the case of *pain*, the main point of reference is an affected part of the body, in the case of *douleur* it is the whole body. A 'bad feeling' engulfing the whole body is likely to be seen as 'very bad', rather than merely 'bad'; and it is more likely to be used as an image of a global 'very bad' feeling affecting the whole person (i.e. roughly speaking, an 'emotional pain') than of a strictly localized 'bad feeling' in a particular part of the body. As discussed earlier, *pain* (in contrast to *it hurts*) does not need to be always localized, but evidence suggests that the conceptual prototype of *pain* (in contrast to that of *douleur*) is indeed localized.

The "localized" prototype of the English word *pain* is reflected in the official definition of the International Association for the Study of Pain, which refers to "actual or potential tissue damage". But French *douleur* does not bring to mind local "damage" (as in the case of torn tissue). The *douleurs rhumaticales* 'rheumatic pains' and *les douleurs de l'accouchement* 'labour pains' mentioned in the entry for *douleur* by the Collins–Robert dictionary seem far more plausible as examples of prototypical physical *douleur* than any localized tissue damage. This leads us to the following explication of *douleur*:

[K]   She felt *douleur* (*elle ressentait de la douleur*).

a.   she felt something bad at this time
b.   like someone can feel when it is like this:
c.   something bad is happening to this someone's body for some time
d.   because of this, this someone feels something very bad in the body for some time
e.   this someone can't not think like this at that time: "I don't want this"

This explication does not separate two different senses, one emotional and one physical, but allows both types of *douleur* to be covered by one formula. The prototype of the experience is physical, but unlike the physical prototype of *pain*, it refers to the body as a whole and not just to part of the body.

It should be noted that this explication of *douleur* does not present *douleur* as a feeling that is **necessarily** intense ('very bad') or extended in time ('feels for some time'), but rather as a feeling that is **prototypically** 'very bad' and lasting 'for some time': the phrases 'very bad' and 'for some time' appear only in component (d), which is part of the semantic prototype of *douleur*, and not in component (a), which should be valid in all cases. This analytical solution is compatible with phrases like *une légère douleur* ('a light *douleur*') and *un moment de douleur* ('a moment of *douleur*'), as well as with the linguistic facts which suggest intensity and duration of a typical *douleur*.

The differences between *pain* and *douleur* can be illustrated with a number of examples from Marcel Proust's *À la recherche du temps perdu* (Proust 1954) and its English translation by James Grieve (Proust 1982; 2002). In the first volume of the novel, the word *douleur* occurs 23 times, and of these, only two refer to physical pain. Furthermore, in one of these two cases *douleur* (in an emotional sense) is contrasted with *douleur physique* (physical "pain"), suggesting that for Proust the emotional sense is unmarked. This is corroborated by the explicit contrast made in the same volume between *la douleur de l'âme* ("pain" of the soul) and *le mal du corps* ("pain" of the body).

Another striking fact is that in the English translation of Proust's volume, in a great majority of cases *douleur* appears to have been rendered not with the word *pain* but with some other words. For example, of the six cases that we checked in context, five have been translated with a word other than pain (*anguish, ache, forlorn, affliction, mourned*), and only one as *pain*.

When one considers all the uses of *douleur* in Proust's volume in context, the translator's reasons for avoiding *pain* in the English version become clear: often, *pain* cannot be used in sentences where *douleur* is perfectly at home in French. For example, the sentence *Ne réveillez pas la plus grande douleur de ma vie* (Proust 1954: 129) (literally, "don't wake up the greatest *douleur* of my life"), referring to emotions, could not very well be rendered in English as "the greatest pain of my life". Grieve rendered it as: "Do not remind me of the bane of my life!" (Proust 1982: 100).

The sentence *Je languissais de douleur* (Proust 1954: 398) ("I was languishing of *douleur*"), which refers to the narrator, distressed, walking slowly in the park, could hardly be rendered as "I was languishing of pain". Grieve translated it as "I dawdled forlornly" (Proust 1982: 321). Similarly, the phrase *la plus cruelle des douleurs* (Proust 1954: 632)—literally "the most cruel of *douleurs*", plural (referring to an emotion born out of the certitude that with time, one will succeed in killing one's love)—could not be credibly rendered in English as "the most cruel of pains". Grieve has translated this as: "the cruellest of all wounds" (Proust 1982: 208).

The sentence referring to the prospect of his beloved being away for Christmas, which made the narrator *fou de douleur* (Proust 1954: 526), literally 'insane with *douleur*', could hardly be translated as "insane with pain". In fact, it has been translated by Grieve as "which gave an unbearable pang" (Proust 1982: 102). Finally, the sentence about the narrator's aunt Léonie, who died *ne causant par sa mort de grande douleur qu'à un seul être, mais à celui-là, sauvage* (Proust 1954: 153), (literally, 'without causing a great *douleur* to anyone except one person, but to this one person, 'wild' *douleur*') has been translated as "in death, she was greatly mourned by just one person" (Proust 1982: 119), without any mention of a "wild pain".

A few more examples of Proust's sentences with *douleur* rendered in English not with *pain* but some other words.

"Tu ne peux t'imaginer ma douleur quand je pense à toi", reprit Bloch.   (Proust 1954: 746)
'You've no idea, Bloch would say, how sad it makes me to think of you.'   (Proust 2002: 327)

Il le faisait en se plaçant non à son point de vue personnel, mais à celui même de l'être qui souffrait, point de vue d'où lui aurait fait horreur le langage de ceux qui continuent à penser à leurs petis intérêts devant la douleur d'autrui.   (Proust 1954: 559)

'He always put himself in the position of the person who was suffering; and this was a position in which he would have been horrified by the language of people who, when faced with the distress of others, go on being engrossed in their own petty concerns.'   (Proust 2002: 135)

Elle avait en ce moment leur visage abattu et navré qui semble succomber sous le poids d'une douleur trop lourde pour elle.   (Proust 1954: 280)

'She had the depressed, grief-stricken expression that seems to mean they [the women in the works of the painter of the Primavera] are burdened with some unbearable affliction.'
(Proust 2002: 222)

Même quand il ne pouvait savoir où elle était allée, il aurait suffi pour calmer l'angoisse qu' il éprouvait alors...   (Proust 1954: 253)

'When he did not manage to discover where she had gone, the anguish that beset him [pain] could even have been soothed...'   (Proust 2002: 316)

Even in European languages, therefore, the conceptualizations of human experience reflected in the English word *pain* do not have to match. A number of dimensions—such as intensity, duration, and localization, and also a focus on the body or on the person as a whole—can differ even between neighbouring and genetically and culturally related languages, such as English and French.

The greater emphasis on the physical and localized (and therefore observable) aspects of the process in English than, for example, in French parallels the differences between English expressions like *to have sex* and French expressions like *faire l'amour* ('to make love'); or between the English *sense* (as in *sense of shame* or *sense of defeat*) and the French *sentiment* ('a feeling of shame, a feeling of defeat'). This greater emphasis on what happens to a body-part rather than to the body as a whole, and to the person, is consistent with the legacy of "British empiricism" (Wierzbicka 2009c; 2010a). Localized physical pain linked with an open wound or torn tissue is easier to ascertain than a global, physical, and emotional experience.

6.7 Comparing *douleur* with *mal* (*avoir mal* and *faire mal*)

As noted earlier, alongside the global concept of *douleur*, French has also the localized concepts of *avoir mal* and *faire mal*, closer in some ways to the English verb *hurt* than to the English noun *pain*. These concepts too are worth examining in some detail, if only because they show that the concept expressed in English as *it hurts* is not a strict conceptual universal either.

While both French expressions, *j'ai mal* (lit. 'I have *mal*') and *ça fait mal* (lit. 'that makes/does *mal*') can be seen as comparable to *it hurts*, the second, which is impersonal, comes closer to it than the first, which starts with the equivalent of 'I have'. But neither *j'ai mal* nor *ça fait mal* favour external body-parts in the way *it hurts* does. For example, both can be used perfectly well with reference to the stomach, whereas, as noted earlier, people don't usually say *My stomach hurts*, instead they normally use expressions involving *ache* or *pain*.

To account for this difference between *ça fait mal* and *it hurts*, we would differentiate their explications as follows:

[L]   *Ça fait mal.*

a.   something bad is happening to a part of my body at this time
b.   I feel something bad in this part of my body because of this
c.   I don't want this

[M]   *It hurts* (=D).

a.   something is happening to a part of my body at this time
b.   because something bad happened to it a very short time before
c.   I feel something very bad in this part of my body because of this
d.   I don't want this

The 'immediate' past tense in components (a) and (b) of *It hurts* suggests an identifiable and observable event involving an observable (and therefore, presumably, external) body-part, whereas the present tense in component (a) of *ça fait mal* allows for a wider range of events, not necessarily identifiable and observable. This would explain why *ça fait mal* is more compatible with internal body-parts than *it hurts*.

Turning now to the French phrase *j'ai mal* (and, more generally, *avoir mal*), we can distinguish its meaning from that of *ça fait mal* as follows:

[N]   *Elle a mal (à l'estomac).*

a.   she feels something bad in a part of the body [stomach] at this time,
b.   like someone can feel when it is like this:
c.   something bad is happening to part of someone's body
d.   because of this, someone feels something bad in that part of the body
e.   this someone thinks at that time: "I don't want this"

This explication presents the phrase *avoir mal* as based on a prototypical cognitive scenario, bringing it a little closer to the English *to feel pain*. The only difference between explications [N] (of *avoir mal*) and [A] (of *feel pain*) is located in component (a). In the case of *pain* [A], the feeling is **prototypically** but not **necessarily** localized (as well as bodily), whereas in the case of *avoir mal*, it is necessarily so ("she feels something bad in a part of the body").

6.8 *Souffrir* and *suffer*

To complete our discussion of the French domain of "pain", we need to take at least a quick look at the verb *souffrir*, which is used in French more widely than *suffer* in English and which is often used interchangeably with *douleur* and *avoir mal* (though always with its own meaning and its own unique conceptual construal). We would articulate this construal as follows:

[O]   *Elle souffrait.*

a.   she felt something very bad at this time
b.   like someone can feel when it is like this:
c.   something very bad is happening to this someone for some time
d.   because of this, this someone feels something very bad in the body for some time
e.   this someone can't think like this during this time:
       "if I do something now, after this it will not be like this"

As compared with *douleur*, the person who *souffre* necessarily feels something very bad (component a); the prototypical cause is not necessarily bodily (c), although the feeling **is** (d); and there is no "rebellious" thought 'I don't want this' (component e). Component (e) of *souffrir* does not imply resignation on the part of the sufferer, but does suggest something like helplessness, which provides a bridge to another sense of *souffrir*, closer to 'endure' and 'undergo'.

The main difference between the French verb *souffrir* and English *to suffer* lies in the greater "physicality" of the former. Thus one can say in French *Où souffrez-vous?* whereas one cannot say in English *Where are you suffering?*. We can account for this greater physicality of *souffrir* in comparison with English *suffer* if we keep a reference to the body in component (d) of the former. Another possible dimension of difference has to do with the duration: English *suffer* appears to imply a greater time span, at least in the prototype. This suggests a contrast between 'for some time' (for *souffrir*) and 'for a long time' (for *suffer*). This leads us to the following tentative explication of the English *suffer*:

[P]   *She was suffering.*

a.   she felt something very bad for some time
b.   like someone can feel when it is like this:
c.   something very bad is happening to this someone for a long time
d.   because of this, this someone feels something very bad for a long time
e.   this someone can't think like this during this time:
       "if I do something now, after this it will not be like this"

6.9 English *pain* vs. Polish *ból* and Russian *bol'*

Bilingual dictionaries equate the English word *pain* with Polish *ból* and Russian *bol'*, but here, too, a closer inspection reveals significant differences in the conceptualization. Beginning with Polish, *ból* is usually opposed in Polish to *radość* 'joy', a word which is situated, so to speak, between *szczęście* (roughly, 'happiness') and *przyjemność* ('pleasure'). This seems to suggest that *ból* is, conceptually, halfway between the English *pain* and the French *douleur*: it is more akin to emotions than *pain* but evokes less intensity than *douleur*. In addition, there is another word in Polish, *męka*, which refers to a very great pain, and this word, too, would be normally translated into French as *douleur* (and into English, as *agony*).

As far as the localization of *ból* is concerned, the situation is somewhat complicated in Polish by morphological and phraseological factors. Thus, to refer to a strictly localized "pain", one would use the verb *boli* ('it hurts') rather than the noun *ból*. However, there are some set phrases referring to particular kinds of localized pain: *ból głowy* (a headache), *ból zęba* (a toothache), *ból gardła* (a sore throat). The phrase *ból głowy* (pain of head.GEN) does not refer to just any kind of *ból* localized in a person's head (e.g. a *ból* resulting from a head injury), but to a particular kind (what in English is called a *headache*). This suggests that *ból głowy* is a nominalization of a verbal expression (*boli mnie głowa*), not a free combination of *ból* and *głowa* ('head'). If the noun *ból* refers to a localized sensation but is not part of an established fixed phrase, the locus in the body would be usually described by means of a locative expression, rather than a genitive. For example:

ból w piersiach   a *ból* in the chest [Prep + LOC]
ból w nogach   a *ból* in the legs [Prep + LOC]
ból w kościach   a *ból* in the bones [Prep + LOC]

This suggests the following explication of *ból* (not as in the set phrases *ból głowy*, *ból zęba*, *ból gardła*, but as a free-standing noun):

[Q]   *Czuła ból* (she felt *ból*).

a.   she felt something bad at this time
b.   like someone can feel when it is like this:
c.   something bad is happening to this someone's body
d.   this someone feels something bad in the body because of this
e.   this someone can't not think like this at this time: "I don't want this"

A reference to duration ('for some time') does not seem justified in the case of *ból*, because *ból* differs in this respect from its "stronger" competitor, *męka*. *Męka* cannot be momentary, and in fact it implies not only some duration, like *douleur*, but a long duration. *Ból*, on the other hand, can be momentary, like *pain* (see Wierzbicka 2012d).

The situation in Russian is similar, with the noun *bol'* standing halfway between English *pain* and French *douleur*, referring in its prototype to a 'bad' (rather than 'very bad') feeling, and evoking a global (rather than localized) bodily feeling as its prototype. Apart from set phrases such as *golovnaja bol'* (a headache), which refer to a particular kind of localized pain, localized pain is normally referred to by means of a verb: *bolit*, comparable to English *hurts* and to French *fait mal*. As for duration, Russian *bol'* (like Polish *ból*) can be either prolonged or momentary, and it also has a "stronger" competitor, *muka*, a word which implies a long duration (as does also the plural form *boli*, very common in Russian). A difference in the conceptualization is also reflected in the contrast between the English word *painkillers* and its Russian counterpart *boleutoljajushchee* (literally, '[means for] appeasing/soothing pain').

To illustrate the lack of semantic and cultural correspondence between the use of the English word *pain* and the Russian word *bol'*, let us note that Vladimir Nabokov, who wrote his famous novel *Lolita* in English and then translated it himself into his native Russian, in many places translated *pain* as *muka* rather than *bol'* (cf. e.g. Nakhimovsky and Paperno 1982: 126–148). Evidently he felt that what would be appropriately described in English as *pain* would in Russian be more naturally described by a "stronger", more extreme word, *muka*. This fact points not only to lexicosemantic differences between English and Russian in this area but also to different cultural scripts for expressing what one feels (cf. Wierzbicka 2009a).

6.10 Concluding remarks

Everywhere in the world, people often feel something bad or even very bad. Everywhere in the world, things happen to parts of people's bodies because of which these people feel something bad in these parts of their bodies. Everywhere in the world, people can often feel something so bad in their bodies that they think something like this: 'something bad is happening to me, I don't want this.'

Speakers of English tend to think about such things in terms of the "*pain* concept", because—along with the expression *it hurts*—this is the main conceptual tool supplied to them by their language. Naturally, Anglophone psychologists and medical practitioners too tend to think about such things in such terms, and of course there is no reason why they shouldn't.

It is good to realize, however, that not all languages have a word corresponding exactly to the English word *pain*, and that other languages may offer somewhat different perspectives on the range of phenomena associated in English with the words *pain*, *hurt*, *ache*, and *sore*. In that sense, 'pain' is not a conceptual universal, even though all people feel, at times, what in English is thought of as 'pain'. From a broader cross-linguistic perspective, the English concept of 'pain' may in fact be somewhat unusual, in so far as it focuses "single-mindedly" on the subjective aspect of the experience (how a person feels), rather than on a combination of the objective and the subjective aspect (what is happening to a person and what the person feels because of this).

The fact that in many languages "pain" is described by means of a verb (comparable to *hurt*) rather than a noun (comparable to *pain*) is significant in this respect—a point made, in relation to Thai, by Fábrega and Tyma (1976*b*):

> Several grammatical features of Thai appear quite significant in this discussion of pain descriptions. First, there does not seem to be a noun form 'pain': the description of pain is totally dependent on verbal morphemes which serve the function of verbs and adjectives. [...] In Thai, then, one does not say "I have a pain" or "I have an ache", as in English, which suggests that the speaker possesses an object or entity. An implication of this is that a general pain description implies a condition which is conceived as active and dynamic. At the same time, the absence of nominal primary pain terms in Thai means that it is more difficult to qualify pain directly through metaphor as is done in English [...]: I have a burning pain [...]
>
> (pp. 328–329)

Fábrega and Tyma's insight into the "dynamic" model of painful experiences embedded in the Thai lexicon and grammar was further developed in a more detailed study of Thai "pain-talk" by Patharakorn (2010). Patharakorn's main conclusion is that Thai, in contrast to English, "construes pain primarily as a process" (p. 55), and that in Thai, "pain [...] is viewed as an active and dynamic process with the speaker's self being highly involved in the process itself" (p. 55).

From an NSM point of view, observations made in terms of phrases such as "active and dynamic" (vs. "passive" and "static") are not sufficiently precise to allow us reliable comparisons of conceptualizations embedded in different languages. They provide, however, valuable clues for more precise cross-linguistic comparisons. In particular, they suggest that in many languages speakers may tend to conceptualize their 'painful' experiences more along the lines of 'it hurts' rather than of 'I feel pain'.

Schematically, these two models (the *hurt*-like one and the *pain*-like one) can be represented as follows:

1. something bad is happening (happened) to part of my body
    I feel something bad **because of this**
2. I feel something bad,
    like someone can feel when something bad is happening to part of this someone's body

The full range of conceptual models embedded in different languages, and detectable through their dominant forms of "pain talk", is no doubt much broader. As Fábrega and Tyma (1976*b*: 323) observed, more than three decades ago:

> The phenomenon of pain touches on the whole question of how the brain and mind "read", interpret, and communicate about the body and its perceived states. It follows logically that cultures and languages are inextricably bound together with the communication of pain.

The English word *pain* does not 'cut nature at its joints'. Its meaning is a conceptual construct, perhaps not uniquely English, but not truly universal either. It is natural, and reasonable, for English-speaking students of what they think of as 'pain' to continue thinking about the phenomena in question as 'pain', and to continue using the English word *pain* as a convenient shorthand. When it comes, however, to identifying the universal aspect of the human condition which Anglophone psychology and medicine associate with the word *pain*, it is also desirable to try to understand it from other perspectives.[6]

By relying on simple and generally understandable words, the NSM methodology allows us to construct a definition of 'pain' which is not only more accessible than a technical definition but also, paradoxically perhaps, more precise and accurate. Contrary to what some professionals and specialists might think, technical words like *sensory* and *tissue* do not bring greater precision to the definitions of 'pain' than simple, non-technical words like *feel*, *body*, and *part*. The meanings of such technical words tend to be complex and to include extraneous material, irrelevant to the concept of *pain*. The exclusive use of simple concepts allows us to eliminate such intrusions and to trim the definition to its conceptual core.

As the explications of the English words *pain*, *hurt*, *ache*, and *sore* presented here show, the mini-language of simple and universal human concepts allows us to elucidate very subtle semantic distinctions drawn by particular languages. At the same time, it allows us to elucidate different perspectives entrenched in different languages, and to make them both faithful to the insiders' point of view and intelligible to outsiders.

Above all, the use of simple and universal human concepts can liberate us from the pervasive Anglocentrism entrenched in the language of contemporary science. It allows us to take a fresh look at the human condition, unencumbered by conceptual intrusions derived from modern English and especially from the technical English dominating contemporary psychology, 'emotionology', and the study of 'pain'.

---

[6] A study on 'Pain in European long-term care facilities: cross-national study in Finland, Italy, and the Netherlands' (Achterberg et al. 2010) reports that "pain is highly prevalent in long-term care facilities in Europe" and that no particular differences between Italy, Finland, and the Netherlands were found: "despite cultural and case-mix differences, pain speaks one language" (p. 70). The authors do not consider the possibility that "pain speaks one language" when questions about pain are conceptualized in, and investigated through, one language (English). There is no reference in the article to the languages in which residents of the long-term care facilities in question were interviewed or the words and expressions which were used in the interviews. Nor do the authors consider the question of possible variation in the cultural scripts for pain expression in the countries under investigation. Given this lack of attention to language and culture issues, the negative results of the study are perhaps not surprising, but they are hardly conclusive.

7

Suggesting, apologizing, complimenting

English speech-act verbs

7.1 Speech acts and speech-act verbs

Words from many areas of the lexicon can shed light on the prevailing social attitudes and values in a given culture and social setting, including words for emotions (such as, to use English examples, *happiness*, *shame*, *guilt*, and *pride*), for "sociality" concepts (*privacy*, *rude*, *nice,* etc.), kinship and other relationship words (*son*, *auntie*, *friend*, *mate*, etc.), terms of address (such as *Sir*, *mate*, *sweetie*), and conversational routines. The same goes for speech-act verbs, i.e. words such as *ask*, *suggest*, *apologize*, *thank*, *promise*, *complain*, and *congratulate*, that provide a "catalogue" of salient kinds of verbal interactions recognized in a particular culture. The words just mentioned are characteristic of contemporary Anglo culture. Cross-linguistic research shows that there is great cross-linguistic variation in the number of speech-act verbs in particular languages, and in their character; cf. Ameka (1999; 2006; 2009) on Ewe, Goddard (2002*b*; 2004*a*) on Malay, Wierzbicka (2003*a*[1991]; 2012*a*; 2012*c*) on English and Russian, Maher (2002) on Italian, and Pedersen (2010) on Swedish. The English language is unusual in having literally hundreds of speech-act verbs, apparently outdoing the other languages of Europe in this respect, let alone most languages from other parts of the world. In other words, the English speech-act lexicon is an area of great lexical elaboration, with many fine-grained meaning differences; consider, for example, *suggest* vs. *recommend*, *promise* vs. *guarantee*, *praise* vs. *compliment*, *insult* vs. *abuse*, *refuse* vs. *decline*.

Though there are many different subclasses of speech-act verbs, most of them work by characterizing the kind of message that the speaker has expressed and linking this with an apparent mental state (wants, thoughts, assumptions). For example, if I say that someone *ordered* me to do something, I am saying, first, that this someone has expressed a message with the content 'I want you to do such-and-such', and, second, that this someone said it as if he or she assumed that I had no choice but to do it and that I recognized this. On the other hand, to say that someone *asked* me to do such-and-such involves attributing more or less the same message, but with different assumptions; roughly, acknowledging that I can choose not to do it if I wish. Other speech-act verbs, such as *marry, sentence, sack,* and *veto,* incorporate reference to culture-specific social roles, institutions, and situations.

Speech-act verbs have been a long-standing topic of interest in the philosophy of language, mainly because, as J. L. Austin (1962) observed in his seminal *How to Do Things With Words,* some speech-act verbs have the property that by using them in a certain way one can actually perform the speech act itself. For example, if I say *I promise to be there tomorrow,* then I have actually *promised.* Likewise, by saying *I apologize* or *I bet you she'll be there,* one can actually *apologize* or *bet.* Verbs that can be used in this fashion, i.e. with a first-person subject, in the present tense, with the effect of carrying out the speech act designated by the verb itself, are known as performative verbs. One of the great challenges of speech-act semantics is to explain how performative verbs can do their work, and also why it is that many speech-act verbs cannot be used performatively, but only descriptively (like ordinary verbs); for example, one can describe how someone said something by saying that he or she *threatened* to do something or *boasted* about something, but the verbs *threaten* and *boast* cannot be used performatively (**I threaten...*, **I boast...*).

Many philosophers (and later, many literary theorists) became very enthusiastic about the concept of "speech acts" because it seemed to offer some relief from the one-dimensional view of verbal interaction as a mere form of "information exchange". Speaking could be seen as a form of social action. But remarkably, to this day the philosophical literature on "speech act theory" remains strongly Anglo-centric in character, in two respects. First, there is little or no awareness of the fact that speech-act verbs differ in meaning across languages; in a recent review article, for example, Tsohatzidis (2010) does not mention a single language other than English. Second, English speech-act verbs are treated, either explicitly or by default, as representing natural categories of social interaction. Linguists have sometimes behaved better in this respect, but there are still many linguistic discussions, including textbooks, such as Fromkin et al. (2012: 181–182), that discuss speech acts in general without reference to any cross-linguistic data (as if all languages could be expected to have equivalents to English words such as *request, promise,* and *apology*). The branch of linguistics known as contrastive pragmatics is a partial exception in this respect, inasmuch as it recognizes that speech acts can be "realized" differently in different languages and cultures. Thus, there are numerous studies of how 'request-ing', 'complimenting', 'thanking', and 'apologizing' are done differently in Spanish and Polish (say), as opposed to English (e.g. Blum-Kulka, House, and Kasper 1989; Blum-Kulka and Kasper 1993; Pütz and Neff-van Aertselaer 2008). This is all well and good, but the irony is that the field still largely accepts English-specific verbs as labels for the categories (or pseudo-categories) being investigated.

In both philosophy of language and linguistic pragmatics, "definitions" of speech acts are almost always flawed by obscurity and implicit circularity—as for example when a key component of *promising* is identified as "undertaking an obligation". There is no reason to believe that 'obligation' is any simpler in its meaning than 'promise' in the first place; and, as for 'undertake', it is just as much a speech act as 'promise'. Overall, therefore, this is defining *per obscurum*. The same goes for other "definitions" in the literature, such as 'express gratitude' for *thank*, and 'attribute credit to' for *praise*. Even ignoring the obscurity and circularity, definitions like these are not sufficiently fine-grained to capture the differences between neighbouring speech-act verbs, such as *praise* vs. *compliment*.

The main exceptions to the shortcomings that have just been reviewed are works in the NSM framework, beginning with Wierzbicka's (1987*b*) *English Speech Act Verbs: A Semantic Dictionary*. This unprecedented work proposed detailed semantic explications for over 250 speech-act verbs, backed by naturally occurring examples from literature and everyday usage. The metalanguage in which the explications were framed has since been greatly improved, however, making it possible to produce improved explications. In addition, the emerging theory of semantic templates provides an enriched approach to characterizing verbal subclasses and linking semantic properties with grammatical ones.

This brings us to a final theme that animates the present chapter: the search for possible semantic correlates of the grammar of speech-act verbs. This also is something of a neglected topic in mainstream linguistics, which has devoted much more attention to "verbs of doing" than to "verbs of saying". Nevertheless, it is a fact that English speech-act verbs have an intriguing set of variable grammatical properties. For example, as mentioned, some can be used performatively (e.g. *I promise I'll...*, *I order you to...*), while others can not (e.g. **I complain...*, **I insult you...*). A second intriguing property is that some speech-act verbs have the addressee in a *to*-phrase (like SAY itself, in this respect), but many others take an "accusative" addressee. Compare: *suggest **to** him/her* vs. *tell him/her*; *complain **to** him/her* vs. *insult him/her*.

7.2 Approaching speech-act verbs, NSM style

As we know from other chapters, the goal of NSM lexical-semantic analysis is to find a satisfactory reductive paraphrase (explication) for the expression being analysed. To achieve the maximum granularity in the analysis, and to guard against circularity and Anglocentrism, the explications rely on a controlled vocabulary of 65 universal semantic primes. A good explication will be well-formed and internally coherent, account for the range of use (distribution) of the word in question, generate the appropriate implications and entailments, and satisfy native speaker intuitions.

TABLE 7.1 **Seven syntactic frames for semantic prime** SAY

I SAY: – – –	[performative frame]
someone SAYS: " – – – "	[direct speech frame]
someone SAYS something	[minimal frame]
someone SAYS something to someone	[addressee frame]
someone SAYS something about something/someone else	[locutionary topic frame]
someone SAYS (some) words to someone else	[directed words frame]
someone SAYS something (not) with words	[verbal means frame]

The semantic foundation of all speech-act verbs is the semantic prime SAY, which many studies have indicated is a lexical-semantic universal. The same applies to another semantic prime in the verbal arena, WORDS, though this is more controversial (cf. Goddard 2011a). The semantic prime WORDS is only needed in the explications of a minority of speech-act verbs, however. The universal grammatical frames for SAY can be tabulated as in Table 7.1.

As we will see, with the exception of the final frame (which is utilized in explications for concepts connected with non-verbal communication), all these frames are needed in explications for different speech-act verbs. Other semantic ingredients of speech-act verbs include the following semantic primes: substantives: I, YOU, SOMEONE, PEOPLE, SOMETHING; the mental predicates WANT, KNOW, THINK, and FEEL, along with the basic predicates DO and HAPPEN; specifiers and quantifiers: THIS, OTHER~ELSE, THE SAME, SOME, MUCH~MANY; the similarity prime LIKE, with its English allolexes AS and WAY; the evaluators GOOD and BAD, and intensifier VERY; and various temporal and logical elements: WHEN~TIME, NOW, AFTER, BECAUSE, CAN, IF, NOT.

7.3 Some English "directives": *order, tell, ask, suggest, recommend*

At least seven subclasses of English speech-act verbs can be identified on the basis of both meaning and grammar, each associated with a different semantic template. In this chapter we will concentrate on two of the most "populous" templates, beginning with the one below. As shown, this template consists of three sections. The top section is the Lexico-Syntactic Frame. This makes it clear that the verb is a "verb of saying", whereby one person says something to an addressee. The parenthesized second line of this frame ('this someone wanted something to happen because of it') appears to correlate with verbs, e.g. *order, tell, thank*, that take the addressee expression without any preposition, as a kind of grammatical object. Next comes the Dictum (from Latin 'thing said') section, which characterizes the content of the speaker's message, and finally the section titled Apparent Mental State, which spells out the psychological state that is being attributed to the speaker.

Speech-act verb template I ("saying something like this to someone else, like someone can say when...")

someone X —— someone Y (e.g. ordered, suggested, asked, apologized,...)

someone X said something to someone else Y at that time	LEXICO-SYNTACTIC FRAME
(this someone wanted something to happen because of it)	
this someone said something like this:	DICTUM
" _ _ _ "	
this someone said it like someone can say something like this	APPARENT
to someone else when this someone thinks like this:	MENTAL STATE
" _ _ _ "	

Most of the verbs that fall under this template can be used performatively. As we shall see shortly, this involves a systematic mapping to a simpler meaning in which the mental state is expressed explicitly.

To see how this template works in practice, we can look at a sample of directive verbs—*order, tell, ask, suggest*—which are often viewed as differing merely in their "strength" or "directness". In fact, the differences involve qualitatively different illocutionary assumptions and intentions. Let's begin with *order*, in uses where the person being addressed appears as the direct object of the verb, as in the examples below (examples in this chapter are from *Collins Wordbanks Online*). Notice that we are not considering the more specialized use of *ordering* food or drink in a restaurant or pub, nor the syntactic frame with an action noun as its direct object, as in *She ordered an investigation/search*, etc.

- Police said a man entered the store armed with a revolver and **ordered** the attendant to lie on the floor.
- After parking his car, he steamed towards the front door of the building and **ordered** the cameramen to "get out of my way".
- What makes you think you can **order** me around?

When someone gives an *order*, they seem to express the assumption that the addressee has no choice but to do as they are told. In addition, however, the illocutionary assumption seems to involve the addressee's recognition or acceptance of this fact. This can be seen if *order* is contrasted with *command*, a speech act which is expected to trigger an immediate, semi-automatic response. Admittedly, the difference is subtle, but it sounds more natural to speak of giving a dog or a horse a *command* than an *order*—a fact which makes sense if *order* implies an appeal to the addressee's consciousness. Even in military contexts, where both verbs can be used freely, *order* sounds better than *command* if there is any direct or implicit appeal to the subordinates' consciousness of their own subordination. For example, *That's an order, soldier!* sounds far more natural than *That's a command, soldier* (Wierzbicka 1987b: 37–39).

From these considerations we arrive at the explication below. Note that in most cases of *ordering* the explicit dictum 'I want you to do this' is conveyed by use of a bare imperative form.

[A]   *X ordered Y to do something (A).*

a.   someone X said something to someone else Y at that time
       this someone wanted something to happen because of it
b.   this someone said something like this:
         "I want you to do this (A)"
c.   this someone said it like someone can say something like this to someone else
         when this someone thinks like this:
           "I know that because I say this, after this, this someone can't not do it
           this someone knows the same"

Now, how can the explication for the descriptive use of *order*, given above, be adapted for when the verb is used performatively? The following explication shows how, and the adaptation it illustrates represents a general pattern which can be described as follows. In a performative use the speaker expresses directly the characteristic content of the Dictum, and in addition explicitly expresses the attitudinal components, in an "I-to-you" style of expression. This explains why, as Searle (1969) puts it, the performative use of a speech act is the most explicit "illocutionary force indicating device" (IFID).

[B]   *I order you to do this (A).*

a.   I say this now: "I want you to do this (A)"
b.   I know that because I say this, after this, you can't not do it
c.   you know the same

We can compare *order* with *tell* in its directive meaning, i.e. *tell to do.* (*Tell* also has an "informative" meaning, i.e. *tell that.*) Unlike *order*, *tell* is a common, versatile, and stylistically plain word. Here are examples:

– He grabbed Nicole and **told** her to get out of the house.
– I **told** him [a taxi driver] to take me to Selkirk in Scotland.
– He **told** the jury to disregard testimony on the two items.

Explication [C] portrays *tell* as expressing the same dictum as *order*, i.e. 'I want you to do this', but with a different apparent attitude. Rather than appearing to assume that the addressee is obliged to (i.e. 'can't not') do as the speaker says, the assumption is simply that the addressee **will** do as the speaker says, once he or she knows what the speaker wants him/her to do. The fact that the speaker's message includes an informative component ('I want you to know it') provides a link with the other, informative, sense of *tell*. It may also be responsible for the fact that, unlike *order*, *tell* always requires an addressee argument. Thus, one cannot say *'Silence', he told* in the same way that one can say *'Silence', he ordered*.

[C] *X told Y to do something (A).*

a. someone X said something to someone else Y at that time
    this someone wanted something to happen because of it
b. this someone said something like this:
    "I want you to do this (A)
    I want you to know it"
c. this someone said it like someone can say something like this to someone else
    when this someone thinks like this:
    "I know that after I say this, this someone will do it because of this"

Assuming that someone will do as one wants may be culturally appropriate in certain situations, but there are many situations in contemporary Anglo culture where speakers wish to disavow such an assumption, i.e. where the speaker's apparent attitude is, roughly speaking, "I don't know if you will do this". Such is the apparent attitude of someone who *asks* (rather than *tells*) someone else to do something. How can such an attitude be conveyed while at the same time expressing the message that 'I want you to do something'?

The Anglo solution is to embed the directive content into a more complex message that simultaneously expresses uncertainty about the addressee's response (Wierzbicka 2003a[1991]; 2006a; 2006d). It is this expressed uncertainty that accounts for the otherwise curious fact that the verb *ask* can be used to report such speech acts (when its other meaning is to depict an information-seeking speech act, i.e. *asking* a question). In other European languages with a "requesting" verb, this verb is quite distinct from the verb for information-seeking.

Here are some examples:

– I **asked** the police to get these kids out of the station, because I felt threatened.
– Most "fancy" restaurants do not advertise takeout but if you **ask** nicely they will do it.
– "Can I come in?" he **asked**.

Consider the following explication for English *ask*, in its "directive" sense.

[D] *X asked Y to do something (A).*

a. someone X said something to someone else Y at that time
    this someone wanted something to happen because of it
b. this someone said something like this:
    "I want you to do this (A), it will be good if you do it
    maybe after this, you will do it
    I don't know, I want to know"

c.   this someone said it like someone can say something like this to someone else
      when this someone thinks like this:
          maybe after I say this, this someone will do it because of this,
          I don't know

We have already discussed the Apparent Mental State section of the explication, but now let us look at the Dictum in more detail. It consists firstly of the same 'I want you to do this' component that is found with *order* and *tell*; but with *ask* this component is paired with 'it will be good if you do it'. The idea is that part of the impression conveyed by *ask* is that the speaker is implying that there is some benefit or value to be realized if the addressee does what is asked. Next in the Dictum comes the component acknowledging the possibility that the addressee will do it ('maybe after this, you will do it'), followed immediately by the third component that expresses uncertainty ('I don't know') and a wish to know ('I want to know'). It is these components that are responsible for the fact that *asking* someone to do something is often (but not invariably) done using a question form.

Now to a verb which, even more than *ask*, can be seen as a hallmark of contemporary English and contemporary Anglo culture, namely, *suggest*. Wierzbicka (2006d) argues that English is unique among European languages not only in possessing a speech-act verb with the precise semantics of *suggest*, but also in having developed a whole range of "suggestive" strategies and formulas. Nothing could be more helpful for many immigrants from non-English speaking countries, she suggests, than learning how to *ask* properly and to *suggest* properly. Otherwise, they run the risk of being perceived as *rude*, *pushy*, *demanding*, and so on. Here are some examples of *suggest* in descriptive uses.

– "Well, then, supposing we go and call on him," **suggested** the Mole.
– "Maybe you should just drop the whole thing and cut your losses," she **suggested**.
– "How about going to see a doctor?" Harry **suggested**.

A *suggestion* is a mild, unassuming speech act, even to the point that, so far as the expressed Dictum is concerned, there is no component 'I want you to do this'. Rather, the speaker expresses the message that it can be good if the addressee does something and, accordingly, that it can be good if the addressee thinks about doing it. There is no assumption that the addressee will necessarily do it. On the contrary, as with *ask* (and consistent with the frequent use of interrogative forms, such as *How about...?* and *Why don't you..?*, for *suggesting*, as well as for *asking*), the speaker appears to wish to disclaim any such assumption. To help capture the difference between the two speech acts, explication [E] for *suggest* includes a further, final component, that acknowledges the addressee's freedom to do as he or she wishes. (Note that the frame explicated below oversimplifies the possible range of roles involved in *suggesting*. It is quite possible for *X to suggest to Y that Z do A*, but for the sake of simplicity we assume that the addressee and the prospective actor are the same.)

[E]   *X suggested to Y (that Y do A).*

a.   someone X said something to someone else Y at that time

b.   this someone said something like this:
  "it can be good if you do this (A), it can be good if you think about it"

c.   this someone said it like someone can say something like this to someone else
  when this someone thinks like this:
   maybe this someone will do it after this, I don't know
   I know that if this someone wants not to do it, this someone can not do it"

To get a clearer impression of the precise content of the attitude attributed to someone when we say that this someone *suggested* something, it is helpful to look at the performative use of *suggest* (i.e. its use in the formula *I suggest...*). This is because, as mentioned earlier, in performative uses all the illocutionary components are expressed directly.

[F]   *I suggest that you do this (A).*

a.   I say this now:
  "it can be good if you do this (A), it can be good if you think about it"

b.   maybe you will do it after this, I don't know

c.   I know that if you want not to do it, you can not do it

Finally, let us look at one further verb in the directive lexicon of English speech acts, *recommend*. Here are some examples.

- A retired judge has **recommended** that Thomson be sacked as national coach as soon as possible.
- We know from a study of 1000 cancer specialists in the United States that 44 per cent of the doctors had already **recommended** to at least one patient that they smoke cannabis.

Recommend provides a nice counterpoint to *suggest*, because someone who *recommends* (like someone who *suggests*) does not express the message 'I want you to do something', but rather a message about the possible value or benefit of doing something. In the case of *recommend*, this message is embedded in a complex configuration that involves the speaker recognizing that the addressee wants to do something, informing the addressee of his/her appraisal of what it would be best to do, and at the same time assuming the position of someone who is knowledgeable about the topic (and whose appraisal should therefore be taken seriously). As for the

Apparent Mental State component, the explication below presents it as a little less "cautious" than that for *suggest*, but as sharing the component that recognizes the addressee's freedom not to follow the recommended course of action.

[G]   *X recommended to Y that Y do A.*

a.   someone X said something to someone else Y at that time
b.   this someone said something like this:
    "I know that you want to do something at some time after this
    I want you to know that I think like this about it:
        "it will be good for you if you do this (A)
        I know much (many things) about things like this"
c.   this someone said it like someone can say something like this to someone else
    when this someone thinks like this:
        "I know that if this someone wants not to do it, this someone can not do it"

This by no means exhausts the inventory of directive and quasi-directive speech-act verbs in English, even common ones. Of those that we haven't covered, perhaps the most significant is *advise* (and related expressions such as *give advice*). For a cross-linguistic study, see Wierzbicka (2012a).

7.4 "Commissives" and related speech acts: *promise, offer, threaten,* and *warn*

The word *promise* is the canonical example of a non-institutional speech-act verb, partly because it was treated extensively by Searle (1965) in an early influential study. It is generally taken as the exemplar of a class of "commissives", so called because they are held to "commit the speaker to some course of action". We restrict ourselves to the frame *promise to (do)*. (*Promise* can also occur in the frame *promise that*, e.g. *I promise that you won't regret it.*) Needless to say, such a characterization leaves a great deal to be desired, if only because it hinges on the complex expression 'commit'. So, can we do better? First, here are some examples:

– He **promised** to pay me back tomorrow.
– "I'll do better tomorrow," I **promise**.
– You have to let me go (to the party). You **promised**!

It seems clear that someone only *promises* to do something when he or she feels that the addressee needs some reassurance or some convincing about it. In other words, to *promise* seems to assume a degree of doubt or uncertainty in the mind of the addressee, dispelling which is, or at least can be, the motivation behind making the *promise*. In view of this, it is clear that a key part of the speaker's message is 'I want you to know that I will do this after this time'. Further, the speaker wants the addressee to accept that he or she (the promiser) sees him- or herself as compelled or obliged to carry out the action, i.e. another part of the speaker's message is: 'I want you to know that I think about it like this: "I can't not do it."' This might seem to be enough, but as various observers have pointed out, someone who *promises* seems to be recognizing that some significance attaches to the issuing of the *promise* as such, that some kind of social sanction or moral discredit will be incurred if the promiser does not make good on the promise. Various proposals have been made in the NSM literature about exactly how this is best captured (e.g. Goddard 1998: 146–147). The proposal embodied in the explication below is that the required effect comes from the final part of the Dictum, namely, 'if I don't do it, this will be very bad'.

The explications below are for the descriptive and performative uses of *promise*, respectively. Note that the speaker's apparent assumption that the addressee wants the speaker to do it but (as the speaker sees it) could be open to doubt, is conveyed in the Apparent Mental State section. The wording of the component ('I know that this someone can think that I do it') does not necessarily imply that the speaker appears to think that such doubt or uncertainty is real, only that it is a possibility.

[H]   *X promised Y (to do A) at that time.*

a.   someone X said something to someone else Y at that time
      this someone wanted something to happen because of it
b.   this someone said something like this:
         "I want you to know that I will do this (A) after this time
         I want you to know that I think about it like this: 'I can't not do it,
            if I don't do it, this will be very bad'"
c.   this someone said it like someone can say something like this to someone else
         when this someone thinks like this:
         "I know that this someone wants me to do this
         I know that this someone can think that I won't do it
         I don't want this someone to think like this"

[I]   *I promise to do A.*

a.   I say this to you now:
         "I want you to know that I will do this (A) after this time
         I think about it like this: 'I can't not do it,
            if I don't do it, this will be very bad'"
b.   I know that you want me to do this
c.   I know that you can think that I won't do it
d.   I don't want you to think like this

In the literature, *promise* is often compared with *threaten*, partly because threats are sometimes issued using the performative formula *I promise*, and partly because *threatening*, like *promising*, hinges on a projected future act of the speaker. It is a considerable overstatement to say, however, that the only difference between *promise* (*vow, pledge, guarantee*, and others) and *threaten* is whether or not the speaker's future act is wanted or unwanted by the addressee (as stated by Palmer 1986: 115). An equally important difference is that someone who *threatens* is by no means obligated to carry out the threat. As Thomas Hobbes (1651, quoted in Traugott 1993: 348) put it: "though the promise of good, bind the promiser; yet threats, that is to say, promises of evil, bind them not." For this reason, one can hardly regard *threaten* as a "commissive" speech act at all. Before we turn to *threaten*, therefore, and to its "neighbour" *warn*, we would do well to consider at least one speech-act verb whereby a speaker does indeed commit him or herself to some future action or situation. We will consider *offer* (other related verbs are *vow, swear (to), pledge*, and *guarantee*).

To *offer* to do something implies declaring oneself able to do something that can be good for the addressee and as being willing to do it, if the addressee wants one to do it. In terms of apparent attitude, the speaker appears to be conscious of the possibilities that the addressee either may or may not want the speaker to do it (i.e. to either *accept* or *decline* the offer). Here are some examples, followed by the proposed explication.

- She **offered** to drive us back to the hotel afterwards if needed.
- Oracle Corp has **offered** a job to Mark Hurd, the former chief executive of Hewlett-Packard.
- He **offered** to give me a pearl necklace.

Collocations which pair *offer* with "positive outcome" words like *job, services, help, advice*, and *explanation*, are common.

[J]   X *offered (to do A)*.
a.   someone X said something to someone else at that time
b.   this someone said something like this:
      "I can do something (A) after this
      I think about it like this: 'if I do it, this can be good for you'
      if you want me to do it, I will do it
      if you say something like this 'I want you to do it', I will do it
c.   this someone said it like someone can say something like this
      to someone else when this someone thinks like this:
        "maybe this someone wants it"

Explication [J], especially its "open-ended" Apparent Mental State components, strongly imply that the speaker is interested in learning what the addressee wants, but the explication stops short of any explicit 'I want to know' component. This is compatible with the fact that *offering* is typically done in the declarative voice, using a modal and/or conditional construction, and not typically in interrogative form. At the same time, it is compatible with the possibility of *offering* using an interrogative; for example, an utterance like *Would you like me to show you around the campus? I'm free this afternoon and it would be no trouble* could be reported using *offer*, e.g. *He offered to show me around the campus.*

Now let us turn to *threaten*, which, as mentioned, is often regarded as a kind of negative and non-performative counterpart of *promise*. Here are some examples of the *threaten to* construction. (There is another syntactic frame with the addressee as direct object and an optional *with*-phrase, e.g. *They threatened me with expulsion from the school. Threaten* also has uses not as a speech act, e.g. *Climate change threatens to destabilize economy.*)

- Teachers have **threatened** to boycott literacy and numeracy tests if school "league tables" aren't stopped.
- Kerry Packer **threatened** to kill me over Fairfax deal: Malcolm Turnbull.
- My wife has **threatened** to keep my kids from me unless I agree to go to marriage counselling with her.

What is the Dictum of *threatening*? It might seem at first that it has a conditional structure ("do this or else"), and it is true that textual examples of *threaten* often include an *if*-clause or an *or*-construction (e.g. *If you don't do it, I'll send you to your room; Do it now or you'll be grounded for a week*) to make it explicit that the speaker is trying to get the addressee to do (or not do) something. At other times, a quasi-directive motivation is implicit. For example, *I'll smack you* can be a threat if, for instance, both mother and child know that the child is not supposed to touch the flowers on the dinner table, and the mother sees the child reaching for them. Nevertheless, there are some instances of *threaten* where the speaker's motivation can be unclear, e.g. *Yesterday a trouble-maker in my class threatened to kill me.*

In explication [K] below, the Dictum of *threaten* is depicted simply as: 'I can do something (A) after this; if I do it, it will be very bad for you.' The wording of the dictum is compatible with an example such as *He threatened to kill himself.* The first line of the Apparent Mental State component ('I want this someone to feel something bad when this someone thinks about this') implies a menacing tone, while the next two lines imply that the unpleasant prospect is being used as leverage to get the addressee to do something, but without being specific about what this might be. Unlike as with *promise*, the verb *threaten* has a final negative evaluation component: 'it is bad if someone says something like this to someone else in this way.' Other speech-act verbs which convey negative evaluations (of various kinds) include *lie*, *slander*, *nag*, *boast*, *blackmail*, *condone*, and *whinge* (AustEng).

[K]   *X threatened (to do A).*

a.   someone X said something to someone else at that time

b.   this someone said something like this:
      "I can do something (A) after this
      if I do it, this will be very bad for you"

c.   this someone said it like someone can say something like this
      to someone else when this someone thinks like this:
          'I want this someone to feel something bad when this someone thinks about this
          I want this someone to do something because of this
          I know that this someone doesn't want to do it'

d.   it is bad if someone says something like this in this way

Coming now to *warn*, for the sake of comparison with *threaten* and *promise*, we will confine ourselves to the *warn (not) to do* construction (and its close partner, *warn against* doing something). It should be noted, however, that *warn* can be used in several other syntactic frames; most notably, one can *warn that* something will happen, as in *She warned me that they were coming* (cf. Wierzbicka 1987b: 177). Here are some examples of the constructions we are interested in.

– Tony Blair has disclosed that his great-grandmother had **warned** him not to marry a Catholic.
– They also **warned** him not to mention the incident.
– He had **warned** her not to sprint at the beginning, to save her energy.
– Her mom **warned** her against marriage.

True warnings (see below) are protective and well-intentioned, but a warning can be, in a sense, disinterested; that is, the speaker need not personally want the addressee to do or not do the relevant action. For instance, my doctor can *warn* me to give up smoking without necessarily conveying the message that he or she wants me to give up smoking. The focus is rather on me. The message is that I should give up smoking for my own good.

Clearly, if someone *warns* me to do or not do something, they (purport to) believe that if I do something, something bad might befall me. It would not be right to formulate the intention in terms of knowing (e.g. to assign warnings an 'informative' intention such as 'I want you to know this'), if only because warnings don't have to convey new information. A warning can be prefaced by *remember*, as in *Remember, this stuff is dangerous. Be careful how you handle it*. The point of *warning* seems to be focused not on what I know, but on what I am thinking about. The person *warning* me seems to want me to think about what I am going to do, to keep something in mind.

What about the Dictum? As noted by Searle (1969: 67), most *warnings* seem to contain or imply an *if*-clause, a condition. Suppose, for example, that you tell me

You'd better be careful to lock your car. There've been lots of break-ins lately. Have you *warned* me to lock my car? Perhaps your utterance could be viewed in that way, but it could also be seen as merely some good advice. If, on the other hand, you articulate a condition and a possible bad consequence there can be no doubt that you have given me a *warning*. For example, both *Better lock your car. If you don't, it might not be here when you get back* and *Lock your car or it won't be there when you get back* are unambiguously *warnings*. Thus, it can be argued that part of the dictum of *warn* is: 'if you do (or: don't do) something, something bad can happen to you.' Notice that it seems more natural to cast the dictum of *warn* in terms of not doing, rather than doing. Admittedly, *warnings* framed in the positive do occur (e.g. *Be careful, you might fall!*), but even in cases like these, there is still an implicit message not to do something (in this case, it is implicit in the word *careful*; roughly, 'Don't stop thinking about what you are doing').

These observations lead to the explication below.

[L]   *X warned Y not to do something (A) (e.g. touch that button).*

a.   someone X said something to someone else Y at that time
      this someone wanted something to happen because of it
b.   this someone said something like this:
         "if you do this (A), something bad can happen to you
         I want you to think about this"
c.   this someone said it like someone can say something like this to someone else
         when this someone thinks like this:
            "I don't want something bad to happen to this someone"

An interesting fact about *warn* is that it can function as a "pseudo-performative" to issue not a *warning*, but a *threat*; for instance, when an assailant says *I'm warning you* (or: *I warn you*). *One word and you're dead.* That these are not true *warnings* can easily be confirmed by a formal test, as well as by native-speaker assessments. The formal test is that, unlike genuine performatives, such sentences cannot be trans-posed (truthfully) into past tense descriptive uses; for example, the sentence just mentioned could not be reported as *He warned me to keep quiet.* Considering the content of its dictum (indicating that something bad can happen and urging the addressee to think about it), the pseudo-performative use of *warn* for *threatening* makes perfect sense.

7.5 "Expressives": *apologize, thank, complain*

With some imprecision, verbs like *apologize, thank,* and even *complain* (along with *congratulate* and some others) can be termed expressives, in the sense that the component 'I feel something (good/bad)' forms part of their Dictum. Though all three of them may seem "plain and natural" from an English speaker's point of view, they are in fact highly culture-specific. As we will see, *apologize* arguably lacks equivalents even in some European languages, such as German, let alone in the languages of more distant cultures. The speech act of *apology* has also assumed considerable importance in Anglophone political discourse.

Here are some examples of the verb.

- Hennessey **apologized** to the policeman, saying: "I am sorry."
- The school has **apologized** to parents for showing a pornographic film by mistake.
- We **apologize** for the inconvenience.

What does a speaker express when he or she *apologizes*, i.e. what is the Dictum of *apologizing*? A naïve first response is that *apologizing* means 'saying sorry', and it is true of course that the words *I'm sorry* can be, and often are, used when making an apology. But until and unless we have a clear idea of what *sorry* means (in this context), such an explanation does not get us far; and furthermore, it is possible to use the words *I'm sorry* to express regret or sympathy, without *apologizing*. Clearly, however, in all its uses the word *sorry* implies that the speaker feels something bad, and this is surely part of the Dictum of *apologizing*. Perhaps, then, *apologizing* is saying that one feels something bad for (on account of) something that one has done? But this would leave the addressee out of the picture. Better to say that the speaker's bad feeling comes from knowing about the bad effect (or potential bad effect) that one's action has had on the addressee. Explication [M] gives the dictum as: 'I know that you can feel something bad because I did something, I want you to know that I feel something bad because of this.' A fine point of detail about this wording is the presence of 'can' in the first component of the Dictum: it does not necessarily imply that one believes that the addressee was hurt, offended, etc., but it does imply that they could have been.

The focus on the addressee's possible bad feelings links in naturally with the apparent motivation behind *apologizing*: the speaker wants to soften any possible bad feeling that the addressee has towards the speaker (hence the role of *apologizing* in the process of reconciliation).

[M]   *X apologized to Y (for doing A).*

a.   someone X said something to someone else Y at that time
b.   this someone said something like this:
      "I feel something bad now because I think like this:
        'I did something (A) before, you can feel something bad because of it'"
c.   this someone said it like someone can say something like this to someone else
      when this someone thinks like this:
        "I know that this someone can feel something bad towards me
        I don't want this"

It might be objected that someone who *apologizes* must be admitting having done something bad, not merely accepting responsibility for doing something that could induce bad feeling in the addressee. From ordinary usage, however, it would seem that admitting "wrong doing", so to speak, is not necessarily implied by *apologizing*. Consider, for example, public signs that *apologize* for the inconvenience of building works in progress. The authorities who put up such signs are surely not characterizing their construction activities as 'doing something bad'. Or consider how ordinary it is to hear someone say: *If I've done something to offend you, I apologize.* Such a person is clearly ready to accept responsibility for causing the addressee to feel something bad, but this does not necessarily entail any real admission of fault.

Given the importance of the performative formula *I apologize*, it is useful to see an explication. As usual, it is adapted from the descriptive explication by the use of the 'I say' performative frame, with the message being re-cast into an "I-to-you" mode of expression, and the mental state components being directly expressed (not merely attributed).

[N]   *I apologize (for doing A).*

a.   I say this to you now:
         "I feel something bad now because I think like this:
            'I did something (A) before, you can feel something bad because of it'"
b.   I know that you can feel something bad towards me now
c.   I don't want this

In cross-cultural perspective, the semantic content of *apologize* seems quite peculiar: it focuses on the possible "hurt feelings" of the addressee, but avoids direct admission of having done something bad; it expresses the wish that the addressee not feel bad towards the speaker but stops short of seeking forgiveness; nor does it include any acknowledgment of indebtedness or commitment to changed behaviour in the future. The speaker's prior act is not characterized as 'I did something bad'. Three thumbnail comparisons with other languages can help bring out these points. The German expression *sich entschuldigen*, by contrast, does seem to imply an admission of something like "guilt" (as implied by the morphology: *Schuld* 'guilt'). Interestingly, German public signs do not use *sich entschuldigen* or related words to "apologize" for inconvenience; rather, they thank the public for their 'understanding' (*Verständnis*). The Malay expression *minta maaf* (lit.) 'ask for pardon', expresses a direct appeal to the addressee. The Japanese verb *ayamaru* acknowledges real adverse effect on the addressee and the need for the speaker to do something to compensate for it.

The striking cross-linguistic differences between *apologize* and comparable verbs in other languages makes it particularly ironic that "apology" has been widely adopted as a category for cross-cultural comparison. The same applies to another English-specific expressive, namely, *thank.*

Consider these examples.

- He **thanked** them for their efforts.
- He apologized to the fans and **thanked** them for their prayers and their support.
- I want to **thank** you again for all your help when I was in California last year.

It should be noted that the speech-act verb *thank* is not in a direct semantic relationship with the formula *Thank you*. There are many occasions where someone has said *thank you*, for instance, in routine service encounters, that would not naturally or normally be reported using the verb *thank*, e.g. by saying *She thanked him*.

The explication presents the Dictum of *thanking*, firstly, as acknowledging that the addressee did something 'because you wanted to do something good for me'. That is, from the speaker's (purported) point of view, it is not only the act that counts, but also the addressee's (imputed) good intention. Along with this, the speaker says, 'I feel something good now because I think like this.' These Dictum components are shared, or substantially shared, with the words *gratitude* and *appreciation* (Wierzbicka 1999a: 104–106), which accounts for the close links between these words and *thank*. It should be noted, therefore, that the Apparent Mental State components of *thank* take the overall meaning content beyond simply 'expressing gratitude' or 'expressing appreciation'. Someone who *thanks* is not merely acknowledging their good feelings about a well-intentioned act: they appear to be experiencing a directed good feeling 'towards' the addressee, and, furthermore, to want the addressee to know this.

[O]   *X thanked Y (for . . .).*

a.   someone X said something to someone else Y at that time
       this someone wanted something to happen because of it
b.   this someone said something like this:
       "I feel something good now because I think like this:
           'you did something before, because
           you wanted to do something good for me'"
c.   this someone said it like someone can say something like this to someone else
       when this someone thinks like this:
           "I feel something good towards this someone now
           I want this someone to know it"

Note that this explication contains no components to the effect that the addressee did not have to do it, or that the act was unexpected, or that the act was beyond the speaker's capacity. Comparisons with the nearest equivalents of *thank* in other languages suggest that the English verb is quite culture-specific in this respect.

The verb *complain* is polysemous. We will explicate the meaning *complain about* (not *complain of*), i.e. the meaning that corresponds to the noun *complaint* in its non-medical sense. For example:

- We **complained** about it [bad service] but it was the same the next day.
- She is always **complaining** about the people at her work.
- There's no point in **complaining** about the weather.

Both the Dictum and the Apparent Mental State components of *complain* require careful phrasing in order to match the range of use of the word. The speaker is focused on some bad effect she has experienced as a result of someone else's actions ('something bad happened to me before because someone else did something'), i.e. the primary focus is not on the other person's actions as such, but their effect on the speaker. This focus is highlighted by the second component of the Dictum: 'I feel something bad because of this.' Associated with this message is the speaker's apparent motivation: 'I want someone to do something because of this.' This formulation allows that this 'someone' could be the person whose action was responsible for the problem (as the speaker sees it), or it could be someone else, for example, the addressee or some other third party. The wording of this component is also compatible with the different possible helpful responses to *complaining*, such as taking remedial action, disciplining the offender, or simply doing something to help assuage the complaining person's bad feelings.

[P]   *X complained to Y (about ...).*

a.   someone X said something to someone else Y at that time
b.   this someone said something like this:
> "something bad happened to me before because someone did something
> I feel something bad because of this"
c.   this someone said it like someone can say something like this to someone else
> when this someone thinks like this:
>> "I want someone to do something because of this"
d.   it can be bad if someone says something like this in this way

7.6 Some English "evaluatives": *praise, criticize, compliment, insult*

As mentioned in section 7.2, not all speech acts follow the semantic template we have been using so far. In this section we look at four speech-act verbs that require a second template. Three distinctive and interrelated aspects of verbs like these bear on the need for a distinctive template: first, it is not possible to formulate a 'model dictum' for them, although—and this is the second point—it is possible, indeed essential, to characterize what the speaker says in evaluative terms (when one *praises*, for example, one says something very good about someone; when one *criticizes*, one says something bad about someone); third, although these speech-acts can be addressed to a particular person, what is more essential to their nature is that their Dicta are **about** someone. In a nutshell, then, these speech-act verbs characterize someone saying something good or bad (evaluative) about someone with a certain Apparent Mental State, typically involving a motivation.

The template structure can be represented as follows:

Speech-act verb template II ("saying something good/bad about someone, like someone can say when...")

someone X —— someone Y (e.g. praised, criticized, complimented,...)

someone X said something good/bad about someone else Y   LEXICO-SYNTACTIC FRAME
   at that time
this someone wanted something to happen because of it
this someone said it like someone can say something like this   APPARENT
   about someone else when this someone thinks like this: MENTAL STATE
    " _ _ _ "
(it is bad if someone says something like this in this way)

Verbs that fall under this template cannot be used performatively, presumably because there is no Dictum component, and they are all semi-transitive. As indicated by the final, parenthesized component in the template shown above, many of them, e.g. *insult*, carry a negative evaluation: 'it is bad if someone says something like this in this way.'

To see how this template works in practice, we will look first at the verb *praise*. Here are some examples.

- In announcing his separation from his wife, Nelson Mandela **praised** her for her support and sacrifice while he was in prison.
- Different children in the class are singled out and **praised** for achieving proficiency in basic skills.
- Police and firefighters **praised** the quick thinking of staff.

The first and primary point about *praise* is that it is not possible to formulate a specific Dictum that would be appropriate for the range of use of the word. To be sure, in many cases speakers *praise* by saying something like 'this someone did something very good', but one can equally *praise* someone for their beauty, intelligence, patience, or knowledge; i.e. the attribute does not have to be literally something that has been done. On the other hand, in *praising* someone's beauty, intelligence, etc., one does somehow seem to be treating it **as if** it were something they have done—at least, that they are responsible and deserve "credit" for it. To accommodate this paradox, the thought that 'this someone did something very good' has been included in the Apparent Mental State section of explication [Q] below.

Linked with this, the next component states that the speaker appears to think that if people knew about it, it would bring credit to this person: 'if other people know

about it, they can think something very good about this someone because of it.'
Notice that the reference to 'other people' implies that *praising* is a speech act with an
implicitly public dimension, even though particular acts of *praising* may be directed
to single individuals. The final component attributes to the praising person the
thought 'I want someone to know this'. This combination of components is compatible with the fact that one may *praise* someone with or without the praised person
being present, as in the first example shown above.

Overall, therefore, the explication for *praise* looks like this:

[Q] *X praised Y (for . . .).*
a.   someone X said something very good about someone else Y at that time
      this someone wanted something to happen because of it
b.   this someone said it like someone can say something like this about someone else
         when this someone thinks like this:
            "this someone did something very good some time before
            if other people know about it, they can think something very good about this
               someone because of it
            I want someone to know this"

It would be a fair observation that most of the semantic content of *praise* is carried
by the Apparent Mental State components. This makes sense (not only for *praise*, but
for the other evaluative speech-act verbs) because there is no Dictum as such, only a
depiction of the speaker saying 'something very good' about the target person.

Criticize can be seen as the negative inverse of *praise*, except that the "strength" of
the evaluation is perhaps not as great, i.e. while *praise* involves 'very good', *criticize*
involves merely 'bad' (not 'very bad'). Here are some examples, followed directly by
an explication.

- She brought a book to work and read it until the boss **criticized** her for wasting the firm's
  time and money.
- Prime Minister Margaret Thatcher has sharply **criticized** France over the deal.
- After the match McEnroe **criticized** some of the umpiring.

[R] *X criticized Y (for . . .).*
a.   someone X said something bad about someone else Y at that time
      this someone wanted something to happen because of it
b.   this someone said it like someone can say something like this about someone else
         when this someone thinks like this:
            "this someone did something bad some time before
            if other people know about it, they can think something bad about this someone
               because of it
            I want someone to know this"

Compliment differs from *praise* and *criticize* in that a *compliment* is typically addressed to the person concerned. In a *compliment* the speaker says something good about the addressee,[1] apparently to express some good feeling towards the addressee. The "addressee orientation" of *compliment* is reflected syntactically in the fact that the complement of *compliment* is usually the person, rather than the thing or aspect chosen for positive comment.

- Deirdre appeared slightly embarrassed when I **complimented** her, so I did not persist.
- His mother **complimented** him on the new jacket he had gotten for his birthday. "It looks handsome," she said, ...

The Apparent Mental State includes awareness that the comment can be pleasing to the addressee and a hint of premeditation ('if I say this, this someone can feel something good because of it'). It also includes a wish to please the addressee ('I want this'). It's a subtle point, but this configuration does not quite amount to saying that the complimenter says it **because** he or she wants to please. Nevertheless, it is enough to distinguish between *complimenting* someone and merely expressing appreciation. (Incidentally, the fact that the speaker appears to assume that his or her opinion matters to the addressee helps explain why a *compliment* can be felt to be presumptuous.)

[S]   *X complimented Y (on his/her Z).*

a.   someone X said something good about someone else Y to this someone else
          at that time
      this someone wanted something to happen because of it
b.   this someone said it like someone can say something like this about someone else
          when this someone thinks like this:
              "if I say this, this someone can feel something good because of it, I want this"

Let us consider *insult*, which comes close to being a converse of *compliment*. As with *compliment*, it involves an awareness of the potential negative impact of speaking in this way and a wish to achieve such an effect. The strength of the effect is stronger, however: 'very bad', not just 'bad'. A difference is that *insulting* (as a kind of speech act) attracts a negative evaluation.

---

[1] Holmes (1988: 446) characterized a compliment as a speech act that "attributes credit to someone other than the speaker, usually the addressee, for some 'good' (possession, characteristic, skill, etc.) which is positively valued by the speaker and the hearer". As Jucker (2009: 1612) notes, the list of "goods" can be continued, i.e. it is unclear whether any non-disjunctive description is possible. Jucker continues: "Explicit personal compliments are the prototypical compliments that say something positive about the addressee."

- I can't even believe I can still call him a friend, you know, after that, you know? He's **insulted** my family, **insulted** me.
- Crowe sparked a massive brawl when he **insulted** locals in a Canadian bar.

[T]   *X insulted Y.*

a.   someone X said something very bad about someone else Y to this someone else
       at that time
       this someone wanted something to happen because of it
b.   this someone said it like someone can say something like this about someone else
       when this someone thinks like this:
          "I want this someone to feel something very bad because I say this"
c.   it is bad if someone says something like this to someone else in this way

7.7 Other templates and speech-act types: *greet* and *marry*

In the foundational texts of philosophical speech-act theory—Austin (1962) and Searle (1969)—formulaic and institutional speech acts such as *greet* and *marry* figured prominently, but these verbs, and others like them, cannot be successfully explicated using the two templates we have developed so far. In this section we will first treat *greet* and *marry*, each of which stands for a distinct subclass with many other members, and then look briefly at several other groups of verbs that again seem to require additional templates.

Searle (1969) says that *greet* is an example of a speech-act verb that lacks any "sincerity conditions". That is, simply by *greeting* someone one is not expressing any psychological state; one is just going through a procedure, a form of words. (Searle contrasted *greeting*, in this respect, with *welcome*. When one *welcomes* someone, one does express a feeling; roughly, that one is pleased that this person has arrived and wants him or her to be pleased too.)

The template exemplified in explication [U] below has several features that are different from anything we have seen so far. The first is that the Lexico-Syntactic Frame is founded on a distinctive valency frame for SAY that involves both words and an addressee, i.e. 'to say some words to someone'. Second, the "new" component 'people do something like this at many times when it is like this' establishes that we are talking about a recognized social practice, appropriate to a particular kind of Typical Social Situation.

The precise details of the social situation associated with *greeting* are tricky to discern and state. Note firstly that stating that 'people do something like this at many times' when the following scenario applies by no means implies that *greetings* only ever occur in this context. One typically *greets* someone one knows upon seeing him or her for the first time on a given day, as a prelude, so to speak, to saying something to this person. But one could also *greet* someone, for example, as a host welcoming a series of people into one's home for a party or other function. In a situation like this, one might actually *greet* someone one does not know or hardly knows, or *greet* someone for a second time on a given day, or *greet* someone when it is highly unlikely that one would be saying anything more to them in the immediate future. None of this is ruled out by the explication, because the characterization it gives is for the typical situation of *greeting*; i.e. saying some words to someone as people typically do in the situation depicted.

[U]   *Someone X greeted Y.*

a.   someone X said some words to someone else Y at that time   LEXICO-SYNTACTIC
       this someone wanted something to happen because of it   FRAME

b.   people do something like this at many times when it is like this: TYPICAL SOCIAL
       someone is somewhere at some time   SITUATION
       this someone sees someone else in the same place at that time
       this someone knows this other someone
       this someone wants to say something to this other someone at this time
       this someone did not say something to this other someone before on the same day [m]

Along with words like *excommunicate, name (a ship), acquit, sentence*, the word *marry* is a classic institutional speech act. Almost all speech-act theorists have recognized that these words belong in a category of their own (often called "declaratory acts"), partly because there are clear institutional preconditions (usually to do with the role and status of the speaker and addressee) that must be satisfied if the speech act is to be successful, partly because successful performance creates a "real" change in the world, and partly because this change is brought about through the pronouncing of a certain form of words.

Reflecting these points, the explication in [V] for *marry* is significantly different from previous examples in its overall structure.[2] First, the Lexico-Syntactic Frame is based around the semantic primes DO, HAPPEN, BECAUSE, and WANT, rather than on SAY. It depicts someone who *marries* two people as doing something as a result of which something happens to these two people, as the actor wants. In this respect, the explication depicts *marry* as much like a "normal" action verb. Next in the template comes a series of Conditions, in this case requiring that the actor has to be a priest or 'someone of another kind like a priest [m]', and also that the two people involved have to be a man and a woman, each of whom is not someone else's husband or wife

---

[2] With the movement for gay marriage, the word *marry* has become something of a contested concept. Arguably, the word has developed a second meaning which is not confined to men and women, but this meaning will not be explicated here.

at the time, and each of whom wants to be the husband or wife of the other, as appropriate. The details of these Conditions are discussed further below. The third section of the template sets out the Dictum/Procedure—so termed because the procedure requires the saying of certain words. Finally there is a Result section, which certifies that the saying of the requisite words resulted in a certain outcome.

[V]   *Someone X married someone Y and someone Z.*

a.   someone X did something at that time   LEXICO-SYNTACTIC FRAME
      because of this, something happened to two people (someone X, someone Y)
            as this someone wanted
b.   someone can do this if this someone is a priest [m]   CONDITIONS
c.   someone can do this if this someone is someone of another kind like a priest [m]
d.   people of other kinds can't do this
e.   someone can't do this if it is not like this:
            one of these two people is a man [m], this man [m] is not someone's husband [m] at
                this time,
            this man [m] wants to be this woman's husband [m]
            the other one of these two people is a woman [m], this woman [m] is not someone's
                wife [m] at this time,
            this woman [m] wants to be this man's wife [m]
f.   when someone does this, this someone says   DICTUM/PROCEDURE
      words like this:
            "this man [m] is now this woman's [m] husband [m], this woman [m] is
                now this man's [m] wife [m]"
g.   because of this, after this, it is like this: RESULT
      this man [m] is this woman's [m] husband [m], this woman [m] is this man's [m] wife [m]

There are a number of aspects of explication [V] that warrant attention. Perhaps the most general, and most interesting, is the observation that it relies on several semantic molecules from the social domain ('man', 'woman', 'husband', 'wife', 'priest') and that one of these, i.e. 'priest', is obviously highly culture-specific. In general, this is only to be expected, assuming that speech-act verbs of this subclass incorporate reference to cultural institutions and authority structures. In similar fashion, one would expect to find items such as 'church', 'judge', and 'king' functioning as semantic molecules in explications for *excommunicate*, *acquit*, and *proclaim*. A substantial study is required to explore this area in sufficient detail, but one could expect it to be richly rewarding in terms of cultural insights.

A second point about the explication for *marry* is that, obviously, it assumes that the words 'husband' and 'wife' are semantically simpler than *marry*, and can be defined independently without circularity. These assumptions are supported by a separate study (Wierzbicka forthcoming) devoted to the semantics of kinship words, in which both 'wife' and 'husband' are successfully explicated without reference to 'marry'. From an intuitive point of view, another argument that can be raised in support of the same point is that one can freely use the words *wife* and *husband* about non-Western societies, without stopping to think about what kind of "marriage" ceremonies they may have, if any.

A third and still more specific point concerns the use of 'priest' as the appropriate semantic molecule for the prototypical marriage celebrant. This is open to discussion, given that in some countries, such as Australia, most marriages are no longer performed by priests (or ministers) but by civil marriage celebrants. The arguments in favour of 'priest' are that the word 'priest' seems to have a secure place in the inventory of English semantic molecules (needed in words such as *church*, *baptize*, *cloister*, *Mass*) and that, intuitively, marriage celebrants are thought of as non-priests who nonetheless have the power to celebrate a marriage. Dictionaries seem to recognize this connection. For example, the *Australian Concise Oxford* (2009) defines 'to marry' as: '(Of a priest, etc., or in *p.p.*) join (persons, on to another) in marriage'; and the *Longman Dictionary* (1987) gives: '(of a priest or official) to perform the ceremony of marriage for (two people)'.

In this section we have identified two additional subclasses of speech acts, which require a distinct template. Together with the two templates developed and exemplified in the bulk of the chapter, this makes four subclasses/templates. But there are clear indications that at least three more will have to be recognized. First, there are speech-act verbs which involve 'saying words to someone' but which—unlike *greet*—are not tied to typical situations. Consider the verbs *address* and *call*, as in *He addressed me as 'Sir'* or *He called me an idiot*. Second, there are speech acts that involve 'saying words', but not necessarily addressing them to anyone, as for example, *quote*, *utter*, *repeat*, *pronounce*. Third, there are speech acts (sometimes termed "responsives") that are made in response to other speech acts. Most notable in English are the multiple verbs for, roughly speaking, "saying no" in different situations, with different implications, such as *refuse*, *deny*, *decline*, *reject*, and *refute*. Other examples of responsives would be *respond* itself, and *reply* and *answer*.

Overall, then, we can be sure that there are at least seven distinct subclasses of speech-act verbs, and possibly a good number more. Despite the semantic spadework begun in Wierzbicka (1987b), and continued in this chapter and in intervening works, the topic of speech-act verbs still has a lot to offer future cohorts of semantic researchers on English and other languages.

7.8 Implications and conclusions

An immediate implication of NSM studies into speech-act verbs, including not only the present chapter but also Wierzbicka (1987b; 2003a; 2012a; 2012c), Goddard (2002b; 2004a), Maher (2002), and Pedersen (2010), is that cross-linguistic and cross-cultural investigations of any kind cannot accept English speech acts or speech-act verbs as analytical categories without imposing Anglocentric bias. This lesson applies with equal force to cross-cultural semantics, lexical typology, and contrastive pragmatics.[3] Treating English speech-act verbs as neutral analytical categories misrepresents the indigenous conceptualization of speech acts of other cultures and imposes an 'outsider perspective'. At the same time, failing to focus attention on the precise meanings of indigenous speech-act terms cuts off a rich source of information and insight into the speech practices of other cultures.

Returning to the questions with which we opened this chapter: how and why has English developed such a large repertoire of speech-act verbs? What can we learn about Anglo culture from a review of its speech-act inventory? At the most general, the sheer number of verbs is probably linked with what Ong (1982) has termed the "chirographic" character of the English language. This term refers to the extent to which the character of a language and culture has been influenced by writing and by discourse practices dependent on writing. Building on Ong's ideas, Wierzbicka (2010*b*) argues that different cultures have "interiorized" writing to different degrees and, more specifically, that English has moved further from orality even than other European languages. Part of the evidence she adduces concerns cultural key words like *story* and *message*, whose content implies conceptualizing something (e.g. roughly, a series of events in the case of *story*, what someone says in the case of *message*) by analogy to a written text. In this connection, it is notable that literacy played a large part in the evolution of the present inventory of English speech-act verbs (Traugott 1994). Many performatives first appeared in written feudal proclamations or court rulings (where, needless to say, they are of special utility) and only much later came to be used in the speech of ordinary people. More broadly, it is notable that from a stylistic or compositional point of view, conciseness and explicitness are highly valued in many genres of "public writing" in English. Having a rich inventory of speech-act verbs at hand allows writers (and speakers) to be highly explicit and at the same time very precise in the way they express or describe the motivations and assumptions accompanying verbal interaction.

---

[3] It is curious and depressing that many scholars in cross-cultural pragmatics have not registered this seemingly basic point and are still oblivious of the scale of semantic differences between "emic" speech-act categories of languages. For example, in a discussion of compliments, Jucker (2009: 1620) observes, "An analysis of compliments always presumes that the researcher knows what a compliment is. Thus even a field linguist cannot set out on his or her investigation of compliments without precise reflections on what constitutes the nature of a compliment." But he offers no advice about how "precise reflections" can be captured or how they can be formulated without Anglocentric bias. Referring to Watts's (2003) interest in "lay speakers' conceptualizations" and to the possibility that researchers might investigate speech acts that are named "compliment" by members of the speech community, Jucker (2009) sees only problems without solutions: "But people may be very inconsistent when they use the term 'compliment'. It is in the nature of lexical items that they have fuzzy denotations."

This applies in particular to public life, as carried on through the media. How often do news headlines consist of speech acts—of phrases such as 'X accuses Y of Z', 'X condemns...', 'X offers...', 'X calls for...', and so on? As Wierzbicka (1987b: 3) remarked, "It would not be an exaggeration to say that public life can be conceived of as a gigantic network of speech acts".

As for the character of the English speech-act inventory, it is notable that several areas appear to be more elaborated than others, and this too seems to have its origins and rationale in cultural history and cultural values. Most elaborated of all, in contemporary English, are the directives and quasi-directives, i.e. verbs like *ask*, *tell*, *suggest*, *recommend*. As suggested by Wierzbicka (2006d; 2008b; 2012c), they can be seen to reflect the pre-eminent value of "personal autonomy" in contemporary English. Pre-17th-century English had relatively few directive speech-act verbs, and among the most notable were verbs like *beseech* and *exhort*, which expressed the speaker's strong wish that the addressee do something. To the modern ear, such verbs smack of putting the addressee under undue "pressure". As we have seen in section 7.2, the contemporary menu of directive and quasi-directive speech-act verbs are "fine tuned to allow the speakers to express their wants in relation to other people without appearing to impose, pressure, intrude, violate someone's autonomy, and so on" (Wierzbicka 2012c). Needless to say, this cultural preoccupation is manifested in other areas of English language structure as well—for example, in the wealth of English interpersonal causative constructions (with *make*, *get*, *have*, and *let*) and associated phraseology (Wierzbicka 2003b; 2006a: ch 6).

If directives and quasi-directives involve nuanced ways of saying things about what one **wants** and about what one wants the addressee to do, a second area of elaboration lies in speech-act verbs that concern nuancing saying things about what one **knows** and about what one's addressee knows. Allan (1986: 193) says that "[t]here are more constatives than any other category of interpersonal act", and although the precise meaning and range of the term 'constative' can be contentious, his general point is well taken. There are a large number of English speech-act verbs concerned with expressing or describing how someone presents what they know or believe (e.g. *tell*, *state*, *assert*, *maintain*, *inform*, *point out*, *claim*) and how someone responds to such speech acts from someone else (e.g. *agree*, *concede*, *admit*, *disagree*, *reject*, *deny*). Outside the realm of speech-act verbs, the highly elaborated English system of epistemic adverbs (e.g. *probably*, *apparently*, *clearly*, *certainly*, *obviously*,) and epistemic formulas (e.g. *I think*, *I suppose*, *I guess*, *I imagine*) (Wierzbicka 2006a: chs 7 and 8) service the same cultural needs, and especially the cultural attention to degrees of certainty and the need to distinguish "what I know" from "what I think". In these respects, as well as in other ways, the speech culture of contemporary English embodies the legacy of the British Enlightenment with its emphasis on epistemic caution, on distinguishing "fact" from "opinion", and on the importance of "evidence" (Wierzbicka 2010a).

8

A stitch in time and *the way of the rice plant*

The semantics of proverbs in English and Malay

8.1 Paremiology meets cross-cultural semantics

Proverbs are multi-word utterances but at the same time they are "word-like", in the sense that their meanings are not the sum of the meanings of their constituent words.[1] In many cultures proverbs are an indispensable part of everyday interaction, yet outside paremiology (the folkloric study of proverbs: Mieder 1994[1987]; 2001) they are a relatively neglected topic. In linguistics, the status of proverbs can best be described as marginal, and although they fare a little better in anthropology, where there is a modest literature (e.g. Arewa and Dundes 1964; White 1987; Briggs 1988; Hasan-Rokem 1992; Obeng 1996), they are hardly mentioned in anthropology textbooks. The low scholarly profile of the proverb is partly due to the ethos of modernity, with its forward-looking approach, its aesthetic of originality, and its rejection of the notion of traditional wisdom. In the late 20th century another potent factor was no doubt the Chomskyan character of mainstream linguistics, which held questions of meaning and culture in disdain, and emphasized linguistic creativity over routinization and formulaicity.

Whether there is full definitional clarity about what exactly qualifies as a "proverb" for the purpose of cross-linguistic comparison is debatable, but there is general agreement that its properties include relative fixity of form, brevity, appealing stylistic features, traditionality, and the status of presenting "folk wisdom" (Norrick 1985: ch. 3). Traditional paremiology has catalogued proverbs, often in their thousands, from many cultures and classified them by form and subject matter. A number of insightful studies in linguistic anthropology and ethnopoetics have inquired into

---

[1] Remarkably, Leibniz recognized that proverbs and other speech formulae are to be treated "like words" so far as semantic analysis is concerned, writing (in 1678): "their whole sense is not gathered from their constituent words . . . [hence] they are to be (separately) analyzed" (Dascal 1987: 162).

culture-specific formal and functional properties, and into the performance dimension—how proverbs are deployed and integrated into ongoing social inter-action (see e.g. Arewa and Dundes 1964; Briggs 1988; Fabian 1990; Obeng 1996). It is clear that culture-specific genres approximating the "proverb" differ somewhat from culture to culture and language to language, as do their functional and performance aspects. For example, when using Mexicano "proverbs" (*dichos*) one of the crucial elements is citing a particular person with whom the proverb is associated, a practice which "emanates from the belief that proverbs are, in a sense, 'owned' by individuals" (Briggs 1988: 106). Mexicano "proverbs" (*dichos*), moreover, are almost invariably rounded off with a series of statements affirming the truth of the proverb. Neither of these features is associated with contemporary uses of English and Malay proverbs, with which we will be dealing in this chapter.

From a formal point of view, the brevity and "semantic compression" (Gándara 2004: 348) of proverbs is one of their most conspicuous features. As unitary, free-standing fixed utterances, they minimize processing demands, and their stylistic characteristics, such as vivid imagery, rhyme, alliteration, parallelism, and contrast, make for easy memorization. Even so, inculcating hundreds or even thousands of proverbial items during language socialization is such a costly investment that it must serve important communicative and, presumably, cognitive functions. As Lee (2007: 481) puts it: "[Proverbs] may reflect typical patterns of reasoning and interpretation among the people who use them. If deeply entrenched within the culture, they also provide ready-made patterns of interpretation that are absorbed by individuals into their own belief and reasoning systems in the course of developmental socialization."

From the vantage point of linguistic semantics, it is striking how little progress has been made on the question of how the meanings of proverbs (in the sense of proverb texts) can be stated, if at all. The simplistic and impressionistic "literal paraphrases" typically offered by proverb dictionaries and researchers, e.g. *Make hay while the sun shines* "Act while propitious conditions prevail" (Norrick 1985: 113), are inadequate in many ways. It is not surprising that some researchers have preferred to say that proverb texts are "semantically incomplete" (Mukařoský 1971[1942–43], cited in Briggs 1988: 132) until or unless they are contextualized by being inserted into real social interaction. One purpose of the present study is to challenge this view. We will seek to demonstrate that using the NSM methodology it is possible to "unpack" the meanings of specific proverb texts in close detail. In general terms, our approach is akin to that of White (1987: 152), who in his study into proverb meaning in English expressed the view that "certain key understandings make up a kind of kernel of proverb meaning, even though such meanings may be shifted or elaborated in particular contexts of use". He continued: "The fact that proverbs represent general-ized knowledge, applied in the interpretation of particular events, suggests that they may tell us something about enduring models of cultural experience."

Although the semantic (symbolic) meanings of proverb texts are amenable to precise description, the full significance of a proverb utterance in context depends also on pragmatic contextualization and on interdiscursive indexicality effects which play out differently in specific cultural, historical, and spatiotemporal settings (cf. Goddard 2002c). In addition to tackling the semantic and genre content of some contemporary English and Malay proverbs, we will discuss how they (or their uses) are positioned very differently in terms of indexical relationships of interdiscursivity in the contemporary Anglo English and Malay settings, i.e. within an ethos of modernity, on the one hand, and in the multi-ethnic polity of a "modernizing" Malaysia, on the other.

8.2 Identifying and characterizing proverbs

Identifying proverbs on linguistic evidence

The ultimate criterion as to whether something qualifies as a *proverb* in the eyes of ordinary people is that it can be referred to as such in ordinary discourse; for example, by means of a metalexical tag such as *As the proverb goes* (or: *says*). Unlike its counterparts in various other languages (Čermák 2004), however, this tag is not particularly common in contemporary English. A related and more frequent tag is *As the old saying goes*, and compatibility with this tag is an intuitively straightforward test which helps delimit the class of items of interest. For example:

(1) a. A stitch in time saves nine, as the old saying goes.
     b. As the old saying goes, "Don't count your chickens before they hatch".

The word *old* is important, because the simpler tag *As the saying goes* can apply to a much broader range of "sayings", including not just proverbs but also well-known quotations and modern sayings, e.g. *Let's cut to the chase, as the (*old) saying goes.* However, even with the inclusion of the modifier *old*, the tag does not delimit proverbs as such, since it can also be used with well-known "old" quotations and other sayings, e.g. *Revenge is sweet, as the old saying goes.* In short, while all *proverbs* are *old sayings*, not all *old sayings* are *proverbs*. (According to various authorities, the following are "modern proverbs": *What comes around goes around*; *If anything can go wrong, it will*; *Shit happens*; *Garbage in, garbage out*; and *Those who can, do, those who can't, teach.* In our view, these do not qualify as *proverbs* because they do not qualify (on linguistic evidence) as *old sayings*.)

A contrast is often drawn between metaphorical proverbs, such as *A stitch in time saves nine*, and "plain" proverbs (sometimes termed maxims), such as *Practice makes perfect.* To separate these classes using linguistic tests is not difficult. Metalexical tags such as *So to speak* and *As it were,* which are diagnostic of "active metaphor" generally (Goddard 2004b), will identify metaphorical proverbs. The metalexical modifier *the proverbial* also works (e.g. *the proverbial stitch in time*) though, ironic-ally, it is not restricted to proverbs but can be applied to any metaphorical but clichéd expression (e.g. *We were up the proverbial creek*).

Norrick (1985: 102) points out: "many scholars have accepted or asserted that the completely metaphorical proverb describing a concrete scene, call it the scenic proverb, represents the archetypal proverb." This proverb type is the most frequent in published compendiums of English proverbs. On the other hand, corpus studies and familiarity ratings indicate that the most common "full" proverbs in contempor-ary English are of the maxim variety (Charteris-Black 1999; Higbee and Millard 1983). In our view, the paradox is easily resolved on two assumptions. From a conceptual point of view, the category *proverb* implies an old saying. Metaphorical proverbs tend to employ archaic imagery and/or vocabulary (e.g. from the farm or the household in pre-industrial days), so this makes them more prototypical. On the other hand, the "modern" attitude militates against actual usage of old-fashioned sounding proverbs.

It would be premature, however, to declare the death of the metaphorical proverb in modern English. They are still used in their full forms, and moreover, as Charteris-Black (1999) has shown, "proverb fragments" (his term is "proverb variations") are a good deal more common than full proverbs (cf. Barlow 2000). For example, in a 330 million-word corpus, the phrase *Birds of a feather* occurred 190 times, compared to 6 occurrences of the full proverb. As Crystal (2006: 8) says: "People may not quote proverbs in full as much as they used to, or treat them with the high respect of an earlier age, but they certainly allude to them" (see later in this section).

Understanding ethno-taxonomies of "proverbial ways of speaking"

Languages differ significantly in their ethno-taxonomies of speech genres, so it would be ethnocentric to uncritically adopt an English word such as *proverb* as the basis for cross-linguistic comparisons in this domain. The appropriate strategy is to seek to identify semantic components that recur across languages, with the aim of building up a typology of "proverbial ways of speaking". To move in this direction we need to turn the semantic microscope onto expressions such as English *proverb* and *old saying*, Malay *pepatah* and *bidalan*, and their nearest counterparts in other languages.

For example, Biblical Hebrew *māšāl* has a much wider referential range than any of the English or Malay terms: it can refer to short rhetorical sayings (e.g. Ezekiel 18: 2), to parables or allegories (e.g. Ezekiel 17: 2), and also to the kind of "poetic rhetorical vision" in Numbers 23: 7. In New Testament Greek, the word *parabolē* (which gave rise to English *parable*) is normally used to render *māšāl*. It can be used to refer to proverbs (e.g. Luke 4: 23), to wisdom sayings (e.g. Luke 5: 36–39), to allegories (e.g. Matthew 22: 1–14), and to the more familiar narrative parables.[2]

---

[2] Thanks to Ghil'ad Zuckermann for these examples from Hebrew scripture. Zuckermann points out that the contemporary Israeli word for proverbs is not *mashal*, but *pitgam* (which in Biblical Hebrew meant 'order, command', from Persian *patigam* 'sent message').

Words similar to Hebrew *māšāl* are found in Aramaic and Arabic. Despite the broader range of use, it seems likely that *māšāl* and its cognates are more restricted than English *proverb* in one respect: they require a metaphorical or analogical element, i.e. involvement of the semantic prime LIKE. Etymologically the Hebrew and Arabic roots *m.š.l* and *m.θ.l* both have the meaning 'like'.

As a first step towards exploring the semantics of ethno-taxonomies of proverbial speech, consider the following set of explications for three English terms: *saying, old saying,* and *proverb*. All begin with the component 'words of one kind'. This use of semantic prime KIND establishes their status as taxonomic or categorical terms (cf. *prayer, riddle, curse, joke, song*). The qualification 'not one word, not many words' excludes single words and lengthy texts: *sayings* have to be relatively short (indeed, the phrase **a long saying* is anomalous). Explication [A] characterizes *sayings* in two additional ways. First, they can be used as brief self-contained utterances, as in component (b). Second, they are recognizable as generally used for the same purpose, as in component (c). Notice that this formulation embraces both "same content" ('saying the same thing') and "same form" ('with the same words').

[A]   *a saying*

a.   words of one kind, not one word, not many words
b.   people can say something in a short time with these words
c.   when someone says something with words of this kind,
        people know that many people say the same thing with the same words

An *old saying*, as explicated in [B], adds a further element to the (c) component, bringing an awareness of the temporal dimension, i.e. that 'for a long time before many people said the same thing many times with the same words'. Naturally, repeated exposure to a saying over a long time means that people can be counted on to know at once what it means. In colloquial terms, people can potentially "get the message" of *an old saying* more or less immediately. This is captured in the additional component (d).

[B]   *an old saying*

a.   words of one kind, not one word, not many words
b.   people can say something in a short time with these words
c.   when someone says something with words of this kind,
        people know that for a long time before many people said the same thing
            many times with the same words
d.   because of this, when someone says something with words of this kind,
        people can know in one moment what this someone wants to say

It has sometimes been said that the concept of a *proverb* is difficult, or even impossible, to define. Explication [C] below is a proposed explication for the English word. It includes the full semantic content of [B] above, along with additional components.

The components in section (c) state that when someone says a *proverb*, they are simultaneously expressing ("co-expressing") some claims about its content—roughly, that it is an item of "traditional wisdom", and that as such, it deserves our consideration. (Components regarding traditionality and wisdom appear as "framing" components in each and every proverb explication presented in this study (section 8.4): they are conveyed or expressed by the medium of the proverb genre itself.)

There is one additional component to the meaning of the word *proverb*, which appears as component (f). It refers to what we have called "semantic compression", and is linked of course with the familiarity and recognizability of proverbs.

[C]   *a proverb*

a.   words of one kind, not one word, not many words
b.   people can say something in a short time with these words
c.   when people say something with words of this kind,
        they say something like this at the same time:
           "many people live for a long time
           because of this, these people can know many things
           this is one of these things
           it can be good for someone if this someone thinks about this at some times"
d.   when someone says something with words of this kind,
        people know that for a long time before many people said the same thing
        many times with the same words
e.   because of this, when someone says something with words of this kind,
        people can know in one moment what this someone wants to say
f.   because of this, when someone says something with words of this kind,
        they can say much in a short time with not many words

In case these explorations into lexical semantics seem unduly specialized, or even tedious, we want to emphasize that words like *saying, old saying*, and *proverb* are the central terms in the English ethno-taxonomy of "proverbial speech". By explicating their conceptual content, we are laying bare the "shared understandings" about these Anglo speech forms and speech practices. From one perspective, this is simply a necessary part of building up an ethnopragmatics of proverbial speech in contemporary Anglo culture. From another perspective, it can help us as English-speaking scholars not to reify the conceptual categories of our own language in order to adopt the comfortable assumption that the conceptual differences between different languages and cultures matter little and that we may as well continue to work through those of our own language. We believe that nothing would advance our understanding of cross-cultural differences in this area faster than some serious contrastive semantics into the ethno-taxonomies of speech genres in different languages.

Let us turn to the question of how proverb meanings can be stated using NSM techniques.

8.3 Semantic explications for some English proverbs

A semantic template for proverb meanings

Consider a classic metaphorical proverb, like *A stitch in time saves nine*. Can its meaning be captured in an extended paraphrase composed from very simple every-day words?

After an extensive trial and error process, we would like to propose and illustrate a five-part semantic template for English proverbs. Its structure can be depicted as in Figure 8.1.

The framing sections recur with exactly the same wording in all the examples to be considered here. Section (a), labelled simply TRADITIONALITY in the explications to follow, establishes that the words used are fixed and that they have long been used by people to express the message content that follows. Section (e), labelled STATUS AS FOLK WISDOM, "caps" the content of each explication with an endorsement of its status as an item of traditional wisdom. Notice that this section presupposes, and in a sense projects, the assumption that there **is** some body of collective traditional knowledge and that aspects of this knowledge can be relevant in certain situations.

a.   for a long time before people said these words at many times   TRADITIONALITY
     they said these words when they wanted to say something like this: – –

     message content: sections [b]–[d]

e.   many people live for a long time   STATUS AS FOLK WISDOM
     because of this, these people can know many things
     this is one of these things
     it can be good for someone if this someone thinks about this at some times

The three middle sections—(b), (c), and (d)—give the content of the individual proverb. To anticipate, we will say that the tripartite structure—RECURRENT SITU-ATION, PROVERBIAL ADVICE, PROVERBIAL ANALOGY—is maximal. Most metaphorical proverbs require all three sections, but maxim-style proverbs (like *Practice makes perfect*) lack the PROVERBIAL ANALOGY, and some metaphorical sayings (like *Out of the frying pan, into the fire*) lack the PROVERBIAL ADVICE. Before considering these

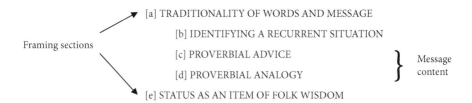

FIGURE 8.1 Structure of semantic template for proverb meanings

variations, however, it will be well to work carefully through a couple of examples of the full structure. (Additional examples are given, in abbreviated form, in Appendix 8.1.)

Semantic explications for some English proverbs

Explication [D] is for *A stitch in time saves nine*. Needless to say, it exhibits a great deal of semantic compression: twenty lines of semantic text are packed into six words.

[D]   *A stitch in time saves nine.*

a.   for a long time before people said these words at many times   TRADITIONALITY
         when they wanted to say something like this:

b.   often it is like this: RECURRENT SITUATION
         someone can't not do many things at some time,
            because this someone did not do one thing at some time before
         this is bad for this someone

c.   because of this, when someone thinks like this at some time: PROVERBIAL ADVICE
         "it is good if I do this"
      it is good if this someone thinks like this at the same time:
         "I want to do it now"

d.   it is like this: PROVERBIAL ANALOGY
         when there is a tear* in someone's clothes*,
            it is good if someone does something to these clothes*
         if this someone does it when the tear* is small, they can do one thing
         if they don't do this one thing at this time, after some time the tear* will not be
            small any more
         because of this, at this time this someone can't not do many things
         this is bad for this someone

e.   many people live for a long time   STATUS AS FOLK WISDOM
      because of this, these people can know many things
      this is one of these things
      it can be good for someone if this someone thinks about this at some times

The RECURRENT SITUATION in section (b) is introduced as follows: 'often it is like this:—' (cf. Burke 1967: 296). The word 'often' can be regarded as equivalent to the expression 'at many times'. The PROVERBIAL ADVICE in section (c) spells out the didactic message (often a way of avoiding the recurrent situation just presented). Then comes the PROVERBIAL ANALOGY in section (d), introduced by 'it is like this: —'; and what follows is usually based on everyday experience. As Taylor (1962[1931]: 10) put it: "A novel application of a familiar scene arrests our attention, imprints itself on our minds, and drives home the lesson."

The wording of the proverb is related to section (d) of the explication, but not necessarily in a simple one-to-one fashion. For example, in the case of *A stitch in time saves nine*, it is not necessary to mention any 'stitching' as such, let alone to refer to the number 'nine'. *A stitch* (i.e. one stitch) stands for doing 'one small thing' as opposed to *nine (stitches)*, which stands for doing 'many things'. To spell out the content of the analogy it **is** necessary, however, to refer to the situation of having a tear in one's clothing, and consequently some semantically complex words ('clothes' and 'tear', marked with an asterisk) are used in this section. In this and subsequent explications, we have tried to keep the number of such words to a minimum, and to use only words which seem essential to spelling out the analogical content in a plain and intuitively appealing fashion. We hypothesize that these concrete lexical items are cognitively "real" in the sense that they are involved in the speaker's actual representation of the analogy.

Explication [E] demonstrates the template for *Make hay while the sun shines*. To save space, only the message content sections of the explication are given.

[E]   *Make hay while the sun shines.*

b.   often it is like this: RECURRENT SITUATION
        someone wants to do something in a place
        this someone can't do it at this time because some other things aren't
            happening in this place at this time

c.   when it is like this, it is good if this someone thinks like this: PROVERBIAL ADVICE
        "when these other things happen, they can happen for a short time
        because of this, when they happen it will be bad if I don't do it at this time"
        it is not good if this someone thinks like this: "I can do it after"

d.   it is like this: PROVERBIAL ANALOGY
        when people in a place want to make [m] hay*,
            they can't do it if the sun [m] is not hot [m] above this place at the same time
        when the sun [m] is hot [m] above a place, it can be like this for a short
            time (not for a long time)
        because of this, it is good if people make [m] hay* at times like this, it is not good
            if they do something else

Briefly let us look now at some simpler proverbs—simpler in the sense that they lack one or other set of semantic components found in the classic metaphorical proverb. Some metaphorical proverbs—like *Out of the frying pan, into the fire* and *Birds of a feather flock together*—simply characterize recurrent situations by pairing them with a proverbial analogy, but without offering any particular advice. Explication [F] illustrates this with *Out of the frying pan, into the fire*. The analogy seems to refer to what speakers describe as a "little critter (or creature)" of some kind. This is rendered in section (c) as a 'small living thing'. Early versions of the saying actually refer to a flounder, e.g. Heywood's (1546) compendium has *As the flounder dothe, Leape out of the frying pan into the fyre.*

[F]   Partial semantic explication for *Out of the frying pan, into the fire.*

b.   often it is like this: RECURRENT SITUATION
        something bad is happening to someone at some time
        this someone does something at this time because this someone wants it
            not to be like this any more
        after this, something very bad happens to this someone because of it

c.   – –   PROVERBIAL ADVICE

d.   it is like this: PROVERBIAL ANALOGY
        if a small living thing is in a frying pan* above a fire [m], it can't
            not feel something bad because of this
        if this small living thing moves in one moment because it wants it not to
            be like this any more, after this it can be in the fire [m] because of this
        if this small living thing is in a fire [m], it can't not feel something very bad
            because of this

As mentioned, many common English proverbs are of the maxim variety, e.g. *Practice makes perfect, Live and let live,* and *Honesty is the best policy.* Consider *Practice makes perfect.* At first blush, it might seem that it consists of plain words used in their plain meanings, and in a sense this is correct; but if we unpack the intended meaning, we find that a RECURRENT SITUATION is implied, along with some highly schematic PROVERBIAL ADVICE. What is missing is the PROVERBIAL ANALOGY.

[G]   Partial semantic explication for *Practice makes perfect.*

b.   often it is like this: RECURRENT SITUATION
        when someone wants to do something, this someone thinks about it like this:
            "I can't do this very well now
            I want to do it very well
            if I do it many times, after this I can do it very well"
        because of this, this someone does it many times
        after this, this someone can do it very well like this someone wanted before

c.   it is good if it is like this   PROVERBIAL ADVICE

Needless to say, these few examples from English (see Appendix 8.1 for more) raise many questions, but in our view they are enough to establish the viability of the general project of explicating proverb meanings via the proposed semantic template.

At this point it is interesting to explore the question whether the same approach can be extended to other languages, especially to languages from cultures that are very different to the Anglo culture associated with the English language. We will explore this question via a study of Malay (Bahasa Melayu), the national language of Malaysia. For other NSM studies of Malay, see Goddard (1996a; 1997b; 2000a; 2001c; 2001d; 2002a; 2002b; 2004a; 2008).

8.4 Malay *peribahasa*

Background

Traditional Malay culture was richly verbal. Linguistic etiquette was elaborate and highly valued, relying on artful indirectness and allusion, as well as on a variety of prescribed formal devices (honorific address forms, lexical variants, etc.). People knew and used innumerable *peribahasa* (roughly, folk sayings and phrases), *pantun* (rhyming four-line verses), and *teka-teki* (riddles), and in the case of the latter two folk genres, they innovated and improvised them freely. Despite modernization, and despite the multi-ethnic, multilingual character of modern Malaysia, many of these practices persist in contemporary Bahasa Melayu, especially as spoken by the Malay population.

In the older Malay oral culture (Sweeney 1987), formulaic speech was ubiquitous.[3] The colonial commentator Swettenham stressed "the Malay's fondness for proverbs, for epigrams and wise saws", adding: "in his conversation he never fails to introduce one or the other, when he sees an opportunity for their fitting application" (1906, cited by Lim 2003: 23). In the last 50 years, *peribahasa* have become emblematic of "Malay" identity. Numerous *peribahasa* dictionaries and guides have been published, both for the general public and for schools. Ding and Arba'eyah (2002) mention 30 books published between the 1950s and 2001, and there are now several websites as well. In tandem with this institutional recognition has come a decline in actual usage. Nonetheless, many *peribahasa* are still in common use—and not only in "traditional" venues and in political contexts. All the usage examples in this study have been garnered from blogs and other internet sources.

Before we propose semantic explications for a selection of Malay "proverbs", it will be helpful to review the Malay ethno-classification and related metalexical indicators. *Peribahasa* is a rather general term, subsuming idioms (*simpulan bahasa*) as well as proverbs in the English sense. For the latter, there are three terms in current use:

> *pepatah*: concise traditional sayings, which can serve as a "clinching" or decisive contribution to discussion; the closest term to English *proverb*;

---

[3] According to Sweeney (1987: 97), pre-modern Malay society was characterized not only by formulaic discourse but by formulaic thought: "the discourse of an oral culture is heavily dependent upon the use of relatively fixed utterances in stylized form, such as proverbs and other "sayings". [. . .] Such utterances are not merely used to underline a point: they *are* the point. The individual *thinks* in these formulas" [emphasis original].

bidalan: explicitly moralistic; similar to *maxim* or *adage* except that they can be
   metaphorical in wording;

perumpamaan (a nominalization on *umpama* 'like'): sayings introduced by one of
   several words meaning 'like', such as *seperti, macam, bagai, bak*, and *ibarat* (the
   last two, like *umpama* itself, are archaic).

Though some Malay writers treat these terms as though they were mutually exclusive
in their referential ranges, this is not really so. For example, those *pepatah* which
strongly imply advice can also be considered *bidalan*; and some *pepatah* can be
prefaced with *seperti* 'like' (or equivalents), in which case they can be termed
perumpamaan.

As in English, Malay sayings can be introduced in various ways. The most generic
is *kata orang* ('people say'), followed by *kata orang-orang tua* ('old people say'). Also
common are metalexical tags employing the categories just mentioned:

(2)   *bak pepatah (Melayu,* etc.)...   'as the (Malay) *pepatah* [goes],...'
       bak peribahasa (Melayu, etc.).... 'as the (Malay) *peribahasa* [goes],...'
       *bidalan lama (*or: *orang tua)*.... 'the old (or: old people's) *bidalan* [goes] ....'
       ibarat kata ....   'the *ibarat* says ...'

There is no Malay term approximating *metaphor* (Goddard 2004a). The word
kiasan applies to any language of allusion or implication, i.e. any indirect mode of
conveying a message, via a process of extrapolation or inference. The colonial scholar
Winstedt wrote the following in his *Malay Proverbs*.

The Malays stress the element of *kiasan* (analogy, simile, metaphor, allusion, moral) and the
two *lapis* (layers or levels of meaning—i.e. the literal and the figurative) in such sayings.

(Winstedt 1981: 6)

Semantic explications for some Malay pepatah *and* bidalan

One of the canonical Malay cultural values is *rendah diri* 'to lower oneself' (Goddard
2000a). A common *peribahasa* referring to and reinforcing this value tells people to
"follow the way of the rice plant (*padi*)". The analogy, which is sometimes spelt out
explicitly, as in (3a), is that the more the rice plant grows full (with grain), the more it
bows over. Sometimes the rice plant is contrasted with the useless 'long grass'
(*lalang*). An online *peribahasa* dictionary gives the explanation in (3b).

(3)   a. *Ikut resmi padi, makin berisi makin tunduk, jangan ikut resmi lalang,*
          semakin tegak tiada berisi.
          'Follow the way of the rice plant, the more it grows full, the more it bows,
          don't follow the way of the long grass, as it grows taller, it remains hollow.'
          [translation, *CG*]

b. *Hendaklah merendah diri walaupun kita berilmu dan berpangkat dan jangan sombong.*

'We should lower ourselves even though we have knowledge and status and not be arrogant.' [translation, *CG*]

As suggested by the gloss in (3b), the proverb implies that the "fuller content" of a person can involve greater knowledge, as well as higher status or greater capabilities (cf. Lim 2003: 44). In usage, it is certainly applied to situations where what is at issue is popularity or recognition. For example, on a Malaysian blog a music fan, commenting on the success of the singer Ning, quotes the "way of the rice plant" saying, then continues in English: *I hope Ning will stay modest if she goes international.* In an online interview, a young self-made millionaire tells how he wants to emulate the low-key style of Bill Gates:

(4)   *Tetapi di Amerika Syarikat seperti Bill Gates sendiri, dia beri ceramah pakai baju T biasa sahaja. Yang penting kejayaan dia. Saya kalau boleh hendak menjadi seperti resmi padi—semakin berisi semakin tunduk.*

'But in the US, like Bill Gates himself, he gives presentations wearing just an ordinary T-shirt. What counts is his success. So if I can, I want to adopt the way of the rice plant—the more it grows full, the more it bows over.'

In explication [H] below, the meaning of the "way of the rice plant" saying is articulated inside the same five-part template developed for English metaphorical proverbs.[4] The RECURRENT SITUATION starts with someone having certain knowledge and certain capabilities, and an appropriate humble or self-lowering attitude. Subsequent to this, this person comes to know more and to be able to do more. When this happens in life, no doubt many people change their way of thinking, but the PROVERBIAL ADVICE delivered here is that to do so is not good. On the contrary, it is good if the person thinks their humble thoughts more often. The PROVERBIAL ANALOGY section sets out the well-known facts about the rice plant.

[H]   *Ikut resmi padi, (semakin berisi, semakin tunduk).*

'Follow the way of the rice plant (the more it grows full, the more it bows over).'

a.   for a long time before people in this place said these words at many times   TRADITIONALITY
      when they wanted to say something like this: – –

b.   it is often like this: RECURRENT SITUATION

---

[4] The only difference is the addition of the specification 'in this place' to the traditionality framing component. This is on account of the highly localized affiliation of Malay proverbs, which have been constructed as emblems of the Malay cultural "brand" (Goddard 2009*b*).

at some time, someone knows some things, this someone can do
   some things
at this time, this someone thinks like this:
   "I know some things, not many things, I can do some things, not many things
   I am not someone above other people, I am someone below other people"
some time after this, this someone knows more, this someone can do more

c.   when it is like this, it is not good if this someone doesn't think like this   PROVERBIAL
    anymore, it is good if this someone thinks like this more often   ADVICE

d.   it is like this: PROVERBIAL ANALOGY
    after a rice-plant* has some rice-seeds*, it bows* over
      [i.e. the top is below the place where it was before]
    after the rice-seeds* are big, it bows* over more

e.   many people live for a long time   STATUS AS FOLK WISDOM
    because of this, these people can know many things
    this is one of these things
    it can be good for someone if this someone thinks about this at some times

Another well-known Malay saying alludes to the transparent hypocrisy of people who instruct others in how to behave well while behaving in the opposite way themselves. It is *Seperti ketam mengajar (menyuruh) anak berjalan betul* 'like a crab teaching (or: telling) its young to walk straight', sometimes continued as follows *tetapi diri sendiri berjalan senget* 'but she herself walks crooked'. A *peribahasa* compendium glosses it as:

(5)   *Memberi nasihat pada orang lain padahal diri sendiri tidak betul.*
    'Giving advice to other people despite being not correct oneself.'

Notice that the "image" in this proverb is not a realistic one, in the sense that no one believes that crabs teach their young anything, let alone to walk straight, cf. English *Like the pot calling the kettle black.* (An even more dramatic "impossible image" is the English *People who live in glass houses shouldn't throw stones.*)

As one might imagine, the "crab teaching its young" proverb finds plenty of application in the political sphere. For example:

(6)   *Di manakah letaknya maruah orang Melayu? Ke manakah perginya budi bahasa? Barangkali Datuk Seri Rais Yatim ada jawapannya. . . . janganlah kita menjadi ketam yang mengajar anaknya berjalan betul; mengajar rakyat berbudi bahasa sedangkan pemimpin2 biadap dan kurang ajar!*

'Where has the dignity and self-respect of the Malays been put? Where has proper behaviour gone? Maybe Datuk Seri Rais Yatim has the answers . . . let's not be the crab that teaches its young to walk straight; instructing the public to be well-mannered while the leaders are discourteous and ill-bred!'

Like some English proverbs, this Malay example lacks any direct PROVERBIAL ADVICE. It gets its "sting" simply by depicting a certain undesirable recurrent situation. A couple of points of detail in the (b) section of explication [I] below are, first, that the person being criticized is someone "higher" than other people (as suggested by the image of a mother/father crab and its young, and by the verbs *mengajar* 'teach, instruct' and *menyuruh* 'tell to do, instruct'); and second, that the hypocritical attitude is presented as being obvious to everyone ('other people can know . . . they can't not know'). This latter element is implied by the analogy with the crab. Everybody knows that a crab doesn't walk straight; in fact, 'people can't not know this'.

[I]   Partial semantic explication for *Seperti ketam mengajar anak berjalan betul.*
       'Like a crab teaching its young to walk straight.'

b.   it is often like this: RECURRENT SITUATION
         someone is above someone else
         this someone says something like this to this other someone about some things:
            "when you do things like this, I want you to do it in one way,
            it is not good if you do it in another way"
         other people can know that when this someone does the same things,
            this someone does these things in this other way
         other people can't not know this
         it is not good if someone is like this

c.   – – –   PROVERBIAL ADVICE
d.   it is like this: PROVERBIAL ANALOGY
         everyone knows that a crab* doesn't ever walk* straight*
         people can't not know this

For a Malay saying that lacks a proverbial analogy, consider the example below. It emphasizes the need for verbal caution, a canonical theme of traditional Malay culture (Goddard 2000a).

(7)   *Ingatlah sebelum berkata-kata . . . ibarat kata . . . binasa badan kerana mulut.*
       'Think before you say anything . . . as the saying goes . . . the body suffers on account of the mouth.'

Variant forms include: *Tersilap cakaplah binasa badan* 'From a slip of speech, the body suffers', and *Binasa badan telajak lidah* [or: *bahasa*] 'The body suffers when the tongue [or: speech] overshoots the mark'.

This saying might seem to employ metaphorical wording, but although the body (*badan*) stands for a person and the mouth (*mulut*) stands for this person's words, this is as far as it goes. There is no implicit analogy about a real body suffering on account of a real mouth.

[J]   Partial semantic explication for *Binasa badan kerana mulut.*
      'The body suffers because of the mouth.'

b.   it is often like this: RECURRENT SITUATION
           someone says something about someone to someone else
           it can be something very small
           this someone does not think about it well before
           afterwards something very bad happens to this someone because of this
c.   because of this, it is not good for someone if this someone says something PROVERBIAL
      when this someone has not thought about it well before   ADVICE

After this exegesis of the meanings of these few Malay proverbs (additional examples are given in Appendix 8.2), the value of the paraphrase technique should be clearer. With familiar English proverbs, it is all too easy to believe that the meanings expressed are pretty simple and pretty obvious. When we encounter proverbs from a different culture, sometimes making reference to unfamiliar analogies and often embodying different value orientations to our own, the value of a meticulous paraphrase which spells out the message content in full detail is more apparent.

8.5 Concluding remarks

We have endeavoured in this chapter to do several things. Firstly, we have tried to show that proverb texts in English and Malay have a determinable semantic content, which can be pinned down and articulated by way of extended paraphrases using the NSM methodology. Secondly, by establishing the viability of a particular semantic template for these explications, we wanted to disclose the internal structure of meanings which are packaged, so to speak, in proverbial genres. This includes the idea that the individual message content is embedded inside a semantic frame that presupposes and projects a claim to traditionality of the words and message, and to the status of the message content as one item (among many such items) of something like "wisdom", i.e. potentially beneficial things that many people know (or can know) on account of having lived for a long time. The semantic template also includes a sub-structure for the message content itself, involving in the maximum case the identification of a recurrent situation, some proverbial advice about what it is good to do in such situations, and an analogy, usually based on a scene from everyday life. The wording of the proverb (if it is of the metaphorical variety) is based on the analogy. These objectives relate to the semantic aspects of proverb texts, in the sense of that aspect of meaning associated with the expressions themselves, as items of the language.

There are of course cultural issues concerning proverbs that go beyond the purely semantic (Goddard 2009b). The resonance and associations of the words themselves often matter to the overall import of a proverb or to the use of a proverb. For example, the agrarian lexicon of many English proverbs conveys a different import from the imagery of rice farming, forest, and fishing in their Malay counterparts. In both cases the words echo the past, but the echoes sound different. Many older English proverbs use (or used) Biblical language (e.g. *Who sows the wind will reap the whirlwind, No man can serve two masters, The love of money is the root of all evil*), and when the sources of such words are recognizable to speakers they carry resonances of faith, religion, and shared identity. Koranic sayings are currently enjoying an upsurge in Malaysia, and in a multilingual and multi-ethnic polity like that in Malaysia, choosing to use a "Malay saying" also provides speakers with a device for positioning themselves and/or their interlocutors within a complex "identity politics".

Moreover, as mentioned at the outset, the status and usage of proverbs and related "echoic" speech forms can be indicative of a broad range of cultural attitudes (mentalities) associated with different social and historical formations. Though some generalizations may be possible, it will not suffice to rely on simple contrasts between "traditional" and "modern" cultures, or between "oral" and "literate" societies. In this connection, Obelkevich's (1994[1987]) study of the social history of proverbs and associated speech genres in Europe is fascinating and instructive. The 16th and early 17th centuries were the golden age for proverbs in England, when they were studied, treasured, and used in abundance by educated people, as well as by the illiterate. Obelkevich charts how the educated classes' enthusiasm for proverbs then began to wane, and in the early 18th century gave way to outright rejection: "the expulsion of the proverb from learned culture is a landmark in social and linguistic history" (p. 230). This development coincided with the onset of the Enlightenment, a loss of reverence for the past, and the abandonment of the notion of traditional collective wisdom. The same period, however, saw the rise of a new and rival genre, the aphorism—more literary, more abstract, more individual. Later, in the Victorian years, there was a short-lived revival of proverbs, and the emergence of a new and even more "personalized" alternative genre, the great quotation. This in turn has gradually lost its gloss, and originality and individuality have triumphed as the leading values of the times. Among educated people, Obelkevich writes, apart from the occasional allusion, proverbs are now taboo:

Only when an old saying can be made to say something new, whether by irony or by more drastic means, are they accepted, but in the process they cease to express the wisdom of the community and become raw material for the wit and originality of the individual speaker.

(Obelkevich 1994[1987]: 239)

In short, not only can the study of proverbs and their meanings open a window onto collective values and worldviews, but the study of shifting attitudes towards proverbs and allied forms provides additional insights of its own.

As in so many aspects of human life, however, issues of meaning are integral and essential to understanding what people do and why. To get a grip on just about any form of communicative practice, we need improved tools for getting a grip on meaning.

Appendix 8.1 Partial explications (message content only) for four additional English proverbs

All that glitters is not gold.

b.   it is often like this: RECURRENT SITUATION
    someone thinks about something for a very short time
    after this, this someone thinks like this:
      "this is something very good, I want to do some things now because of this"
    because of this, this someone does some things at this time
    after this, when this someone knows more about it, this someone can't think like this any more
    this someone knows that it is not something very good
    this is bad for this someone

c.   because of this, it is not good if someone thinks like this about something   PROVERBIAL ADVICE
    after a very short time:
    "this is something very good, I want to do some things now because of this"

d.   it is like this: PROVERBIAL ANALOGY
    when many people see some things, they think about these things after a very short time:
      "this is gold [m], I want it to be mine"
    they think like this because these things glitter* like gold [m] glitters*
    when they think more about it, they can't think like this any more
    they know at that time that these things are not *gold

Too many cooks spoil the broth.[5]

b.   it is often like this: RECURRENT SITUATION
    there are many people in one place
    these people want something to happen in this place
    they know that it can't happen if they don't do some things
    because of this, they all want to do these things
    for some time they all do the same things at the same time in the same place

---

[5] *Too many cooks spoil the broth* is sometimes said to have an antonym in *Many hands make light work*. Notice, therefore, that the recurrent situation and proverbial advice in the explication would not apply to the prototypical situations for *Many hands make light work*, i.e. sharing a "distributed" physical task such as moving a heavy load.

because of this, none of these people can do these things well

because of this, it doesn't happen as they want

this is bad

c.   because of this, when many people all want the same thing to happen,   PROVERBIAL ADVICE

it is not good for these people if they all do the same things in the same place at the

same time

d.   it is like this: PROVERBIAL ANALOGY

sometimes some people do some things at the same time in the same place

because they want to make [m] some good things for people to eat [m]

if these people all do the same things at the same time, none of them can do these things well

because of this, they can't make [m] something good

this is bad

You can't teach an old dog new tricks.

b.   it is often like this: RECURRENT SITUATION

someone says some things to someone else for a long time,

because they want this other someone to know how to do something well

this other someone can't know it well,

because this other someone was born [m] a very long time before

c.   because of this, it is not good if someone thinks about someone else like this,   PROVERBIAL

if this other someone has lived for a very long time: ADVICE

"I want this someone to know how to do something well

because of this, I will say some things to this someone for some time"

it can be good to think something like this:

"this someone knows how to do many other things well"

d.   it is like this: PROVERBIAL ANALOGY

when someone does some things because this someone wants a dog [m] to

learn* to do something, this dog [m] can't learn* it,

if this dog [m] was born [m] a very long time before

if this dog [m] was born [m] a very long time before, this dog [m] can do many other things well

Where there's smoke, there's fire.

b.   it is often like this: RECURRENT SITUATION

someone knows that something is happening in the place where this someone is

this someone thinks like this about it:

"I know that something of this kind can't happen

if something else of another kind didn't happen before

if it is like this, I want to know more about it"

because of this, this someone can know what happened before

this is good

c.   when someone knows that things of some kinds are happening in a place,   PROVERBIAL

it can be good if this someone thinks like this about it   ADVICE

d.   it is like this: PROVERBIAL ANALOGY
     people know that there can't be smoke* in a place, if there was not fire [m]
      in this place before
     because of this, when people see smoke* in a place,
     they can know that there was fire [m] in this place before

Appendix 8.2 Partial explications (message content only) for four additional Malay proverbs

Ada gula, ada semut 'Where there's sugar, there's ants'. This saying is said to have two related interpretations, given informally in (a) and (b) below (from www.bahasa-melayu.com/pe ribahasa/a.html, accessed 20/12/06). The explication applies to the first interpretation.

a.   *Orang berharta dan berkedudukan mempunyai banyak kawan.*
    'Someone with valuable possessions and status will have many friends.'

b.   *Di tempat orang mudah mendapat rezeki, di situlah orang bertumpu.*
    'In a place where it's easy to find a living, that's where people will gather.'

b.   it is often like this: RECURRENT SITUATION
     when someone has many good things, many people want to be with this someone,
      many people want to do things with this someone
     these people want this because they want to have some of this other someone's things
     they don't want this because they feel something good towards this someone
c.   – –   PROVERBIAL ADVICE
d.   it is like this: PROVERBIAL ANALOGY
     when there is sugar [m] in a place, often there are many ants* in this place
     the ants* are in this place because they want to have sugar [m], not because of anything else
     everyone knows this

Seperti katak di bawah tempurung 'like a frog under a coconut shell', one of the most famous Malay *peribahasa*.

b.   it is often like this: RECURRENT SITUATION
     someone lives in one small place for a long time
     afterwards this someone can think like this:
      "I know everything about this place
      I know everything about people in this place"
     when this someone thinks like this, this someone feels something good
     because of this, this someone doesn't think about other places, this someone doesn't want
      to know about other places
     this is not good
c.   – –   PROVERBIAL ADVICE
d.   it is like this: PROVERBIAL ANALOGY
     if a frog* is under* a coconut shell*, it can think like this:

"I can see everything in this place"
this frog* doesn't know that there are other places
it doesn't know that there are many other things in these other places

Keluar mulut harimau, masuk mulut buaya 'Out from the tiger's mouth, into the crocodile's mouth'. This is another well-known Malay saying, with several variants.

b.   it is often like this: RECURRENT SITUATION
        someone thinks like this at some time:
            "something very bad can happen to me now
            I don't want it to happen to me"
        because of this, this someone does something
        because of this, afterwards this very bad thing doesn't happen to this someone
        another very bad thing happens to this someone
        this someone did not think before that it could be like this

c.   – –   PROVERBIAL ADVICE

d.   it is like this: PROVERBIAL ANALOGY
        when someone is somewhere where there is a tiger*, this someone thinks like this:
            "something very bad can happen to me here now
            I want to be somewhere else where there is no tiger*"
        because of this, this someone does something
        after this, when this someone is somewhere else, there is a crocodile* in this other place
        this someone did not think before that it could be like this

Bila gajah dan gajah berlawan, kancil juga yang mati tersepit 'When elephant fights elephant, it's the mousedeer that's squashed to death'.

b.   it is often like this: RECURRENT SITUATION
        two kinds of people are in one place
        one kind are big people, they can do many things as they want
        the other kind are small people, they can't do many things as they want
        some of these big people want to do some bad things to some of the other big people
        because of this, they do something for some time
        the other big people do the same at the same time
        when big people do things like this in this place, very bad things happen to the small people
            because they are in the same place at the same time

c.   when big people in a place do things like this,   PROVERBIAL ADVICE
        if someone is someone small,
            it is good for this someone if this someone can be not in this place

d.   it is like this: PROVERBIAL ANALOGY
        two kinds of animals [m] live in the jungle*
        one kind are elephants*, they are big
        the other kind are mousedeer*, they are small
        the elephants* are above the mousedeer*
        when elephants* fight*, very bad things can happen to the mousedeer* because of this
        the mousedeer* can die because of this

9

The meaning of "abstract nouns"

Locke, Bentham, and contemporary semantics

Though therefore it be the mind that makes the collection, 'tis the name which is as it were the knot that ties them fast together.

(John Locke, *An Essay Concerning Human Understanding*, book III, v, §10)

To language, then—to language alone—it is that fictitious entities owe their existence; their impossible, yet indispensable existence.

(Jeremy Bentham, *Works*, vol. VIII, §vi)

9.1 "Abstract" and "concrete" in the linguistic and logical literature

The distinction between "abstract nouns" and "concrete nouns" is deeply entrenched in linguistic terminology and is usually taken for granted in linguistic descriptions, but it is far from clear what exactly is meant by "abstract nouns" and "concrete nouns".

Linguists generally prefer to rely on illustrations, rather than on definitions: "abstract nouns" are those like *goodness, beauty*, etc., whereas "concrete nouns" are those like *tree, bed*, or *dog*. Two linguistic authorities who have offered definitions are Quirk et al. (1972) in their *Grammar of Contemporary English* and David Crystal (1994[1992]) in his *Encyclopedic Dictionary of Language and Languages*. Quirk et al. (1972: 48) state that "nouns [...] refer to entities that are regarded as stable, whether these are concrete (physical) like *house, table, paper*, or abstract (of the mind) like *hope, botany, length*". In their formulation, then, it is the entities referred to by nouns which can be divided into "concrete (physical)" and "abstract". But this of course begs the question: how does one distinguish these two kinds of "entities", and what exactly is meant by "abstract entities"? The word *concrete* is at least provided with a quasi-explanatory comment (i.e. 'physical'), but the word *abstract* is not provided with any explanation at all.

Crystal (1994[1992]: 78) writes:

concrete Descriptive of nouns which refer to physical entities (*book, car, egg*); contrasts with abstract, which applies to nouns lacking physical reference (*information, idea, certainty*). The distinction is not clear-cut, as many nouns have properties which would allow either inter-pretation (*structure, music, version*).

Is this intended to mean that nouns like *structure, music,* and *version* are polysemous, or that they are inherently vague? Crystal does not explain, and in any case it is not clear how the criterion of "physical reference" could apply to nouns like *structure, music,* or *version* on any interpretation.

Logicians have traditionally distinguished between "abstract names" and "concrete names", but the definitions they have proposed are equally problematic. For example, John Stuart Mill in his classic *System of Logic* (1843) wrote:

> The second general division of names [after that between "general" and "individual" ones— *AW/CG*] is into *concrete* and *abstract*. A concrete name is a name which stands for a thing; an abstract name is a name which stands for an attribute of a thing. Thus *John, the sea, this table,* are names of things. *White,* also, is the name of a thing, or rather of things. *Whiteness,* again, is the name of a quality or attribute of those things. *Man* is a name of many things; *humanity* is a name of an attribute of things; *old age* is a name of one of their attributes.   (Mill 1961[1843]: 17)

This is all very well, but what exactly does it mean to say that "an abstract name is a name which stands for an attribute of a thing"? Mill himself notes: "it may be objected to our definition of an abstract name that not only the names which we have called abstract, but adjectives, which we have placed in the concrete class, are names of attributes" (p. 18). Mill tries to counter this objection by arguing that in fact only *whiteness* is the name of an attribute, and *white* is not, but this explanation is obscure, given that we have no independent definition of the word *attribute*.

What is clear is that for Mill, *whiteness* is an "abstract name" whereas both *snow* and *white* are "concrete names". This is at odds with the basic intuition of ordinary speakers that, for example, *snow* is 'something' ('something of one kind'), whereas *white* is not 'something'. It is also at odds with the evidence of grammar: people's use of words like *snow* (nouns) is quite different from their use of words like *white* (adjectives). From a linguistic point of view, then, Mill's distinctions are arbitrary and unhelpful: they are anchored neither in linguistic evidence nor in the speakers' intuitions.

Given the absence of clear criteria for distinguishing "abstract nouns" from "concrete nouns", it is remarkable how often these categories have been taken for granted. In psycholinguistics, in particular, various accounts have been developed on how "concrete" and "abstract" words are stored, accessed, retrieved, and so on, in the mental lexicon (e.g. Kroll and Merves 1986; Altarriba and Bauer 2004). Likewise, linguists continue to use the time-honoured term "abstract nouns" with hardly a qualm about its ill-defined status. The question is: does the putative category of "abstract noun" deserve to be preserved in 21st-century linguistics, and if so, on what basis? We believe that it does, and in this chapter we seek, *inter alia,* to show on what basis this can be done, building on the ideas put forward by John Locke (1690) in his *An Essay Concerning Human Understanding.*[1]

9.2 Abstract nouns and mental ontologies

Before recalling Locke's seminal ideas, let us start with a simple linguistic example. Consider the meaning of the English noun *illness*, in comparison with that of the adjective *ill*, from which the noun is obviously derived. The *Collins Cobuild English Language Dictionary* (1991) assigns to *illness* the following definition: "*illness* is the experience of being ill for a period of time", thus seemingly suggesting that the meaning of the noun *illness* adds to the meaning of the adjective *ill* the idea of 'experience'. This cannot be right, however, since one can speak just as easily of "the experience of being ill" as of "the experience of illness". Evidently, the *Collins Cobuild* definition uses the word 'experience' simply as a nominalizing device, thus implying that the only difference between *illness* and *ill* is grammatical, and that *illness* means in effect the same as *ill*.

But if *illness* means *ill*, what does a word like *disease* (which is not derived from any adjective) mean, and how is the close semantic relationship between *disease* and *illness* to be explained? Sadly, here the *Collins Cobuild* offers the following set of answers:

1. *Disease* or *a disease* is an illness in people, animals, or plants which is caused by bacteria or infection, rather than by an accident.
2. An *illness* is a particular disease that people can suffer from, such as a cold, measles, or pneumonia.
3. Someone who is *ill* is suffering from a disease or health problem which makes them unable to work or live normally.

---

[1] Our focus here is the semantic structure of "abstract nouns", but it must be said that the traditional notional definitions of "concrete noun" also leave much to be desired. Our approach can be sketched under three points. First, we note that the traditional dichotomy between concrete nouns (e.g. *bed, apple, cat, gold, water*) and abstract nouns (e.g. *death, beauty, disease, trauma, heat*) applies primarily to nouns based on the substantive SOMETHING, often but not always in combination with KIND. Second, we observe that we can find a workable criterion to separate the classes by reference to "localizability", i.e. the applicability or inapplicability of the question 'where is it?' For example, the sentence *Where is the bed?* is perfectly ordinary, whereas one such as **Where is the death?* is unacceptable. Third, we acknowledge that various caveats need to be added. For example, we need to exclude elliptical and rhetorical sentences, such as *Where is your courage/intelligence/decency?*, which obviously do not refer to a place at all. We also have to recognize that 'being somewhere' is not the same as 'happening somewhere'; for example, *earthquake* is not a concrete noun, but if someone asks about an earthquake, *Where is it?*, the question means 'where is it happening?' With these caveats in place, we can say that the "locational frame" ('where is it?') allows us to identify a class of "concrete nouns" broadly coinciding with that envisaged in traditional grammar. Importantly, if something is somewhere, then this something can be pointed at ('this shirt', 'this tree', 'this water'). This gives expressions based on such nouns the property described in technical language as "referentiality": their intended referents can in principle be pointed at and thus identified jointly by a gesture visible to other people and by the words 'this something' ('this shirt', 'this tree', etc.).

Thus, *ill* is defined via *disease*, *disease* via an *illness*, and an *illness* again via *disease*.

Obviously, the approach illustrated by the *Dictionary* does not work and leads us into a blind alley. Apart from everything else, this failure to come to grips with the relationships like that between *disease* and *illness* has unfortunate consequences for language teaching. For example, Russian makes no lexical distinction analogous to that between *illness* and *disease*, and for Russian learners of English it is really important to find out what the two words mean and how their meanings differ. But monolingual English dictionaries will not help them, and bilingual ones only take the confusion further, by (understandably but unhelpfully) identifying both *illness* and *disease* with *bolezn'* (cf. e.g. *Oxford English–Russian Dictionary* 1980; 1984).

To find a way out of the blind alley we need to acknowledge that a concept like 'disease' is not based directly on any adjectival (or verbal) meaning, but rather belongs to a mental ontology (Chilton 2004) created in the English language by its repertoire of abstract nouns; and also that in fact the same applies to a derived abstract noun like *illness*.

The concept of a "mental ontology" is important here, and we will return to it at various points later. For the moment, we want to highlight the fact (which was discussed with great perspicacity by Locke) that the meanings of abstract nouns generally don't match across language boundaries. To be sure, the meanings of concrete nouns often do not match either: for example, the English *butterfly* does not mean the same as the Russian *babočka* (which could be a moth), and the English *cheese* does not mean the same as the Russian *syr* (e.g. *cottage cheese* is not *syr* but *tvorog*: cf. Jakobson 1959). Nonetheless, as discussed by Locke, generally speaking, concrete nouns are much more likely to match than abstract nouns (see section 9.5), and the discrepancy between (on the one hand) the English words *illness* and *disease* and (on the other) the Russian *bolezn'* is a good case in point.

Furthermore, the deep and pervasive discrepancies between the meanings of abstract nouns in different languages matter much more than those in the area of the concrete lexicon—another point which was crystal clear to Locke, who saw better than anyone else its consequences for law, ethics, science, and philosophy:

The terms of our law, which are not empty sounds, will hardly find words that answer them in the Spanish or Italian, no scanty languages; much less, I think, could any one translate them into the Caribbee or Westoe tongues: and the *versura* of the Romans, or *corban* of the Jews, have no words in other languages to answer them; the reason whereof is plain, from what has been said. Nay, if we look a little more nearly into this matter, and exactly compare different languages, we shall find that though they have words which in translations and dictionaries are supposed to answer one another, yet there is scarce one of ten amongst the names of complex ideas, especially of mixed modes, that stands for the same precise idea, which the word does that in dictionaries it is rendered by [...] and we shall find this much more so in the names of more abstract and compounded ideas, such as are the greatest part of those which make up moral discourses: whose names, when men come curiously to compare with those they are translated into, in other languages, they will find very few of them exactly to correspond in the whole extent of their significations.   (Locke 1959[1690]: book III, v, §8)

The importance of these observations, and especially of their implications for today's globalized world where one language (English) is rapidly becoming the world language, can hardly be overestimated (Wierzbicka 2006a; 2010a). Like other languages, English carries with it particular mental ontologies, and given the role of English in the contemporary world and its close association with science (as a global pursuit), it is particularly important for the language-based status of these ontologies to be recognized and acknowledged. With these broader considerations in mind, we propose here an approach to the semantics of abstract nouns which frees us from circularity, obscurity, and false cross-linguistic equations, and at the same time allows us to explain mental ontologies entrenched in the English language to native speakers of other languages and to unwitting adherents of other mental frameworks.

9.3 Example 1: *illness* and *disease*

As a starting point, we propose that abstract nouns such as *illness* and *disease* contain in their meaning a semantic component which can be represented as 'something', and also an explicit reference to a particular 'word'—in the case of *illness*, a reference to the word *illness*, and in that of *disease*, a reference to the word *disease*. At first sight, this may seem circular, but as it will become clear as we proceed, it is not. We do not define the word *ill* via the word *ill*, we only propose that the noun *illness* refers in its meaning both to the concept 'ill' and to a particular, language-specific word which establishes the condition of being ill as an identifiable mental entity. The proposal can be formalized as in explication [A] below.

As we have seen at various places in this book, some explications make use of productive semantic molecules, which are marked in explications by the notation '[m]'. These intermediate-level meanings function as building blocks in the composition of numerous complex meanings. We now want to identify another way in which a complex meaning can find its way into an explication—i.e. in the case that there is a genuine relationship of semantic derivation between one word and another morphologically derived from it. In such cases, the base word can function as an element in an explication, and we indicate this in explications by the notation '[d]'.[2]

---

[2] To clarify the difference between the use of a "derivational base" and a "semantic molecule", it can be added that the former is a highly localized and specialized phenomenon. Each derivational base is confined to a handful of morphologically related words. Semantic molecules, on the other hand, range widely across the lexicon and are not visible in the surface morphology.

[A]   *illness*

a.   something

b.   people can say what this something is with the word *illness*

c.   someone can say something about something with this word when this someone thinks
        like this:

d.   "it can be like this:

e.   someone is ill [d] for some time"

The adjective 'ill' in component (e) is of course semantically complex, and, as we will see in a moment, it can be explicated separately, in simpler terms, The explication given in [A] assumes that the meaning of the noun *illness* builds on that of the adjective but is not identical with it. Rather, the noun "reifies" a potential situation whose description involves the adjective. In the explication the reification is shown by starting with the substantive component 'something', which is linked with a particular identifying word, in (b). The word is then characterized, in (c), as a discourse tool, so to speak (a way of saying something about something), associated with a particular way of thinking which invokes a certain potential situation ((d) and (e)).

It is of course not an accident that the meaning of the adjective *ill* is included in that of the abstract noun *illness*. The derivational morphology reflects the semantic relationship between the two, as it does in the case of hundreds of other adjectives and abstract nouns in English (and in many other languages). We suggest that the adjective *ill* can be explicated as follows.

[B]   *She was ill.*

a.   something bad was happening to her body for some time

b.   because of this, she felt something bad in her body during this time

c.   because of this, she couldn't do many things during this time like she could at other
        times

The adjective can be used about a particular person, in a particular situation. The derived abstract noun, on the other hand, refers to a hypothetical person in a potential situation, not anchored in any particular time.

As Locke (1959[1690]) argued in relation to what he called "mixed modes": "who can doubt but the ideas of *sacrilege* or *adultery* might be framed in the minds of men, and have names given them, and so these species of names be constituted, before either of them was ever committed [...] And I think nobody can deny but that the *resurrection* was a species of mixed modes in the mind, before it really existed" (book III, v, §5). The component 'it can be like this', which we posit for these abstract nouns, tallies well with Locke's argument. The usefulness, and indeed necessity, of such an approach to the semantics of abstract nouns becomes particularly clear when we seek to explicate abstract nouns like *disease*, which are not derived from an adjective or a verb. We propose the following explication. Note that components (a)–(d), the framing components associated with the word's status as an abstract noun, are exactly the same as for *illness*.

[C]   *disease*

a.   something

b.   people can say what this something is with the word *disease*

c.   someone can say something about something with this word when this someone thinks like this:

d.   "it can be like this:

e.   something bad of one kind is happening to some people's bodies for a long time

f.   it is happening because something bad is happening inside these people's bodies"

Comparing the explications, it can be seen that the concept of *illness* emphasizes individual persons and their bodily feelings and capabilities, whereas that of *disease* focuses on objective causes which can adversely affect many people's bodies in more or less predictable ways; cf. the contrast between the expressions *contagious disease* vs. **contagious illness*. This is consistent with the easy extension of *disease* from people to animals and plants, and with the more "scientific" character of the *disease* concept. The explications proposed here recognize an existential and experiential dimension in *illness*, and the absence of any such component to *disease*; cf. the contrast between *I feel ill* vs. **I feel diseased*. They are also consistent with the intuitions reflected in the *Collins Cobuild* definitions, which link *illness* with someone's experience ("the experience of being ill for a period of time"), and *disease* with bacteria and infection. Unlike those definitions, however, the NSM explications proposed here articulate those intuitions without circularity or obscurity, and in a way which makes the conceptual similarities and differences between *illness* and *disease* transparent.

The explications above are proposed for *illness* and *disease* as **non-countable** nouns, as in the following examples. Example (1) presents the opening sentences of Susan Sontag's (2002) *Illness as Metaphor* and *Aids and its Metaphors*.

(1) **Illness** is the night-side of life, a more onerous citizenship. Everyone who is born holds dual citizenship, in the kingdom of the well and in the kingdom of the sick. (Sontag 2002: 1)

(2) Death and **disease** are often beautiful, like (. . .) the hectic glow of consumption. (Thoreau, quoted in Sontag 2002: 20)

(3) The romantic view is that **illness** exacerbates consciousness. (Sontag 2002: 36)

Both *illness* and *disease* can also be used as countable nouns, as in the following examples (also from *Illness as Metaphor*):

(4) Two **diseases** have been spectacularly, and similarly, encumbered by the trappings of metaphor: tuberculosis and cancer. (Sontag 2002: 5)

(5) Once that **illness** was TB; now it is insanity that is thought to bring consciousness to a state of paroxysmic enlightenment. (Sontag 2002: 37)

We would suggest that when *illness* and *disease* are used as countable nouns, the first line of their explications should read as 'something of one kind', rather than simply 'something', as follows:

[D]   *an illness*

a.   something of one kind
b.   people can say what this something is with the word *illness*
c.   someone can say something about something with this word when this someone thinks like this:
d.   "it can be like this:
e.   someone is ill [d] for some time"

[E]   *a disease*

a.   something of one kind
b.   people can say what this something is with the word *disease*
c.   someone can say something about something with this word when this someone thinks like this:
d.   "it can be like this:
e.   something bad of one kind is happening to some people's bodies for a long time
f.   it is happening because something bad is happening inside these people's bodies"

Of course, nouns do not divide neatly into two classes, "countable" and "uncountable", and the grammatical semantics of "countability" in a given language can be in fact quite complex. For "concrete nouns", we have studied this complexity in considerable detail in earlier work (see Wierzbicka 1985a; 1988; Goddard 2009c; 2009e; forthcoming a). For abstract nouns, a full picture requires further investigation, but we are confident that what matters most in the present context is the distinction between 'something' and 'something of one kind' (see also section 9.6).

We would now like to discuss in greater detail the language-specificity of abstract nouns, and to illustrate how particular abstract nouns can function as dominant discourse topics.

9.4 Example 2: the post-Holocaust "*trauma* discourse" in English-speaking countries

The importance of abstract nouns is highlighted by the fact that these words often have no counterparts in other languages and yet seem quite central, almost indispensable, to the thinking of those who are familiar with them. A good illustration of this point, which has profound implications for intercultural communication, is the English word *trauma*, and the "trauma discourse" of the last half-century or so.

As discussed, for example, by Eva Hoffman (2004), the use of the word *trauma* is one of the hallmarks of Holocaust literature in English-speaking countries. It is a term which provided the children of survivors with an interpretive key to the legacy of their parents' generation—a legacy of "scars and wounds", of "the splintered signs of acute suffering of grief and loss", rather than "thoughts or images".

> Such things, in our contemporary parlance, have come to be called trauma. "Trauma" is the contemporary master term in the psychology of suffering, the chief way we understand the personal aftermath of atrocity and abuse. The survivors of such events, we take it for granted, have been traumatized; and Holocaust survivors are the chief exemplars of such damage. "Trauma" is our culture's way of extricating one set of meanings from the Holocaust legacy, and from genocide. But it was not always so, and it is worth pausing to ponder the history of this influential idea and what it may tell us about the conditions of extreme violence and its survival. (Hoffman 2004: 35)

It is also worth pausing to ponder what the history of the idea of *trauma* and of "trauma discourse" in a variety of contexts (psychological, historical, international, humanitarian, and so on) can tell us about the meaning and power of abstract nouns, and about their influence in human thinking and human affairs.

Hoffman notes further that "in the first decades after the war, neither the term nor the concept had entered the wider, non-medical vocabulary, and there was no general awareness that certain kinds of extreme abuse and violence [...] might have an impact that lasts beyond its occasion or wrench the psyche of its target out of its customary position and perceptions" (p. 35). But once the term *trauma* did enter the general non-medical vocabulary, "trauma discourse" spread widely in Anglophone countries: the concept of *trauma* started to be applied to all sorts of historical and geographical contexts, and its referent came to be seen as something that exists, rather than a way of thinking about what can happen to some people in certain circumstances.

Hoffman comments on the history of the idea created and popularized by the word *trauma* as follows:

> [...] after a period when "trauma" was the unquestioned term of explanation for all forms of postviolent conditions and all cultural contexts, in recent years, in the next swing of the pendulum or conceptual correction, a fledgling critique of the "trauma discourse" has begun to be advanced. The critique comes mostly from a very interesting source: the cadres of humanitarian aid personnel and assorted counselors who have been exported by Western countries to sites of war and violence all over our perennially violent globe. On the basis of their first-hand observations, these fieldworkers in landscapes after battle have begun to note, and to tell us, that reactions to atrocity do not always follow a course that can be easily classified under the rubric of "trauma"; and that, even if they are administered with the best

intentions, the Western, psychological models for addressing loss and mourning are some-times entirely inappropriate to local cultures. To the villagers of Bosnia or the Congo, "the discourse of trauma," with its vision of the resolutely separate self, and its techniques of depth-psychological probing may seem a very strange—indeed, and alien—invention.

(Hoffman 2004: 269–270)

So are "traumas" fact or fiction? Something real that happens to people or a way of thinking created by the invention of a word?

These are crude and unhelpful alternatives. The framing components of an explication can, we suggest, facilitate a better understanding of what is going on.

[F]   *trauma*

a.   something
b.   people can say what this something is with the word *trauma*
c.   someone can say something about something with this word when this someone thinks like this:
d.   "it can be like this: . . ."

As this partial explication indicates, a word like *trauma* stands indeed for a way of thinking. It is entirely possible, however, indeed likely, that when such a way of thinking emerges in a given historical context and becomes firmly entrenched in it, it reflects some new realities. This seems to be Hoffman's own conclusion in relation to *trauma*—that it is a new way of thinking, capturing some distinct new reality, above all, new forms of historical experience. Thus, she compares the use of the concept of *trauma* in the Holocaust literature with the use of the concept *tragedy* (*tragedia*) in the Polish war literature, and links the two not only with different ways of thinking but also with differences in historical experience:

War is always utterly deplorable, and the suffering it causes always incalculable. And yet that suffering can come in different valences, different affective tonalities. For all the enormous losses that non-Jewish Poles incurred in the Second World War, and for all the intense cult of memory in that country, the war there is remembered as tragedy rather than trauma. It is interesting in this respect that there is no non-Jewish "second generation" in Poland; that is, no group that conceives of itself as the inheritors of the war's psychological—rather than historical—legacy. But perhaps tragic suffering is more resolvable than the traumatic kind. For tragedy, of course, involves a conflict—agon—between opposing principles and agents. Trauma is produced by persecution of subjects to whom all agency and principle have been denied. Tragic struggle may entail moral agony, but it leaves the sense of identity and dignity intact. Violent abuse can lead to a deeper penetration and fragmentation of the psychic cells, of the victim's self and soul.   (Hoffman 2004: 41)

Thus, according to Hoffman, the concept 'trauma' fits certain kinds of experience better than others. At the same time, it is a concept which embodies a certain **analysis** of experience, that is, a certain way of thinking, identifiable through the abstract noun *trauma.* To capture the specific content of the *trauma* concept, we propose that a full explication would read as follows:

[G]   *trauma*

a.   something

b.   people can say what this something is with the word *trauma*

c.   someone can say something about something with this word when this someone thinks like this:

d.   "it can be like this:

e.   something very bad happens to someone for some time

f.   at this time, this someone thinks like this:

g.   "I want these bad things not to be happening
           I want to do something because of this
           I know that I can't do anything"

h.   because of this, after this, this someone feels something very bad for a long time

i.   this someone can't say anything about it to other people for a long time

j.   this someone doesn't want to think about it for a long time

k.   because of all these things, this someone is not like this someone was before

l.   this someone can't feel many good things like this someone could before"

This explication may appear long, but we would argue that its length is a reflection of the inherent complexity and specificity of the concept. We will run briefly through the components in the potential scenario. Components (e)–(g) indicate that the "*trauma* concept" is grounded in someone's experience of something very bad happening to them, under conditions in which they experience what Hoffman (2004) calls an absolute "denial of agency". Subsequently, as stated in component (h), the victim experiences sustained and intense bad feelings, but he or she is inhibited in speaking about it to others and instead tries to put it out of mind (components (i) and (j)). Together, these experiences enact a deep existential change in the person: 'because of all these things, this someone is not like this someone was before'; in particular, the person's capacity to 'feel many good things' is impaired.

Another contemporary writer who has written in an informed and insightful way about the word *trauma* and the way of thinking embedded in its meaning is the British historian Catherine Merridale. In her acclaimed book *Night of Stone: Death and Memory in Twentieth-Century Russia* (2001), she writes:

The idea of psychological damage—mental distress, trauma (a central theme of Holocaust writing)—is something that most Russians reject. Even psychologists and doctors have their doubts, and for many of the older ones who trained while Stalin was alive, the concept itself is entirely strange. They cannot picture it, this trauma, and they do not understand its privileged place in the Western understanding of violence and its consequences. I have tried to explore why this might be. Part of the answer is that even the idea of mental illness remains largely taboo in Russia. But it is also possible that this particular diagnosis and its treatment are so alien to the Russian way of thinking about life, death, and individual need that notions of psychological trauma are genuinely irrelevant to Russian minds, as foreign as the imported machinery that seizes up and fails in a Siberian winter.   (Merridale 2001: 16)

Foreign concepts like *trauma* can of course be imported, either through loanwords or through calques, but in both cases the word carrying the concept plays a funda-mental importance. The top component of the meaning of the abstract noun ('something') shows how this noun reifies a certain way of thinking, and the second one ('people can say what this something is with the word...') how the different ingredients of this way of thinking become cemented into one 'something' by means of a particular word. The explication proposed in [G] above does not stipulate that the 'something' in question exists, but it shows how the use of an abstract noun can firmly establish this 'something' in the mental ontology of discourse.

9.5 Locke on the semantics of abstract nouns

The approach to the semantics of abstract nouns outlined here corresponds to a considerable degree to that advanced in John Locke's (1690) *An Essay Concerning Human Understanding*. Locke's paradigm example of what he called "mixed modes" was *parricide*, on which he commented as follows:

[...] 'tis by their names, that men commonly regulate their account of their distinct species of mixed modes, seldom allowing or considering any number of simple *ideas* to make one complex one, but such collections as there be names for. Thus, though the killing of an old man be as fit in nature to be united into one complex idea as the killing a man's father; yet there being no name standing precisely for the one, as there is the name of *parricide* to mark the other, it is not taken for a particular complex idea, nor a distinct species of actions, for that of killing a young man, or any other man.   (1959[1690]: book II, xxii, §4)

Thus, according to Locke, the idea of "father-killing" as a distinct kind of act is due to the existence of the word *parricide*: it is the word which ties together the simpler ideas of 'father' and 'killing' into one, and thus creates an impression that there is such a thing as "father-killing" (in contrast to "old-man-killing"), or as he says elsewhere in the *Essay*, "son-killing", "daughter-killing", or "neighbour-killing":

[...] what union is there in nature between the idea of the relation of a father with killing than that of a son, or neighbour; that those are combined into one complex *idea*, and thereby made the essence of the distinct species *parricide*, whilst the other make no distinct species at all? [...] Thus the mind in mixed modes arbitrarily unites into complex ideas such as it finds convenient, whilst others that have altogether as much union in nature are left loose, and never combined into one *idea*, because they have no need of one name.   (book III, v, §6)

Again and again Locke emphasizes that it is the mind which "makes" ideas such as 'parricide', 'incest', 'adultery', 'sacrilege' and so on, and that it does this by choosing some simpler ideas, combining them into one and tying them together by a name (cf. e.g. book III, v, §6). He also emphasizes, again and again, that such making of new ideas is "arbitrary" but not random: it is arbitrary in relation to "nature", but is dictated by the interests and communicative needs of the speakers of a particular language.

> Nobody can doubt but that these *ideas* of mixed modes are made by a voluntary collection of *ideas* put together in the mind, independent of any original patterns in nature, who will but reflect that this sort of complex *ideas* may be made, abstracted, and have names given them, and so a species be constituted before any one individual of that species ever existed. Who can doubt but the ideas of sacrilege, of adultery, might be framed in the mind of men and have names given them, and so these species of mixed modes be constituted, before either of them was ever committed; and might be as well discoursed of and reasoned about, and as certain truths discovered of them, whilst yet they had no being but in the understanding, as well as now, that they have but too frequently a real existence? Whereby it is plain how much *the sorts of mixed* modes are the creatures of the understanding.   (book III, v, §5)

Thus, various types of actions and events tend to be treated by people as distinct categories solely because there are in a given language certain abstract nouns corresponding to them. Such categories "are the creatures of the understanding" but they are treated as "essences": "'tis the mind that combines several scattered independent Ideas into one complex one; and by the common name it gives them makes them the essence of a certain species, without regulating itself by any connection they have in nature" (book III, v, §§5–6).

Locke pleads: "who can doubt" and "nobody can deny", but what he presents as indubitable and undeniable has of course often been denied (or ignored)—in his own times, and in the three centuries which followed the publication of the *Essay*. For example, when philosophers publish books with titles like *What Emotions Really Are*, they seem to assume that "emotions" really exist and that they form a category created by the "patterns of nature", rather than being created by their own minds and by the lexicon of the modern English language. According to the approach developed here, which incorporates Locke's basic ideas concerning "mixed modes" into an NSM analysis of the semantics of abstract nouns, the meaning of an abstract word like *parricide* (or *patricide*) can be portrayed as follows. (Notice that 'kill' and 'father' are functioning in this explication as semantic molecules.)

[H]   *parricide (patricide)*

a.   something

b.   people can say what this something is with the word *parricide (patricide)*

c.   someone can say something about something with this word when this someone thinks like this:

d.   "it can be like this:
e.   someone thinks like this: 'it will be good if I kill [m] my father [m]'
f.   because of this, after this, this someone does it
g.   it is very bad if it is like this"
h.   when people think about it, they can't not feel something very bad

There is no need for detailed discussion of the content of this explication at this stage, except perhaps for two points. Component (e) portrays the mental state of the perpetrator not simply as 'I want to kill my father', which could be compatible with an impulse in a moment of rage, but as a more considered thought, tinged with something like self-justification: 'it will be good if I kill [m] my father [m].' Component (h) adds a dimension of social abhorrence, above and beyond the strong disapproval already expressed in component (g).

This analysis corresponds to Locke's insofar as it treats the seemingly unitary idea of 'patricide' as dependent on the word *parricide* (*patricide*), and as entrenching a particular way of thinking, based around a potential state of affairs: 'it can be like this ...'.

We would like to emphasize, furthermore, something that is only implicit in Locke's account: that the meaning of a "complex idea" embedded in an abstract noun is never just a sum of a number of simple ideas. We will consider in some detail an example analogous to Locke's favourite example of *parricide*, namely, the concept of *suicide*. The general point is that *suicide* is more than 'killing oneself' (just as *parricide* is more than 'killing one's father').

To compare the meaning of *suicide* with that of the verbal phrase *to kill oneself*, we need to briefly first consider the meaning of the verb *to kill*. The NSM tradition (which rejects the standard story that 'kill = cause to die') proposes, in essence, the following analysis (see e.g. Wierzbicka 1975; 1980; Goddard 2011b):

[I]   *Bill killed Harry.*
a.   at some time, Bill did something to Harry
b.   because of this, something happened to Harry at that time
c.   because of this, something happened in Harry's body
d.   because of this, after this Harry was not living any more

It might seem that to explicate a sentence like *Bill killed himself* it would be sufficient to replace 'Harry' with 'Bill' in the explication above ('Bill did something to Bill' etc.), but this is an illusion. From a semantic point of view, 'killing oneself' is not simply an instance of 'killing someone'. For example, the question *Did he kill someone?* could be answered in the negative: *No, he only killed himself.* (It could also be answered, rhetorically, in the positive, but only with heavy stress on *himself*; "yes, *himself*".) In contrast to sentences about someone killing someone else, a sentence like *He killed himself* suggests that the killing is intentional, and moreover, it implies a specific motivation which can only be adequately portrayed with the word *I*, namely: 'I don't want to live any more'.[3] These considerations bring us to the following explication:

[J]   *He killed himself.*

a.   this someone (= he) did something, like someone can do when this someone wants to kill [m] someone

b.   this someone did it because this someone thought like this:

c.   "I don't want to live any more"

d.   because this someone did this, something happened to this someone as this someone wanted

e.   because of this, after this, this someone didn't live any more

According to explication [J], the idea of 'killing oneself' focuses on a specific action, described through an analogy with that of 'killing someone'. To the action so described there is added a particular "self-centred" motivation.

The idea of *suicide* is somewhat different. Here, the self-centred motivation is paramount, and the analogy with 'killing someone' is less salient. In the case of *killing oneself*, this analogy with 'someone' comes at the outset, in component (a). By contrast, in *committing suicide*, it comes towards the end of the explication (see explication [K] below), and what is foregrounded is the general idea: 'it can be like this: someone can think like this', followed by a self-centred motivation, as set out in (f). Thus, in *suicide*, this self-centred motivation is attributed not to the specific person in question as such, but to the whole category of people about whom the word *suicide* can be used.

Notice that this motivation is not exactly the same as the corresponding component in the previous explication. In the case of 'killing oneself', the thought is 'I don't want to live any more'; but with *suicide*, the thought is framed in a way which suggests both greater consideration and something akin to self-justification: 'it will be good if I don't live any more'. Furthermore, the word *suicide* implies a negative evaluation and an emotive tone that is not present with the more factual 'killing oneself'. There is a negative evaluation of the whole situation, expressed in component (j): 'it is bad if it is like this.' As well, there is a broader social attitude towards the phenomenon of *suicide*, as expressed in the final component (k): 'when people think about it, they can't not feel something bad'.

---

[3] The motivation implied by a sentence like *He killed himself* cannot be satisfactorily portrayed as 'I want to kill someone, this someone is myself', because this would distort the sentence's meaning. Nor can it be portrayed as 'I want to kill me', which is ungrammatical in English ('I want to kill myself' would be more plausible, but it would rely on the very construction we are trying to explicate).

[K]   *He committed suicide.*

a.   he did something
b.   people can say what this something is with the word *suicide*
c.   someone can say something about something with this word when this someone thinks
      like this:
d.   "it can be like this:
e.   someone thinks like this:
f.   'it will be good if I don't live any more
                 because of this, I want something to happen to me
                 it can happen if I do something
                 I want to do it'
g.   because this someone thinks like this, this someone does something
                 like someone can do when this someone wants to kill [m] someone
h.   because of this, something happens to this someone as this someone wanted
i.   because of this, after this, this someone doesn't live any more
j.   it is bad if it is like this"
k.   when people think about it, they can't not feel something bad

As the explications above show, the abstract noun *suicide* does not simply "tie together" the idea of 'killing' with the idea of 'oneself', but introduces various additional semantic elements. But Locke's main points stand: it is the mind which "makes the patterns for sorting and naming of things" and which makes "the connection between the loose parts of those complex ideas"; and also, while "it be the mind that makes the collection, 'tis the name which is as it were the knot that ties them fast together" (book III, v, §10).

A noun such as *illness*, *death*, or *suicide* stands for a potential or hypothetical state of affairs which is not anchored in a particular place, time, or person. In this respect, abstract nouns differ both from adjectives like *ill*, and from verbs like *kill* and *die*. When *illness*, *death*, and *suicide* are combined with a possessive pronoun such as *her*, the individual case is seen through the prism of the abstract concept, thus the meanings of sentences (a) and (b) in the pairs below are not identical:

(6a)   She was ill at that time, and this worried him.
(6b)   She was ill at that time, and her illness worried him.

(7a)   She died. This affected him deeply.
(7b)   She died. Her death affected him deeply.

(8a)   She killed herself. This affected him deeply.
(8b)   She committed suicide. Her suicide affected him deeply.

A phrase like *her illness* (*her death*, *her suicide*) indicates that the speaker is thinking about the event through the prism of the more general thought which includes in its content the elements 'something', 'word', and 'it can be like this'. Obviously, the specifics of the analysis proposed here go beyond what was proposed by Locke, but the use of NSM aside, in the main our approach follows his.

A final aspect on which our approach tallies well with Locke's concerns is what we might term "referentiality differences" between concrete and abstract nouns.[4] The assumptions embedded in "concrete nouns" (e.g. *trees, water*) appear to be that there is a pre-existing category—"pre-existing", that is, in the sense of being "independent of discourse"—and that speakers may choose to say something about things of this kind (or about something of this kind). There are no corresponding assumptions embedded in "abstract nouns", such as *death* or *heat*. Here, the speaker wants to say something **with** the words *death* or *heat*, but not **about** death or heat. Rather, he or she wants to say something about people (who can die), or about things or places (which can be hot). While on the surface, speakers can make predications about *death, heat*, etc., in the deep semantic structure of these sentences these speakers are always saying something about something "concrete": for example, about people who die, about places or things which are hot. Such predications may incorporate an element of the hypothetical ('it can be like this'), but they are not predications **about** "abstract ideas", as such.

Compare Locke's statement:

the common use of language [...] permits not any two abstract words, or names of abstract ideas, to be affirmed one of another. For [...] how certain soever it is that man is an animal, or rational, or white, yet everyone at first hearing perceives the falsehood of these propositions: *humanity is animality*, or *rationality*, or *whiteness*: and this is as evident as any of the most allowed maxims. All our affirmations then are only in concrete....   (book III, viii, §1)

It is important to note that the analysis proposed in the present study departs from Locke's insofar as it distinguishes "reification" effected by the use of abstract nouns from "categorization", in a strict sense of the word. Locke keeps talking about "sorts" or "species". The explications proposed here, on the other hand, present the mental referent of uncountable abstract nouns like *illness, disease, death*, or *parricide* as

---

[4] Our account of "abstract" and "concrete" nouns is also in keeping with Locke's distinction between "the names of substances" (i.e. words like *gold, water, ice, horse, mule, herb, star*) and "the names of mixed modes" (i.e. abstract nouns like *gratitude, glory, adultery, sacrilege, incest*). In Locke's view, even the names of substances depend "on such collections of ideas as men have made, and not on any real nature of things" (book III, vi, §1), and accordingly, "our distinct species are nothing but distinct complex ideas, with distinct names annexed to them" (book III, vi, §13). To emphasize the fact that such ideas are essentially "man-made" and dependent on languages, he introduced the term "nominal essence", which he contrasted with any "real essence". Nonetheless, Locke stresses that the names of substances are far less arbitrary and language-specific than those of "mixed modes" (i.e. abstract nouns): "The names of [...] mixed modes stand for ideas perfectly arbitrary; those of substances are not perfectly so, but refer to a pattern, though with some latitude" (book III, iv, §17); and again: "But though those nominal essences of substances are made by the mind, they are not yet made so arbitrarily as those of mixed modes" (book III, vi, §28).

'something', rather than 'something of one kind'. We have argued that abstract nouns can effect both "reification" and "categorization", but that the two should be distinguished, and **can** be distinguished in a principled way on the basis of linguistic evidence such as the grammatical feature of countability (see section 9.6 for more discussion).

9.6 Further explications and issues

We now consider a further set of examples. Though it would be premature to contemplate a full typology of abstract nouns, we have chosen this selection with an eye to various cross-cutting factors. We first consider a further brace of examples (*death, depression, violence, problem*) that conform to the same semantic template we have been working with so far. We would like to draw attention to the fact that in all these examples the "topic substantive" of the potential scenario evoked by the abstract noun is 'someone' or 'people'. Most abstract nouns—it would seem—are about people, in a broad sense. This is not surprising. As humans we are interested, for the most part, in other humans. In relation to abstract nouns which exhibit a morphological relationship with other words, we would like to emphasize that in addition to examples like *illness* and *death*, where the morphological relationship corresponds to a semantic one, there are plenty of cases where a morphological relationship does not correspond to a direct semantic "embedding", as with *depressed* and *depression*, *violence* and *violent*, *security* and *secure*, and many others.

The next two sections canvass two kinds of abstract nouns that diverge from the general semantic template we have been using so far. First we look at *size* and *temperature*, arguing that they exemplify a somewhat different top-level semantic structure. They are, we suggest, essentially epistemic categories (classifying kinds of "knowledge about" referents), rather than discourse topics evoking potential scenarios. Then we look briefly at non-taxonomic (collective) abstract nouns, such as *emotions* and *sports*.

Additional examples of abstract nouns based on potential scenarios

We will use the following sketches to adumbrate a number of points in connection with abstract noun explications. Our main point is that even what appear to be simply "nominalized" versions of a verb or adjective often include additional semantic content, above and beyond the "abstract noun" framing components. Consider the example of *death* and *die*. It might seem that the potential scenario evoked by *death* can be stated simply as 'it can be like this: someone dies'. We would suggest, however, that there is a bit more to it. On reflection, one realizes that the topic of *death* arises only in the context of speaking about someone's "life". Specifically, *death* evokes a frame in which the event of someone dying is seen as following a period during which someone has lived for some time.

[L]   *death*

a.   something
b.   people can say what this something is with the word *death*
c.   someone can say something about something with this word when this someone thinks
      like this:
d.   "it can be like this:
e.   someone lives for some time, after this, this someone dies"

Sometimes, the relationship between abstract noun and its apparent derivational base is much more complex. Consider, for example, the adjective *depressed* and the noun *depression*. The adjective can be explicated as in [M1].

[M1]   *depressed* (as in *She came home from the meeting depressed*)

a.   she thought like this at that time:
b.   "I know now that some good things can't happen
c.   this is bad
d.   I don't want it to be like this
e.   I know that I can't do anything because of this"
f.   when she thought like this, she felt something bad
      like people feel at many times when they think like this

Let us now consider an explication, given in [M2] below, for the abstract noun *depression* (as in *She was suffering from depression*). *Depression* differs from *depressed* in several ways. Most importantly, it refers to what is seen as a pathological and incapacitating condition, similar to a physical illness. This is portrayed in components (e)–(g) of the potential scenario in [M2]. To be sure, this condition is also associated with a particular way of thinking linked with "very bad feelings", and this is shown in (h)–(k). But the details of the way of thinking associated with *depression*—the "hopeless" thoughts depicted in components (i) and (j)—are not quite the same as those associated with the adjective *depressed*: they are much more far-reaching and much more "personal".

[M2]   *depression* (as in *suffering from depression*)

a.   something
b.   people can say what this something is with the word *depression*
c.   someone can say something about something with this word when this someone thinks
      like this:
d.   "it can be like this:
e.   something very bad is happening to someone for some time,
f.   like something very bad can be happening in someone's body
g.   this someone can't do many things because of this
h.   this someone thinks like this during this time:

i.   "I know that it is like this: good things can't happen to me, I can't do anything
           good
j.   this is very bad"
k.   when this someone thinks like this, this someone feels something very bad
           like people can feel when they think like this for some time"

According to this explication, the concept of *depression* refers to a condition which cannot be reduced to thoughts and feelings alone, but which is likely to have some basis in what is happening inside the person's body. It invites the assumption that some sort of external (medical) intervention may be needed, as with an "illness" or a "disease" (see Obeyesekere 1985 for an illuminating discussion of the cultural specificities of the "*depression* concept"). Note that despite its morphological affinity with the word *depressed*, the explication for *depression* does not make any use of 'depressed' as a derivational base.

Now consider the following explication for *violence* (Goddard 2009g[2006]; Wierzbicka in press *b*), as it appears in sentences like *Violence is not the solution* and *There's too much violence on TV*. The scenario involves 'something happening in a place', but not just any something: it happens on account of people doing some bad things to other people in this place—component (e). These acts are attributed to the fact that the actors 'feel something very bad at this time'—component (f) (emotions such as rage, hatred, or jealousy come to mind in this context). Further, the actors are capable of knowing that their actions can bring about very bad physical consequences for the other people concerned—component (g).

[N]   *violence*

a.   something
b.   people can say what this something is with the word *violence*
c.   someone can say something about something with this word when this someone thinks
      like this:
d.   "it can be like this:
e.   something happens in a place for some time because some people do some bad
          things to some other people in this place at that time
f.   these people do these things because they feel something very bad at that time
g.   something very bad can happen to these other people's bodies because of this,
          these people know this
h.   it is very bad when it is like this"

Again, despite the morphological affinity with the word *violent*, the explication for *violence* does not make any use of 'violent' as a derivational base. The same applies to the explications for *security* proposed in Goddard (2009f), which do not employ 'secure' as a derivational base. Here, as in other areas of the lexicon, a formal morphological relationship is no guarantee of an exactly parallel semantic relationship. Detailed analysis is required in each and every case.

As a final example, of a rather different kind, we will consider the word *problem*, as used in sentences such as *He has a problem* or *That's your problem*. In sentences of this kind, the meaning of the word *problem* cannot be separated from that of the pseudo-possessive construction as a whole: *someone **has** a problem, it is **somebody's** problem*. Our proposed explication is as follows:

[O] *He has a problem.*

a.   it is like this: he can think like this about something:
b.   "something bad is happening now
c.   I want to do something because of this
d.   I don't know what I can do
e.   I know that I can't not do something"

It is interesting to note that, according to Russian linguist Anna Zalizniak, the relevant meaning of the English word *problem* has been borrowed by Russian, and has been spreading in Russian speech. Zalizniak argues that this meaning carries with it a cultural concept important for Anglo-American culture and incompatible with the traditional Russian "linguistic picture of the world" linked with Russian cultural key words such as *gore* (roughly, "a great misfortune combined with deep unhappiness, one can't do anything about it"). Zalizniak suggests that, in recent times, under the influence of English, habitual thinking in terms of *u menja gore* ('I have a *gore*') appears to be increasingly giving way to thinking in terms of *u menja problema* 'I have a problem' (implied: "I should do something about it").

Semantic exploration of the abstract noun domain is still in its early stages, but already we would hazard the generalization that most of them involve 'someone' or 'people' in one way or another. A substantial number appear to involve 'people' and 'place' (or 'places') in various ways. For example, words like *culture, language*, and *government* all involve what one could term a "bounded social entity"— essentially, people in a place (Goddard 2005*b*; 2011*a*). Another grouping consists of words that describe "social conditions", such as *war, peace, prosperity*, and the like. Some abstract nouns focus not on a (hypothetical) 'someone' or on 'people' but purely on things or events—highly analytical words such as *structure, function, cause, result*—but these are probably a minority. Likewise, there may be some abstract nouns that concern conditions in a place without any regard to 'people', but again we venture to suggest that these are small in number compared with the vast number of abstract nouns pertaining to human activities and to the "human condition".

Abstract nouns representing "epistemic categories"

As we have argued, most abstract nouns are essentially reified discourse topics, labelled with a word, and associated with thinking about various potential scenarios (introduced by 'it can be like this: –'). The top-level structure is:

a.   something (of one kind)
b.   people can say what this something is with the word *XXX*
c.   someone can say something about something with this word when this someone thinks
     like this:
d.   "it can be like this: - -"

This structure seems to be appropriate for a great variety of abstract nouns that designate what may be termed "situations" or "contingencies".

We do not claim, however, that this is the only "top-level" structure associated with abstract nouns. We will illustrate with the words *size* and *temperature* (interesting also on account of the role that the semantic molecule 'number [m]' plays in both concepts).

Consider sentences like *What size was it?* and *What size shoes do you take?* The word *size* in such contexts implies "sizes": a set of categories that can be indicated either with a special set of words (e.g. 'large', 'medium', 'small', 'extra small') or by means of a set of numbers (e.g. size 8, size 10, size 12). This is especially clear if we compare the questions *What size is it?* and *How big is it?* The former could not apply to, for example, a leaf, or a rock, or a hole in the ground, or to any other things which do not "come" in discrete size categories. (Notice that we must be careful to recognize that *size* also has a second meaning in English, in sentences like *I was surprised by the size of it.* This usage does not presuppose any discrete categories, but is clearly different because it implies bigness.)

We propose the following explication for *size* (as in the *size* of a shirt, a pair of shoes, etc.).

[P]   *size* (of something of one kind)

a.   something
b.   people can say what this something is with the word *size*
c.   someone can say something about something with this word
        when someone wants to know something of one kind about this something
d.   at many times when people want to know something like this, people say things like this:
        "this is something big", "this is something very big"
        "this is something small", "this is something very small"
e.   at some times when people want to know something like this, people say things with
        number [m] words

In this explication, component (c) indicates a somewhat different discourse function than that we have seen so far. Rather than the word *size* providing a way of 'saying something about something' when the speaker is thinking in a certain way, the canonical context for the word *size* is more specific, with a more "informative" function: to 'say something about something when someone wants to know something of one kind about this something'. The reference to knowing 'something of one kind' of course invites the question "of what kind?". Component (d) lays the groundwork for an answer, by itemizing a set of frequently heard comments about various objects, i.e. that such-and-such is 'something big', 'something very big', 'something small', 'something very small'. This indicates the relevant "field" or dimension of attention and it also grounds the concept of *size* in the simplest ordinary language terms. (It is no coincidence that in Chinese, for example, the nearest equivalent to the English word *size* has the form: *dà xiǎo* [big-small]). Component (e) provides that dicta of this kind can sometimes be expressed 'with number [m] words'. (The semantic molecule 'number' is explicated in Goddard 2009d, along with a range of related numerical concepts.)

As for a question such as *What size is it (= this something)?*, someone who asks such a question is essentially saying: "when someone wants to say something like this about this something, I want to know what this someone can say."

The concept of *temperature* is rather similar to that of *size*. Note that we are here concerned with the meaning of *(the) temperature* in sentences like *What's the temperature?* and *The temperature was rising*. This meaning is focused primarily on places. Notice the definite article, characteristic of this meaning. There is a secondary meaning, which appears in sentences like *I took his temperature*. This second meaning (roughly, "body temperature") is usually found in combination with a possessor expression, such as a possessive pronoun, and there is normally no possibility of it occurring with the definite article. Moreover, body *temperatures* may range, informally speaking, from normal, to 'hot', and to 'very hot', but there is no need for appraisals on the "cold" side of things.

Returning to the place-based meaning of *temperature*, we would propose the following explication.

[Q]   *temperature*

a.   something

b.   people can say what this something is with the word *temperature*

c.   someone can say something about a place with this word
       when someone wants to know something of one kind about this place

d.   at many times when people want to know something like this, people say things like this:
       "it is hot [m] in this place at this time", "it is very hot [m] in this place at this time"
       "it is cold [m] in this place at this time", "it is very cold [m] in this place at this time"

e.   at some times when people want to know something like this, people say things with
       number [m] words

Words like *size* and *temperature* can be compared with other "quantitative" concepts, such as *length, height, weight,* and *age,* all of which (we would expect) can be explicated along the lines proposed above. Wierzbicka (2005*b*; 2006*c*; 2008*a*) has proposed that the abstract noun *colour* has a similar top-level structure, i.e. that the concept of *colour* represents a kind of "knowledge category", though obviously the "*colour* concept" does not rely on numbers in any way. (Possibly other metalinguistic words like *shape* could yield to a similar treatment.)

Non-taxonomic (collective) abstract nouns

As we saw in section 9.3, uncountable abstract nouns imply, generally speaking, reification without categorization, that is, their top component is simply 'something', while countable abstract nouns have the top component 'something of one kind'.[5] For example:

violence – something
          people can say what this something is with the word *violence*
a disease – (one) something of one kind
          people can say what this something is with the word *disease*

It would be wrong to give the impression, however, that all abstract nouns can be accommodated in one or other of these structures, or that "countability" with abstract nouns is a simple yes/no phenomenon. Here an analogy with the concrete lexicon can be helpful. Previous NSM work has shown that the concrete lexicon consists of multiple classes and subclasses, some of which are better described as "collective", rather than as "taxonomic" (Wierzbicka 1984; 1985*a*; 1988; 1996; Goddard 2009*e*; forthcoming *a*). For example, explications for words from subclasses such as *furniture* (*cutlery, jewellery,* etc.) and *vegetables* (*cosmetics, medicines,* etc.) begin with the topmost component 'things of many kinds' (not with 'something of one kind'). Words like these represent groupings of heterogeneous kinds that can be thought of as constituting a single class on account of shared functions, similar origins, spatial contiguity, and other factors. These two subclasses also enable us to draw attention to certain subtleties in the grammar of countability. For example, though *furniture* is a "mass" (non-count) noun, it allows a unitizer construction, e.g. *an item of furniture.* And while *vegetables* looks on the surface like a regular count noun, when counting vegetables, one counts not individuals but kinds (for example, a sentence like *We always have two vegetables for dinner* cannot be used in reference to two carrots or

---

[5] Though most countable abstract nouns require only a single-level taxonomy, there are certain areas in the English abstract noun lexicon where the categorization is deeper. This occurs when a countable abstract noun functions as the taxonomic head for a further (sub)kind. For example, the English semantic molecules 'game' and 'dance' appear to function as taxonomic heads; explications for *cricket, chess, football,* etc. must begin with 'a game [m] of one kind'; and explications for *waltz, tango, foxtrot* with 'a dance [m] of one kind'.

two zucchinis, or the like; it must indicate the presence of two **kinds** of *vegetable*, such as carrots and peas). Many fine details of this kind are highly language-specific. The point is that to sort out the various classificatory relations embedded in the concrete nominal lexicon of a particular language is a complex task which demands painstaking study. The same applies to the abstract nominal lexicon. The few observations we make here are highly preliminary.

Non-taxonomic classifications reflected in the abstract lexicon can be illustrated with the word *emotions*, which can be compared in many respects to a collective word like *vegetables*. Roughly:

vegetables – things of many kinds [that people can eat]
emotions   – things of many kinds [that people can feel]

The phrase *many emotions* implies "many *different* emotions", not "many instances of the same emotion". Thus, the word *emotions* (in the plural) implies a heterogeneous collection of kinds, like *vegetables* or *cosmetics* in this respect.[6] Other collective abstract nouns, similar to *emotions*, include *sciences* and *sports*. It is also interesting to observe the existence of some plural-only (*pluralia tantum*) abstract nouns, such as the expressions *the humanities, the arts,* and *the professions* (notice the definite article, another formal property of interest) (Wierzbicka 2011a).

Clearly, to explore these distinctions and the broader topic of non-taxonomic abstract nouns is not a task that we can undertake here. Rather we would like to return to our main theme: the affiliations between our general analyses of abstract nouns and the thinking of John Locke and his successors in the 17th and 18th centuries. Chief among these successors, so far as abstract nouns are concerned, was Jeremy Bentham.

9.7 "Fictitious entities", vagueness, and translatability

In his introduction to *Bentham's Theory of Fictions*, C. K. Ogden (1951[1932]: ix) assigns to Bentham a place of honour in the history of philosophy with a "linguistic bias", right next to his "five great predecessors": Bacon, Hobbes, Locke, Berkeley, and Hume. The purpose of his commentary and his edition of *Bentham's Theory of Fictions*, Ogden says, is "to give some indication of the debt which future generations may acknowledge to Jeremy Bentham, when he has taken his place as sixth in line of the great tradition—and in some respects its most original representative" (p. ix).[7]

---

[6] This means, incidentally for present purposes, but importantly in other contexts, that words like *happiness, sadness, joy, fear,* and *anger* do not stand, conceptually, for 'an emotion of one kind'. They can of course be classified together under the heading *emotions*, just as *cabbage, carrots,* and *peas* can be classified together under the heading *vegetables*, but such classifications do not reflect a relationship of taxonomic hierarchy.

[7] Bentham's writings on fictions are distributed across multiple locations in his collected *Works*, and it was one of Ogden's (1951) chief purposes to bring them together into a single volume. When quoting

As the authors of the present study, we feel like representatives of those "future generations", wishing to acknowledge their debt to Bentham. Our work on the natural semantic metalanguage—in effect, on the shared conceptual and grammatical core of all languages—is closely related in spirit to Bentham's "debabelization project" (Ogden 1951[1932]: cxii; cf. Ogden 1931), and to his project of developing "an entirely new system of logic" (Ogden 1951[1932]: lxiv), linguistically oriented and according a fundamental role to cross-linguistic evidence. Equally, our work on the semantics of abstract nouns is closely related in spirit to Bentham's "theory of fictions".

Bentham's most practical concern was the reform of legal jargon, and among language-based "fictions" he was particularly concerned with "legal fictions", that is, "fictions" which arise from the reification of abstract nouns and which are often accorded unjustified legal authority.

By habit, wherever a man sees a *name*, he is led to figure himself a corresponding object, of the reality of which the *name* is accepted by him, as it were of course, in the character of a *certificate*. From this delusion, endless is the confusion, the error, the dissension, the hostility, that have been derived.   (*Works*, vol. I, p. 205; Ogden 1951[1932]: cxiii)

While for practical reasons Bentham focused in particular on "legal fictions", his general "linguistic theory of fictions" applied, as Ogden (1951[1932]: cxlix) stressed, "in every branch of human thought".

Bentham took as a starting point a division of nouns into two classes, corresponding in essence to "concrete nouns" and "abstract nouns":

Every noun-substantive is a name, a name either of an individual object, or of a sort or aggregate of objects. [...] By this name an existence is ascribed to the individual object, or sort of object, of which it is the name. In the case where [...] the object is a tangible one, here there is no fiction—as this man, this beast, this bird, this fish, this star; or this sort of man, this sort of beast, this sort of bird, this sort of fish, this sort of star; the object spoken of may be termed a real entity. On the other hand in the case in which the object is not a tangible one, the object, the existence of which is thus asserted, not being a real existing one, the object, if it must be termed an entity [...] it may, for distinction's sake, be termed a fictitious entity. Take, for example, *this motion, this operation, this quality, this obligation, this right*. Thus then we have two sorts of names, with two corresponding sorts of entities. Names of real entities, names of fictitious entities.   (*Works*, vol. III, p. 327; Ogden 1951[1932]: 59–60)

Bentham emphasized both the usefulness of "fictitious entities" called into existence by abstract nouns and the fact that they are "continually confounded with real ones" (*Works*, vol. VIII, p. 126). To converse about abstract matters, people need abstract nouns. The abstract nouns lead people to speak about abstract matters as if

Bentham, we provide the reference to his *Works* (now available online) and to Ogden's compendium, which forms the second part of his *Bentham's Theory of Fictions*.

they were speaking about "real entities". This saves time and makes conversation about complex and abstract matters feasible. But the utility of abstract nouns should not prevent us from recognizing that their logical and linguistic status is quite different from that of concrete nouns.

Entities are either *real* or *fictitious* [...] By *fictitious entities* are here meant, not any of those which will be presented by the name of *fabulous*, i.e. imaginary *persons*, such as *Heathen Gods*, *Genii*, and *Fairies*, but such as *quality—property* (in the sense in which it is nearly synonymous to *quality*), *relation, power, obligation, duty, right*, and so forth. Incorrect as it would be if the entities in question were considered as being, in point of reality, upon a footing with *real* entities as above distinguished, the supposition of a sort of *verbal* reality, so to speak, as belonging to these fictitious entities is a supposition without which the matter of language could never have been formed, nor between man and man any converse carried on other than such as hath place between brute and brute.

Fictitious as they are, entities of this description could not be spoken of at all if they were not spoken of as *real* ones. (*Works*, vol. VIII: 126; Ogden 1951[1932]: 137)

We will illustrate the way Bentham applied his distinction between "real entities" and "fictitious entities" to the language of law with his discussion of the English noun *right* and the role it plays in English discourse:

The word *right* is the name of a fictitious entity; one of those objects the existence of which is feigned for the purpose of discourse—by a fiction so necessary that without it human discourse could not be carried on.

A man is said to have it, to hold it, to possess it, to acquire it, to lose it. It is thus spoken of as if it were a portion of matter such as a man may take into his hand, keep it for a time and let it go again. According to a phrase more common in law language than in ordinary language, a man is even spoken of as being *invested* with it. Vestment is clothing: invested with it makes it an article of clothing, and is as much as to say 'is clothed with it.'
(*Works*, vol. III, p. 218; Ogden 1951[1932]: 118)

Bentham made it clear that when he said that *rights* were "fictitious entities" he didn't wish to imply that they were not important. Of course they were important, but it was also important to understand what sentences with the word *right* or *rights* really meant.

Give us our rights, say the thousands and the millions. *Give us our rights*, they say, and they do well to say so. Yet, of all who say so, not one perhaps can say, not one perhaps ever conceived clearly, what it is he thus calls for—what sort of thing *a right* is. (*Works*, vol. III, p. 594; Ogden 1951[1932]: lxxviii)

As Ogden (p. lxxix) notes in his comment on this passage: "they do well to say so, because although rights, as entities, are fictitious, any sentence in which rights are spoken of can be translated [...] into a statement at another level in which all the referents are real entities."

Needless to say, as semanticists we are not concerned with any ontological differences between "real entities" and "fictitious entities", but rather with the meanings of words and sentences. But our semantic analysis of abstract nouns, and of sentences including such nouns, connects with Bentham's distinction between "real entities" and "fictitious entities". As we would put it, sentences with the word *rights* are not "**about** rights"; rather, they are, at the deep, semantic level, about people who think in a certain way, who want some things, who can or can't do some things, and so on. Or, to use Ogden's formulation, "any sentence in which rights are spoken of can be translated into a statement at another level" about people who think, want, and so on.

Speaking more generally, any sentence including an abstract noun can be translated into one without such a noun—indeed, it **has** to be so translated (or paraphrased) if its meaning is to be elucidated. To see this, it is sufficient to consider a situation when a young child is asking for an explanation of an abstract concept, for example: "What is 'mortality'?", "What is 'euphoria'?", "What is 'talent'?". The only way to answer such a question (at least, the only one which makes sense) is to paraphrase the abstract nouns away and to offer explanations phrased in terms of people, things (tangible things), bodies, or places. Informally, one could reply as follows:

mortality—"people use this word when they want to say that after people have lived for some time, they die"

euphoria—"people use this word when they want to say that someone feels very happy and is very excited because of this"

a talent—"people use this word when they want to say that someone can do something very well, better than other people, but not because they have done it before"

What applies to *euphoria*, *mortality*, and *talent* applies of course also to *rights*. To explain to a child what the word *rights* means, one would have to talk in the first place about what people want to do, and about what they can or cannot do.

The fact that sentences with abstract nouns can in principle be translated into (paraphrased in terms of) sentences without such nouns is particularly important given that, as mentioned earlier, abstract nouns tend to be highly language-specific in their meaning. The English word *right(s)* is a very good case in point.

Contra Jackendoff (1999), who has claimed in a number of publications that 'rights' and 'obligations' are universal human concepts, both concepts are in fact highly language-specific. While, as evidence suggests, in all languages one can say that someone "can" do something (with the same range of interpretations as in English), most languages of the world do not have a word corresponding in meaning to the English noun *right* (Wierzbicka 2006a, 2007a). Furthermore, even in a language which does seem to have a counterpart of *right*, for example French, this counterpart may not have exactly the same meaning as the English *right*—and it is truly remarkable that Bentham noticed this fact and saw its significance. In particular, he noted (with a certain disapproval) a mixture of a factual and a deontic (as well as evaluative) component in the English noun *right*, due to a close semantic link between the noun *right* and the adjective *right* (the opposite of *wrong*). The lack of a clear distinction between 'it is like this' and 'it ought to be like this' in the meaning of the English noun *right* often causes (in Bentham's view) conceptual confusion.

In the English language, an imperfection, perhaps peculiar to that language, contributes to the keeping up of this confusion. In English, in speaking of a certain man and a certain coat, or a certain piece of land, I may say it is right he should have this coat or this piece of land. But in this case, beyond doubt, nothing more do I express than my satisfaction at the idea of his having this same coat or land.

This imperfection does not extend itself to other languages. Take the French, for instance. A Frenchman will not say, *Il est droit que cet homme ait cet habit*: what he will say is, *Il est juste que cet homme ait cet habit. Cet appartient de droit à cet homme.*

(Works, vol. III, p. 218; Ogden 1951[1932]: 120)

While we as semanticists would not wish to follow Bentham in describing the semantics of the English noun *right* "an imperfection", we would agree with him that its meaning is language-specific, and in particular, that it is different from that of the French *droit*.

As discussed in the entry on 'law/right' in the monumental work entitled "European Vocabulary of Philosophies: A Dictionary of Untranslatables" (*Vocabulaire européen des philosophies: dictionnaire des intraduisibles*, Cassin 2004), the modern English concept of *right* is quite different from e.g. the French *droit*, and bears the imprint of historical, legal, and philosophical traditions quite distinct from those which prevailed, through centuries, on the "Continent".

Crucially, the specific aspects of the philosophical and legal traditions reflected in philosophical and legal registers of English have also shaped ordinary English, making the colloquial English word *right* unique in its emphasis on what is good and desirable for the individual and what an individual is "entitled" to. In particular, the "Dictionary of Untranslatables" links the uniqueness of the English concept with the "history of English liberty", with the tradition of the Magna Carta (1215) and the Bill of Rights (1689), "with the supremacy of the Parliament over the monarchy" (or of "the King in Parliament"), and with Hobbes's political philosophy which posited a link between a 'right' and 'liberty' (an individual's 'liberty' to do what they want to do and not to do what they don't want to do).

Thus, as the "Dictionary of Untranslatables" puts it: "The conceptual system of the English law, whose fundamental lines of division are reproduced in linguistic usage, presents itself above all as an embodiment of this peculiar experience, and reflects a logic which is both very old and extremely durable" [translation, *AW*].

As illustrated by Montesquieu's famous definition of *liberté*, the French *droit* emphasizes what one can do, rather than what one wants to do. According to this definition, *liberté c'est le droit de faire tout ce que les lois permettent* "liberty is the 'right' (*droit*) to do all that is permitted by laws (*les lois*)". In English, however, the word *rights* is invested with a moral force which is independent of the law: in this perspective, people's 'rights' (to do what they want) can be violated not only by some actions incompatible with the law but also by arbitrary, unjust laws; a "right" stands not only for what is guaranteed by the law, but also, for what is "right". For this reason, no doubt, an expression like *le droit du plus fort* 'the *droit* of the stronger' cannot be rendered in English as 'the right of the stronger' or as 'the right of the jungle'. There can be a 'law of the jungle' (an unjust law), but not a 'right of the jungle': unlike a *droit*, a *right* is "right".

What matters most in the present context is that any sentence including the untranslatable English noun *right* can be paraphrased in terms of words which are fully translatable, and that its meaning can in this way be explained to anyone, including children born and raised in English-speaking societies, immigrants to such societies, and learners of English anywhere in the world.

Such translatability has important consequences for international discourses on human rights, law, ethics, and science. The fact that English key words such as *right*, *security*, *experience*, or *fairness* are all significantly English-specific in their meanings poses a barrier to intercultural and international understanding in a world in which English is rapidly becoming the global lingua franca, especially if their language-specific character is not recognized and their meanings are not explained (Wierzbicka 2008*b*; Goddard 2009*f*).

It is important to recognize, however, that while sentences with abstract nouns can in principle be "translated" into sentences without such nouns, the resulting translations do have a sense which is vaguer and less definite than that of sentences with concrete nouns or pronouns. Consider, for example, an English sentence like *She loves life*. According to the analysis developed here, one can assign to it the following explicatory paraphrase:

[R]   *She loves life.*

a.   she loves something
b.   people can say what this something is with the word *life*
c.   someone can say something about something with this word when this someone thinks like this:
d.   "it can be like this:
e.   someone lives for some time
f.   many things happen to this someone during this time
g   this someone does many things during this time"

The paraphrase seems all right, as far as it goes, but one may still ask: What exactly is it that the speaker loves? It is true to say that the paraphrase does not really spell this out and so it is vague and indeterminate, but this does not mean that the explication is inadequate. On the contrary, a good explicatory paraphrase needs to match exactly the level of vagueness and indeterminacy of the sentence whose meaning it seeks to portray. It has be to recognized that in the case of sentences with abstract nouns, an explicatory paraphrase lays bare the inherent vagueness and indeterminacy of those sentences due to the semantics of abstract nouns as such. This vagueness and indeterminacy is of course compounded in sentences in which all substantives are abstract and in passages composed of such sentences. Consider, for example, the following passage from a newspaper article (*The Australian*, 23–24 Feb. 2008, p. 33) on the subject of "the impact of the tsunami of doubt swamping investment markets [in Australia]":

The forces driving the retreat of market values are real and in the present, and that, to some degree explains the disconnect between a relatively solid suite of interim profit reports over the last week and the continuing leakage of value through another hard week on local and global equity markets. Profit reports are necessarily a reflection of previous trading conditions. [...] The negative sentiment dragging down share values is, in various sectors, quite well founded. But, at the same time, there are pockets of bleakness where there needn't be, and they have been allowed to infect sentiment needlessly [...].

The only "real entity" referred to in this passage, and thus the only one which anchors this passage in reality, is 'Australia': presumably, whatever is said in these sentences is said about Australia (at a particular time). What exactly is being said, however, is not quite clear, and the condensation of abstract nouns in the passage, virtually to the exclusion of any other substantives, allows the author to write many sentences without actually saying anything precise that could be pinned down.

The inherent semantic indeterminacy of abstract nouns, laid bare in their explications, does not mean that the meanings of these nouns cannot be explicated in a stable and rigorous manner. They can, just as the meanings of semantically indeterminate words and phrases like *more or less*, *approximately*, or *roughly* can, be rigorously explicated (Wierzbicka 2003a[1991]: ch. 9). Nonetheless, the explications of such words support Locke's (1690) contention that what he called "the names of mixed modes" (essentially, abstract nouns) are "liable to great uncertainty and obscurity in their signification" (book III, ix, §6). Commenting first on the words *murder* and *sacrilege*, and then *glory* and *gratitude*, Locke wrote:

Though the names *glory* and *gratitude* be the same in every man's mouth through a whole country, yet the complex collective idea, which every one thinks on, or intends by that name, is apparently very different in men using the same language.   (book III, ix, §8)

According to Locke, this "uncertainty" of the intended signification of abstract nouns is related to the way children learn them:

as for mixed modes, especially the most material of them, *moral words*, the sounds are usually learn'd first, then to know what complex ideas they stand for, they are either beholden to the explication of others, or (which happens for the most part) are left to their own observation and industry; which being little laid out in the search of the true and precise meaning of names, these moral words are, in most men's mouths, little more than bare sounds; or when they have any, 'tis for the most part but a very loose and undetermined, and consequently obscure and confused signification.   (book III, ix, §9)

Arguably, to a larger or smaller degree, this applies to all abstract nouns.

9.8 Final remarks

In this chapter we have sought to open up a new field for modern semantics, or rather, to reopen a field that was explored in the 17th and 18th centuries but has since then largely lain fallow. The explications presented in this chapter show that while abstract nouns are not indefinable, their semantic structure is different from that of "concrete nouns", and also, that it is different in ways consistent with both Locke's account of "mixed modes" and Bentham's of "fictitious entities". We have reached these conclusions following the pathways of modern linguistic semantics.

The chapter of John Locke's *Essay* entitled "of abstract and concrete terms" starts with the following sentence: "The ordinary words of language, and our common use of them, would have given us light into the nature of our ideas if they had been but considered with attention" (book III, viii, §1). Like Locke and other 17th–18th-century thinkers, we too believe that inquiries into language—if considered "with attention"—can shed great light on the "nature of our ideas", or in modern parlance, "conceptual semantics".[8]

We would add two provisos. The first is that our inquiries need not only attention but also a sound and coherent methodology. In our view, the NSM semantic methodology, developed over the past 35 years, satisfies this requirement. Applying

---

[8] Expanding on the connection between words (lexical semantics) and ideas (conceptual analysis), Locke (1690) wrote: "I must confess then, that when I first began this discourse of the understanding, and a good while after, I had not the least thought, that any consideration of words was at all necessary to it. But when having passed over the original composition of our *ideas*, I began to examine the extent and certainty of our knowledge, I found it had so near a connexion with words, that unless their force and manner of signification were first well observed, there could be very little said clearly and pertinently concerning knowledge: which being conversant about truth, had constantly to do with propositions. And though it terminated in things, yet it was for the most part, so much by the intervention of words, that they seem'd scarce separable from our general knowledge. At least they interpose themselves so much between our understandings and the truth, which it would contemplate and apprehend, that like the *medium*, through which visible objects pass, their obscurity and disorder does not seldom cast a mist before our eyes, and impose upon our understandings" (book III, ix, §21).

this methodology in the directions indicated by Locke, Bentham, and others opens up new vistas for systematic empirical research into the content and functions of abstract nouns. Our second proviso is that linguistic semantics must concern itself not solely with the words of "our language", but rather with the words of many languages. Only in this way can we gain a full picture of "human understanding", and only in this way can we ensure that the idiosyncratic features of our own language are not interfering with or distorting our inquiries (cf. Wierzbicka 2014).

10

Broader horizons

Beyond lexical semantics

This book has been dedicated to words and their meanings. We have also touched on grammatical matters here and there, and interested readers will find that there is a substantial NSM literature on grammar (e.g. Wierzbicka 1988; 1996: chs 13–15; 2003b; 2006a: chs 6–8; 2006b; 2009h; Goddard and Wierzbicka 2002c; Goddard 2015; in press; Ye 2004c; Priestley 2008; 2012a). Since the metalanguage of semantic primes can be used for explicating all meanings, whether they are expressed lexically or grammatically, NSM offers an integrated approach to lexicon and grammar. As Leibniz foresaw, however, the metalanguage of semantic primes (his *alphabetum cogitationum humanarum* 'alphabet of human thoughts') has even broader potentials. It provides a new intellectual technology with "unrivalled power with respect to the development of ideas, storing these ideas, and distinguishing between them" (Leibniz 1890[1675], vol. 7: 7; cf. Wierzbicka 2001a). In this chapter we survey some of the ways in which semantic primes can be used for exploring cultural norms and values, for clarifying thinking in the human sciences, and for helping to document and conserve the unique human concepts of endangered languages. We begin, however, by reprising the main theme of this book, i.e. the importance of words and their meanings in people's lives—this time from the perspective of literature.

10.1 Words and meanings in human life

No one is more aware of the centrality of words to human life than writers—paradoxically, much more so than most linguists. For many writers—as for "ordinary people"—words are what language is primarily all about. "I gotta use words when I talk to you," wrote T. S. Eliot (in *Sweeney Agonistes*), and Tom Stoppard (in *Rosencrantz and Guildenstern are Dead*) countered Shakespeare's distrustful "Words words words" with "Words words words. They're all we have to go on." An important theme in such celebration of words is the recognition that words enshrine and crystallize particular ideas, and that they affect people's thinking. "Ideas are enclosed and almost bound in words like precious stones in a ring," mused Italian poet Giacomo Leopardi, and English novelist Aldous Huxley wrote: "Words are magical in the way they affect the minds of those who use them." These and other quotations were marshalled by Vivian Cook (2009) in his *It's All in a Word*.

Under the influence of the logical tradition, in which the meanings of words are understood primarily in terms of "denotata", even linguistic semantics has often overlooked the basic fact that words enshrine ideas—ways of thinking—rather than relating directly to parts of "external reality" as such, and conversely, that ideas are often stabilized in a given society through words. From the point of view of individual speakers born into a community sharing a certain set of words, these words consti-tute and create a shared conceptual and emotional currency—a basis for mutual understanding in many areas and a common framework for both agreements and disagreements, both good and bad feelings.

In her memoir *Reaching One Thousand: A Story of Love, Motherhood and Autism*, Australian writer Rachel Robertson (2012) reflects on the discomfort she felt when she first received an official letter recognizing her as a "carer" of her autistic child:

To use the term carer about the mother of a young child is to mark her out as different from other mothers. Not that she cares more or less for her child, but rather that her role is not the seemingly simple and socially valued role of mothering one's own child but a more complex and invisible one of providing life-long care for a child who may never become independent. [...] The relationship is constructed and defined as unequal – giver and recipient – in the way that the relationship between a parent and her non-disabled child is not, even though the dynamic of independence is the same. [...]

Now I think of it, I have never used the term carer about myself, even though I have ticked that box on the various government forms that I have had to complete over the years. I'm a member of Carers Australia and support the political and educational work that carers' associations undertake. Yet I am still ambivalent about the word. (p. 97)

As Robertson's reflections illustrate, it can matter a great deal to people whether they are described as a "mother" or as a "carer" of a disabled child. New words such as *carer* (which entered the English lexicon only a few decades ago) carry with them new ways of thinking about people and of conceptualizing human relations, and the choice of one word rather than another can have a profound (though not always obvious) effect on people's thinking.

Evidently, words matter a great deal—and if some people (including scholars) who live their lives within the confines of one language do not recognize this fact, for "language migrants" and "language travellers" (Besemeres 1998; 2002; 2008) it is often blindingly obvious, as the testimony of many bilingual writers illustrates.

Here is one example from a language memoir by the American writer Katherine Russell Rich (2009), *Dreaming in Hindi*, recalling her experiences at an educational institution in Delhi:

To the Indians at the Institute, sexual harassment was a terrifying concept. Even its name, with its clacking, hissing sounds, was ominous. The idea behind it, actionable sexual attentions, was purely Western, and no one understood precisely what it meant. But academic advisers who materialised throughout the year had made it clear that in America, whence most students came, this was the most serious of all offenses. Lawsuits from across the seas could come flaming down on any staff member who abetted the behaviour. Careers could be singed to charred stumps. In Delhi, an afternoon of role-playing was planned, to armor the students.

(Rich 2009: 27)

"Sexual harassment" is a relatively new concept in English, too, and the expression illustrates how new ways of thinking can congeal into new concepts, stabilize through new phrases and words, and then travel as loan concepts to other languages.

Another example from Rich's language memoir concerns the word *privacy*:

"There's no word for 'privacy' in any of the Indian languages", we'd been told during orientation, though I surely would have figured that out pretty fast on my own. A month into moving here, I'd begun to suspect that the whole town belonged to the Central Intelligence caste. "Madam, are you living in Sector Eleven?" a rickshaw driver asked. "My friend said he took you there from the bank two weeks ago." "Madam, who was that man who walked you home last night?" the candy shop owner inquired. I had to think, then remembered—just Swami-ji. "He is my teacher," I said with an extreme annoyance that went unnoticed. The guy was too busy nodding, as if calculating implications.   (p. 70)

The absence of a word meaning 'privacy' in languages other than English has often been commented on before (cf. Wierzbicka 2003a[1991]; 2008b; Pavlenko 2011b). But Rich's account is particularly interesting in that it vividly brings to light the link between words, ways of thinking, and ways of living. (See also J. M. Coetzee's remarks (1997: 126) on the key role that the Anglo notion of 'privacy' played in his bilingual and bicultural life as a boy growing up in South Africa.)

Testimonies of bilingual writers are often ignored or dismissed by cognitive scientists and psychologists who see them as insufficiently "scientific". There are, however, some outstanding exceptions, such as cognitive psychologist Merlin Donald, who writes (for discussion, see Besemeres 2010):

The best writers have pushed the subjective exploration of the mind much further than would be permissible in clinical...psychology. [Their] portrayals of it...are possibly the most authoritative descriptions we have.... [S]uch testimony constitutes our primary ethological database.   (Donald 2001: 78–85)

What applies to insightful writers' subjective exploration of the mind in general applies with special force to bilingual writers' exploration of their own subjective experience of living with two conceptual vocabularies. Eva Hoffman's discussion of non-matching social categories such as *friend* in English and *przyjaciel* in Polish is a particularly illuminating example here (1989), and so is Luc Sante's (1998) discussion of emotional words (and emotional worlds) in his three languages, French, Walloon, and English:

To speak of my family, for example, I can hardly employ English without omitting an emotional essence that remains locked in French, although I can't use French either, unless I am willing to sacrifice my critical intelligence. [...] French is an archeological site of emotions, a pipeline to my infant self. It preserves the very rawest, deepest, least guarded feelings. (p. 265)

In my family, the use of someone's first name was nearly always an indication of anger or the prelude to bad news. My parents addressed me as *fifi*, *chou* (cabbage), *lapin* (rabbit), *vî tchèt* (Walloon: old cat), *petit coeur* [little heart].   (Sante 1998: 266)

The literary scholar Mary Besemeres comments on these passages (which come from Sante's 1998 memoir *The Factory of Facts*: "The habitual use of such words by Sante's parents in place of his name suggests a world of relations in which the parents' feelings for their child are at the fore, not his individual identity" (Besemeres 2010: 492).

The idea that the words of the world's many languages may carry with them ways of thinking unfamiliar to speakers of English is sometimes ridiculed by Anglophone scholars and authors who have no experience of living in the two languages, and whose mental horizon is defined by the words of English alone. For example, the *Economist* correspondent and author Robert Lane Greene (2012) writes:

[...] a lot of people believe that the language that you speak alters your thought in really profound and deep ways. It's one of the most common themes of the 20th century, and it came from a couple of linguists working early in the century. Since then you have people who will come up and tell you, with a totally straight face: 'These people have no word for x so they can't think about it.'

Greene misses here the crucial point that words embody **habitual** ways of thinking, **shared** by people in a speech community. We can indeed think about things for which we don't have words, but words suggest to us certain ways of thinking about reality and create shared conceptual currency for the speakers of a language.

In a perfunctory fashion Greene rejects the testimony of bilingual writers writing in English but capable of thinking and experiencing the world through two languages, such as Bharati Mukherjee, of whom he writes:

Bharati Mukherjee claims that some of these Bengali words [such as the word *bhoi*, roughly 'fear/terror'] have a resonance that is impossible to carry over into English. But that's not really true. She's a good writer in English so she should know that you can do the job with slightly different tools in any language.

Greene's condescending "she should know" addressed to a writer of Bharati Mukherjee's depth, subtlety, and experience defies comment, especially given that he has no arguments (other than superficial references to Noam Chomsky and Stephen Pinker) to challenge her insight.

Different ways of thinking and feeling entrenched in different languages—in different conversational routines and the like, but also in different words—are existentially and experientially beyond question to people living with two or more languages and cultures, and for whom, in the words of psycholinguist Aneta Pavlenko, "their own linguistic experience illuminates ways in which languages shape and affect thought" (Pavlenko 2011a: 9; see also Pavlenko 2005; 2006; Besemeres and Wierzbicka 2007). To make differences of this kind transparent to those who don't have such experiences themselves and whose "critical intelligence" (to use Luc Sante's words) makes them distrustful of the experience of others, we need not only subjective testimonies but also rigorous semantic analyses, and this in turn requires a rigorous semantic methodology. NSM provides such a methodology, enabling us to show precisely how, for example, the words *privacy, friend,* or *harassment* differ from their would-be counterparts in other languages (Wierzbicka 2008b; 1997; 2009f). It also provides a methodology for identifying differences in meaning which cannot be the subject of testimonies from people living with two languages.

In her memoir *Things I've Been Silent About,* the Iranian-American writer Azar Nafisi (2008) recalls how her mother, advised by a psychiatrist to be tolerant towards her teenage children ("you know how teenagers are"), replies tartly: "In my time, teenagers didn't exist." In many countries of the world, teenagers still "don't exist", in the sense that there is no such word and no corresponding concept: evidence suggests that the concept of 'children' is universal, but the concept of 'teenager' is a conceptual creation of modern Anglo culture, solidified in a particular word. The NSM methodology allows us to identify the meaning of this word, and thus the way of thinking ingrained in it, in a precise, clear, and verifiable manner.

For concepts ingrained in this way in the words of living languages like present-day English, such verification can include testing NSM explications against the intuitions of native speakers as well as validating them through substitution in a wide range of contexts. For concepts from languages which are no longer spoken but for which we have rich literary records, for example, ancient Greek or 16th-century English, only the second of these methods can be used. As Helen Bromhead's (2009) book *The Reign of Truth and Faith: Epistemic Expressions in 16th and 17th century English* illustrates, however, for such languages, too, careful and rigorous NSM-based analysis can bring to light past ways of thinking and demonstrate differences in the prevailing worldviews of different epochs (reflected in their vocabularies) in an illuminating and precise manner.

Given all this, two questions which naturally arise are the following: How can the findings and the general approach of NSM semantics be brought to bear on practical lexicography, so that dictionaries can become more accurate and more helpful? And how can NSM be applied in practical language teaching? Space does not allow us to pursue these matters here, but the interested reader can follow up with Wierzbicka (1996: ch. 9), Bullock (2011), Goddard and Wierzbicka (2007b), Goddard (2010c).

10.2 Cultural scripts for culturally shaped "ways of speaking"

The language of semantic primes can be used not only for explaining the meaning of words and other vehicles of linguistic meaning (such as fixed phrases, conversational routines, and grammatical constructions) but also as a notation for writing 'cultural scripts', i.e. hypotheses about cultural shared assumptions, norms, and expectations which help regulate interaction in different cultural settings. It has long been recognized that people in different cultures and societies not only speak different languages and use different words but also use these languages in different ways.

The most influential approach to these different culture-specific 'ways of speaking' is the 'ethnography of communication' (Hymes 1968[1962]; Gumperz and Hymes 1986[1972]; Bauman and Sherzer 1974; Carbaugh 2005). This tradition emphasizes that to be a competent speaker includes knowing how to speak in culturally appropriate ways to different people about different things in different settings. To describe and explain such phenomena, ethnographers usually posit culture-specific norms of interaction and interpretation. A stumbling block for standard ethnography of communication (and even for innovative versions, such as Donal Carbaugh's Cultural Discourse Analysis) is how to state or articulate these norms without falling foul of excessive abstraction, ambiguity, or Anglocentrism. Frequently used terms of description such as 'formality', 'politeness', 'respect' 'deference', 'face', 'hierarchy', and 'involvement' (Irvine 1979; Janney and Arndt 1993; Besnier 1994) are all prone to these problems. Above all, because the concepts designated by these specialist English words cannot be translated easily into the languages involved, they cannot disclose what anthropologists call an "insider perspective", i.e. an interpretation from the point of view of the people concerned. The metalanguage of semantic primes can help overcome these problems by providing a precise and culture-independent way of formulating cultural rules for speaking. In NSM theory, cultural rules of this kind are known as cultural scripts. Wierzbicka summed it up like this:

Cultural scripts are representations of cultural norms which are widely held in a given society and are reflected in its language. They constitute a certain "naïve axiology", that is, a naïve set of assumptions about what it is good and bad to do or say, and even to think and feel. Any given speech community has such shared assumptions, and although not everyone necessarily agrees with them, everyone is familiar with them because they are reflected in the language itself.   (Wierzbicka 2007e: 56)

The theory of cultural scripts (also known as ethnopragmatics) can be seen as a "sister theory" to NSM semantics. It has been described and developed in many studies, in relation to a large variety of languages and cultures (Wierzbicka 1994b; 1994c; 1994d; Goddard 2006d; Goddard and Wierzbicka 1997; 2004). It is hardly possible to review all this literature here so we will just offer a couple of examples, which can help illuminate another interesting point: namely, that cultural norms and speech practices (describable by cultural scripts) are usually closely tied up, in diverse ways, with word meanings, phraseology, and conversational routines. One of the main priorities of ethnopragmatics is to de-naturalize the pragmatics of English, which is often unwittingly taken as a baseline or default against which other cultures' interactional practices are compared. We will therefore begin by adducing an example of an Anglo cultural script.

Arguably one of the primary Anglo cultural values can be described as 'personal autonomy'. This, however, is a technical expression, unknown to most ordinary speakers of English. As such, it cannot represent an insider perspective on the cultural value in question, nor is it directly translatable across languages. These difficulties can be overcome if the basic insight behind the claim that "Anglo English values personal autonomy" is unpacked into simple cross-translatable words using the cultural script technique. As one can see, a cultural script is introduced by a framing expression like 'at many times people think like this'. After this comes the content of a widely known and assumed-to-be-shared attitude.

[A]   *An Anglo English cultural script for "personal autonomy"*

a.   at many times people think like this:
b.   when someone does something, it is good if this someone can think like this:
c.   "I am doing this because I want to do it"

As argued extensively elsewhere, the script above (and a suite of related sub-scripts) is connected with various well-known facts about English interactional style, such as the general dispreference for using the bare imperative ("telling people what to do") and the elaborate range of "interrogative-directive" and "suggestive" formulas, such as those displayed in (1) and (2) (Wierzbicka 2003a[1991]; 2006d). These Anglo English "request strategies" are not arbitrary properties of the English language, much less the result of any "universals of politeness", but rather have their roots and rationale in Anglo cultural values.

(1)   *Will you ... please?*   *Won't you ... ?*
       Would you ... ?   *Do you want to ... ?*
       Could you ... ?   *Why don't you ... ?*
       Would you mind ... ?   *I wonder if ...*
       Would you like to ... ?

(2)   *You might like to ...*   *I would suggest ...*
       You could consider ...   *Have you thought of ... ?*
       Perhaps you could ...

The two scripts below have been proposed as high-level scripts of Russian and Colombian Spanish culture, respectively. The Russian script expresses a cultural endorsement of, roughly speaking, an "expressive" stance in speech and action

(Wierzbicka 2002*a*), while the Colombian Spanish script endorses displays of something like "personal warmth" (Travis 2004; 2006).

[B]   *A Russian cultural script connected with "expressiveness"*

a.   at many times people think like this:

b.   it is good if someone wants other people to know what this someone thinks

c.   it is good if someone wants other people to know what this someone feels

[C]   *A Colombian Spanish cultural script connected with "interpersonal warmth"*

a.   at many times people think like this:

b.   when I feel something good towards someone, it is good if this someone knows it

c.   because of this, it is good if I do some things when I am with this someone, it is good if I say some things when I am with this someone

As with the Anglo English script given above, it can be argued that the high-level concerns captured in these scripts are played out by way of a whole family of related speech practices in their respective speech cultures. High-level scripts such as these, furthermore, are often closely associated with cultural key words, such as English *freedom* (and *free*), Russian *iskrennost'*, roughly "sincerity", and Spanish *calor humano* "human warmth", respectively.

We conclude this brief treatment of cultural scripts with four points. First, in any speech community there will be a large number of interrelated cultural scripts "in circulation", as it were, some of them more important than others, some tailored to specific situations, settings, and types of interlocutors, some in a state of flux or in competition with other cultural scripts. No speech culture can be reduced, in any sense, to a small number of formulas, and no speech culture is static either. Nonetheless, using the methods of ethnopragmatics and cultural semantics, it is possible to disentangle and articulate cultural scripts in a way that makes sense of speech practices.

Second, given the heterogeneity of any society, it is obvious that not every member of Anglo, Russian, or Colombian Spanish culture would accept or endorse the scripts cited above. The claim is that even those who do not personally accept or identify with the content of a script are nonetheless familiar with it, i.e. that it forms part of the interpretative backdrop to discourse and social behaviour in a particular cultural context.

Third, the cultural scripts method has been applied to a large number of languages and to a large number of speech practices. Languages include English (e.g. Wierzbicka 2003*a*[1991]; 2002*b*; 2006*a*; 2006*d*; Goddard 2006*a*; 2009*a*; 2012*b*; Peeters 2000; 2004*b*), Singapore English (Wong 2004*b*; 2008), Spanish (Travis 2004; 2006), French (Peeters 2000; 2012; 2013), Russian (Wierzbicka 2002*a*; 2009*b*; 2011*b*; 2012*a*), Polish (Wierzbicka 1999*a*: ch. 6), Chinese (Ye 2004*a*; 2004*b*; 2006), Japanese (Hasada 1996; 2006), Malay (Goddard 1997*b*; 2000*a*; 2004*a*), Korean

(Yoon 2004; 2007c), Ewe (Ameka 2006; 2009; Ameka and Breedveld 2004), Koromu, PNG (Priestley 2008; 2013), Roper Kriol (Nicholls 2011: ch. 6), and Danish (Levisen 2010; 2012). Particular cultural scripts are of course not necessarily unique to any given culture. On the contrary, similar or identical scripts can recur in many different cultures, reflecting similarities and affiliations at the 'trait' level between different cultures. It should also perhaps be stated that cultural scripts change and develop over time and vary across geographical and social space.

Fourth, because cultural scripts formulated in semantic primes can be readily translated into any language, they can have practical application in real-world situations of trying to bridge some kind of cultural gap, with immigrants, language learners, in international negotiations, etc. (Goddard and Wierzbicka 2004; 2007b; Wierzbicka 2008b; 2012b; Goddard 2010c).

10.3 Semantics, psychology, and psycholinguistics

People often wonder what relation there is between the conceptual and linguistic analysis of NSM semantics and the discipline of psychology.

The findings of NSM semantics indeed afford many opportunities for research using psycholinguistic methods, but while some psychologists (Wisniewski, Lamb, and Middleton 2003; Middleton et al. 2004; Boster 2005) recognize this, overall the uptake of NSM ideas by psychologists and psycholinguists has not been very significant to date. To some extent this is attributable to the disciplinary divide between experimental psychology and linguistics. Linguists tend to prefer analysis of naturally occurring data, often—these days—marshalled with the help of computerized corpus techniques. They also employ a range of well-established analytical constructs and procedures, such as the concept of lexical polysemy, the distinction between polysemy (distinct but related meanings) and generality of meaning, recognizing the existence of "lexicalized" word combinations whose meaning is not the sum of the parts, and using collocational preferences as clues to meaning. NSM linguists draw on all these standard (albeit sometimes contested) linguistic concepts in their work, as readers will know from many studies in this book, as well as deploying their own unique tools: conceptual analysis into semantic primes and molecules and the test of substitution without change of meaning. Psychologists, by contrast, usually distrust the use of naturalistic data and prefer to use data gathered in controlled (experimental or quasi-experimental) conditions. They strongly prefer quantitative methods. Many have scant knowledge of linguistics and are uncomfortable with what they see as the excessive mentalism and subjectivity of linguistic analysis.

For our part, we believe that much standard psychological and psycholinguistic research on meaning is methodologically shaky, for reasons explained briefly below. We are certainly not prepared to fall in with the assumption of some psychologists that all statements and claims about meaning remain hypothetical until or unless they are "verified" by experiments. On the other hand, it is true that because explications are intelligible to native speakers, they are amenable to experiments that directly expose speakers to the analysis itself using recognition, matching, and rating tasks. Well-designed psycholinguistic experiments could help test the validity of explications and clarify the role of lexical semantic structures in thinking. It is important to recognize, however, that the meanings of everyday words are not immediately transparent to ordinary language users. They lie "under the hood" of people's consciousness, not on its surface. As well, explications are unfamiliar in form and in genre. They clash with expectations based on people's experiences with dictionaries and with prestige academic language generally. With proper attention to experimental design, e.g. via pre-training and familiarization, these issues could no doubt be overcome. The caveats about experimental design must be taken seriously, however, as it is likely that many and varied factors could influence the results, aside from the validity of the semantic components.

In terms of test items, it would be interesting to explore the advantages and drawbacks of presenting explications all at once, as opposed to using one component at a time. It is true that as a representation of meaning, an explication stands or falls as a whole, and that much often hinges on the interplay between components. These effects would be compromised by using isolated components or partial explications. On the other hand, single components present reduced processing difficulty for the respondents. One promising component-based design would be a semantic questionnaire in which respondents are presented with a test item and a list of several components and are asked to rate the appropriateness of each component on a Likert scale. Preliminary work along these lines is already under way (Gladkova, Vanhatalo, and Goddard 2015).

We also want to mention the possibility that focus groups and semi-structured interviews may provide effective methodologies for working with full explications. NSM explications are usually developed, in part, dialogically, i.e. by an iterative process in consultation with collaborators, workshop participants, and students. It may be that the dialogical process makes it easier to access unconscious or semi-conscious linguistic knowledge. It would also be interesting to explore the possibility that individuals may differ markedly in their degree of "semantic aptitude" on different tasks.

Using NSM to improve psychological experiments on subjective experience

Much research in psychology and psycholinguistics depends on verbal responses of one kind or another. This is only natural—indeed, it is inevitable. Subjective experience can only be accessed from the inside, and can only be reported and communicated via language. Even non-verbal data such as facial expressions, behavioural observations, and physiological measurements (skin conductance, hormonal states, neurological states, etc.) cannot be correlated with particular mental states without some kind of subjective attributions.

This point is not affected by the fact that physiology presumably plays a role in explaining some subjective experiences, such as emotions. Barrett et al. (2007: 374–377) spell out the logic as follows:

> Describing how emotion experiences are caused does not substitute for a description of what is felt, and in fact, an adequate description of what people feel is required so that scientists know what to explain in the first place [...] To know what emotion feels like, it is necessary to ask people what they experience [...] to examine people's verbal behaviors regarding their own mental state, in the form of self-reports [...] [self-reports] are useful—and indeed essential— for revealing the ontological structure of consciousness [...]

Self-reports of course require a language. When interpreting the self-reports of people whose native language is not English, if their words are simply converted into their assumed English counterparts, this effectively "re-codes" those reports and in the process alters them. Such re-coding is a routine practice in psychological studies of emotion across cultures. For example, Scherer and collaborators administered a questionnaire in eight European countries with the aim of assessing the frequency and quality of emotional experience (Scherer, Wallbott, and Summerfield 1986). Information was sought on four supposedly universal categories, each characterized by a pair of English words: *joy/happiness, sadness/grief, fear/fright, anger/rage*. The technique of translation and back-translation was used "to guarantee equivalence across languages" (Aebischer and Wallbott 1986: 32), but numerous semantic studies have shown that ordinary translation and back-translation cannot guarantee full equivalence of meaning. In the German version of the questionnaire, for example, one of the words used for the category *fear/fright*, with the sanction of the back-translation procedure, was *Angst* (Scherer 1986: 177), but the meaning of *Angst* is quite different from that of either *fear* or *fright* (Wierzbicka 1999a: 123–165).

In our view, this flawed translation methodology should be abandoned altogether. We can—indeed, must—continue to gather self-reports about mental states in terms of indigenous categories, but what we cannot do any longer is to assume that the content of these categories can be matched in a simple fashion with the categories of the English language. The semantic content of language-specific categories must be analysed and explicated into configurations of semantic primes, which can then be transposed without distortion across languages.

In many cases, scenarios and reporting protocols can be framed directly in terms of semantic primes and other lexical universals and near-universals. For example, rather than asking people how often and in what circumstances they *feel angry*, we can ask about how often and in what circumstances they think something like 'someone is doing something bad, I don't want this', and about how often and in what circumstances they think something like 'I want to do something bad to this person because of it'. Likewise, rather than asking people how often and in what circumstances they *feel happy* or *feel satisfied*, we can ask about how often and in what circumstances they 'feel something good' or 'feel something very good', or specifically about how often and in what circumstances they think something like 'some good things happened to me, I can do many things now as I want', or 'some very good things happened to me, I don't want anything more now'. In this way, we effectively "deconstruct emotions for the sake of comparative research" (Shweder 2004).

Framing the reporting protocols in semantic primes would make them cross-translatable and, at the same time, more fine-grained. Some psychologists have recognized this. For example, discussing scenarios for eliciting emotion descriptors in different languages and cultures, Boster (2005: 219) says: "Any propositions should be expressed in something approaching Wierzbicka's (1992[a]) semantic metalanguage, employing simple, clear terms with universal (or near universal) significance."

In short, as we see things, the NSM paradigm can stimulate cross-disciplinary research and open the way for the development of new experimental and quasi-experimental methodologies.

A cautionary note

Despite the potential for controlled data-gathering methods to yield valuable information for the study of meaning, we think it necessary to sound a cautionary note. Research into meaning must be precisely that, i.e. it must focus on people's concepts and ways of thinking (as embedded in language), not on people's behaviours, "naming practices", responses to stimuli, etc. We mention this because many researchers in psychology and psycholinguistics tend to gravitate towards experimental designs that collect people's verbal responses (often single-word responses) to standardized sets of external stimuli, such as models and other props, colour chips, pictures, drawings, or video clips (Berlin and Kay 1969; Levinson 2003; Levinson and Meira 2003; Levinson and Wilkins 2006; Majid and Bowerman 2007; Majid, Enfield, and van Staden 2006; Majid 2012). This "stimulus-based elicitation" has been energetically promoted in recent years by researchers in the Max Planck Institute of Psycholinguistics (Nijmegen). It allows a linguist to collect "lexical data" economically and in a form that can be readily compared with data from other languages.

Despite these attractions, we see multiple problems with stimulus-based elicitation. The first and most fundamental is that it is not designed to access meanings at all, i.e. to tap into people's concepts. Merely mapping out a word's range of use against a set of pre-selected stimuli offers no method for getting inside speakers' heads, for accessing ideas.[1] Second, it is hard to see how the method can

---

[1] As Evans and Sasse (2007[2003]) observe, meaning cannot be "read off" from external data. To access meaning requires a hermeneutic process, preferably involving creative engagement with native speakers and the opportunity to access an open-ended set of examples in everyday contexts.

accommodate, or even recognize, the existence of lexical polysemy, which is funda-mental to understanding how the lexicon really works. Third, the method is designed to work with things that can be seen and handled. It is not readily extendable to words for psychological attributes, emotions, values and social relations, and the like.

Fourth, researchers using this approach are often unwilling to acknowledge that even concrete nouns like *cup* or *bird* are not names of particular things but names of categories, and that categories are essentially "creatures of the mind".[2] They tend to assume that, as Gentner and Boroditsky (2001: 241) put it, "concrete nouns are in many cases simply names for pre-existing natural referents". Yet cross-linguistic analysis shows that even words for apparently "natural referents" incorporate anthropocentric and culture-specific perspectives, for example, ethnogeographical words such as *moun-tain* and *river*, and ethnobiological words like *mouse* and *butterfly* (Bromhead 2011b; Goddard 2011b: ch. 7; Wierzbicka 1996: chs 11 and 12; 2013). Fifth, unless rigorously controlled, the language in which the researchers describe and interpret their results necessarily imposes its own language-specific perspective. Typically the language of description is English, and no effort is made to control for and eliminate English-specific words. This means that English becomes, in effect, the default standard against which the meanings of other languages are calibrated (Wierzbicka 2014).

This is not to suggest that studies using standardized stimuli cannot be valuable and revealing. They can be—but in order to be constructive they need to work hand in hand with conceptual semantics. Ultimately, if we want to understand "word-to-referent mapping" in different languages, we have to formulate explicit and testable hypotheses about what the words mean.

Before leaving the topic of NSM's potential engagements and collaborations with psychology, we want to mention three other frontiers, where, it seems to us, pro-ductive work is waiting to be done. The first is the project of cultural psychology, which lies at the intersection of psychology and cultural anthropology. It has been characterized by one of its founders, Richard Shweder (2003: 27), as the study of "the distinctive mentalities and modes of psychological functioning of members of differ-ent communities". One of its assumptions is that the semantic constructs of different languages provide culture-specific cognitive frameworks (cultural models, in the sense of Holland and Quinn 1987) through which people interpret their interpersonal experiences, encode them in memory, and negotiate them in narratives of life experience. That is, that everyday words and expressions form part of "the implicit

---

[2] John Locke (1959[1690]) saw this clearly: "'tis evident", he wrote, "that **men** make sorts of things" (III, vi, 35). Having discussed various kinds of birds common in England and commonly distinguished in English, Locke concluded: "This, then, in short, is the case: nature makes many particular things, which do agree one with another, in many sensible qualities [...], but [...] 'tis men who, taking occasion from the qualities they find united in them [...] range them into sorts, in order to their naming, for the convenience of comprehensive signs, [...] and in this, I think, consists the whole business of genres and species" (III, vi, 36).

meanings (the goals, values, and pictures of the world) that give shape to psychological processes" (Shweder 2003: 28). The connection with NSM semantics, which provides the tools to access everyday meanings in diverse languages, will be obvious. Similar connections exist with another interdisciplinary field, psychological anthropology (e.g. Strauss and Quinn 1997; Quinn 2002).

A second cross-over area between NSM semantics and psychology concerns language acquisition and conceptual development in early childhood. Though this is a much-contested area of scholarship in psychology, some leading researchers hold views that are highly compatible with the stance and findings of NSM semantics. For example, in her book *The Origin of Concepts*, Susan Carey (2009) posits the existence of innate "conceptual primitives" which underlie "core cognition" and which provide "the developmental foundation of human conceptual understanding" (p. 11). For discussion, see Wierzbicka (2015). Other excursions of NSM into child language development include Goddard (2001*b*) and Tien (2010).

Finally, we would like to mention the possibility (still untested) that NSM findings about the core elements of cognition and communication may have clinical applications, for example, in helping people recover from communication impairment due to stroke and other forms of brain damage.

10.4 Clarifying thinking in the human sciences

Anglophone scholars in the human sciences often unwittingly frame their research hypotheses in English-specific terms. For example, when evolutionary biologists postulate a "universal sense of right and wrong" (Hauser 2006) or puzzle over the evolutionary origins of "animal altruism" (e.g. Field 2001; Orr 2010), there is little awareness of the problematical fact that their words *right*, *wrong*, and *altruism* are English-specific constructs that lack precise equivalents in many languages of the world, including many European languages. Conceptual Anglocentrism is not widely recognized as a problem for science, but in our view it ought to be. It hardly seems optimal for scientific hypotheses to be locked, so to speak, into a single language.

Using ill-defined terms such as *altruism* (*cooperation*, *collaboration*, *reciprocity*, *sociality*, etc.) in scientific discourse routinely leads to confusion and misunderstandings. To illustrate: Orr (2010) says that "Darwin recognized that altruism posed a potentially fatal challenge to his theory of natural selection", and also: "One of the most striking examples of animal altruism and one that troubled Darwin no end, occurs among the insects". Darwin himself, however, never used the language of altruism, speaking rather of 'sympathy', 'self-sacrifice', 'social instincts', 'parental and filial affections', and 'social affections'. Orr also writes that the Russian zoologist Peter Kropotkin "found an astonishing amount of altruism in nature", but in his classic book *Mutual Aid: A Factor in Evolution*, Kropotkin (1902) never used the word *altruism* (Russian, *al'truism*), and his key word *vzaimopomoshch'* (roughly, 'mutual aid') does not mean the same as either *altruism* or *cooperation*.

Anglocentrism and conceptual unclarity in the human sciences can both be alleviated by using NSM as an auxiliary metalanguage for conceptual clarification. This would enable scholars to define any English-specific terms that they might want to use through simple and universal concepts or (when appropriate) to formulate claims directly through conceptual universals, without going through English-specific concepts at all. To illustrate: Kropotkin's idea of mutual aid was intended as a generalization from field observations (wolves hunting together, collective migrations of deer in Siberia, and the like). His core idea can be formulated in NSM in the first text below. This is quite different from the ethical ideal of 'altruism' developed in Victorian England and stabilized in colloquial English (Dixon 2008), which can be explicated as in the second text.

[D]   Kropotkin's idea of 'mutual aid' *vzaimopomoshch'*

a.   at many times, it is like this in a place:
b.   some living things of one kind do things for some time with many other
            living things of the same kind
c.   this is good for these living things
d.   they do it like this because they want to do it like this

[E]   The ethical ideal of *altruism* in colloquial English

a.   it is good if it is like this:
b.   someone thinks like this at many times:
c.   "I want to do good things for other people"
d.   because of this, this someone does many good things for other people

The different introductory frames reflect the difference between Kropotkin's empirical generalization ('at many times it is like this in a place') as opposed to an ethical ideal ('it is good if it is like this'). In terms of content, Kropotkin's 'mutual aid' concerns 'doing something **with** (someone else)', which happens to be of mutual benefit, whereas ethical altruism concerns 'doing something **good for** (someone else)'.

'Altruism' is not the only term to be used in multiple ways and at "cross-purposes" in human sciences discourse. Similar confusions are evident in use of terms like 'cooperation', 'reciprocity', 'collaboration', and the like, which are commonly used, with somewhat shifting and variable meanings, in debates about evolutionary psychology. These confusions can be disentangled and made transparent through NSM (cf. Wierzbicka 2014).

Recently, psychiatrist Horacio Fábrega (forthcoming; cf. 2013) has foreshadowed how NSM may help advance scientific thinking about the evolution of the human mind. Fábrega's special interest lies in the conceptualization of "psychiatric conditions" among early humans (which he doesn't want to label "mental illness" because he wants to avoid the culturally shaped implications of this modern English phrase). What is particularly relevant from a semantic point of view is that Fábrega is trying to look not just at behaviours but at what may have happened inside our ancestors' minds, and moreover to look at it from their own perspective rather than from a modern perspective. His questions concern the subjectivity of early humans—their thoughts and feelings.

The project of getting inside the heads of early humans and trying to understand (or speculate about) their own self-understanding is unusually bold. At the same time, it is not altogether different from an attempt to get inside the heads of speakers of an endangered (or dead) language and to endeavour to see the world from their point of view. For an Anglophone scholar, the first step towards either of these goals must be to divest oneself from the layers of culturally shaped English in one's own mind, and to try to imagine possible conceptual perspectives of people whose thinking was not similarly shaped by English and Anglo culture. For example, there is good evidence that the languages of hunter-gatherers (in Australia, Papua, or Africa) do not have words corresponding to *depression, self-esteem, phobia,* or *paranoia*. Presumably, it is safe to assume that there were no such words and concepts in the thought of early humans and pre-humans in ancestral environments. Fábrega suggests that in trying to model that thought from within, we need a simple metalanguage such as NSM:

One can presume that to the extent that NSM grips the logical and semantic core of human thought that underlies all languages its resources serve as a model or exemplum of what language and communication may have been like in early human history. Something like NSM, then, probably undergirded early modes of thought and language use.

(Fábrega forthcoming: 86)

Fábrega points out that NSM presupposes a mental or psychological faculty, and is consistent in this respect with "ideas about cognitive modules (e.g. theory of mind, social cognition more generally) and underpinnings of cognitive models of persons and minds" put forward in evolutionary social sciences. At the same time, he notes, "the 'folk psychology' that permeates NSM formulations of behaviour is miles away from similar-sounding ideas about minds, persons, and which are regnant in modern Western societies."

Referring in particular to "conditions of psychiatric interest", Fábrega sketches conceptual components couched in terms of semantic primes such as 'someone', 'something', 'bad', 'happen', 'do', 'want', and 'feel', saying that "NSM delineates a conceptual space around a social context wherein conditions of psychiatric interest would have been placed" (Fábrega forthcoming: 88). Another way to look at it is to say that, in Fábrega's words, "NSM enables one to get inside the heads of hominins as they acquired resources for representing and sharing ideas" (p. 92).

We will offer just a single example here, which connects with the previous discussion of "altruism" concepts. Various writers on human evolution and the importance of "pro-social thinking" (e.g. Harman 2010) appear to suggest that many human groups across time and space share a consensus that can be articulated, in NSM terms, as: 'it is good if people want to do good things for (some) other people.' Presumably, it could be argued that from an evolutionary point of view, "pro-social" thinking of this kind would make good sense. Speaking of the changing contexts of behaviour among early humans Fábrega writes:

[I]ndividuals at the threshold of Upper Paleolithic social life were experiencing emerging categories of awareness of self, other, personal and social identity, and the value and disvalue of social commitment compared to selfish pursuits. It was behavioral milieus such as these which became emotionally and cognitively associated with scrutiny of oneself, one's situation, and the actions and belief psychologies of group members.   (Fábrega forthcoming: 106)

Thinking along these lines, one might consider the following scenario. At some time in human prehistory, when our ancestors started to live in relatively small groups (rather than in large "hordes"), there may have emerged (in some places) "pro-social" thinking along the following lines:

I live with many people
these people do many good things for me
it is good if I do some good things for these people

Or, drawing on Fábrega's (ch. 36) discussion of the probable emergence in early hominins of a "social self based on high group interdependence", we could suggest that the key evolutionary breakthrough in human "moral" thinking may be more faithfully represented in the following, fuller formula, which reflects (in its second and third lines) something like "group thinking":

I live with many people
all these people are like one something
I am part of this something
these people do many good things for me
it is good if I do some good things for these people

This is all, needless to say, contested territory. The purpose of the present discussion is not to express particular views on the subject matter as such, but to show that the debates can be sharpened and clarified by drawing on the conceptual language of NSM.

10.5 Capturing endangered concepts

With language endangerment moving up the mainstream linguistic agenda, recent years have seen a resurgence of interest in linguistic fieldwork and language documentation (Austin 2003–10; Gippert, Himmelmann, and Mosel 2006; Ameka, Dench, and Evans 2006; Grenoble and Furbee 2010; Crowley 2007; Bowern 2008; Sakel and Everett 2012; Thieberger 2012). Endangered languages, and the fieldworkers trying to document them, have an urgent need for useful techniques for grappling with meaning analysis. We believe that NSM semantics, and in particular its empirical findings about lexical universals, can make an important contribution to linguistic fieldwork. The technique of reductive paraphrase makes meanings tangible, concrete, and amenable to discussion with consultants and language teachers. The same approach can enable the analyst to cut through perennial confusions about when it is or isn't justified to recognize polysemy. Skilfully used, it can bring to light culture-specific conceptualizations and ways of thinking that are embedded in the lexicons and grammars of different languages, and thus help to fulfil the promise of field linguistics to document the untold diversity of human ways of knowing, thinking, and feeling.

Despite their best intentions, in our opinion, field linguists are often not prepared to face up to the fact that indigenous concepts cannot be faithfully portrayed using English-specific vocabulary, especially not the Latinate vocabulary favoured in technical and academic discourse. To ensure that "endangered concepts" are preserved for a wider audience (as part of the common human heritage), it may be necessary to describe them in a widely accessible language such as English but it is not necessary to use technical or sophisticated Latinate English, which is bound to impart an Anglocentric perspective. Rather, we think, field linguists should always strive to find ways to express their hypotheses and insights about indigenous meanings in terms that are simple and cross-translatable, even if this comes at the cost of their being lengthier and less sophisticated in tone. We will illustrate with just two examples, both drawn from the spatial domain.

It is often assumed that in the spatial domain it is a straightforward matter to move from extensional data, such as audiovisual recordings, maps, and photographs, to an authentic intensional (cognitive) representation. Evans and Sasse (2007[2003]) argue against this view, insisting that meaning is a matter of **construal** and hence demands a hermeneutic process. On this point we are in full agreement with them. We would not agree, however, that it is appropriate to render an indigenous meaning (even "roughly") using a complex English expression such as "significant geographical discontinuity", as they do in the following passage:

[I]n Kayardild, there is a suffix -*ngurrnga,* added to directional terms based on compass points, meaning roughly 'beyond a significant geographical discontinuity'. Thus *ringurrnga* 'east-*ngurrnga*' can be used for an island, emerging from the sea to the east, but also to a stand of mangroves, or sandhills, as one leaves a saltpan travelling east. Though it is possible to photograph or map particular instances of *ringurrnga,* the underlying meaning—what is construed as a significant geographical discontinuity—cannot simply be taken for granted,

or immediately inferred from a couple of instances, and to really get to the bottom of it we need
to probe an open-ended set of examples.   (Evans and Sasse 2007[2003]: 67)

It would be preferable, in our view, to see the Kayardild concept expressed by the
-*ngurrnga* suffix unpacked into terms that can be expressed in Kayardild itself. It
seems to us that this can be done using a scenario-based approach, roughly as
follows: someone in a place wants to be in another place on one side (e.g. to the
east or south) of the place where he or she is to begin with, this someone knows that
to reach this other place (i.e. to be in this place after some time), he or she first has to
move through some other places, and this someone also knows that this can't be done
without making special efforts, e.g. swimming, canoeing, climbing. This is not a full
or precise explanation, but it goes some way to breaking down the meaning implied
by the expression "geographical discontinuity" in a fashion that could conceivably
correspond to a Kayardild way of thinking about it.

For another example, we will attempt to rethink two of the glosses used by Hinton
(2001) in an article about directional suffixes in the endangered American indigenous
language Karuk. The two suffixes and their glosses are: -*vara* 'in through a tubular
space' and -*kiv* 'out through a tubular space'. Glosses like these are common in the
literature on complex directional morphology, but they are distinctly peculiar,
obscure, and unidiomatic even in English. What is a "tubular space"? Can such a
gloss capture an indigenous Karuk meaning if (as we assume to be the case) Karuk
does not have any words like "tubular" and "space"? Again, we would suggest that
a plausible unpacking of the intended meaning is based on a motional scenario, in
this case the scenario of something moving for some time 'inside something long'.
For -*vara,* the result of such movement is that the moving thing ends up inside
something else, for -*kiv,* it ends up no longer being inside something else. Again,
these ideas may be incomplete or mistaken in some respects, but at least they are
formulated in a way that can plausibly represent indigenous Karuk meanings (unlike
formulations that rely on the expression "tubular space").

We also want to draw attention to the importance of identifying and documenting
the cultural key words of endangered languages. Fieldwork manuals in linguistics pay
surprisingly little attention to the importance of locating and exploring culturally
important words, or to the challenges involved in doing so. (This is due largely to the
field manuals' concentration on grammar and phonology, at the expense of lexicon.)
We would be first to acknowledge that unravelling the semantics of a cultural
key word is a formidable challenge, and that it may be necessary to settle for an
approximation at first. Still, there are some guidelines that can be helpful, and chief
among them, in our opinion, is the goal of producing a formulation that is phrased as
simply as possible (not necessarily exclusively in semantic primes, but as close as
possible) and that relies as little as possible on disjunction. The problem with an
excess of disjunctions can be illustrated with the following quotation about the

Hawaiian cultural key concept *mauli*. Wilson and Kamanā (2001: 61) describe it as follows:

Some features of *mauli* are covered by the English word "culture", but *mauli* also includes worldview, spirituality, physical movement, morality, personal relationships, and other central features of a person's life and the life of a people.

This statement is undoubtedly useful as an indication of the cultural centrality of the *mauli* concept, but the string of abstract English words ("culture", "worldview", "spirituality", "morality", etc.) is too vague and diffuse, and above all too Anglo-centric, to convey any sense of a powerful and unitary culture-specific meaning. The same applies to descriptions of a more celebrated cultural key word from Oceania, *mana*, which has been variously glossed by anthropologists as "power, authority, influence, prestige, efficacy" (cf. Keesing 1984). The Māori linguist Haumihiata Mason (2008: 35) has even rendered *mana* as "identity" and "integrity" in his poetic motto: *Tōku reo, tōku mana, Ki te ngaro tōku reo, ka ngaro ko au* 'My language is my identity, my integrity, Without my language I am lost.' The wide range of these glosses highlights the fact that they all fail to capture the uniqueness of the Māori concept.

We are not in a position to offer any suggestions about Hawaaian *mauli*, but Goddard and Wierzbicka (2014: 110) propose the following explication for *mana* in Māori (cf. Moorefield 2005: 76–77):

[F]   *mana* [Māori]

a.   something
b.   people can't see it, people can't know well what it is
c.   it can be part of some things, it can be part of some people
d.   if someone has this part, this someone can do many things not like other people
e.   when people think about this something, they can't not feel something good

This explication is framed exclusively in semantic primes, and thus all its terms are independent of English, transposable into Māori, and can plausibly represent part of the traditional Māori worldview. In more conventional English, the main ideas could be captured by a paraphrase as follows: "a mysterious, invisible power that can be a part of certain special things and certain special people". The latter paraphrase includes some complex English words (especially 'power'), but it is a useful approximation: more intelligible (more "focused") than disjunctive explanations, and capable of conveying a sense of the unique conceptualization behind the *mana* concept.

Semantic primes and universal (or near-universal) semantic molecules can also play an important role as an aide to communication with consultants and as a medium of empowerment. Many fieldwork guides emphasize the importance of communication and meaningful engagement with language consultants (cf. Mosel n.d.; Grenoble and Furbee 2010; Hellwig 2010). What is often lacking in these discussions are guidelines on how to talk more effectively with consultants about meaning. We want to offer a very simple idea: that the metalanguage of semantic primes can be the basis for a way of talking with consultants about meanings in their own language.

The approach has been used in lexical semantic analysis by Harkins (2001) in her work on emotion terminology in Arrernte (Central Australia), by Junker (2003; 2007; 2008; also Junker and Blacksmith 2006) in various lexicographic and grammatical projects in East Cree, and in a more low-key fashion by various NSM-influenced fieldworkers in Southeast Asia and elsewhere.

In Harkins' (2001) study, a group of speakers "formulated statements of meaning in their own language, without proceeding via English" (p. 199), developing for each emotion word a "*ayeye akweke angketye nhenhe-ke* 'story small word this-DAT', that is, a little story, script or mini-narrative" (p. 206). As Harkins noted, these "little stories" showed "a surprising degree of convergence with the kinds of semantic explications produced through more formal NSM analyses". The following is an example, for the term *arnkelye,* which can be glossed in different contexts as 'resentful' or 'sulky' (Harkins 2001: 207).[3]

[G]   *X arnkelye-irre-me:* [Arrernte]

a.   *X re awelhe-me-le itirre-ke Y-ke alakenhe* [X 3sg feel-NPP-SS think-PC Y-DAT thus]
b.   *Y-le akenge mpwarre-ke-nge* [Y-ERG rotten make/do-PC-DS]
c.   *the akurne ile-tyehnge Y renhe ikwere-nge* [1sA bad do-SBSQ Y 3sO 2sDAT-ABL]
d.   *X alakenhe itirre-me-le, X akurne awlhe-me Y-ke* [X thus think-NPP-SS X bad feel-NPP Y-DAT]

a.   X is feeling something because X thought like this about Y:
b.   "Y did something very bad
c.   I will do something bad to Y because of this"
d.   when X is thinking like this, X feels something bad towards Y

Commenting on the explication, Harkins noted that the middle components "identify the most typical thoughts of someone experiencing *arnkelye:* a strongly negative evaluation and a burning desire for retaliation. Note that the offending action doesn't have to be something that personally affects the experiencer of *arnkelye,* of course, this is very often the case, but one can also feel *arnkelye* about other kinds of very bad deeds" (p. 207).

Harkins (2001) concluded her article with a section titled "Practical Semantics", which included the following comment:

---

[3] The Arrernte consultants themselves chose to use X and Y as "false initials" to represent the hypothetical participants in the scenario "for reasons of anonymity" (Harkins 2001: 207).

But perhaps more importantly, it has demonstrated something of the practicality of the NSM approach in facilitating intercultural discussion and understanding of people's emotional life and behaviour in cultural context, and, furthermore, as a tool for stating meanings in the language of inquiry. This is a practical tool that fieldworkers and research participants can use in their own language and cultural setting – a far cry from some popular notions of semantics as an abstract, ivory-tower activity.   (Harkins 2001: 211–212)

Of course field situations are different from one another in many ways, and in some local traditions it may be difficult to talk about what someone means (i.e. wants to say) by using certain words, even in relation to real-world or highly contextualized examples (cf. Foley 2003). Nevertheless, in many cultural contexts the idea of explaining in simple words is likely to have a foothold in traditional ways of speaking to very young children and/or in ways of using simplified language variants with linguistic outsiders. Even if not, it is always going to be a more practical proposition to communicate with indigenous consultants using shared simple words (with equivalents in both languages) than to try to adapt the kind of technical linguistic jargon that linguists usually fall back on when talking about meanings among themselves. At the same time, casting questions of meaning into semantic primes (with equivalents in both languages) can help safeguard the analyst against the conceptual biases of his/her own language.

In summary, we see that there is much to be gained, and very little to be lost, if field linguists were to cut themselves loose from complex academic English and start trying to capture their emerging understandings of indigenous meanings using a metalanguage based on simple translatable words.

10.6 The way ahead for semantics

In line with the "narrative turn" in the humanities and social sciences, which his own work did much to initiate, Jerome Bruner (2002) has declared: "Story is the coin and currency of cultures." With all due respect to Bruner, a great champion of meaning in places and times hostile to it, it is not stories but **words** which are the coin and currency of cultures. As philosopher Ernest Gellner (1981: 9) has written, however, in the introduction to a volume entitled *Universals of Human Thought*: "Unconvertible currencies are not suitable for trade." As we have seen in this book, a key (and unique) characteristic of NSM is that it is convertible. Simple and universal words, with meanings like 'before' and 'after', 'big' and 'small', and 'good' and 'bad', are the most dependable conceptual coins for interaction across languages and cultures. Within a particular society or language community, on the other hand, language-specific words, including cultural key words, can be the most useful currency for communication. As we have seen in this book, the meanings of complex language-specific words are richer, subtler, and more intricate by far than envisaged by conventional lexical semantics.

What is the future for linguistic semantics? The field is often characterized as the poor cousin of contemporary linguistics, and understandably so. Compared with phonology, morphology, and syntax, it is strikingly underdeveloped and enjoys a correspondingly lower level of disciplinary prestige. As we have emphasized in Chapter 1, we see the plight of lexical semantics as largely due to methodological failings—above all, the failure to take seriously the central problem of semantic metalanguage.

In many ways, the current state of linguistic semantics is analogous to that of phonetics prior to the adoption of the International Phonetic Alphabet. Without any standardization of the terms of description (without a reliable system of "semantic transcription", in Igor Mel'čuk's (2012: 90) phrase), researchers muddle along by relying on ad hoc comparisons with the home language of the investigators. (To make matters worse, many of them are even not aware of what they are doing, i.e. they do not appreciate the epistemological consequences of framing their semantic descriptions in English-bound terminology: cf. Chapter 1.) We do not mean to denigrate or disrespect colleagues who are committed to semantics, and especially to cross-linguistic semantics. On the contrary, they are to be commended for their commitment and perspicacity, but in our opinion they can be compared with craftspeople who are attempting to do their work, if not in the dark, then in the half-light. In our view, the NSM methodology—rigorous, precise, and anchored in empirical findings about shared human conceptual universals—is the way to bring linguistic semantics out of the shadows.

Although there are still obstacles ahead, the trajectory of the NSM program over the past 35 years has been generally upward; for example, the system is now included in various encyclopedias, handbooks, introductory textbooks, and the like (Goddard 2006*c*; 2009*g*[2006]; 2010*d*; 2010*e*; 2011*b*; Goddard and Schalley 2010; Goddard and Wierzbicka 2002*b*; 2011; Wierzbicka 2009*b*; 2009*h*; 2010*d*; 2010*e*; 2012*c*; Gladkova 2011; Allan 2001; Löbner 2002; Riemer 2010; Murphy 2010). Some obstacles are sociological, e.g. established figures who continue to marginalize NSM and refuse to engage in dialogue. Others are pedagogical: even receptive scholars who see the advantages and attractions of the NSM approach may have difficulty in gaining enough hands-on familiarity with the method to apply it successfully in their own work. Though NSM explications are crafted from simple materials, the investigative processes needed to develop a suite of good explications in a given area are highly demanding and require well-developed analytical skills. It is to be hoped that the continuing growth and outreach of the NSM research community and new pedagogical resources, such as Goddard (2011*b*), will help overcome these difficulties.

As for ourselves, we have high confidence that the 'alphabet of human thoughts' has finally been discovered, essentially in full. Continually heartened by the interest and enthusiasm of talented young scholars in NSM,[4] we see a bright future for an approach to linguistics that in an earlier work Wierzbicka (2001a: 232) described as follows:

a linguistics grounded in language universals, and centred on meaning and translation, a linguistics which begins with the study of words, difficult as these may be to define, and which is prepared to serve, and guide, lexicography, a linguistics which combines an interest in universal grammar with in-depth empirical study of lexical and grammatical systems of real languages, in all their specificity and richness.

We hope in the present work to have given further impetus to this 'linguistics which begins with the study of words'.

---

[4] It was also encouraging that in 2010 NSM was honoured by two high-profile international prizes awarded to Anna Wierzbicka: the Dobrushin prize, established in Russia primarily for mathematicians, and the Polish Science Foundation prize.

References

Achterberg, Wilco P., Giovani Gambassi, Harriet Finne-Soveri, Rosa Liperoti, Anja Noro, Dinnus H. M. Frijters, Antonio Cherubini, Giusy Dell'Aquila, and Miel W. Ribbe (2010). Pain in European long-term care facilities: cross-national study in Finland, Italy, and the Netherlands. *Pain* 148(1): 70–74.

Aebischer, Verena, and Harold G. Wallbott (1986). Measuring emotional experiences: questionnaire design and procedure, and the nature of the sample. In Klaus R. Scherer, Harold G. Wallbott, and Angela B. Summerfield (eds), *Experiencing Emotion: A Cross-Cultural Study*. Cambridge: Cambridge University Press, 28–38.

Alexander, Dennis (2006). Literal, figurative, metaphorical: a semantic inquiry into the semantic field of *game* and *play* in English. Ph.D thesis, University of New England.

Allan, Keith (1986). *Linguistic Meaning*. London: Routledge and Kegan Paul.

Allan, Keith (2001). *Natural Language Semantics*. Oxford: Blackwell.

Altarriba, Jeanette, and Lisa M. Bauer (2004). The distinctiveness of emotion concepts: a comparison between emotion, abstract, and concrete words. *American Journal of Psychology* 117(3): 389–410.

Amberber, Mengistu (2008). Semantic primes in Amharic. In Cliff Goddard (ed.), *Cross-Linguistic Semantics*. Amsterdam: John Benjamins, 83–119.

Ameka, Felix K. (1999). "Partir, c'est mourir un peu": universal and culture specific features of leave taking. In Jacob Mey and Andrzej Boguslawski (eds), *'E Pluribus Una': The One in the Many*. Special issue of *RASK, International Journal of Language and Communication*, 9/10: 257–284.

Ameka, Felix K. (2002). Cultural scripting of body parts for emotions: on "jealousy" and related emotions in Ewe. *Pragmatics and Cognition* 10(1–2): 1–25.

Ameka, Felix K. (2006). "When I die, don't cry": the ethnopragmatics of "gratitude" in West African languages. In Cliff Goddard (ed.), *Ethnopragmatics: Understanding Discourse in Cultural Context*. Berlin: Mouton de Gruyter, 231–266.

Ameka, Felix K. (2009). Access rituals in West African communities: an ethnopragmatic perspective. In Gunter Senft and Ellen B. Basso (eds), *Ritual Communication*. New York: Berg, 127–152.

Ameka, Felix K., and Anneke Breedveld (2004). Areal cultural scripts for social interaction in West African communities. *Intercultural Pragmatics* 1(2): 167–188.

Ameka, Felix K., Alan Dench, and Nicholas Evans (eds) (2006). *Catching Language: The Standing Challenge of Grammar Writing*. Berlin: Mouton de Gruyter.

Andersen, Elaine S. (1978). Lexical universals of body-part terminology. In Joseph H. Greenberg (ed.), *Universals of Human Language*, vol. 3: *Word Structure*. Stanford, Calif.: Stanford University Press, 335–368.

Annas, Julia (1999). *Platonic Ethics, Old and New*. Ithaca, NY: Cornell University Press.

Annas, Julia (2004). Happiness as achievement. *Daedalus* 133(2): 44–51.

Apresjan, Jurij D. (1992). *Lexical Semantics: User's Guide to Contemporary Russian Vocabulary.* Ann Arbor, Mich.: Karoma. [Originally published 1974 as *Leksiceskaja Semantika: Sinonimeceskie Sredstva Jazyka.* Moscow: Nauka.]

Apresjan, Jurij D. (2000). *Systematic Lexicography.* Translated by Kevin Windle. Oxford: Oxford University Press.

Apresjan, Jurij D. (2004). *Novyj Ob"jasnitel'nyj Slovar' Sinonimov Russkogo Jazyka* [New Explanatory Dictionary of the Synonyms of the Russian Language]. Moscow: Jazyki Russkoj Kul'tury.

Apresjan, Jurij D. (2006). *Jazykovaja Kartina Mira i Sistemnaja Leksikografija* [A Linguistic Picture of the World and Systematic Lexicography]. Moscow: Jazyki Slavjanskix Kul'tur.

Arendt, Hannah (1973). *The Origins of Totalitarianism.* New York: Harcourt, Brace, Jovanovich.

Arewa, E. Ojo, and Alan Dundes (1964). Proverbs and the ethnography of speaking folklore. *American Anthropologist* 66(6), pt 2: 70–85.

Arnauld, Antoine, and Pierre Nicole (1996[1662]). *Logic or the Art of Thinking.* Translated by Jill Vance Buroker. Cambridge: Cambridge University Press.

Austin, John L. (1962). *How to Do Things with Words: The William James Lectures Delivered at Harvard University in 1955.* Oxford: Oxford University Press.

Austin, Peter K. (ed.) (2003–10). *Language Documentation and Description*, vols 1–9. London: Hans Rausing Endangered Languages Project, School of Oriental and African Studies.

Australian Concise Oxford Dictionary (2009). Melbourne: Oxford University Press.

Barfield, Owen (1953). *History in English Words.* London: Faber and Faber.

Barlow, Michael (2000). Usage, blends, and grammar. In Michael Barlow and Suzanne E. Kemmer (eds), *Usage-Based Models of Language.* Stanford, Calif.: CSLI, 7–28.

Barrett, Lisa Feldman, Batja Mesquita, Kevin N. Ochsner, and James J. Gross (2007). The experience of emotion. *Annual Review of Psychology* 58: 373–403.

Barrios Rodríguez, María Auxiliadora and Cliff Goddard (2013). "Degrad verbs" in Spanish and English: Collocations, Lexical Functions and contrastive NSM semantic analysis. *Functions of Language* 20(2): 219–249.

Bauman, Richard, and Joel Sherzer (eds) (1974). *Explorations in the Ethnography of Speaking.* Cambridge: Cambridge University Press.

Ben-Amos, Dan (1969). Analytical categories and ethnic genres. *Genre* 2(3): 275–301.

Bentham, Jeremy (1843). In John Bowring (ed.), *The Works of Jeremy Bentham.* 11 vols. Edinburgh: William Tait.

Berlin, Brent (1992). *Ethnobiological Classification.* Princeton, NJ: Princeton University Press.

Berlin, Brent, and Paul Kay (1969). *Basic Color Terms: Their Universality and Evolution.* Berkeley: University of California Press.

Berlin, Isaiah (1976). *Vico and Herder: Two Studies in the History of Ideas.* London: Hogarth.

Besemeres, Mary (1998). Language and self in cross-cultural autobiography: Eva Hoffman's *Lost in Translation. Canadian Slavonic Papers* 40(3–4): 327–344.

Besemeres, Mary (2002). *Translating One's Self: Language and Selfhood in Cross-Cultural Autobiography.* Oxford: Peter Lang.

Besemeres, Mary (2005). Anglos abroad: memoirs of immersion in a foreign language. *Biography* 28(1): 27–42.

Besemeres, Mary (2008). Australian "immersion" narratives: memoirs of contemporary language travel. In Desley Deacon, Penny Russell, and Angela Woollacott (eds), *Transnational Ties: Australian Lives in the World.* Canberra: ANU E-Press, 245–257.

Besemeres, Mary (2010). Emotions in bilingual life narratives. In Vivian Cook and Benedetta Bassetti (eds), *Language and Bilingual Cognition*. New York: Psychology Press (Taylor and Francis), 479–506.

Besemeres, Mary, and Anna Wierzbicka (eds) (2007). *Translating Lives: Living with Two Languages and Cultures*. St Lucia: University of Queensland Press.

Besemeres, Mary, and Anna Wierzbicka (2009). The concept of frustration: a culture-specific emotion and a cultural key word. In Agata Błachnio and Aneta Przepiórka (eds), *Closer to Emotions III*. Lublin, Poland: Catholic University of Lublin (Wydawnictwo KUL), 211–226.

Besnier, Niko (1994). Involvement in linguistic practice: an ethnographic appraisal. *Journal of Pragmatics* 22: 279–299.

Biggam, Carol P. (2004). Prototypes and foci in the encoding of colour. In Christian J. Kay and Jeremy J. Smith (eds), Categorization in the History of English. Amsterdam: John Benjamins, 19–40.

Biswas-Diener, Robert, Ed Diener, and Maya Tamir (2004). The psychology of subjective well-being. *Dædalus* 133(2): 18–25.

Bloomfield, Leonard (1933). *Language*. New York: Holt, Rinehart and Winston.

Blum-Kulka, Shoshana, Juliane House, and Gabriele Kasper (eds) (1989). *Cross-Cultural Pragmatics: Requests and Apologies*. Norwood, NJ: Ablex.

Blum-Kulka, Shoshana, and Gabriele Kasper (1993). *Interlanguage Pragmatics*. Oxford: Oxford University Press.

Bogusławski, Andrzej (1966). *Semantyczne Pojęcie Liczebnika i Jego Morfologia w Języku Rosyjskim*. Wrocław: Ossolineum.

Bogusławski, Andrzej (1970). On semantic primitives and meaningfulness. In Algirdas Julien Greimas, Roman Jakobson, Maria-Renata Mayenowa, and Stefan Żółkiewski (eds), *Sign, Language and Culture*. The Hague: Mouton, 143–152.

Bohnemeyer, Jürgen (1998a). Time relations in discourse: evidence from a comparative approach to Yukatek Maya. Ph.D thesis, Katholieke Universitet Brabant.

Bohnemeyer, Jürgen (1998b). Temporal reference from a radical pragmatics point of view: why Yucatec Maya does not need to express "after" and "before". *Cognitive Linguistics* 9(3): 239–282.

Bohnemeyer, Jürgen (2003). NSM without the strong lexicalization hypothesis. *Theoretical Linguistics* 29(3): 223–226.

Bolinger, Dwight (1965). The atomization of meaning. *Language* 41(4): 555–573.

Boster, James S. (2005). Emotion categories across languages. In Henri Cohen and Claire Lefebvre (eds), *Handbook of Categorization in Cognitive Science*. Amsterdam: Elsevier, 187–222.

Bowern, Claire (2008). *Linguistic Fieldwork: A Practical Guide*. New York: Palgrave Macmillan.

Brand, Paul, and Philip Yancy (1997). *The Gift of Pain: Why We Hurt and What We Can Do About It*. Grand Rapids, Mich.: Zondervan.

Briggs, Charles (1988). *Competence in Performance: The Creativity of Tradition in Mexicano Verbal Art*. Philadelphia: University of Pennsylvania Press.

Bromhead, Helen (2009). *The Reign of Truth and Faith: Epistemic Expressions in 16th and 17th Century English*. Berlin: Mouton de Gruyter.

Bromhead, Helen (2011*a*). The bush in Australian English. *Australian Journal of Linguistics* 31(4): 445–471.

Bromhead, Helen (2011*b*). Ethnogeographical categories in English and Pitjantjatjara/Yankunytjatjara. *Language Sciences* 33(1): 58–75.

Brown, Cecil H. (1976). General principles of human anatomical partonomy and speculations on the growth of partonomic nomenclature. *American Anthropologist* 3: 400–424.

Brown, Donald E. (1991). *Human Universals*. Philadelphia: Temple University Press.

Bruner, Jerome (1990). *Acts of Meaning*. Cambridge, Mass.: Harvard University Press.

Bruner, Jerome (2002). *Making Stories: Law, Literature, Life*. New York: Farrar, Straus and Giroux.

Bugenhagen, Robert D. (2002). The syntax of semantic primitives in Mangaaba-Mbula. In Cliff Goddard and Anna Wierzbicka (eds), *Meaning and Universal Grammar: Theory and Empirical Findings*, vol. 2. Amsterdam: John Benjamins, 1–64.

Bullock, David (2011). NSM + LDOCE: a non-circular dictionary of English. *International Journal of Lexicography* 24(2): 226–240.

Bulmer, Ralph (1968). Karam colour categories. *Kivung* 1(3): 120–133.

Burke, Kenneth (1967). *The Philosophy of Literary Form: Studies in Symbolic Action*, 2nd edn. Baton Rouge: Louisiana State University Press.

Burling, Robbins (1969). Cognition and componential analysis: God's truth or hocus-pocus? In Stephen Tyler (ed.), *Cognitive Anthropology*. New York: Holt, Rinehart and Wilson, 419–428.

Carbaugh, Donal (2005). *Cultures in Conversation*. Mahwah, NJ: Lawrence Erlbaum.

Carbaugh, Donal (2007). Cultural Discourse Analysis: the investigation of communication practices with special attention to intercultural encounters. *Journal of Intercultural Communication Research* 36: 167–182.

Carey, Susan (2009). *The Origin of Concepts*. Oxford: Oxford University Press.

Carlyle, Thomas (2000[1843]). *Past and Present*, ed. Richard D. Altick. New York: New York University Press.

Cassin, Barbara (ed.) (2004). *Vocabulaire européen des philosophies: dictionnaire des intraduisibles* [European Vocabulary of Philosophies: A Dictionary of Untranslatables]. Paris: Éditions du Seuil; Le Robert.

Čermák, František (2004). Text introducers of proverbs and other idioms. In C. Földes and Jan Wirrer (eds), *Phraseologismen als Gegenstand sprach- und kulturwissenschaftlicher Forschung*. Baltmannsweiler: Schneider Verlag Hohengehren, 27–46.

Chappell, Hilary (2002). The universal syntax of semantic primes in Mandarin Chinese. In Cliff Goddard and Anna Wierzbicka (eds), *Meaning and Universal Grammar: Theory and Empirical Findings*, vol. 1. Amsterdam: John Benjamins, 243–322.

Charteris-Black, Jonathan (1999). The survival of English proverbs: a corpus based account. *DeProverbio* 5(2). http://www.deproverbio.com/display.php?a=3&r=96 [viewed 12 Nov. 2006 and 29 Aug. 2012].

Chilton, Paul (2004). *Analysing Political Discourse: Theory and Practice*. London: Routledge.

Coetzee, John M. (1997). *Boyhood: Scenes from Provincial Life*. London: Secker and Warburg.

Coleridge, Samuel Taylor (1825). *Aids to Reflection*. London: Taylor and Hessey.

Collins Cobuild English Language Dictionary (1991). London: HarperCollins.

Collins Robert English–French Dictionary (1987). London: HarperCollins.

Collins Wordbanks Online. http://www.collinslanguage.com/content-solutions/wordbanks

Conklin, Harold G. (1964). Hanunóo colour categories. In Dell H. Hymes (ed.), *Language in Culture and Society.* New York: Harper and Row, 189–192.

Cook, Vivian (2009). *It's All in a Word.* London: Profile Books.

Cordell, William H., Kelly K. Keene, Beverley K. Giles, James B. Jones, James H. Jones, and Edward J. Brizendine (2002). The high prevalence of pain in emergency medical care. *American Journal of Emergency Medicine* 20(3): 165–169.

Crowley, Terry (2007). *Field Linguistics: A Beginner's Guide.* Edited and prepared for publication by Nick Thieberger. Oxford: Oxford University Press.

Cruse, D. A. (1986). *Lexical Semantics.* Cambridge: Cambridge University Press.

Crystal, David (1994[1992]). *An Encyclopedic Dictionary of Language and Languages.* Harmondsworth: Penguin.

Crystal, David (2003). *English as a Global Language.* Cambridge: Cambridge University Press.

Crystal, David (2006). *As They Say in Zanzibar.* London: HarperCollins.

Dalai Lama XIV and Howard C. Cutler (1998). *The Art of Happiness: A Handbook for Living.* Sydney: Hodder Headline.

Dalai Lama XIV with Rajiv Mehrotra (2008). *All You Ever Wanted to Know From His Holiness the Dalai Lama on Happiness, Life, Living, and Much More: Conversations with Rajiv Mehrotra.* Carlsbad, Calif.: Hay House.

D'Andrade, Roy (1995). *The Development of Cognitive Anthropology.* New York: Cambridge University Press.

Darwin, Charles (1989[1871]). *The Descent of Man,* vol. 21. In Paul H. Barrett and Richard B. Freeman (eds), *The Works of Charles Darwin.* London: Pickering and Chatto.

Dascal, Marcelo (1987). *Leibniz: Language, Signs and Thought.* Amsterdam: John Benjamins.

Diller, Anthony (1980). Cross-cultural pain semantics. *Pain* 9(1): 9–26.

Dimmendaal, Gerrit J. (1995). Studying lexical-semantic fields in languages: nature versus nurture, or where does culture come in these days? *Frankfurter Afrikanistische Blätter* 7: 1–29.

Ding Choo Ming and Arba'eyah Abdul Rahman (2002). Daripada Kamus Peribahasa Melayu Digital ATMA kepada Perkamusan Bahasa Berkomputer [From the digital ATMA Malay Proverb Dictionary to computerized lexicography]. *Dewan Bahasa* 2(7): 48–59.

Dirven, René, Roslyn M. Frank, and Martin Pütz (eds) (2003). *Cognitive Models in Language and Thought.* Berlin: Mouton de Gruyter.

Dixon, R. M. W. (1982). *Where Have All the Adjectives Gone? and other Essays in Semantics and Syntax.* Berlin: Mouton de Gruyter.

Dixon, R. M. W., and Alexandra Y. Aikhenvald (2002). Word: a typological framework. In R. M. W. Dixon and Alexandra Y. Aikhenvald (eds), *Word: A Cross-Linguistic Typology.* Cambridge: Cambridge University Press, 1–41.

Dixon, Thomas (2008). *The Invention of Altruism: Making Moral Meanings in Victorian Britain.* Oxford: British Academy/Oxford University Press.

Donald, Merlin (2001). *A Mind So Rare: The Evolution of Human Consciousness.* New York: Farrar, Straus and Giroux.

Dowrick, Christopher (2004). *Beyond Depression: A New Approach to Understanding and Management.* Oxford: Oxford University Press.

Dugatkin, Lee Alan (2006). *The Altruism Equation: Seven Scientists Search for the Origins of Goodness.* Princeton, NJ: Princeton University Press.

Durie, Mark, Bukhari Daud, and Mawardi Hasan (1994). Acehnese. In Cliff Goddard and Anna Wierzbicka (eds), *Semantic and Lexical Universals: Theory and Empirical Findings.* Amsterdam: John Benjamins, 171–202.

Durst, Uwe (1999). BAD as a semantic primitive: evidence from Biblical Hebrew. *Pragmatics & Cognition* 7(2): 375–403.

Eisler, Rudolf (1961). *Kant-Lexikon.* Hildesheim: Georg Olms.

Enfield, Nick J. (2002). Combinatoric properties of Natural Semantic Metalanguage expressions in Lao. In Cliff Goddard and Anna Wierzbicka (eds), *Meaning and Universal Grammar: Theory and Empirical Findings*, vol. 2. Amsterdam: John Benjamins, 145–256.

Evans, Nicholas (2007). Standing up your mind: remembering in Dalabon. In Mengistu Amberber (ed.), *The Language of Memory in a Crosslinguistic Perspective.* Amsterdam: John Benjamins, 67–95.

Evans, Nicholas, and Steven C. Levinson (2009). The myth of language universals: language diversity and its importance for cognitive science. *Behavioral and Brain Sciences* 32: 429–492.

Evans, Nicholas, and Hans-Jürgen Sasse (2007[2003]). Searching for meaning in the Library of Babel: field semantics and problems of digital archiving. In Peter K. Austin (ed.), *Language Description and Documentation*, vol. 4. London: School of Oriental and African Studies, 58–99.

Everett, Daniel L. (2005). Cultural constraints on grammar and cognition in Pirahã. *Current Anthropology* 46(4): 621–646.

Fabian, Johannes (1990). *Power and Performance: Ethnographic Explorations through Proverbial Wisdom and Theater in Shaba (Zaire).* Madison: University of Wisconsin Press.

Fábrega, Horacio, Jr (2013). *Conditions of Psychiatric Interest in Early Human History.* Lewiston: Edwin Mellen Press.

Fábrega, Horacio, Jr (forthcoming). *Early Evolution of Medicine.*

Fábrega, Horacio, Jr, and Stephen Tyma (1976a). Language and cultural influences in the description of pain. *British Journal of Medical Psychology* 49: 349–371.

Fábrega, Horacio, Jr, and Stephen Tyma (1976b). Culture, language and the shaping of illness: an illustration based on pain. *Journal of Psychosomatic Research* 20: 323–337.

Fernandez, Ephrem, and Ajay Wasan (2010). The anger of pain sufferers: attributions to agents and appraisals of wrongdoings. In Michael Potegal, Gerhard Stemmler, and Charles Spielberger (eds), *International Handbook of Anger: Constituent and Concomitant Biological, Psychological, and Social Processes.* New York: Springer, 449–464.

Field, Alexander J. (2001). *Altruistically Inclined? The Behavioral Sciences, Evolutionary Theory, and the Origins of Reciprocity.* Michigan, Ill.: University of Michigan Press.

Fillmore, Charles J. (1985). Frames and the semantics of understanding. *Quaderni di semantica* 6: 222–254.

Fletcher, William H. (2007). Concordancing the web: promises and problems, tools and techniques. In Marianne Hundt, Nadja Nesselhauf, and Carolin Biewer (eds), *Corpus Linguistics and the Web.* Amsterdam: Rodopi, 25–45.

Foley, William A. (1997). *Anthropological Linguistics: An Introduction.* Oxford: Blackwell.

Foley, William A. (2003). Genre, register and language documentation in literate and pre-literate communities. In Peter K. Austin (ed.), *Language Documentation and Description*, vol. 1. London: SOAS, 85–98.

Freud, Sigmund (1949). *Civilisation and its Discontents*. Translated by Joan Riviere. London: Hogarth Press.

Fromkin, Victoria, Robert Rodman, Nina Hyams, Peter Collins, Mengistu Amberber, and Felicity Cox (2012). *An Introduction to Language* (Australia and New Zealand 7th edn). Melbourne: Cengage Learning.

Gándara, Lelia (2004). "They that sow the wind...": proverbs and sayings in argumentation. *Discourse & Society* 15(2/3): 345–359.

Geeraerts, Dirk (1994). Polysemy. In Ron E. Asher and J. M. Y. (Seumas) Simpson (eds), *The Encyclopedia of Language and Linguistics*. Oxford: Pergamon Press, 3227–3228.

Geeraerts, Dirk (2006). Componential analysis. In Keith Brown (ed.), *Encyclopedia of Languages and Linguistics*, 2nd edn. Oxford: Elsevier, 709–712.

Geertz, Clifford (2000). *Available Light: Anthropological Reflections on Philosophical Topics*. Princeton, NJ: Princeton University Press.

Gellner, Ernest (1981). Relativism and universals. In Barbara Lloyd and John Gay (eds), *Universals of Human Thought: Some African Evidence*. Cambridge: Cambridge University Press, 1–20.

Gelman, Susan A. (2005). *The Essential Child: Origins of Essentialism on Everyday Thought*. New York: Oxford University Press.

Gentner, Dedre, and Lera Boroditsky (2001). Individuation, relativity, and early word learning. In M. Bowerman and S. Levinson (eds), *Language Acquisition and Conceptual Development*. Cambridge: Cambridge University Press, 215–256.

Gibbs, Raymond W., Jr, and Gerard J. Steen (eds) (1999). *Metaphor in Cognitive Linguistics*. Amsterdam: John Benjamins.

Gippert, Jost, Nikolaus P. Himmelmann, and Ulrike Mosel (eds) (2006). *Essentials of Language Documentation*. Berlin: Mouton de Gruyter.

Gladkova, Anna (2010a). A linguist's view of "pride". *Emotion Review* 2(2): 178–179.

Gladkova, Anna (2010b). "Sympathy", "compassion", and "empathy" in English and Russian: a linguistic and cultural analysis. *Culture & Psychology* 16(2): 267–285.

Gladkova, Anna (2010c). *Russkaja Kul'turnaja Semantika: Ėmocii, Cennosti, Žiznennye Usta-novki* [Russian Cultural Semantics: Emotions, Values, Attitudes]. Moscow: Languages of Slavic Cultures.

Gladkova, Anna (2011). Cultural variation in language use. In Gisle Andersen and Karin Aijmer (eds), *Pragmatics of Society*. Berlin: Mouton de Gruyter, 571–592.

Gladkova, Anna (2012). Universals and specifics of "time" in Russian. In Luna Filipović and Kasia M. Jaszczolt (eds), *Space and Time across Languages and Cultures*, vol. 2: *Language, Culture and Cognition*. Amsterdam: John Benjamins, 167–188.

Gladkova, Anna, Ulla Vanhatalo and Cliff Goddard (2015). The semantics of interjections: an experimental study with Natural Semantic Metalanguage. *Applied Psycholinguistics*. Published online in First View, 21/07/2015: 1–25, doi:10.1017/S0142716415000260.

Goddard, Cliff (1991). Anger in the Western Desert: a case study in the cross-cultural semantics of emotion. *Man* 26: 602–619.

Goddard, Cliff (1994*a*). Lexical primitives in Yankunytjatjara. In Cliff Goddard and Anna Wierzbicka (eds), *Semantic and Lexical Universals: Theory and Empirical Findings*. Amsterdam: John Benjamins, 229–262.

Goddard, Cliff (1994*b*). Semantic theory and semantic universals. In Cliff Goddard and Anna Wierzbicka (eds), *Semantic and Lexical Universals: Theory and Empirical Findings*. Amsterdam: John Benjamins, 7–30.

Goddard, Cliff (1996*a*). The "social emotions" of Malay (Bahasa Melayu). *Ethos* 24 (3): 426–464.

Goddard, Cliff (1996*b*). *Pitjantjatjara/Yankunytjatjara to English Dictionary*, revised 2nd edn. Alice Springs: Institute for Aboriginal Development.

Goddard, Cliff (1997*a*). Contrastive semantics and cultural psychology: "surprise" in Malay and English. *Culture & Psychology* 3(2): 153–181.

Goddard, Cliff (1997*b*). Cultural values and "cultural scripts" in Malay (*Bahasa Melayu*). *Journal of Pragmatics* 27(2): 183–201.

Goddard, Cliff (1998). *Semantic Analysis: A Practical Introduction*. Oxford: Oxford University Press.

Goddard, Cliff (1999). Review article: Color categories in thought and language. *Linguistic Typology* 3: 259–269.

Goddard, Cliff (2000*a*). "Cultural scripts" and communicative style in Malay (*Bahasa Melayu*). *Anthropological Linguistics* 42(1): 81–106.

Goddard, Cliff (2000*b*). Polysemy: a problem of definition. In Yael Ravin and Claudia Leacock (eds), *Polysemy: Theoretical and Computational Approaches*. Oxford: Oxford University Press, 129–151.

Goddard, Cliff (2001*a*). Lexico-semantic universals: a critical overview. *Linguistic Typology* 5(1): 1–66.

Goddard, Cliff (2001*b*). Conceptual primes in early language development. In Martin Pütz, Susanne Niemeier, and René Dirven (eds), *Applied Cognitive Linguistics I: Theory and Language Acquisition*. Berlin: Mouton de Gruyter, 193–227.

Goddard, Cliff (2001*c*). The polyfunctional Malay focus particle *pun*. *Multilingua* 20(1): 27–59.

Goddard, Cliff (2001*d*). *Sabar, ikhlas, setia*—patient, sincere, loyal? A contrastive semantic study of some "virtues" in Malay and English. *Journal of Pragmatics* 33: 653–681.

Goddard, Cliff (2002*a*). Semantic primes and universal grammar in Malay (*Bahasa Melayu*). In Cliff Goddard and Anna Wierzbicka (eds), *Meaning and Universal Grammar: Theory and Empirical Findings*, vol. 1. Amsterdam: John Benjamins, 87–172.

Goddard, Cliff (2002*b*). Directive speech-acts in Malay: an ethnopragmatic perspective. *Les cahiers de praxématique* 38: 113–143.

Goddard, Cliff (2002*c*). Ethnosyntax, ethnopragmatics, sign-functions, and culture. In Nick J. Enfield (ed.), *Ethnosyntax: Explorations in Grammar and Culture*. Oxford: Oxford University Press, 52–73.

Goddard, Cliff (2004*a*). Speech-acts, values and cultural scripts: a study in Malay ethnopragmatics. In Robert Cribb (ed.), *Asia Examined: Proceedings of the 15th Biennial Conference of the ASAA, 2004, Canberra, Australia*. Canberra: Asian Studies Association of Australia and Research School of Pacific and Asian Studies, Australian National University. http://coombs.anu.edu.au/SpecialProj/ASAA/biennial-conference/2004/Goddard-C-ASAA2004.pdf

Goddard, Cliff (2004*b*). The ethnopragmatics and semantics of "active metaphors". *Journal of Pragmatics* 36: 1211–1230.

Goddard, Cliff (2005*a*). Componential analysis. In Jef Verschueren and Jan-Ola Östman (eds), *Handbook of Pragmatics 2003–2005*, 2nd edn. Amsterdam: John Benjamins.

Goddard, Cliff (2005*b*). The lexical semantics of "culture". *Language Sciences* 27(1): 57–73.

Goddard, Cliff (2006*a*). "Lift your game, Martina!" Deadpan jocular irony and the ethnopragmatics of Australian English. In Cliff Goddard (ed.), *Ethnopragmatics: Understanding Discourse in Cultural Context*. Berlin: Mouton de Gruyter, 65–97.

Goddard, Cliff (2006*b*). Verbal explication and the place of NSM semantics in cognitive linguistics. In June Luchjenbroers (ed.), *Cognitive Linguistics Investigations: Across Languages, Fields, and Philosophical Boundaries*. Amsterdam: John Benjamins, 189–218.

Goddard, Cliff (2006*c*). Natural Semantic Metalanguage. In Keith Brown (ed.), *Encyclopedia of Language and Linguistics*, 2nd edn. Oxford: Elsevier, 544–551.

Goddard, Cliff (ed.) (2006*d*). *Ethnopragmatics: Understanding Discourse in Cultural Context*. Berlin: Mouton de Gruyter.

Goddard, Cliff (2007*a*). A culture-neutral metalanguage for mental state concepts. In Andrea C. Schalley and Drew Khlentzos (eds), *Mental States*, vol. 2: *Language and Cognitive Structure*. Amsterdam: John Benjamins, 11–35.

Goddard, Cliff (2007*b*). Semantic primes and conceptual ontology. In Dietmar Zaefferer and Andrea C. Schalley (eds), *Ontolinguistics: How Ontological Status Shapes the Linguistic Coding of Concepts*. Berlin: Mouton de Gruyter, 145–174.

Goddard, Cliff (2008*a*). Contrastive semantics and cultural psychology: English *heart* vs. Malay *hati*. In Farzad Sharifian, Rene Dirven, Ning Yu, and Susanne Niemeier (eds), *Culture, Body, and Language: Conceptualizations of Internal Body Organs Across Cultures and Languages*. Berlin: Mouton de Gruyter, 75–102.

Goddard, Cliff (ed.) (2008*b*). *Cross-Linguistic Semantics*. Amsterdam: John Benjamins.

Goddard, Cliff (2009*a*). *Not taking yourself too seriously* in Australian English: semantic explications, cultural scripts, corpus evidence. *Intercultural Pragmatics* 6(1): 29–53.

Goddard, Cliff (2009*b*). "Like a crab teaching its young to walk straight": proverbiality, semantics and indexicality in English and Malay. In Gunter Senft and Ellen A. Basso (eds), *Ritual Communication*. New York: Berg, 103–126.

Goddard, Cliff (2009*c*). *A piece of cheese, a grain of sand*: the semantics of mass nouns and unitizers. In Francis Jeffry Pelletier (ed.), *Kinds, Things and Stuff*. New York: Oxford University Press, 132–165.

Goddard, Cliff (2009*d*). The conceptual semantics of numbers and counting: an NSM analysis. *Functions of Language* 16(2): 193–224.

Goddard, Cliff (2009*e*). *Vegetables, furniture, weapons*: the semantics of functional macro-categories. Paper presented at the Australian Linguistic Society Annual Conference, 9 July 2009, Melbourne.

Goddard, Cliff (2009*f*). When key terms in global discourse have English-specific meanings: a case study of "security". Paper presented at the international conference "Cross-Culturally Speaking, Speaking Cross-Culturally", 6 July 2009, Macquarie University.

Goddard, Cliff (2009*g*[2006]). Cultural scripts. In Gunter Senft, Jan-Ola Östman, and Jef Verschueren (eds), *Culture and Language Use*. Amsterdam: John Benjamins, 68–80.

Goddard, Cliff (2010*a*). Universals and variation in the lexicon of mental state concepts. In Barbara C. Malt and Phillip Wolff (eds), *Words and the Mind: How Words Capture Human Experience*. New York: Oxford University Press, 72–92.

Goddard, Cliff (2010*b*). Semantic molecules and semantic complexity (with special reference to "environmental" molecules). *Review of Cognitive Linguistics* 8(1): 123–155.

Goddard, Cliff (2010*c*). Cultural scripts: applications to language teaching and intercultural communication. *Studies in Pragmatics* 3: 105–119.

Goddard, Cliff (2010*d*). The Natural Semantic Metalanguage approach. In B. Heine and H. Narrog (eds), *The Oxford Handbook of Linguistic Analysis*. Oxford: Oxford University Press, 459–484.

Goddard, Cliff (2010*e*). Semantic primes (primitives). In Patrick Colm Hogan (ed.), *The Cambridge Encyclopedia of Language Sciences*. Cambridge: Cambridge University Press, 740–741.

Goddard, Cliff (2011*a*). The lexical semantics of "language" (with special reference to "words"). *Language Sciences* 33(1): 40–57.

Goddard, Cliff (2011*b*). *Semantic Analysis: A Practical Introduction*, 2nd edn. Oxford: Oxford University Press.

Goddard, Cliff (2012*a*). Semantic primes, semantic molecules, semantic templates: key concepts in the NSM approach to lexical typology. *Linguistics* 50(3): 711–743.

Goddard, Cliff (2012*b*). "Early interactions" in Australian English, American English, and English English: cultural differences and cultural scripts. *Journal of Pragmatics* 44: 1038–1050.

Goddard, Cliff (2015). Verb classes and valency alternations (NSM approach), with special reference to English physical activity verbs. In Bernard Comrie and Andrej Malchukov (eds), *Valency Classes: A Comparative Handbook*. Berlin: Mouton de Gruyter, 1649–1680.

Goddard, Cliff (in press). Furniture, vegetables, weapons: Functional collective superordinates in the English lexicon. In Zhengdao Ye (ed.), *The Semantics of Nouns*. Oxford: Oxford University Press.

Goddard, Cliff, and Andrea C. Schalley (2010). Semantic analysis. In Nitin Indurkhya and Fred J. Damerau (eds), *Handbook of Natural Language Processing*, 2nd edn. London: CRC Press, Taylor and Francis, 92–120.

Goddard, Cliff, and Anna Wierzbicka (eds) (1994). *Semantic and Lexical Universals: Theory and Empirical Findings*. Amsterdam: John Benjamins.

Goddard, Cliff, and Anna Wierzbicka (1997). Discourse and culture. In Teun A. van Dijk (ed.), *Discourse as Social Interaction*. London: Sage, 231–257.

Goddard, Cliff, and Anna Wierzbicka (2002*a*). Semantic primes and universal grammar. In Cliff Goddard and Anna Wierzbicka (eds), *Meaning and Universal Grammar: Theory and Empirical Findings*, vol. 1. Amsterdam: John Benjamins, 41–85.

Goddard, Cliff, and Anna Wierzbicka (2002*b*). Lexical decomposition II: conceptual axiology. In D. Alan Cruse, Franz Hundsnurscher, Michael Job, and Peter Rolf Lutzeier (eds), *Lexicology. An International Handbook*. Berlin: Walter de Gruyter, 256–268.

Goddard, Cliff and Anna Wierzbicka (eds) (2002*c*). *Meaning and Universal Grammar: Theory and Empirical Findings*, vols 1 and 2. Amsterdam: John Benjamins.

Goddard, Cliff and Anna Wierzbicka (eds) (2004). *Cultural Scripts*. Special issue of *Intercultural Pragmatics*, 1(2).

Goddard, Cliff, and Anna Wierzbicka (2007a). NSM analyses of the semantics of physical qualities: *sweet, hot, hard, heavy, rough, sharp* in cross-linguistic perspective. *Studies in Language* 31(4): 765–800.

Goddard, Cliff, and Anna Wierzbicka (2007b). Semantic primes and cultural scripts in language learning and intercultural communication. In Farzad Sharifian and Gary B. Palmer (eds), *Applied Cultural Linguistics*. Amsterdam: John Benjamins, 105–124.

Goddard, Cliff, and Anna Wierzbicka (2008). Universal human concepts as a basis for contrastive linguistic semantics. In Maria de los Ángeles Gómez-González, J. Lachlan Mackenzie, and Elsa M. Gonzáles Álvarez (eds), *Current Trends in Contrastive Linguistics: Functional and Cognitive Perspectives*. Amsterdam: John Benjamins, 205–226.

Goddard, Cliff, and Anna Wierzbicka (2009). Contrastive semantics of physical activity verbs: 'cutting' and 'chopping' in English, Polish, and Japanese. *Language Sciences* 31: 60–96.

Goddard, Cliff, and Anna Wierzbicka (2010). 'Want' is a semantic and conceptual universal (response to Khanina). *Studies in Language* 34(1): 108–123.

Goddard, Cliff, and Anna Wierzbicka (2011). Semantics and cognition. *Wiley Interdiscipinary Reviews: Cognitive Science* 2(2), 125–135.

Goddard, Cliff, and Anna Wierzbicka (2014). Semantic fieldwork and lexical universals. *Studies in Language* 38(1): 80–127.

Goddard, Cliff and Zhengdao Ye (eds) (in press) *"Happiness" and "Pain" Across Languages and Cultures*. Amsterdam: John Benjamins.

Goodenough, Ward H. (1956). Componential analysis and the study of meaning. *Language* 32(1): 195–216.

Greene, Robert Lane (2012). Robert Lane Greene on language and the mind [interview by Sophie Roell]. *The Browser*. [http://old.thebrowser.com/interviews/robert-lane-greene-on-language-and-mind]

Grenoble, Lenore A., and N. Louanna Furbee (eds) (2010). *Language Documentation: Practice and Values*. Amsterdam: John Benjamins.

Grimsley, Ronald (1972). Rousseau and the problem of happiness. In Maurice R. Cranston and Richard S. Peters (eds), *Hobbes and Rousseau: A Collection of Critical Essays*. Garden City, NY: Anchor Books, 437–461.

Gumperz, John J., and Dell H. Hymes (eds) (1986[1972]). *Directions in Sociolinguistics: The Ethnography of Communication*. Oxford: Basil Blackwell.

Habib, Sandy (2011). Contrastive lexical-conceptual analysis of folk religious concepts in English, Arabic and Hebrew: NSM approach. Ph.D thesis, University of New England.

Hale, Kenneth L. (1959). Unpublished field notes. MIT Archives.

Hale, Kenneth L. (1995). *An Elementary Warlpiri Dictionary*. Alice Springs: Institute for Aboriginal Development.

Hale, Kenneth L., and Joseph B. Casagrande (1967). Semantic relationships in Papago folk-definitions. In Dell Hymes and William E. Bittle (eds), *Studies in Southwestern Ethnolinguistics*. The Hague: Mouton, 165–193.

Halliday, M. A. K. (1998). On the grammar of pain. *Functions of Language* 5(1): 1–32.

Hanks, Patrick W. (2007). General Introduction. *Lexicology: Critical Concepts in Linguistics*, vol. 1. London: Routledge, 1–23.

Hargrave, Susanne (1982). A report on colour term research in five Aboriginal languages. In *Work Papers of SIL-AAB Series B8*. Darwin: Summer Institute of Linguistics, Australian Aborigines Branch.

Harkins, Jean (2001). Talking about anger in Central Australia. In Jean Harkins and Anna Wierzbicka (eds), *Emotions in Crosslinguistic Perspective*. Berlin: Mouton de Gruyter, 201–220.

Harkins, Jean, and Wilkins, David P. (1994). Mparntwe Arrernte and the search for lexical universals. In Cliff Goddard and Anna Wierzbicka (eds), *Semantic and Lexical Universals*. Amsterdam: John Benjamins, 285–310.

Harman, Oren (2010). *The Price of Altruism: George Price and the Search for the Origins of Kindness*. New York: W. H. Norton.

Hasada, Rie (1996). Some aspects of Japanese cultural ethos embedded in nonverbal communicative behaviour. In Fernando Poyatos (ed.), *Nonverbal Communication in Translation*. Amsterdam: John Benjamins, 83–103.

Hasada, Rie (2006). Cultural scripts: glimpses into the Japanese emotion world. In Cliff Goddard (ed.), *Ethnopragmatics: Understanding Discourse in Cultural Context*. Berlin: Mouton de Gruyter, 171–198.

Hasada, Rie (2008). Two "virtuous emotions" in Japanese: *nasake/joo* and *jihi*. In Cliff Goddard (ed.), *Cross-Linguistic Semantics*. Amsterdam: John Benjamins, 331–347.

Hasan-Rokem, Galit (1992). Proverb. In Richard Bauman (ed.), *Folklore, Cultural Performances, and Popular Entertainments: A Communications-Centered Handbook*. Oxford: Oxford University Press, 128–133.

Hauser, Marc D. (2006). *Moral Minds: How Nature Designed Our Universal Sense of Right and Wrong*. New York: HarperCollins.

Haviland, John (1979). Guugu Yimidhirr. In R. M. W. Dixon and Barry J. Blake (eds), *Handbook of Australian Languages*. Canberra: Australian National University Press, 27–182.

Hellwig, Birgit (2010). Meaning and translation in linguistic fieldwork. *Studies in Language* 34(4): 802–831.

Henderson, John, and Veronica Dobson (1994). *Eastern and Central Arrernte to English Dictionary*. Alice Springs: Institute for Aboriginal Development.

Higbee, Kenneth L., and Richard Millard (1983). Visual imagery and familiarity ratings for 203 sayings. *American Journal of Psychology* 96(20): 211–222.

Hinton, Leanne (2001). The Karuk language. In Leanne Hinton and Kenneth Hale (eds), *The Green Book of Language Revitalization in Practice*. Boston: Academic Press, 191–194.

Hjelmslev, Louis (1961[1943]). *Prolegomena to a Theory of Language*, 2nd edn. Translated by Francis J. Whitfield. Madison: University of Wisconsin Press. [First published in Danish in 1943; first English translation published 1953, as *IJAL* Memoir 7.]

Hobsbawm, Eric (1973[1962]). *The Age of Revolution: Europe 1789–1848*, 2nd edn. London: Cardinal.

Hoffman, Eva (1989). *Lost in Translation: A Life in a New Language*. New York: Dutton.

Hoffman, Eva (2004). *After Such Knowledge: Memory, History, and the Legacy of the Holocaust*. New York: Public Affairs.

Holland, Dorothy, and Naomi Quinn (eds) (1987). *Cultural Models in Language and Thought.* Cambridge: Cambridge University Press.

Holmes, Janet (1988). Paying compliments: a sex-preferential strategy. *Journal of Pragmatics* 12(4): 445–465.

Hymes, Dell H. (1968[1962]). The ethnography of speaking. In Joshua A. Fishman (ed.), *Readings in the Sociology of Language.* The Hague: Mouton, 99–138.

Inglehart, Ronald (1990). *Culture Shift in Advanced Industrial Society.* Princeton, NJ: Princeton University Press.

International Association for the Study of Pain website. http://www.iasp-pain.org/AM/Template.cfm?Section=Pain_Definitions

Iordanskaja, Lidija N., and Igor A. Mel'čuk (2007). *Smysl i Sočetaemost' v Slovane [Le sens et la cooccurrence dans le dictionnaire].* Moscow: Jazyki Slavjanskix Kul'tur.

Irvine, Judith T. (1979). Formality and informality in communicative events. *American Anthropologist* 81(4): 773–790.

Isaacs, Jennifer (1999). *Spirit Country: Contemporary Australian Aboriginal Art.* Melbourne: Hardie Grant Books.

Jackendoff, Ray (1983). *Semantics and Cognition.* Cambridge, Mass.: MIT Press.

Jackendoff, Ray (1990). *Semantic Structures.* Cambridge, Mass.: MIT Press.

Jackendoff, Ray (1999). The natural logic of rights and obligations. In Ray Jackendoff, Paul Bloom, and Karen Wynn (eds), *Language, Logic, and Concepts: Essays in Memory of John Macnamara.* Cambridge, Mass.: MIT Press, 67–95.

Jackendoff, Ray (2002). *Foundations of Language: Brain, Meaning, Grammar, Evolution.* New York: Oxford University Press.

Jackendoff, Ray (2007). Conceptual semantics and Natural Semantic Metalanguage theory have different goals. *Intercultural Pragmatics* 4(3): 411–418.

Jackendoff, Ray (2010). *Meaning and the Lexicon: The Parallel Architecture 1975–2010.* Oxford: Oxford University Press.

Jakobson, Roman (1959). On linguistic aspects of translation. In Reuben A. Brower (ed.), *On Translation.* Cambridge, Mass.: Harvard University Press, 232–239.

Janney, Richard, and Horst Arndt (1993). Universality and relativity in cross-cultural politeness research: a historical perspective. *Multilingua* 12(1): 13–50.

Jones, Howard Mumford (1953). *The Pursuit of Happiness.* Ithaca, NY: Cornell University Press.

Jones, Rhys, and Betty Meehan (1978). Anbarra concept of colour. In Lester Richard Hiatt (ed.), *Australian Aboriginal Concepts.* Canberra: Australian Institute of Aboriginal Studies, 20–29.

Jucker, Andreas H. (2009). Speech act research between armchair, field and laboratory: the case of compliments. *Journal of Pragmatics* 41(8): 1611–1635.

Judt, Tony (2010). Words. *New York Review of Books* 57(12).

Junker, Marie-Odile (2003). A Native American view of the "mind" as seen in the lexicon of cognition in East Cree. *Cognitive Linguistics* 14(2–3): 167–194.

Junker, Marie-Odile (2007). The language of memory in East Cree. In Mengistu Amberber (ed.), *The Language of Memory in a Crosslinguistic Perspective.* Amsterdam: John Benjamins, 235–261.

Junker, Marie-Odile (2008). Semantic primes and their grammar in a polysynthetic language: East Cree. In Cliff Goddard (ed.), *Cross-Linguistic Semantics*. Amsterdam: John Benjamins, 163–204.

Junker, Marie-Odile, and Louise Blacksmith (2006). Are there emotional universals? Evidence from the Native American language East Cree. *Culture & Psychology* 12(3): 275–303.

Jurafsky, Daniel (1996). Universal tendencies in the semantics of the diminutive. *Language* 72: 533–578.

Kay, Paul (2004). NSM and the meaning of color words. *Theoretical Linguistics* 29(3): 237–248.

Kay, Paul, and Brent Berlin. (1997). Science ≠ imperialism: there are nontrivial constraints on color naming. A response to B. A. C. Saunders and J. van Brakel's "Are there non-trivial constraints on color categorization?" *Behavioral and Brain Sciences* 20(2): 196–201.

Kay, Paul, Brent Berlin, Luisa Maffi, and William R. Merrifield (1997). Color naming across languages. In Clyde L. Hardin and Luisa Maffi (eds), *Color Categories in Thought and Language*. Cambridge: Cambridge University Press, 21–56.

Kecskes, Istvan, and Liliana Albertazzi (eds) (2007). *Cognitive Aspects of Bilingualism*. Heidelberg: Springer.

Keesing, Roger M. (1994). Radical cultural difference: anthropology's myth? In Martin Pütz (ed.), *Language Contact and Language Conflict*. Amsterdam: John Benjamins, 3–24.

Kempson, Ruth (1977). *Semantic Theory*. Cambridge: Cambridge University Press.

Kenny, Neil (2004). *The Uses of Curiosity in Early Modern France and Germany*. Oxford: Oxford University Press.

Kerttula, Seija (2005). Semantic basicness in contrastive corpus studies. Paper presented at the 4th International Contrastive Linguistics Conference, 21 Sept. 2005, Santiago de Compostela, Spain.

Kerttula, Seija (2007). Meanings shaped by neurophysiological emphases: a matter of taste. In Matti Rissanen, Mariana Hintikka, Leena Kahlas-Tarkka, and Rod McConchie (eds), *Change in Meaning and the Meaning of Change: Studies in Semantics and Grammar from Old to Present-Day English*. Helsinki: Société Néophilologique, 113–137.

Ketovuori, Heikki, and Pekka J. Pöntinen (1981). A pain vocabulary in Finnish: the Finnish pain questionnaire. *Pain* 11: 247–253.

Khanina, Olesya (2008). How universal is *wanting*? *Studies in Language* 32(4): 818–865.

Khanina, Olesya (2010). Reply to Goddard and Wierzbicka. *Studies in Language* 33(1): 124–130.

Koptjevskaja-Tamm, Maria (2008). Approaching lexical typology. In Martine Vanhove (ed.), *From Polysemy to Semantic Change: Towards a Typology of Lexical Semantic Associations*. Amsterdam: John Benjamins, 3–54.

Koptjevskaja-Tamm, Maria, and Ekaterina V. Rakhilina (n.d.). "Some like it hot": on semantics of temperature in Russian and Swedish. http://www.ling.su.se/staff/tamm/art-KoptjT-Rakhilina1.pdf [viewed Sept. 2005].

Koptjevskaja-Tamm, Maria, and Ekaterina V. Rakhilina (2006). "Some like it hot": on the semantics of temperature adjectives in Russian and Swedish. *Sprachtypologie und Universalienforschungi* 59(2): 253–269.

Kroll, Judith F., and Jill S. Merves (1986). Lexical access for concrete and abstract words. *Journal of Experimental Psychology: Learning, Memory, and Cognition* 12(1): 92–107.

Kropotkin, Peter (1902). *Mutual Aid: A Factor of Evolution*. London: William Heinemann.

Kuschel, Rolf, and Torben Monberg (1974). "We don't talk much about colour here": a study of colour semantics on Bellona Island. *Man* 9: 213–242.

Lakoff, George (1972). Hedges: a study in meaning criteria and the logic of fuzzy concepts. *Chicago Linguistic Society* 8: 183–228.

Lakoff, George (1987). *Women, Fire and Dangerous Things*. Chicago: University of Chicago Press.

Lakoff, George, and Mark Johnson (1999). *Philosophy in the Flesh: The Embodied Mind and its Challenge to Western Thought*. New York: Basic Books.

Langacker, Ronald W. (1987). *Foundations of Cognitive Grammar*. Stanford, Calif.: Stanford University Press.

Langlois, Annie (2004). *Alive and Kicking: Areyonga Teenage Pitjantjatjara*. Canberra: Pacific Linguistics.

Lascaratou, Chryssoula (2008). The function of language in the experience of pain. In Chryssoula Lascaratou, Anna Despotopoulou, and Elly Ifantidou (eds), *Reconstructing Pain and Joy: Linguistic, Literary, and Cultural Perspectives*. Newcastle upon Tyne: Cambridge Scholars, 35–57.

Laughren, Mary, Kenneth Hale, and Warlpiri Lexicography Group (2006). *Warlpiri–English Encyclopaedic Dictionary* [electronic files]. St Lucia: University of Queensland.

Lazarus, Richard S. (1995). Emotions express a social relationship, but it is an individual mind that creates them. *Psychological Inquiry* 6(3): 253–265.

Lee, Penny (2007). Formulaic language in cultural perspective. In Paul Skandera (ed.), *Phraseology and Culture in English*. Berlin: Mouton de Gruyter, 471–496.

Leech, Geoffrey (1974). *Semantics*. Harmondsworth: Penguin.

Lefevere, André (1977). *Translating Literature: The German Tradition from Luther to Rosenzweig*. Assen: Van Gorcum. [Chapter: Arthur Schopenhauer, "Equivalence and atomisation of the original", 98–101.]

Lehrer, Adrienne (1974). *Semantic Fields and Lexical Structure*. Amsterdam: North-Holland.

Leibniz, Gottfried Wilhelm (1890[1675]). In Carl Immanuel Gerhardt (ed.), *Die philosophischen Schriften von Gottfried Wilhelm Leibniz*, vols 1–7. Hildesheim: Georg Olms, 1960–1961.

Leibniz, Gottfried Wilhelm (1903). Table of definitions. In Louis Couturat (ed.), *Opuscules et fragments inédits de Leibniz*. Paris. [Reprinted 1961, Hildesheim: Georg Olms.]

Leibniz, Gottfried Wilhelm (1999[1685]). Logica de notionibus. In Ursula Goldenbaum (ed.), *Philosophscyen Schriften und Briefe*, series 6, vol. 4, pt 3. Berlin: Akademie, 1211–1299.

Levin, Beth, and Malka Rappaport Hovav (2005). *Argument Realization*. Cambridge: Cambridge University Press.

Levinson, Stephen C. (2003). *Space in Language and Cognition: Explorations in Cognitive Diversity*. Cambridge: Cambridge University Press.

Levinson, Stephen C., and Sérgio Meira (2003). "Natural concepts" in the spatial topological domain: adpositional meanings in cross-linguistic perspective. An exercise in semantic typology. *Language* 79(3): 485–516.

Levinson, Stephen C., and David P. Wilkins (2006). *Grammars of Space: Explorations in Cognitive Diversity*. Cambridge: Cambridge University Press.

Levisen, Carsten (2011). The Danish universe of meaning: semantics, cognition and cultural values. Ph.D thesis, University of New England.

Levisen, Carsten (2012). *Cultural Semantics and Social Cognition: A Case Study on the Danish Universe of Meaning*. Berlin: Mouton de Gruyter.

Levy, Robert I. (1973). *Tahitians: Mind and Experience in the Society Islands*. Chicago: Chicago University Press.

Lewis, C. S. (1960). *Studies in Words*. Cambridge: Cambridge University Press.

Lewycka, Marina (2005). *A Short History of Tractors in Ukrainian*. London: Viking Penguin.

Lim, Kim Hui (2003). *Budi* as the Malay mind: a philosophical study of Malay ways of reasoning and emotion in *peribahasa*. Ph.D dissertation. University of Hamburg.

Löbner, Sebastien (2002). *Understanding Semantics*. London: Hodder Arnold.

Locke, John (1959[1690]). *An Essay Concerning Human Understanding*. Oxford: Clarendon Press.

Longman Dictionary of Contemporary English (1987). 2nd edn. Harlow: Longman.

Lounsbury, Floyd G. (1956). A semantic analysis of the Pawnee kinship usage. *Language* 32(1): 158–194.

Lucy, John A. (1997). The linguistics of "color". In Clyde L. Hardin and Luisa Maffi (eds), *Color Categories in Thought and Language*. Cambridge: Cambridge University Press, 320–346.

Lutz, Catherine A. (1988). *Unnatural Emotions: Everyday Sentiments on a Micronesian Atoll and Their Challenge to Western Theory*. Chicago: University of Chicago Press.

Lyons, John (1968). *An Introduction to Theoretical Linguistics*. Cambridge: Cambridge University Press.

Lyons, John (1977). *Semantics*. Cambridge: Cambridge University Press.

Maher, Brigid (2002). Natural Semantic Metalanguage theory and some Italian speech act verbs. *Studies in Pragmatics* (journal of the Pragmatics Society of Japan) 4: 33–48.

Majid, Asifa (2012). A guide to stimulus-based elicitation for semantic categories. In Nicholas Thieberger (ed.), *The Oxford Handbook of Linguistic Fieldwork*. Oxford: Oxford University Press, 54–71.

Majid, Asifa, and Melissa Bowerman (eds) (2007). *Cutting and Breaking Events: A Crosslinguistic Perspective*. Special Issue of *Cognitive Linguistics*, 18(2).

Majid, Asifa, Melissa Bowerman, Miriam van Staden, and James S. Boster (2007). The semantic categories of cutting and breaking events: a crosslinguistic perspective. *Cognitive Linguistics* 18(2): 133–152.

Majid, Asifa, Nick J. Enfield, and Miriam van Staden (eds) (2006). *Parts of the Body: Cross-Linguistic Categorization*. Special issue of *Language Sciences*, 28(2–3).

Majsak, Timur A., and Ekatarina V. Rakhilina (2007). *Glagoly Dviženija v Vode: Leksičeskaja Tipologija* [Verbs of Movement in Water: Lexical Typology]. Moscow: Indrik.

Marmaridou, Sophia (2006). On the conceptual, cultural and discursive motivation of Greek pain lexicalizations. *Cognitive Linguistics* 17(3): 393–434.

Mason, Te Haumihiata (2008). The incorporation of *Mātauranga Māori* or Māori knowledge into *Te Mātāpuna*, the first monolingual Māori dictionary for adults. In R. Amery and J. Nash (eds), *Warra Wiltaniappendi Strengthening Languages: Proceedings of the Inaugural Indigenous Languages Conference 2007*. Adelaide: University of Adelaide, 35–39.

Matthews, Stephen, and Virginia Yip (1994). *Cantonese: A Comprehensive Grammar*. New York: Routledge.

McCawley, James D. (1972). A program for logic. In Donald Davidson and Gilbert Hartman (eds), *Semantics of Natural Language*. Dordrecht: Reidel, 489–544.

McCrum, Robert (1998). *My Year Off: Rediscovering Life after a Stroke.* New York: W. W. Norton.

McMahon, Darrin M. (2006). *Happiness: A History.* New York: Atlantic Monthly Press.

Mel'čuk, Igor (1981). Meaning-text models: a recent trend in Soviet linguistics. *Annual Review of Anthropology* 10: 27–62.

Mel'čuk, Igor (1988). Semantic description of lexical units in an explanatory combinatorial dictionary: basic principles and heuristic criteria. *International Journal of Lexicography* 1: 165–188.

Mel'čuk, Igor (2006). Explanatory combinatorial dictionary. In Giandomenico Sica (ed.), *Open Problems in Linguistic and Lexicography*. Monza: Polimetrica, 225–355.

Mel'čuk, Igor (2012). *Semantics: From Meaning to Text.* Amsterdam: John Benjamins.

Mel'čuk, Igor, Nadia Arbatchewsky-Jumarie, Lidija Iordanskaja, Suzanne Mantha, and Alain Polguère (1984–99). *Dictionnaire explicatif et combinatoire du français contemporain: recherches lexico-sémantiques I–IV.* Montreal: Presses de l'Université de Montréal.

Mel'čuk, Igor, and Aleksandr Žolkovskij (1984). *Tolkovo-Kombinatornyj Slovar' Sovremennogo Russkogo Jazyka* [Explanatory-Combinatorial Dictionary of the Contemporary Russian Language]. Vienna: Wiener Slawistischer Almanach.

Melzack, Ronald (1975). The McGill Pain Questionnaire: major properties and scoring methods. *Pain* 1(3): 277–299.

Merridale, Catherine (2001). *Night of Stone: Death and Memory in Twentieth-Century Russia.* New York: Viking Adult.

Merskey, Harold (1994). Logic, truth and language in concepts of pain. *Quality of Life Research* 3, Supplement *Chronic Pain*, S69–S76.

Merton, Thomas (1955[1948]). *The Seven Storey Mountain.* New York: Harcourt Brace Jovanovich.

Metherell, Mark (2009). Helpline for nagging pain. *Sydney Morning Herald*, 23 Nov. http://www.smh.com.au/national/helpline-for-nagging-pain-20091122-isvq.8html [viewed 23 Nov. 2009].

Middleton, Erica L., Edward J. Wisniewski, Kelly A. Trindel, and Mutsumi Imai (2004). Separating the chaff from the oats: evidence for a conceptual distinction between count noun and mass noun aggregates. *Journal of Memory and Language* 50: 371–394.

Mieder, Wolfgang (ed.) (1994[1987]). *Wise Words: Essays on the Proverb.* New York: Garland.

Mieder, Wolfgang (2001). *International Proverb Scholarship: An Annotated Bibliography, Supplement III (1990–2000).* New York: Peter Lang.

Mill, John Stuart (1961[1843]). *A System of Logic, Ratiocinative and Inductive: Being a Connected View of the Principles of Evidence and the Methods of Scientific Investigation*, 8th edn. London: Longmans.

Moorfield, John C. (2005). *Te Aka: Maori–English, English–Maori Dictionary and Index.* Auckland: Pearson Longman.

Morphy, Howard (2006). From dull to brilliant: the aesthetics of spiritual power among the Yolngu. In Howard Morphy and Morgan Perkins (eds), *The Anthropology of Art: A Reader.*

Malden, Mass.: Blackwell, 302–320. [Repr. from Jeremy Coote and Anthony Shelton (eds), *Anthropology, Art and Aesthetics*. Oxford: Clarendon Press, 1992, 181–208.]

Mosel, Ulrike (1994). Samoan. In Cliff Goddard and Anna Wierzbicka (eds), *Semantic and Lexical Universals: Theory and Empirical Findings*. Amsterdam: John Benjamins, 331–360.

Mosel, Ulrike (n.d.). Morphosyntactic analysis in the field: a guide to the guides. http://www. linguistik.uni-kiel.de/sldr/stuff/sldr_mosel_handout.pdf [viewed 22 Apr. 2012].

Murphy, M. Lynne (2010). *Lexical Meaning*. Cambridge: Cambridge University Press.

Myers, David G., and Ed Diener (1995). Who is happy? *Psychological Science* 6(1): 10–19.

Myhill, John (1996). Is BAD a semantic primitive? Evidence from Biblical Hebrew. *Lexicology* 2(2): 99–126.

Nabokov, Vladimir (1961). *Nikolai Gogol'*. New York: New Directions.

Nafisi, Azar (2008). *Things I've Been Silent About: Memories of a Prodigal Daughter*. New York: Random House.

Nakhimovsky, Alexander D., and Slava Paperno (1982). *An English–Russian Dictionary of Nabokov's Lolita*. Ann Arbor, Mich.: Ardis.

Napaljarri, Peggy Rockman, and Lee Cataldi (1994). *Yimikirli: Warlpiri Dreamings and Histories*. San Francisco, Calif.: HarperCollins.

Narayan, Mary C. (2010). Culture's effects on pain assessment and management. *American Journal of Nursing* 110(4): 38–47.

Nash, David (1986). *Topics in Warlpiri Grammar*. New York: Garland.

Nicholls, Sophie (2003). The semantics of 'pain' and 'suffering'. BA Hons thesis, University of New England.

Nicholls, Sophie (2011). Referring expressions and referential practice in Roper Kriol (Northern Territory, Australia). Ph.D thesis, University of New England. [https://e-publications.une. edu.au/vital/access/manager/Repository/une:9244]

Nida, Eugene Albert (1975). *Componential Analysis of Meaning: An Introduction to Semantic Structures*. The Hague: Mouton.

Nietzsche, Friedrich (1939). *Der Wille Zur Macht*. Leipzig: Alfred Kröner.

Nietzsche, Friedrich (1973[1886]). *Beyond Good and Evil*. Translated by R. J. Hollingdale, with an introduction and commentary. Harmondsworth: Penguin.

Nietzsche, Friedrich (2000[1872]). *The Birth of Tragedy*. Oxford: Oxford University Press.

Norrick, Neal R. (1985). *How Proverbs Mean: Semantic Studies in English Proverbs*. Berlin: Mouton de Gruyter.

Nussbaum, Martha C. (2004). Mill between Aristotle and Bentham. *Dædalus* 133(2): 60–68.

Obama, Barack (2008). *The Audacity of Hope: Thoughts on Reclaiming the American Dream*. Melbourne: Text.

Obelkevich, James (1994 [1987]). Proverbs and social history. In Wolfgang Mieder (ed.), *Wise Words: Essays on the Proverb*. New York: Garland, 211–252.

Obeng, Samuel Gyasi (1996). The proverb as a mitigating and politeness strategy in Akan discourse. *Anthropological Linguistics* 38(3): 523–549.

Obeyesekere, Gananath (1985). Depression, Buddhism, and the work of culture in Sri Lanka. In Arthur Kleinman and Byron Good (eds), *Culture and Depression: Studies in the Anthropology and Cross-Cultural Psychiatry of Affect and Disorder*. Berkeley: University of California Press, 134–152.

Ogden, Charles Kay (1931). *Debabelization. With a Survey of Contemporary Opinion on the Problem of a Universal Language.* London: Kegan Paul, Trench and Trubner.

Ogden, Charles Kay (1951[1932]). *Bentham's Theory of Fictions*, with Introduction, 2nd edn. London: Routledge and Kegan Paul.

O'Grady, William, and John Archibald (2009). *Contemporary Linguistic Analysis: An Introduction*, 6th edn. Toronto: Pearson-Longman.

Ong, Walter J. (1982). *Orality and Literacy: The Technologizing of the Word.* London: Methuen.

Orr, H. Allen (2010). Is goodness in your genes? Review of Oren Harman's *The Price of Altruism: George Price and the Search for the Origins of Kindness. New York Review of Books* 62.15: 32.

Oxford English–Russian Dictionary (1984). Ed. Paul Stephen Falla. Oxford: Clarendon Press.

Oxford Russian–English Dictionary (1980). Ed. Marcus Wheeler and B. O. Begaun. Oxford: Oxford University Press.

Padučeva, Elena V. (2004). *Dinamičeskie Modeli v Semantike Leksiki* [Dynamic Models in Lexical Semantics]. Moscow: Jazyki Slavjanskoj Kultury.

Palmer, Frank R. (1986). *Mood and Modality.* Cambridge: Cambridge University Press.

Pascal, Blaise (1954[1667]). De l'esprit géometrique et de l'art de persuader. In Jacques Chevalier (ed.), *Oevres complètes.* Paris: Gallimard, 575–604.

Patharakorn, Patharaorn (2010). Pain language: a Thai case study. MA thesis, University of Queensland.

Pavlenko, Aneta (2005). *Emotions and Multilingualism.* Cambridge: Cambridge University Press.

Pavlenko, Aneta (ed.) (2006). *Bilingual Minds: Emotional Experiences, Expressions, and Representation.* Bristol: Multilingual Matters.

Pavlenko, Aneta (2011a). Introduction: Bilingualism and thought in the 20th century. In Aneta Pavlenko (ed.), *Thinking and Speaking in Two Languages.* Bristol: Multilingual Matters, 1–28.

Pavlenko, Aneta (2011b). (Re)-naming the world: word-to-referent mapping in second language speakers. In Aneta Pavlenko (ed.), *Thinking and Speaking in Two Languages.* Bristol: Multilingual Matters, 199–237.

Pavlenko, Aneta (2011c). Thinking and speaking in two languages: overview of the field. In Aneta Pavlenko (ed.), *Thinking and Speaking in Two Languages.* Bristol: Multilingual Matters, 237–257.

Pedersen, Jan (2010). The different Swedish *tack*: an ethnographic investigation of Swedish thanking and related concepts. *Journal of Pragmatics* 42(5): 1258–1265.

Peeters, Bert (2000). "S'engager" vs. "to show restraint": linguistic and cultural relativity in discourse management. In Susanne Neimeier and René Dirven (eds), *Evidence for Linguistic Relativity.* Amsterdam: John Benjamins, 193–222.

Peeters, Bert (2004a). Tall poppies and equalitarianism in Australian discourse: from key word to cultural value. *English World Wide* 25: 1–25.

Peeters, Bert (2004b). "Thou shalt not be a tall poppy": describing an Australian communicative (and behavioral) norm. *Intercultural Pragmatics* 1: 71–92.

Peeters, Bert (2006a). "She'll be right" vs. "On va s'arranger": étude ethnophraséologique. *Revue de sémantique et pragmatique* 19/20: 71–89.

Peeters, Bert (ed.) (2006*b*). *Semantic Primes and Universal Grammar: Empirical Findings from the Romance Languages*. Amsterdam: John Benjamins.

Peeters, Bert (2012). Les petites idées d'un petit belge, ou quand *petit* ne renvoie pas à la taille. In Franck Neveu, Valelia Muni Toke, Peter Blumenthal, Thomas Klingler, Pierluigi Ligas, Sophie Prévost, and Sandra Teston-Bonnard (eds), *CMLF 2012: 3e Congrès Mondial de Linguistique Française*. Paris: EDP Sciences, 1893–1907. http://dx.doi.org/10.1051/shsconf/20120100071.

Peeters, Bert (2013). La langue de bois: un pèlerinage ethnolexicologique. In Pierre Marillaud and Robert Gauthier (dir.), *La mauvaise parole. 33e Colloque d'Albi Langages et Signification*. Albi/Toulouse: CALS/CPST, 196–210.

Pinker, Steven (1994). *The Language Instinct*. New York: William Morrow.

Potkay, Adam (2007). *The Story of Joy: From the Bible to Late Romanticism*. Cambridge: Cambridge University Press.

Priestley, Carol (2002). Insides and emotion in Koromu. In Nick J. Enfield and Anna Wierzbicka (eds), *The Body in Description of Emotion: Cross-Linguistic Studies*. Special issue of *Pragmatics and Cognition*, 10(1/2): 243–270.

Priestley, Carol (2008). The semantics of "inalienable possession" in Koromu (PNG). In Cliff Goddard (ed.), *Cross-Linguistic Semantics*. Amsterdam: John Benjamins, 277–299.

Priestley, Carol (2012*a*). The expression of potential event modality in the Papuan language of Koromu. In Maia Ponsonnet, Loan Dao, and Margit Bowler (eds), *The 42nd Australian Linguistics Society Conference Proceedings—2011*. Canberra: ANU Research Repository, https://digitalcollections.anu.edu.au

Priestley, Carol (2012*b*). Koromu temporal expressions: semantic and cultural perspectives. In Luna Filipović and Kasia M. Jaszczolt (eds), *Space and Time Across Languages and Cultures*, vol. 2: *Language, Culture and Cognition*. Amsterdam: John Benjamins, 143–165.

Priestley, Carol (2013) Social categories, shared experience, reciprocity and endangered meanings: examples from Koromu (PNG). *Australian Journal of Linguistics* 33: 257–281.

Priestley, Carol (2014). The semantics and morphosyntax of tare "hurt/pain" in Koromu (PNG): Verbal and nominal constructions. *International Journal of Language and Culture* 1(2): 253–271.

Priestley, Carol (in press). Body parts in the Papuan language of Koromu (Kesawai). In Zhengdao Ye (ed.) *The Semantics of Nouns*. Oxford: Oxford University Press.

Proust, Marcel (1954). *À la recherche du temps perdu*. Paris: Gallimard.

Proust, Marcel (1982). *A Search for Lost Time: Swann's Way*. Translated by James Grieve. Canberra: Australian National University.

Proust, Marcel (2002). *In the Shadow of Young Girls in Flower*. Translated by James Grieve. London: Allen Lane.

Pullum, Geoffrey K. (1991). *The Great Eskimo Vocabulary Hoax and Other Irreverent Essays on the Study of Language*. Chicago: University of Chicago Press.

Pütz, Martin, and JoAnne Neff-van Aertselaer (eds) (2008). *Developing Contrastive Pragmatics: Interlanguage and Cross-Cultural Perspectives*. Berlin: Mouton de Gruyter.

Quinn, Naomi (2002). Cultural selves. Paper presented at the New York Academy of Sciences conference "The Self: From Soul to Brain". New York. [Revised version published in Joseph

E. LeDoux, Jacek Debiec, and Henry Moss (eds), *Annals of the New York Academy of Sciences* 1001 (Oct. 2003): 145–176.]

Quirk, Randolph, Sidney Greenbaum, Geoffrey Leech, and Jan Svartvik (1972). *A Grammar of Contemporary English*. London: Longman.

Radford, Andrew, Martin Atkinson, David Britain, Harald Clahsen, and Andrew J. Spencer (2009). *Linguistics: An Introduction*, 2nd edn. Cambridge: Cambridge University Press.

Rajagopalan, Kannavillil (2009). Pragmatics today: from a component of linguistics to a perspective on language. In Bruce Fraser and Ken Turner (eds), *Language in Life, and a Life in Language: Jacob Mey—A Festschrift*. Bingley, UK: Emerald, 335–342.

Rappaport Hovav, Malka, and Beth Levin (2010). Reflections on manner/result complementarity. In Malka Rappaport Hovav, Edit Doran, and Ivy Sichel (eds), *Lexical Semantics, Syntax, and Event Structure*. Oxford: Oxford University Press, 21–38.

Regier, Terry, Paul Kay, and Richard S. Cook (2005). Focal colors are universal after all. *Proceedings of the National Academy of Sciences* 102(203): 8386–8391.

Reznikova, Tatiana, Ekaterina V. Rakhilina, and Anastasia Bonch-Osmololovskaya (2012). Towards a typology of pain predicates. *Linguistics* 50(3): 421–465.

Rich, Katherine Russell (2009). *Dreaming in Hindi: Coming Awake in Another Language*. Orlando, Fla.: Houghton Mifflin Harcourt.

Riemer, Andrew (1992). *Inside Outside*. Pymble, NSW: Angus and Robertson.

Riemer, Nick (2010). *Introducing Semantics*. Cambridge: Cambridge University Press.

Robertson, Rachel (2012). *Reaching One Thousand: A Story of Love, Motherhood and Autism*. Collingwood, Victoria: Black.

Rosaldo, Michelle (1980). *Knowledge and Passion: Ilongot Notions of Self and Social Life*. Cambridge: Cambridge University Press.

Rosch, Eleanor (1978). Principles of categorization. In Eleanor Rosch and B. B. Lloyd (eds), *Cognition and Categorization*. Hillsdale, NJ: Lawrence Erlbaum, 27–48.

Rosch, Eleanor, and Carolyn B. Mervis (1975). Family resemblances: studies in the internal structure of categories. *Cognitive Psychology* 7: 613–661.

Rousseau, Jean-Jacques (1994). Political fragments, pt 6, sect. 3. In *Social Contract, Discourse on the Virtue Most Necessary for a Hero, Political Fragments, and Geneva Manuscript*, vol. 4: *The Collected Writings of Rousseau*. Edited by Roger D. Masters and Christopher Kelly; translated by Judith R. Bush, Roger D. Masters, and Christopher Kelly. Hanover, NH: University Press of New England.

Sakel, Jeanette, and Daniel L. Everett (2012). *Linguistic Fieldwork: A Student Guide*. Cambridge: Cambridge University Press.

Salkever, Stephen G. (1978). Rousseau and the concept of happiness. *Polity* 11(1): 27–45.

Sante, Luc (1998). *The Factory of Facts*. New York: Pantheon.

Saunders, Barbara A. C. (1992). *The Invention of Basic Colour Terms*. Utrecht: ISOR.

Saunders, Barbara A. C., and Jaap van Brakel (1995). Translating the World Color Survey. In Karin Geuijen, Diederick Raven, and Jan de Wolf (eds), *Post-modernism and Anthropology*. Assen: van Corcum.

Ščerba, Lev V. (1940). Opyt obščej teorii leksikografii [An Outline of a General Lexicographic Theory]. *Izvestija Akademii Nauk SSSR, Otdelenie Literatury i Jazyka* [*Bulletin of the Academy of Sciences of the USSR: Department of Literature and Language*], 3: 89–17.

[Translated by Donna M. T. Cr. Farina (1995), as "Towards a general theory of lexicography", *International Journal of Lexicography* 8(4): 315–350.]

Scheffler, Harold W. (1978). *Australian Kin Classification*. Cambridge: Cambridge University Press.

Scherer, Klaus R. (1986). Studying emotion empirically: issues and a paradigm for research. In Klaus R. Scherer, Harald G. Wallbott, and Angela B. Summerfield (eds), *Experiencing Emotion: A Cross-Cultural Study*. Cambridge: Cambridge University Press, 3–27.

Scherer, Klaus R., Harald G. Wallbott, and Angela B. Summerfield (eds) (1986). *Experiencing Emotion: A Cross-Cultural Study*. Cambridge: Cambridge University Press.

Schmied, Josef (2006). New ways of analysing ESL on the WWW with WebCorp and Web-PhraseCount. In Antoinette Renouf and Andrew Kehoe (eds), *The Changing Face of Corpus Linguistics*. Amsterdam: Rodopi, 309–324.

Schopenhauer, Arthur (1913[1844]). *Die Welt als Wille und Vorstellung*, Band 2. Munich: Georg Müller.

Schopenhauer, Arthur (1966[1844]). *The World as Will and Representation* [*Die Welt als Wille und Vorstellung*], vol 2. Translated by E. F. J. Payne. New York: Dover.

Scott, Kim (2007). Strangers at home. In Mary Besemeres and Anna Wierzbicka (eds), *Translating Lives: Living with Two Languages and Cultures*. St Lucia: University of Queensland Press, 1–11.

Searle, John (1965). What is a speech act? In Max Black (ed.), *Philosophy in America*. London: Allen and Unwin, 221–239.

Searle, John (1969). *Speech Acts: An Essay in the Philosophy of Language*. Cambridge: Cambridge University Press.

Sheffield, Frisbee C. C. (2008). Introduction. In Margaret Campbell Howatson and Frisbee C. C. Sheffield (eds), *Plato: The Symposium*. Cambridge: Cambridge University Press, 1–21.

Shi-xu (2000). To feel or not to feel, that is the question. *Culture & Psychology* 6(3): 375–383.

Shweder, Richard A. (2003). *Why Do Men Barbeque? Recipes for Cultural Psychology*. Cambridge, Mass.: Harvard University Press.

Shweder, Richard A. (2004). Deconstructing the emotions for the sake of comparative research. In Anthony S. R. Manstead, Nico Frijda, and Agneta Fischer (eds), *Feelings and Emotions*. Cambridge: Cambridge University Press, 81–97.

Shweder, Richard A., Jonathan Haidt, Randall Horton, and Craig Joseph (2008). The cultural psychology of the emotions: ancient and renewed. In Michael Lewis, Jeannette M. Haviland-Jones, and Lisa Feldman Barrett (eds), *Handbook of Emotions*, 3rd edn. New York: Guilford Press, 409–427.

Simpson, Jane (2006). How do we know what they see? http://blogs.usyd.edu.au/elac/2006/09/how_do_we_know_what_they_see_f.html

Sommerville, Margaret A. (2001). *Death Talk: The Case Against Euthanasia and Physician-Assisted Suicide*. Montreal: McGill-Queen's University Press.

Sontag, Susan (2002). *Illness as Metaphor and Aids and its Metaphors*. London: Penguin Classics.

Stevenson, Burton (1958). *Stevenson's Book of Quotations: Classical and Modern*. London: Cassell.

Stollznow, Karenina (2006). Key words in the discourse of discrimination: a semantic and pragmatic analysis. Ph.D thesis, University of New England.

Strauss, Claudia, and Naomi Quinn (1997). *A Cognitive Theory of Cultural Meaning*. Cambridge: Cambridge University Press.

Strong, Jenny, T. Mathews, Roland Sussex, F. New, S. Hoey, and Geoffrey Mitchell (2009). Pain language and gender differences when describing a past pain event. *Pain* 145(1–2): 86–95.

Sussex, Roland (2009). The language of pain in applied linguistics. Review article of Chryssoula Lascaratou's *The Language of Pain* (Amsterdam: John Benjamins, 2007). *Australian Review of Applied Linguistics* 32(1): 6.1–6.14.

Sutrop, Urmas (1999). Temperature terms in the Baltic area. In Mati Erelt (ed.), *Estonian: Typological Studies III*. Tartu: Tartu Ülikool, 185–203.

Swadesh, Morris (1972[1960]). What is glottochronology? In Joel Sherzer (ed.), *The Origin and Diversification of Languages*. London: Routledge and Kegan Paul, 271–292.

Sweeney, Amin (1987). *A Full Hearing: Orality and Literacy in the Malay World*. Berkeley: University of California Press.

Swettenham, Frank (1906). *British Malaya: An Account of the Origin and Progress of British Influence in Malaya*. London: John Lane.

Tarski, Alfred (1956[1935]). The concept of truth in formalized languages. In *Logic, Semantics, Metamathematics: Papers from 1923 to 1938*. Translated by J. H. Woodger. Oxford: Clarendon Press, 152–278.

Taylor, Archer (1962[1931]). *The Proverb, and an Index to "The Proverb"*. Hatboro, Penn.: Folklore Associates.

Taylor, John R. (1995). *Linguistic Categorization: Prototypes in Linguistic Theory*, 2nd edn. Oxford: Oxford University Press.

Taylor, John R., and Robert E. MacLaury (1995). *Language and the Cognitive Construal of the World*. Berlin: Mouton de Gruyter.

Thieberger, Nicholas (ed.) (2012). *The Oxford Handbook of Linguistic Fieldwork*. Oxford: Oxford University Press.

Tien, Adrian (2010). *Lexical Semantics of Children's Mandarin Chinese during the First Four Years*. Munich: Lincom Academic.

Todd, Olivier (1996). *Albert Camus: une vie*. Paris: Gallimard.

Tolstoy, Leo N. (1940). *Voskresenie* [Resurrection]. Leningrad: Xudožestvennaja Literatura.

Tolstoy, Leo N. (2009). *Resurrection*. Translated by Louise Maude. London: Oxford University Press.

Traugott, Elizabeth C. (1993). The conflict promises/threatens to escalate into war. *Proceedings of the 19th Annual Meeting of the Berkeley Linguistics Society*, 348–358.

Traugott, Elizabeth C. (1994). Subjectification and the development of modal meanings. Paper presented at the Australian Linguistics Institute, La Trobe University, Melbourne.

Travis, Catherine E. (2002). La Metalengua Semántica Natural: the Natural Semantic Metalanguage of Spanish. In Cliff Goddard and Anna Wierzbicka (eds), *Meaning and Universal Grammar: Theory and Empirical Findings*, vol. 1. Amsterdam: John Benjamins, 173–242.

Travis, Catherine E. (2004). The ethnopragmatics of the diminutive in conversational Colombian Spanish. *Intercultural Pragmatics* 1(2): 249–274.

Travis, Catherine E. (2005). *Discourse Markers in Colombian Spanish: A Study in Polysemy*. Berlin: Mouton de Gruyter.

Travis, Catherine E. (2006). The communicative realization of *confianza* and *calor humano* in Colombian Spanish. In Cliff Goddard (ed.), *Ethnopragmatics: Understanding Discourse in Cultural Context*. Berlin: Mouton de Gruyter, 199–230.

Trésor de la langue française: dictionnaire de la langue de XIXe et du XXe Siècle (1789–1960) (1971–1994). [Treasury of the French Language: Comprehensive Etymological and Historical Dictionary of the French Language, originally published in 16 vols.] French Online Dictionary: http://atilf.atilf.fr/

Tsiolkas, Christos (2008). *The Slap*. Crows Nest, NSW: Allen and Unwin.

Tsohatzidis, Savas L. (2010). Speech Act Theory: some current options. *Intercultural Pragmatics* 7(2): 341–362.

Vanhatalo, Ulla, Heli Tissari and Anna Idström (2014). Revisiting the universality of Natural Semantic Metalanguage: a view through Finnish. *SKY Journal of linguistics* 27: 67–94.

Varela, Francisco J., Evan T. Thompson, and Eleanor Rosch (1991). *The Embodied Mind: Cognitive Science and Human Experience*. Boston, Mass.: MIT Press.

Watts, Richard J. (2003). *Politeness*. Cambridge: Cambridge University Press.

Weber, Max (1958[1904]). *The Protestant Ethic and the Spirit of Capitalism*. Translated by Talcott Parsons, 1930. New York: Charles Scribner's Sons.

Weber, Max (1993[1894]). Die Deutschen Landarbeiter in *Gesamtausgabe*, Abteilung 1, *Schriften und Reden*, Band 4, *Landarbeiterfrage, Nationalstaat und Volkswirtschaftspolitik. Schriften und Reden 1892–1899*. Edited by Wolfgang J. Mommsen and Rita Aldenhoff. Tübingen: J. C. B. Mohr/Paul Siebeck, 339–340.

Weber, Sandy E. (1996). Cultural aspects of pain in childbearing women. *Journal of Obstetric Gynecologic and Neonatal Nursing* 25(1): 67–72.

Weissman, David E., Deb Gordon, and Shiva Bidar-Sielaff (2004). Cultural aspects of pain management. *Journal of Palliative Medicine* 7(5): 715–716.

White, Geoffrey M. (1987). Proverbs and cultural models: an American psychology of problem solving. In Dorothy Holland and Naomi Quinn (eds), *Cultural Models in Language and Thought*. Cambridge, Mass.: Cambridge University Press, 151–172.

Wierzbicka, Anna (1972). *Semantic Primitives*. Translated by Anna Wierzbicka and John Besemeres. Frankfurt: Athenäum.

Wierzbicka, Anna (1975). Why "kill" does not mean "cause to die": the semantics of action sentences. *Foundations of Language* 13(4): 491–528.

Wierzbicka, Anna (1980). *Lingua Mentalis: The Semantics of Natural Language*. Sydney: Academic Press.

Wierzbicka, Anna (1984). Apples are not a "kind of fruit": the semantics of human categorization. *American Ethnologist* 11(2): 313–328.

Wierzbicka, Anna (1985a). *Lexicography and Conceptual Analysis*. Ann Arbor, Mich.: Karoma.

Wierzbicka, Anna (1985b). Different cultures, different languages, different speech acts: Polish vs. English. *Journal of Pragmatics* 9: 145–178.

Wierzbicka, Anna (1987a). Boys will be boys: "radical semantics" vs. "radical pragmatics". *Language* 63(1): 95–114.

Wierzbicka, Anna (1987*b*). *English Speech Act Verbs: A Semantic Dictionary.* Sydney: Academic Press.

Wierzbicka, Anna (1988). *The Semantics of Grammar.* Amsterdam: John Benjamins.

Wierzbicka, Anna (1990). The meaning of colour terms: semantics, culture, and cognition. *Cognitive Linguistics* 1(1): 99–150.

Wierzbicka, Anna (1992*a*). *Semantics, Culture, and Cognition: Universal Human Concepts in Culture-Specific Configurations.* Oxford: Oxford University Press.

Wierzbicka, Anna (1992*b*). Semantic primitives and semantic fields. In Adrienne Lehrer and Eva Feder Kittay (eds), *Frames, Fields, and Contrasts: New Essays in Semantic and Lexical Organization.* Hillsdale, NJ: Lawrence Erlbaum, 209–227.

Wierzbicka, Anna (1992*c*). Defining emotion concepts. *Cognitive Science* 16: 539–581.

Wierzbicka, Anna (1994*a*). Semantic primitives across languages: a critical review. In Cliff Goddard and Anna Wierzbicka (eds), *Semantic and Lexical Universals: Theory and Empirical Findings.* Amsterdam: John Benjamins, 445–500.

Wierzbicka, Anna (1994*b*). "Cultural scripts": a semantic approach to cultural analysis and cross-cultural communication. *Pragmatics and Language Learning*, Monograph Series, 5: 1–24.

Wierzbicka, Anna (1994*c*). "Cultural scripts": a new approach to the study of cross-cultural communication. In Martin Pütz (ed.), *Language Contact and Language Conflict.* Amsterdam: John Benjamins, 69–87.

Wierzbicka, Anna (1994*d*). Emotion, language, and "cultural scripts". In Shinobu Kitayama and Hazel Rose Markus (eds), *Emotion and Culture: Empirical Studies of Mutual Influence.* Washington, DC: American Psychological Association, 130–198.

Wierzbicka, Anna (1996). *Semantics: Primes and Universals.* Oxford: Oxford University Press.

Wierzbicka, Anna (1997). *Understanding Cultures Through Their Key Words: English, Russian, Polish, German, Japanese.* New York: Oxford University Press.

Wierzbicka, Anna (1999*a*). *Emotions Across Languages and Cultures: Diversity and Universals.* Cambridge: Cambridge University Press.

Wierzbicka, Anna (1999*b*). "Universals of colour" from a linguistic point of view. *Behavioral and Brain Science* 22: 724–725.

Wierzbicka, Anna (2001*a*). Leibnizian linguistics. In István Kenesei and Robert M. Harnish (eds), *Perspectives on Semantics, Pragmatics, and Discourse: A Festschrift for Ferenc Kiefer.* Amsterdam: John Benjamins, 229–253.

Wierzbicka, Anna (2001*b*). Introduction. In Jean Harkins and Anna Wierzbicka (eds), *Emotions in Crosslinguistic Perspective.* Berlin: Mouton de Gruyter, 1–34.

Wierzbicka, Anna (2002*a*). Russian cultural scripts: the theory of cultural scripts and its applications. *Ethos* 30(4): 401–432.

Wierzbicka, Anna (2002*b*). Australian cultural scripts: *bloody* revisited. *Journal of Pragmatics* 34(9): 1167–1209.

Wierzbicka, Anna (2002*c*). Philosophy and discourse: the rise of *really* and the fall of *truly*. In Christine Béal (ed.), *Langue, discours, culture.* Special issue of *Les cahiers de praxématique*, 38: 85–112.

Wierzbicka, Anna (2002*d*). Semantic primes and universal grammar in Polish. In Cliff Goddard and Anna Wierzbicka (eds), *Meaning and Universal Grammar: Theory and Empirical Findings*, vol. 2. Amsterdam: John Benjamins, 65–144.

Wierzbicka, Anna (2003*a*[1991]). *Cross-Cultural Pragmatics: The Semantics of Human Inter-action*, 2nd edn. Berlin: Mouton de Gruyter.

Wierzbicka, Anna (2003*b*[1998]). The semantics of English causative constructions in a universal-typological perspective. In Michael Tomasello (ed.), *The New Psychology of Language: Cognitive and Functional Approaches to Language Structure*. Mahwah, NJ: Lawrence Erlbaum, 113–153.

Wierzbicka, Anna (2004*a*). Prototypes save. In Bas Aarts, David Denison, Evelien Keizer, and Gergana Popova (eds), *Fuzzy Grammar: A Reader*. Oxford: Oxford University Press, 461–478.

Wierzbicka, Anna (2004*b*). Jewish cultural scripts and the interpretation of the Bible. *Journal of Pragmatics* 36: 575–599.

Wierzbicka, Anna (2004*c*). "Happiness" in cross-linguistic and cross-cultural perspective. *Dædalus* 133(2): 34–43.

Wierzbicka, Anna (2005*a*). Comments on Daniel L. Everett, "Cultural constraints on grammar and cognition in Pirahã", *Current Anthropology* 46(4): 641.

Wierzbicka, Anna (2005*b*). There are no "color universals", but there are universals of visual semantics. *Anthropological Linguistics* 47(2): 217–244.

Wierzbicka, Anna (2006*a*). *English: Meaning and Culture*. New York: Oxford University Press.

Wierzbicka, Anna (2006*b*). Shape in grammar revisited. *Studies in Language* 30(1): 115–177.

Wierzbicka, Anna (2006*c*). The semantics of colour: a new paradigm. In Carole P. Biggam and Christian J. Kay (eds), *Progress in Colour Studies*, vol. 1: *Language and Culture*. Amsterdam: John Benjamins, 1–24.

Wierzbicka, Anna (2006*d*). Anglo scripts against "putting pressure" on other people and their linguistic manifestations. In Cliff Goddard (ed.), *Ethnopragmatics: Understanding Discourse in Cultural Context*. Berlin: Mouton de Gruyter, 31–63.

Wierzbicka, Anna (2007*a*). Theory and empirical findings: a response to Jackendoff. *Intercultural Pragmatics* 4(3): 399–409.

Wierzbicka, Anna (2007*b*). NSM Semantics versus Conceptual Semantics: goals and standards (A response to Jackendoff). *Intercultural Pragmatics* 4(4): 521–529.

Wierzbicka, Anna (2007*c*). Bodies and their parts: an NSM approach to semantic typology. *Language Sciences* 29(1): 14–65.

Wierzbicka, Anna (2007*d*). Shape and colour in language and thought. In Andrea C. Schalley and Drew Khlentzos (eds), *Mental States*, vol. 2: *Language and Cognitive Structure*. Amsterdam: John Benjamins, 37–60.

Wierzbicka, Anna (2007*e*). Reasonably well: "NSM" as a tool for the study of phraseology and of its cultural underpinnings. In Paul Skandera (ed.), *Phraseology and Culture in English*. Berlin: Mouton de Gruyter, 49–78.

Wierzbicka, Anna (2007*f*). Two languages, two cultures, one (?) self: between Polish and English. In Mary Besemeres and Anna Wierzbicka (eds), *Translating Lives: Living with Two Languages and Cultures*. St Lucia: University of Queensland Press, 96–113.

Wierzbicka, Anna (2008*a*). Why there are no "colour universals" in language and thought. *Journal of the Royal Anthropological Institute* 14: 407–425.

Wierzbicka, Anna (2008*b*). A conceptual basis for intercultural pragmatics and world-wide understanding. In Martin Pütz and JoAnne Neff-van Aertselaer (eds), *Developing*

Contrastive Pragmatics: Interlanguage and Cross-Cultural Perspectives. Berlin: Mouton de Gruyter, 3–45.

Wierzbicka, Anna (2009*a*). Language and metalanguage: key issues in emotion research. *Emotion Review* 1(1): 3–14.

Wierzbicka, Anna (2009*b*). The theory of the mental lexicon. In Sebastian Kempgen, Peter Kosta, Tilman Berger, and Karl Gutschmidt (eds), *Die Slavischen Sprachen: Eine Internationales Handbuch zu ihrer Struktur, ihrer Geschichte und ihrer Erforsching* [The Slavic Languages: An International Handbook of their Structure, their History and their Investigation]. Berlin: Mouton de Gruyter, 848–863.

Wierzbicka, Anna (2009*c*). Exploring English phraseology with two tools: NSM semantic methodology and Google. *Journal of English Linguistics* 37(2): 101–129.

Wierzbicka, Anna (2009*d*). All people eat and drink: Does this mean that "eat" and "drink" are universal human concepts? In John Newman (ed.), *The Linguistics of Eating and Drinking*. Amsterdam: John Benjamins, 65–89.

Wierzbicka, Anna (2009*e*). What makes a good life? A cross-linguistic and cross-cultural perspective. *Journal of Positive Psychology* 4(4): 260–272.

Wierzbicka, Anna (2009*f*). The language of "bullying" and "harassment". *Quadrant* 53(12): 102–107.

Wierzbicka, Anna (2009*g*). Pragmatics and cultural values: the hot centre of Russian discourse. In Bruce Fraser and Ken Turner (eds), *Language in Life, and a Life in Language: Jacob Mey—A Festschrift*. Bingley, UK: Emerald, 423–434.

Wierzbicka, Anna (2009*h*). Case in NSM: a reanalysis of the Polish dative. In Andrej Malchukov and Andrew Spencer (eds), *The Oxford Handbook of Case*. Oxford: Oxford University Press, 151–169.

Wierzbicka, Anna (2010*a*). *Experience, Evidence, Sense: The Hidden Cultural Legacy of English*. New York: Oxford University Press.

Wierzbicka, Anna (2010*b*). On emotions and on definitions: a response to Izard. *Emotion Review* 2(4): 379–380.

Wierzbicka, Anna (2010*c*). "Story" : an English cultural keyword and a key interpretive tool of Anglo culture. *Narrative Inquiry* 20(1): 153–181.

Wierzbicka, Anna (2010*d*). Cultural scripts. In Louise Cummings (ed.), *The Pragmatics Encyclopedia*. London: Routledge, 92–95.

Wierzbicka, Anna (2010*e*). Cultural scripts and Intercultural Communication. In Anna Trosborg (ed.), *Pragmatics Across Languages and Cultures*. Berlin: Mouton de Gruyter, 43–78.

Wierzbicka, Anna (2011*a*). Defining "the humanities". *Culture & Psychology* 17(1): 31–46.

Wierzbicka, Anna (2011*b*). Arguing in Russian: why Solzhenitsyn's fictional arguments defy translation. *Russian Journal of Communication* 4: 8–37.

Wierzbicka, Anna (2011*c*). Prototypes and invariants (Prototipy i invarianty). Ch. 3 of Anna Wierzbicka, *Semantičeskie Universalii i Bazisnye Koncepty* [Semantic Universals and Basic Concepts]. Moscow: Jazyki Slavjanskoj Kultury. [In Russian.]

Wierzbicka, Anna (2012*a*). "Advice" in English and in Russian: a contrastive and cross-cultural perspective. In Holger Limberg and Miriam A. Locher (eds), *Advice in Discourse*. Amsterdam: John Benjamins, 309–332.

Wierzbicka, Anna (2012*b*). When cultural scripts clash: miscommunication in "multicultural" Australia. In Barbara Kryk-Kastovsky (ed.), *Intercultural Miscommunication Past and Present*. Frankfurt am Main: Peter Lang, 121–148.

Wierzbicka, Anna (2012*c*). The history of English seen as the history of ideas: cultural change reflected in different translations of the New Testament. In Terttu Nevalainen and Elizabeth Closs Traugott (eds), *The Oxford Handbook of the History of English*. New York: Oxford University Press, 434–445.

Wierzbicka, Anna (2012*d*). Is "pain" a human universal? Conceptualization of "pain" in English, French, and Polish. *Colloquia Communia* 1(92): 29–53.

Wierzbicka, Anna (2013). Polish *zwierzęta* 'animals' and *jabłka* 'apples': an ethnosemantic inquiry. In Adam Głaz, David S. Danaher and Przemysław Łozowski (eds), *The Linguistic Worldview: Ethnolinguistics, Cognition, and Culture*. London: Versita, 137–159.

Wierzbicka, Anna (2014). *Imprisoned in English: The hazards of English as a default language*. New York: Oxford University Press.

Wierzbicka, Anna (2015). Innate conceptual primitives manifested in the languages of the world and in infant cognition. In Eric Margolis and Stephen Laurence (eds), *The Conceptual Mind: New directions in the study of concepts*. Cambridge, Mass: MIT Press, 379–412.

Wierzbicka, Anna (in press *a*). Deconstructing "colour", exploring indigenous meanings. In D. Young (ed.), *Rematerializing Colour*. Wantage, UK: Sean Kingston.

Wierzbicka, Anna (in press *b*). Back to 'mother' and 'father': overcoming the Eurocentrism of kinship studies through eight lexical universals. *Current Anthropology*.

Williams, Raymond (1976). *Keywords: A Vocabulary of Culture and Society*. London: Croom Helm.

Wilson, Margaret (2002). Six views of embodied cognition. *Psychological Bulletin and Review* 9(4): 626–636.

Wilson, William H., and Kaijanoe Kamanā (2001). "Mai Loko Mai O ka 'I'ini: Proceeding from a dream": the 'Aha Pūnana Leo Connection in Hawaiian language revitalization. In Leanne Hinton and Kenneth L. Hale (eds), *The Green Book of Language: Revitalization in Practice*. Boston: Academic Press, 147–178.

Winstedt, Richard Olaf (1981). *Malay Proverbs*. Singapore: Graham Brash.

Wisniewski, Edward J., Christopher A. Lamb, and Erica L. Middleton (2003). On the conceptual basis for the count and mass noun distinction. *Language and Cognitive Processes* 18 (5/6): 583–624.

Wong, Jock Onn (2004*a*). The particles of Singapore English: a semantic and cultural interpretation. *Journal of Pragmatics* 9: 739–793.

Wong, Jock Onn (2004*b*). Cultural scripts, ways of speaking and perceptions of personal autonomy: Anglo English vs. Singapore English. *Intercultural Pragmatics* 1(2): 231–248.

Wong, Jock Onn (2005). "Why you so Singlish one?" A semantic and cultural interpretation of the Singapore English particle *one*. *Language in Society* 34(2): 239–275.

Wong, Jock Onn (2008). Anglo English and Singapore English tags: their meanings and cultural significance. *Pragmatics & Cognition* 16(1): 88–117.

Wong, Jock Onn (2010). The triple articulation of language. *Journal of Pragmatics* 42(11): 2932–2944.

Ye, Zhengdao (2001). An inquiry into "sadness" in Chinese. In Jean Harkins and Anna Wierzbicka (eds), *Emotions in Crosslinguistic Perspective*. Berlin: Mouton de Gruyter, 359–404.

Ye, Zhengdao (2004a). Chinese categorization of interpersonal relationships and the cultural logic of Chinese social interaction: an indigenous perspective. *Intercultural Pragmatics* 1(2): 211–230.

Ye, Zhengdao (2004b). The Chinese folk model of facial expressions: a linguistic perspective. *Culture & Psychology* 10(2): 195–222.

Ye, Zhengdao (2004c). When "empty words" are not empty: examples from the semantic analysis of some "emotional adverbs" in Mandarin Chinese. *Australian Journal of Linguistics* 24(2): 139–161.

Ye, Zhengdao (2006). Why the "inscrutable" Chinese face? Emotionality and facial expressions in Chinese. In Cliff Goddard (ed.), *Ethnopragmatics: Understanding Discourse in Cultural Context*. Berlin: Mouton de Gruyter, 127–169.

Ye, Zhengdao (2007a). "Memorisation", learning and cultural cognition: the notion of *bèi* ("auditory memorisation") in the written Chinese tradition. In Mengistu Amberber (ed.), *The Language of Memory in a Crosslinguistic Perspective*. Amsterdam: John Benjamins, 139–180.

Ye, Zhengdao (2007b). Taste as a gateway to Chinese cognition. In Andrea C. Schalley and Drew Khlentzos (eds), *Mental States*, vol. 2: *Language and Cognitive Structure*. Amsterdam: John Benjamins, 109–132.

Ye, Zhengdao (2010). Eating and drinking in Mandarin and Shanghainese: a lexical-conceptual analysis. In Wayne Christensen, Elizabeth Schier, and John Sutton (eds), *ASCS09: Proceedings of the 9th Conference of the Australasian Society for Cognitive Science*. Sydney: Macquarie Centre for Cognitive Science, 375–383.

Yoon, Kyung-Joo (2004). Not just words: Korean social models and the use of honorifics. *Intercultural Pragmatics* 1(2): 189–210.

Yoon, Kyung-Joo (2006). *Constructing a Korean Natural Semantic Metalanguage*. Seoul: Hankook.

Yoon, Kyung-Joo (2007a). My experience of living in a different culture: the life of a Korean migrant in Australia. In Mary Besemeres and Anna Wierzbicka (eds), *Translating Lives: Living with Two Languages and Cultures*. St Lucia: University of Queensland Press, 114–127.

Yoon, Kyung-Joo (2007b). Do you *remember* where you put the key? The Korean model of *remembering*. In Mengistu Amberber (ed.), *The Language of Memory in a Crosslinguistic Perspective*. Amsterdam: Benjamins, 209–233.

Yoon, Kyung-Joo (2007c). Korean ethnopsychology reflected in the concept of *ceng* "affection": semantic and cultural interpretation. *Discourse and Cognition* 14(3): 81–103.

Yoon, Kyung-Joo (2008). The Natural Semantic Metalanguage of Korean. In Cliff Goddard (ed.), *Cross-Linguistic Semantics*. Amsterdam: John Benjamins, 121–162.

Young, Diana (2005). The smell of green-ness; cultural synaesthesia in the Western Desert. In Regina Bendix and Donalds Brenneis (eds), *The Senses*. Special issue of *Etnofoor*, 18(1): 61–77.

Zalizniak, Anna, Irina Levontina, and Aleksej D. Šmelev (2005). *Ključevye Idei Russkoj Jazykovoj Kartiny Mira* [Keywords of the Russian Linguistic Model of the World]. Moscow: Jazyki Slavjanskix Kul'tur.

Index

Printed and bound by CPI Group (UK) Ltd, Croydon, CR0 4YY